EUROPE EMERGES

TRANSITION TOWARD AN INDUSTRIAL WORLD-WIDE SOCIETY

600–1750

EUROPE EMERGES

TRANSITION TOWARD AN INDUSTRIAL WORLD-WIDE SOCIETY 600–1750

Robert L. Reynolds

THE UNIVERSITY OF WISCONSIN PRESS

Madison, Milwaukee, and London, 1967

Published by the University of Wisconsin Press
Madison, Milwaukee, and London
U.S.A.: Box 1379, Madison, Wisconsin 53701
U.K.: 26–28 Hallam Street, London, W.1

First printing (cloth), 1961 ___
Second printing (cloth and paper), 1967

Printed in the United States of America
Library of Congress Catalog Card Number 61-6175

My wife and I
made this book
together

FOREWORD

A DOZEN years ago I began seriously to work out a course for freshmen in the Integrated Liberal Studies program at the University of Wisconsin. The proposed course was to bridge the centuries from the late Roman Empire to the global commercial, industrial, and political pattern which was rapidly emerging under European domination by the time of George Washington. To a great extent this book is the result of that course.

Medieval European economic history is stressed; all the earlier parts of the book deal with Europe (as does much of the rest too), with a focus upon the western parts of Europe.

This field has received much attention for two generations. Many diligent scholars have cultivated it intensively. But since the surviving evidence is much of it thin, difficult to understand in its multiplicity of obsolete vocabularies and archaeological remains, it has lent itself to a variety of interpretations, being important for supporting or weakening ideologies passionately and even bloodily supported today by great and antagonistic sections of the human race. Because its appreciation requires so many special trainings that are hard to master, the material will, as I present it, contain much that has scarcely been noticed outside narrow circles of specialists—and among them is still drawing both support and attack, either to win support or to draw controversy.

The emphasis I have placed on business—banking, bookkeeping, insurance, government finance, mercantile practices—in the days of the Crusades is in line with scholarly research in the last thirty years. The evidence is still being collected, still being presented and weighed, but in many respects the picture now seems less like the world seen by Sir Walter Scott and more like that seen by the *Wall Street Journal* than could have been anticipated.

Technology is stressed, again in line with the research and findings of numerous scholars whose efforts are still being exerted in a difficult field. The results so far presented from current research are revising more and more the older, still influential ideas that stress the novelty of the steps made in the Industrial Revolution. The new findings do not lessen the significance of the latter, but they do increase the stature of the medieval craftsman and make the development since the earlier eighteenth century far more intelligible than a sudden-jump concept allowed.

I also seek to correct the commonplace distortion in the view of Europe which sees it as for thirteen centuries or more to have been "manorial," "feudal," "static," "backward." A person today is backward, feudal, static, medieval, who so designates all the centuries and patterns of society and economy during which were born and flourished Petrarch, Francis Bacon, Bede, Ivan IV, Gutenberg, Newton, Calvin, Jacob Fugger, Cortes, Francis of Assisi, John Winthrop, Clovis, Snorri Sturlasson, Galileo, Aquinas, Louis XIV, Brian Boru, Michelangelo, Villon, Sobieski, Anselm, Camoëns, and even the fathers of Benjamin Franklin and George Washington.

The rest of the work here is condensed in treatment of details because it must expand so largely in coverage to include the peoples of the whole earth.

The main theme in human history over the last six hundred years has been, as this book conceives it, the emergence of the Europeans as leaders, drivers, persuaders, shapers, crushers, builders, of all the economies and societies of all the peoples. What those other economies and societies were and, on broad lines, what they did to and what was done to them by European economy and society in the first generations of contact are the interest of the rest of the book.

There is heavier emphasis on power and its politics than it has been popular to emphasize for some time, but to develop the story otherwise is to put in Little Eva and Uncle Tom while leaving out Simon Legree and the bloodhounds—and Gettysburg. The expansion of the Europeans has often been told before, but to leave out the Muscovites of Great Russia has always seemed to me a feat comparable to erecting the Empire State Building with a complete gap where the fourth floor belongs. Brief as the survey herein must be, the Russians are included alongside their fellow Europeans, the Spanish and Portuguese, Dutch, French, and English, and their frontiersmen stand with their peers such as Brazil's Bandeiristas, South Africa's Boers, or our mountain men—and the Strogonovs with the Hudson's Bay Company and John Jacob Astor.

Finally, the colonial societies, on the verge of political detachment from the European states, are briefly analyzed.

There is no Conclusion; we are writing that from day to day.

R. L. R.

Port Washington, Wisconsin
August, 1960

CONTENTS

LIST OF MAPS

I am indebted to the Cartographic Laboratory, University of Wisconsin, for assistance in the preliminary planning of the maps for this book and to Howard E. Loy, Madison, for drawing the maps from my plans. I am grateful to Professor Kuo-P'ing Chou for her design of Chinese characters and to Mrs. Isobel Korbel of the University of Wisconsin Press for her unflagging editorial assistance.

Section I

BASIC ASSETS: ABOUT 600 A.D.

HISTORIANS, writing a description in a European language of a part of Europe's past, usually neither take up space nor make an effort to sketch the geographical features, climatic conditions, soils and minerals, roads and harbors, beasts and plants, tools, techniques, and products, or clothes, foods, and housing of the time and area described. Fiction writers and dramatists weave in such items far more commonly and often far better than does the professional historian. For the professional historian assumes that the reader naturally knows enough about such matters to serve the purpose, and the reader is likely to assume so too. With rare exceptions these assumptions are invalid. No one, historian or reader, naturally knows anything of the sort. For instance, an Italian or Polish historian, who knows a great deal about eleventh-century Italy or Poland, will almost certainly be most inaccurate in what he knows about such a place as eleventh-century Highland Scotland—if he has ever felt the need to learn anything about it at all.

It is not necessarily true, but it is also commonly assumed—and no quarrel will be made here with the assumption—that tools and technology, or food, clothing, and housing facilities, can be overlooked in tracing such things as intellectual or constitutional history. However, it is obviously a mistake to assume that economic and social matters can be described without initial provision of an appraisal of the things people lived with and used as they went along as well as a subsequent running account of changes.

Later on in this work brief sketches will be given of the geographies and climates, tools and technologies of the other regions into which the Europeans pushed their influence as they grew more and more assertive.

But first of all, prosaic as inventories must be, a general appraisal of Europe must be included here, rather like the one a prospective purchaser of control of the assets, tangible and intangible, of a great corporation would wish made before striking his bargain. Europe will receive first and most detailed attention because it was this corporation—to push the parallel a bit farther—which started as a small, rural, partially dependent operation in a narrow part of the globe and has since emerged to dominate all others.

It is this growth—for it still goes on—which is the unremitting economic and social revolution to which the title of this book refers.

3

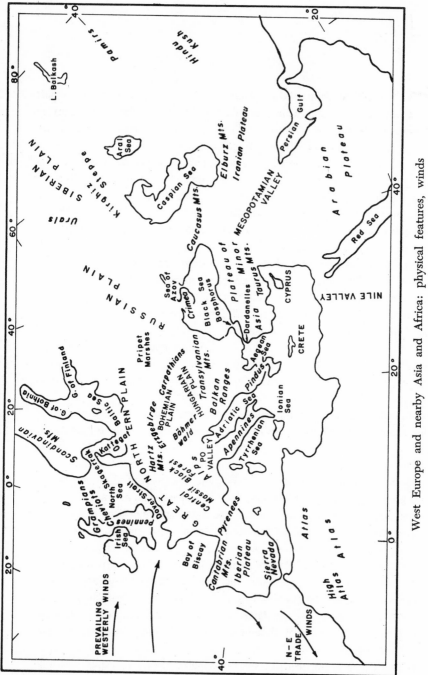

West Europe and nearby Asia and Africa: physical features, winds

CHAPTER I

Climate,
Physical Features

A COMMUNITY is not a geographical entity and very often does not coincide with one. This has been true of the European community. It has never coincided with "Europe," and the community of "Europeans" has never occupied all of geographical Europe —in some periods it has covered far less than half. Yet it has come by conquest and migration to extend itself over vast areas far from its homeland. Our interest at first will be centered on this community of a few millions of persons, in 600 A.D., which was just starting to form itself out of the survivors of older communities and parts of still other neighboring groups.

Language usage, rather than an inherent logic of land formation, forms the entity we commonly call Europe. The Atlantic Ocean is a truly natural western demarcation for Europe, but its eastern line of demarcation from the mass now called Asia consists of artificial lines drawn a few generations ago, across hundreds of miles of plains and forests, through lines of hills or down river channels, by lesser local officials of the Czarist Russian government in order to mark off their respective provinces.

Its southern line of demarcation conventionally makes the Mediterranean Sea the geographical feature which cuts Europe off from Africa. But actually the sea has more often united than divided the peoples north and south of it. Physically they are all of the same breed, and often have shared languages, political ideas and allegiances, religious faiths, intellectual interests, and commercial and industrial networks. In sharp contrast, the Sahara can be thought of as an abysmally deep barrier. Historically it is the true barrier between the Euro-Asians on the north and the very different peoples to its south.

5

What are the surface features and the climatic zones of the "Europe" which lies between the Sahara and the Arctic Ocean? A glance at any good map of Europe's physical or climatic features shows plains and mountain chains, bays and plateaus, isotherms and rainfall belts, all in seeming splendid disarray from any pattern. There are palm-growing spots in England and Ireland, spots with really low annual rainfall around the North Sea, year-round ski slopes in Sicily, and so on.

Yet a broad statement can be sustained that climatic zones and surface features all tend to run in bands east and west. The Sahara runs easterly and westerly; so do the folds of the Atlas Mountains; so also does the trough of the Mediterranean, into which, to be sure, plateaus and lesser mountain ranges project from the north coasts to form the Iberian, Italian, and Balkan Peninsulas and the offshore islands.

Across the north of those three peninsulas lie the generally easterly-westerly mountain ranges that act as a broken, twisted ridgepole. These ranges cut off the lands touching the Mediterranean and its special sort of climate from the lands which look across the Great Northern Plain to the English Channel and the North and Baltic seas. Then across these seas, still oriented roughly easterly-westerly, is the same northern plain emerging from its sea-covered lowest parts into the northernmost belt of Europe, where are the Scandinavian and offshore mountain chains and the low Arctic plains of the entire British Isles, and of Sweden, Finland, and northern European Russia.

We will return to topography, but first we will consider whether climatic zones also tend to run in bands east and west and what effect these climatic zones have had on the peoples experiencing them.

Departing from the Sahara and moving just north from it, we come to the Mediterranean Sea and the region of "Mediterranean climate," named by climatologists from this, its largest expanse on the globe. It covers both sides of the sea, and extends up to the southern valleys of the ridgepole mountains in mainland Europe, where the Alps lie in the center with the Pyrenees to their west and the Balkans to their east. The belt of "Mediterranean climate" actually stretches right on eastward into Asia, north of the driest deserts of Arabia and the Indian Ocean coasts, and provides the homeland for the peoples of Islam. (Patches of "Mediterranean climate" exist elsewhere over the earth—for example, in the southern part of the state of California.)

This climate is characterized by a two-season alternation of rain and sun. In the summer, for months on end, the skies are blue, the winds light, the rains few and scanty. During this season vegetation ripens, browns, and then dries out, while the narrow, leathery leaves of such trees as eucalyptus, live oak, and olive hoard their moisture. Then, usually in October and November, as the sun is dropping back south, the winds of the next more northerly belt of climate follow, bringing gray skies, week-long storms which pile up towering but choppy waves in the seas and which fill gulches with rushing water.

Historically this climate has strongly affected the peoples living around the Mediterranean. The winter storms make navigation of the sea hazardous. Hot, clear summers and wet winters have compelled the people to develop an economy—at least so far as the growing of crops is concerned—that can fit such a climate, for there is a need to raise crops which can grow in the wet season, or at least be started then, and which can be harvested in the dry season.

There must also be a pattern of pasturing animals which will take into account the presence of good pastures for some of the time in some places, of poor pastures at other times in the same places, and of alternative pastures which can be reached from those which have turned dry. Housing, clothing, the habits of everyday life, are all strongly affected by such necessities.

In such an area the rivers are, by and large, seasonal. In the wet season there is too much water in the water courses; in the dry season there is too little. The rivers in Mediterranean climate areas are not very dependable as sources for water supply or for navigation unless they receive a constant supply of water from mountain snows not too far away.

In contrast to the Mediterranean area, western Europe north of the mountain ridgepole lies in a temperate zone, and nowhere else in the latitudes of prevailing westerly winds does the land rise from an ocean on its west in a gradual slope which stretches inland for hundreds of miles. In every other part of the world, in such latitudes there are mountains very close to the sea on the west coast of each land mass, mountains which form a barrier against the moisture-laden ocean winds coming in, as on the northwest coast of the United States, where winds coming in off the Pacific are tripped by mountain ranges and drop much of their moisture before they have reached the interior. East of such mountains (in their "rain shadow") dry plains or desert are created.

But in western Europe the land slopes gently up from the sea; the westerly cyclones penetrate hundreds of miles into the interior, dropping their moisture a little at a time. All the way inland, as far as Warsaw and even Moscow, the winds still carry moisture picked up in the North Atlantic. In addition, storm systems, sweeping Arctic Ocean winds across the plains, bring chill, but also precipitation. In deepest winter, when the belt of prevailing westerlies has shifted to south of the Alps, such spells of near-Arctic storms can carry real cold and consequent suffering far south into Spain, Italy, or the Balkans. But on the whole the winds bring in air which does not vary greatly in temperature and which gives the land a relatively warm climate in the winter and a rather cool one in the summer; the top and the bottom of the temperature curves are relatively near one another. In the North Atlantic the winds have blown over the warm waters of the equatorial current which comes from the south and swings north toward Norway and the North Sea—so that even in Norway the water is warmer than that found due west on the coast of Labrador or in the Hudson's Bay region—and over that relatively warm water the winds have picked up a good deal of heat.

This equalization of the temperature has had a great effect on the way people have lived. For example, they have been able to pasture their cattle outside for most of the months of the year. Houses have had to be built and clothing made to guard against both the damp chill of the winters and the damp and chill of the summers. The houses have needed sloping roofs to shed water and snow, while social life has been centered indoors—in the Great Hall for the wealthy, in the hut or the tavern for the poor. Much reliance has been placed on woolen clothing, which in turn has called for the raising of sheep and the making of woolen cloth. But still, the weather is seldom so severe in the winter as to prevent men from moving about, so that normal exchanges between farms and towns, marketing and commerce, have always been possible with little interruption throughout twelve months of the year.

Because of the constant rainfall and moderation of climate the rivers in Europe north of the mountain ridgepole run at a fairly even level throughout the year, ice-free and full. As a consequence, transportation of men and goods by water has been easy and reasonably certain.

Just as the Mediterranean climate zone runs off to the east of the Mediterranean Sea, so do the subbelts of climate in the zone found north of the Alps continue on to the east of northern Europe. Hardwood forests and prairies, with sparsely covered dry chalk ridges found frequently in Gaul and Britain, characterized the higher lands north of the Alps and, moving eastward beyond the Carpathians, the prairies, constantly broadening, became the great grass plains of Scythia, ranged by the herds and flocks and war parties of Sarmatians, Huns, Avars, Khazars, Bulgars, and Magyars—the Russian steppes.

North in turn were the denser dark forests, with drear moors and

wasted dune lands, which were found in the southern parts of the glaciated areas. Rich vales and productive clearings where the soil was good
hardly made up for the general difficulty of life. Most northerly of all,
softwood forests, swamps and lakes, unproductive soils, and a short,
clouded, wet, chill growing season characterized the belt nearest the
Arctic Ocean. Both of these northernmost zones—the dark coniferous
forest or *taiga,* and the *tundra*—will receive further attention when the
mass of Asia proper is considered some chapters later.

The European coastline proper is the most indented of any of similar
extent in the world. Nowhere in Britain is it possible to be much more
than sixty miles from salt water; on the continent of Europe it is not
possible, unless one travels eastward, to go more than a few days' journey
away from one body of salt water before coming closer to salt water on
the other side. Europe has access to the sea from all inland areas in a
fashion not found in any other land mass of similar size. The sinking of
the coastal plain of the north (or the deepening of the seas) has permitted
the ocean to come far up the river valleys to form in particular the estuaries of England, France, and Germany. Salt-water estuaries running
deep into the land greatly facilitate inland Europe's relatively easy access
to the sea.

For centuries fortified places have characterized each north European
estuary at the point where bridging or fording of the river was first
possible when ascending a stream. Even in an age of small boats, cargo
was transferred at such points, partly for redistribution of merchandise
and partly because government officials could halt craft trying to run
under fortified bridges and make traders pay customs and other duties.
London is a good example of such a fortified place, situated where the
Thames could first be bridged and where tidewater met fresh water
coming down the stream.

The chief feature of the northern parts of Europe is the Great Northern
Plain, whereas in the Mediterranean regions there is far less level land
in relation to total area. There are some southern plains which have always been important, however, the most famous of them being the
Lombard Plain in North Italy. Here the Apennines, the backbone mountain chain of the Italian peninsula, curve southeastward and the Alps to
the north curve eastward, leaving a broad bay which has been filled in
by the rivers coming down from both mountain chains. These rivers now
run together to form the great Po River. The Po Valley, otherwise known
as the Lombard Plain, is nevertheless relatively narrow, and on clear

days the mountains on both sides can be seen from its center. Much of the land was marshy until protected by dikes, but after being properly drained the whole plain is highly productive. In addition to this there are small plains along the Italian, Greek, and Spanish coasts which are locally very important, as, for example, the famous one around the Bay of Naples. But their small size makes them have limited significance in the over-all economy of Europe.

The Great Northern Plain, which lies to the north of the Alpine ridges, is a great expanse shaped somewhat like a horn of plenty, with its point at the southwest and flaring out to the north and east. On a map showing only the land, the plain looks narrower than it is in actual fact, for it goes on out under the sea around the British Isles as well as across them, up under the North Sea (save for the canyon of the Rhine River which stretches out beneath that sea), on under the Baltic Sea, and finally under the Arctic Ocean.

The Great Northern Plain has relatively easy slopes; starting at the west coast and moving inland there is a general rise uphill to the south and east. However, the plain is not uninterrupted, for in many localities there are old mountain and plateau systems which have been eroded until they are now mere stumps. In some places these old mountain areas are still fairly rough, but while none of them is particularly rocky or snow covered, they are likely to be sharply rolling and covered with such forests as the Black Forest in Germany.

These mountains do not spread over the plain in such a fashion as to interfere with the use of the rivers as an interlocking system for water transportation. In fact, very short, easy low-level portages between the different river systems are found all the way from the Atlantic to Siberia. In modern times it has been simple, wherever such portage routes existed, to link the river systems by canals.

The northern part of the Northern Plain was repeatedly overrun by glaciers at the same time as was the northern part of the United States. The glaciers smoothed out the roughness in the landscape, cut down big hills, and filled up valleys, thus producing for Europe to the north of about central France a topography much like that of southern Wisconsin. Farther north the glaciers left the land looking like that of northern Wisconsin, Minnesota, and Ontario. But while lakes and swamps are still a common feature in parts of the Northern Plain, they were much more prominent in 500 A.D. than they are now, for men have greatly modified their own geographical environment in this matter.

A few of the lesser mountain systems are worthy of mention here, either because of their mineral content or because of their effect upon the lives of peoples living near them. Among these is the system which provides the backbone for the island of Britain. These mountains are very rich in minerals. In primitive times they were of some importance in barring peoples on one side from being in close touch with those on the other, but since that time they have had no significance as a barrier to travel back and forth. The Irish mountains are low and lie around the edges of the island rather than in the center; as a result the population on the whole looks inward, toward the Shannon River valley, rather than outward. The Scandinavian peninsula has its ridge of mountains running very close to the sea on the Atlantic or Norwegian side, with a glacial plain full of lakes and bogs on the Swedish or eastern side. This plain actually runs on out under the Baltic Sea. A very important old and low mountain system is that of the Urals, far to the east. Before the sixteen hundreds these mountains were almost unknown, save by a few fur traders, but since that time have become most important because of their rich mineral deposits. The mountains of present-day Germany and Czechoslovakia have always been important to men. The Hartz Mountains in north central Germany are so low and worn down that they scarcely impress one as being mountainous, but their minerals were historically significant. Of even greater importance than these have been the mountains which surround Bohemia and the Carpathians around Hungary. Both of these systems contain rich deposits of minerals and enclose rich basins of land well suited to agriculture and the raising of livestock.

Seas, valleys, river systems, and mountain passes all have their places in an appraisal of transportation resources. As already noted, Europe has a great salt lake and bay system to the north composed of the Gulf of Finland, the Gulf of Bothnia, the Baltic and North Seas, while to its south lie the great waterways of the Black Sea and Mediterranean. Europe's endowment in salt water lakes is matched to a degree in the United States by the great salt bay or gulf to the south—the Gulf of Mexico, and to the north by the Great Lakes, which serve much the same purpose as does the Baltic complex of waters in Europe.

From the mountains lying between the Great North Plain and the Mediterranean basin the slope of land is very sharp. Rivers flowing south toward the Mediterranean are largely unnavigable except in a few stretches; not only is the water running down them very swift, but also they alternate between being very full of fast-running water and rolling boulders and being dry gulches when there has been no rain.

On the other hand the easy-flowing rivers of the Great North Plain serve everywhere to connect inland areas with the northern seas. In an age when sea-going vessels were small, these rivers were practically the same as the open sea so far as freight and military traffic were concerned. Both sea rovers and merchandise could sail from the sea to Paris, or on past London, or deep into Germany, while freight could be loaded far upstream and shipped out through the estuaries and on across the sea.

While the Mediterranean rivers were not useful as water courses, their valleys have been very useful. People and freight could move on land along the sides of the rivers, and could make use of the openings between hills and mountains made by the water.

On the west of Europe is the salt-water route through the Straits of Gibraltar and around the Iberian Peninsula which was used by very primitive men and was never entirely abandoned. However, until the time of the modern steamship it was not actually so easy a route as it looks to be on the map, for the west coasts of Europe were and are perilous, with great tides and swells and fierce storms; many stretches of coastland are dangerously fringed with reefs, and harbor entrances are treacherous. Before aids to navigation had become reasonably accurate and dependable, small ships risked much when they ventured over the horizon out of sight of land, and the dangers which existed near the coasts seemed preferable. Even at Gibraltar itself the winds, tides, and currents can at times make passage difficult. In addition to the perils which nature provided there were dangers provided by mankind, for the coastal peoples practiced piracy until quite modern times, while for centuries after 700 A.D. the Straits were controlled by Mohammedans, who were generally hostile to Europeans. For all these reasons, until the late twelve hundreds the sea route around the Iberian peninsula had less traffic than might be expected.

To a certain extent, similar conditions restricted mercantile shipping around the Danish peninsula where cargoes were, by preference, unloaded at one side of its base, carried across the land neck, and reloaded on the other side.

As a means of communication from one part of Europe to another, the water routes were very important, but so also were the land routes. North-south communication by way of gaps in the mountain ridgepole was particularly important. However, the pattern of routes in 500 or 600 A.D. was somewhat different from that found today; while many of the most important routes have always been in use, there are many others which have only become available as man from medieval times to the present has cut tunnels and built approaches.

Mountain passes through the Pyrenees were difficult, especially those in the central parts of that chain, and the best land routes from France to Spain have always been along the coasts at the two ends of the mountain range. However, neither of these routes has ever been of first importance in European commerce since they compete with coastwise shipping and do not connect areas of major production.

North of the Pyrenees, the wide, low gap going from east to west across southern France from the region of Narbonne to the estuary of the Garonne River, with its fine port at Bordeaux, has been a useful route since Neolithic and Bronze Age times. Yet this route has never carried a great share of Europe's commerce, for at the west end of the route either ocean shipments or long overland shipments are necessary to carry cargoes to first-rank markets.

A route which has always been heavily used is that which ascends the Rhone River valley from the Mediterranean, skirting the Alps, rising just to the east, and leading easily into the Great Northern Plain. The Rhone is not much help as a river, being essentially of Mediterranean character, with too steep a pitch over long stretches, but it has always been easy to make roads along its valley. Furthermore, its headwaters are at a short distance, over fairly level ground, from the headwaters of the Seine River, which flows on toward Paris, from the English Channel and Britain, and from the Rhine River, which leads into northern Germany and on to the northern seas.

All the passes over the Alps, connecting Italy with France on the west and Germany on the north, are relatively difficult. The valleys below the passes proper are narrow and rocky, calling for the construction of bridges over torrents and of roads along shelves in cliffs, as well as for the provision of shelters and food for men and animals along the way. Many of the passes used today were unused, or crossed only by goatherds, until relatively late in our period of history. However, several of them, such as the Mount Cenis Pass through the western Alps, were used a great deal for trade and war in spite of all difficulties.

Best of all were several of the passes from northern Italy eastward. Those going from Italy into what is now Yugoslavia were the most accessible, being low and broad enough to allow cattle to be driven through

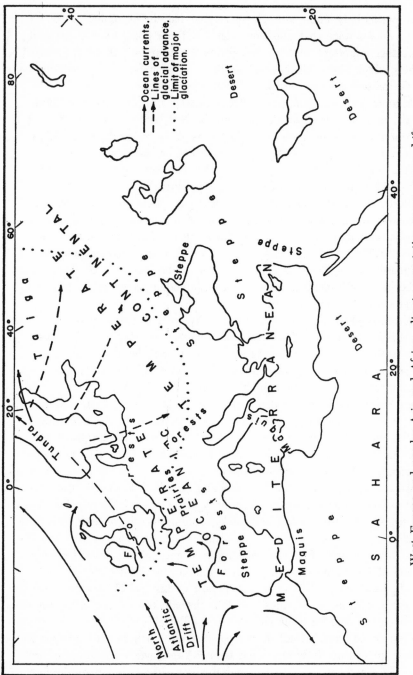

West Europe and nearby Asia and Africa: climate, vegetation zones, ocean drift

for market in the good seasons. The Brenner Pass, which has always been the main route from the lower Po Valley to the German lands of Bavaria and Austria, was an avenue taken by merchants and migrating peoples in the Stone Age. It is still taken by merchants and generals in our own time. To a great degree it fed the trade which in the Middle Ages built up Venice on the south and to the north such famous German cities as Nuremberg and Augsburg.

East of Italy the mountain ridgepole rather frays out. It breaks into a complex of mountains and valleys stretching across the whole of the northern Balkans and over to the Black Sea, with pockets and blind alleys and difficult passes to be found throughout the area. However, there are several routes which have always served to connect northern Europe with the Mediterranean seas. Of these the most famous starts south near Belgrade on the Danube and, working southward up-valley, finally leads into the route which comes out in northern Greece at Salonika. A fork on this route leads eastward across lower spurs of the Balkan mountains until it reaches level ground and goes on into Constantinople. It was the route of the famed Orient Express when that train was running.

Mention has been made above of the way in which the Great Northern Plain, as one travels eastward through Poland and around the Carpathian Mountains, flares wider and wider to the south; then it touches the Black Sea. Of all the routes around or through the mountain ridgepole, this was the easiest for early men to travel, for the rivers which flow north are the typical rivers of the Great Northern Plain; the rivers which flow south to the Black Sea are of the same sort—the Bug, the Dniester, the Dnieper, and the Don. And when on the Black Sea, a mariner, merchant, or admiral is on a salt lake which flows through a salt river past Constantinople (Istanbul) and through the Dardanelles into the Mediterranean Sea itself. A general observation can be made that in all ages down to the present this route has been of prime importance except when blocked because of political or military barriers. But it has been so blocked throughout much of the history of western Europe

Before leaving the subject of Europe's transportation facilities, some attention should be given the Roman road system. While those roads had been man made, they were so fixed a part of the land and so enduring that they could be, and were, regarded by some heathen Europeans in the five and six hundreds as having been made by the gods. Main state highways had stretched between all the important urban centers within the boundaries of the old Roman Empire. They had been so well engineered and constructed that, despite neglect lasting for generations, for great distances they continued to serve much as they had from the beginning. To be sure, the neglect of bridges, and the bad stretches where the roads were exposed to erosion or river action, made these great highways less than perfect avenues for moving men and goods. The secondary and local Roman roads went out of existence after a few generations, but the main roads remained in use for centuries until medieval road builders and modern railroad builders began either to run new tracks parallel to the Roman routes or, to a very great extent, to run new constructions right over the tops of the Roman foundations.

In the present day we are not likely to think of forests as barriers between one part of a country or countryside and another, since they are now so easily penetrated with bulldozers and concrete highways. As a result we are likely to underestimate their strength as barriers or their value as resources. However, in Europe, in the period with which we begin, forests were tremendous barriers when attacked by men with stone hatchets as their only tools, or by small populations with limited transport facilities. Even sweeping forest fires could not be relied upon to clear land and convert woodland to pasture and the plow. The great forests in Europe, as they existed in the six, seven, and eight hundreds and pretty widely thereafter, have disappeared. Men have cut them down and put the soil to other use. Where the forests once dominated, clumps of trees miles across still stand; but the great forests are gone.

In many parts of Gaul, Italy, and Spain coverage of the land with forests was quite certainly more extensive in the five, six, and seven hundreds than it had been earlier in Roman Imperial history. Shrinkage of the population inside the old Roman Empire during the two, three, and four hundreds had caused the abandonment of villages and of whole countrysides. As in New England today, where old pasture fences can be found running off through the second-growth woods, so in some of the best land in Gaul and Italy whole areas had reverted to forest. Lands which were richly productive had been let go; the people had died or moved off, the forest had correspondingly increased.

Forest barriers seem to have had a great deal to do with the way in which settlement took place in the period of the great migrations of peoples, from 400 to 700 A.D., holding up the migration of some German tribes in some directions or deflecting their movements to one side and around. It has been suggested that the language frontier between the

...nd reliance on crops which can take root in the wet sea-
...uition in the dry season. In the Roman epoch there had
...ble engineering of drainage-irrigation works. But in the
...ch we begin, because of political weakness, the thinning
...lation, disturbance of communications and of farm life,
...part of the old channels and terraces had been allowed
...epair.

...e lands men have developed a method of caring for their
...known as "transhumance"—the moving of most of the
...the lowlands, where the grass is green in the winter, to
...where grazing can be found in the dry season. Since all
...animals must be driven to the highlands during the sum-
...e engaged in crop cultivation lose the work of the animals
...l grain farms during a part of the summer and early fall
...mportant is the loss of the animal droppings which help
...tility of the soil upon which grain crops are grown.
...e dry season has one beneficial effect upon the soil. Be-
...oisture is drawn up from quite deep in the ground, bring-
...portant soluble minerals, so that in the short run there is
...hing or washing them out of the soil. But there is one dan-
...es—that the soil may be washed or blown away, especially
...as been deforestation and overpasturing by goats and sheep.
...urn to the north we find that a great deal of the land has
...to a depth of several hundred feet by the gravel, clay, and
...down by glaciers from the northernmost parts of Europe
...Germany, and northern France. Also, during periods which
...y, a fairly large amount of wind deposit had built up rich
...born earth coverage—in some of the districts along the
...rmany and elsewhere. There has also been an overlaying
...tal areas with water-deposited soils.
...rn-down mountain districts in the north most of the surface
...ough to hold soil, although rock outcrops, cliffs, and barren
...to be found. However, in general the mountain country was
...try, almost always more valuable, as it is today, for its timber
...erals under the soil than for top soils and the crops which
...own on them. These districts have been used for pasturing,
...ively recent times terracing of the less steep slopes has been

...much of the Great Northern Plain is fairly level country,
...lowing where the soil is worth plowing, and where the plow

French-speaking and German-speaking peoples in part follows the line
of old forests. On the other hand, the Rhine River was German on both
sides very soon after the migration of peoples began. In England The
Weald, a great forest, was a barrier which cut off Kent, to the south
and east, from the rest of England, while north of Kent the Thames
River was a highway.

While forests acted as barriers holding up the movement of peoples,
more locally they acted as barriers between political groups. That was
in part intentional. It was customary among the barbarians—and to a
degree was a factor that Roman frontier generals also relied upon—to
leave an area of waste and forest dozens of miles wide between the lands
of any one tribe and those of its neighbors. On a smaller scale this was
also the case with villages and other lesser units of population, for in
forested areas a village was typically fenced in by a forest which served
for a defense against bandits, pirates, and foreign invaders as well as for
other purposes to be mentioned later. In Anglo-Saxon law it was required
that a man approaching a village through the forests keep blowing his
horn or whistling or hallooing. Should he neglect to do this, an arrow
shot at him was taken to be his own responsibility, for along the path
were stationed village guards who were to shoot, without asking, any
persons who were not coming as friends. Friends would show their status
by making a noise.

In summary, what were the basic physical assets with which Europe
was supplied about 600 A.D.? It was well arranged for the movement of
materials and only minor improvements were needed—most of all harbor
works, amelioration of roads, bridges, and passes, with ingenuity and energy expended to devise and operate canals and locks—to make it the
finest workshop men in such a large community had yet had in world
history.

There was value in the relative mildness of the climate and also in
its very variety which would eventually allow a wide range of goods
to be produced under conditions which would facilitate intraregional
and interregional exchanges. But those values were largely there for
the future to find. They were to be seen when traders began to exploit
them.

Meantime, under men's feet, were the assets which at the time—and
ever since, to be sure—made Europe valuable: the minerals and the
soils.

CHAPTER II

Soils, Fisheries, Metals, and Minerals

A MAP of the resources of a great area such as Europe must be continuously modified as man and nature work to change it. We can appreciate the need to fill in the picture of a district with symbols, for example, indicating that it supplies gold when a gold strike has been made there by prospectors, and we can see the justice in removing those symbols from that area after it has been mined out. Or we can appreciate the need to add, and then to remove, symbols indicating timber land, wheat land, and dairying land as successive generations put a given area to different uses (as has been done, for instance, in southern Wisconsin).

It is not so clearly self-evident, however, that the resource maps of the whole world are forever changing moment by moment as larger or smaller modifications of pre-existing tools, uses, transportation, political organization, and the like are made—or even thought of. But that has been the case for centuries now, and the following survey of Europe's basic resources, as of about 600 A.D., with some comments in passing upon subsequent modifications of our survey's picture, will illustrate this fact.

About 600 A.D. Europe's resources in soil then being used to grow crops and feed livestock were only a small part of what they have since become, or even of what they were by 1200 A.D. Most of the soil on the surface of Europe has been built up, often to many hundreds of feet in depth, by the action of wind, of water, or by glaciers. Its dryness and its wetness, its drainage both on the surface and in the subsoil, have determined whether or not man could use it to produce the crops he needs. Then too, in areas which have been well covered with plants and trees, the accumulation of humus has made the soil easier to work and more fruitful.

18

Soils, Fi...

20

Historically man's own wo... portance in determining its ... and constructive. How he pas... of crops he grows and the w... ditching and damming and d... on its fertility. Man can eithe... ful fertilizing or by "mining" ...

Over-all, men had not muc... 600 A.D. Since that time they ... continent. There are several o... action has been as important—... or the fertile parts of the island... been as much made by man as ... very large part of the land which ... century is so used and so usable ... of years, tremendously increased ... ditching, draining, terracing, and ...

In the Mediterranean region a g... tainous or semimountainous. Tha... stricted. A very large proportion ... nearly everywhere it is subject to t... There are some plains with soil v... rich in minerals, or alluvial and also ... draining. Some of the best soils are ... bases of mountains which come do... lands catch and hold water in such ... lem, its removal calling for ditching ... By the time of the late Roman Emp... come infected by malarial mosquitoe... impossible to put laborers in gangs ... and rehabilitation as farming areas. ... lowland areas were out of cultivation ... ern times.

Because of great differences in rain... sons, there are draining and irrigatio... the Mediterranean area. The same ar... problem of an oversupply of running ... season may be short of water—even sh... for crop raising—in the summer. This ...

ing techniques, ... son and reach fr... been a considera... period with whi... out of the popu... a considerable ... to fall into disr...

In these sam... cattle which is ... livestock from ... the highlands ... or many of the... mer, the peopl... on the lowlan... months. Also i... sustain the fer...

However, th... cause of it, m... ing with it im... no fear of lead... ger at all tim... where there h...

When we ... been covered ... sand brought ... to England, ... had been dr... loess—wind-... Rhine in Ge... of some coas...

In the wo... was level er... places were ... timber coun... and for min... could be g... and in rela... worked ou...

However... good for p...

can defeat the obstacles in its way. Over considerable areas the glaciers dropped poor soil full of sand or rocks, where cultivation was difficult or not worth while until the pressure of population, especially in very modern times, made it worth improving. A great deal of the total surface in the glaciated areas was poorly drained, with lakes, marshes, and swamps with sour soils to be found over great sections. Especially along the Baltic and North Sea coasts there were wind-blown and sea-deposited sand dunes and infertile moors. Tidal marshes are extensive along the flat lands which shelve out under the North Sea in England and in the Netherlands opposite.

At the time with which we start, much of the best land in the northern area of Europe was covered with such heavy forests, or with such thick prairie sod that it was very difficult to cultivate with the tools then available. Men could make small clearings in the forests by girdling trees and burning them, and they could patch-cultivate in the prairies. But until at least the five, six, and seven hundreds, cultivation of the best lands in the north was difficult.

Before that time most planting had been done on the relatively thin soil of ridges. For example, chalk downs with thin, dry topsoil are common enough in parts of England and France, and it was on these that much of the crop growing was carried on, not only in Neolithic times, but on through Roman Imperial days. It was in the five and six hundreds that conversion of the great prairies and the best of the forest lands into plowable land was begun, for it was at this time that it began to be technologically possible to do so.

The north enjoyed mild enough temperatures and enough rainfall for domestic animals to be kept in the same neighborhood through all seasons of the year. To be sure, they had to be sheltered against the worst weather, and fodder had to be stored for those weeks or months when they could not be foraging on their own; but the manure of the whole year could be saved, part of it on the lands where the animals grazed and part of it in barns and cowsheds from which it could be removed and used for fertilization of the soil. By this means the quality of the soil and the crops could be better maintained.

However, the poor quality of the fodder for the animals (for they did not have our fodder crops or anything like our means for storage of good fodder to use over the lean months) made it necessary to cull out the flocks and herds in the late fall, thereby cutting down the number of livestock to be fed. This operation produced a more or less vicious circle: the limited amount of fodder restricted the number of animals which could be carried over into the following year. This meant a restriction upon the amount of animal power available for the following year, and of course upon the amount of manure to be produced. The resultant restriction in animal power and in supply of manure in turn cut down on the amount of fodder which would be available in the succeeding years. It was not possible to make any substantial increase in the amount of land to be used, or of population to live on that land, until some break-out from this circle could be achieved. The break-out was tied up with bringing into cultivation the more favored areas in the prairies and forests, where some margin could be built up in successive years, which in turn could be built up to an increasingly large margin as the decades went on. This break-out came with the development in many areas of the manorial crop-rotation pattern of cultivation, which had its own tools and techniques and organization of society.

Maintenance of the fertility of the soil in the north was a problem aggravated by the steady drenching of the soil by rain. The rain, while beneficial in many ways, tended to leach out soluble minerals, washing them deeper into the ground or off the top soil and down the rivers, so that men had to work to keep up the fertility of the northern soils in order to combat this effect.

Europe has always been richly provided with fisheries, both fresh and salt water, though the endowment is more generous in some regions than in others.

Lakes, especially in glaciated mountain valleys or on the newly glaciated plain in the north, the abundantly watered northern rivers, and also the carefully maintained fish ponds so widely found, all have been fished in all generations. Estuaries and tidal flats fringe the whole Atlantic coast, and are generously productive of large and small fish, of mollusks, of shrimps, crabs, and lobsters.

The rivers which enter the Mediterranean and the offshore waters of that sea are far less generous than the northern rivers and seas. Although there are little settlements of fishermen from the Bosphorus to Gibraltar in nearly every cove where a few small boats can be sheltered or beached, the average yield is thin for all the risk and work invested. The case is different both with the rivers which drain southward into the Black Sea and with the offshore waters of that sea. Both are highly productive, and when trade channels have been open those waters have furnished dried, salted, smoked fish and caviar to other more-southerly regions.

Among the richest of all fishing waters in the world are those off Europe's western shores, especially on the wide continental shelf which runs out under the ocean, or in shallow banks or narrows where prodigious schools of spawning herring pass. There are many varieties, some prized for immediate consumption and many others, more valuable still, which can be easily and cheaply preserved for storage or shipment abroad.

As soon as western Europeans began to use iron, great reliance was placed on small local deposits found in bogs, or what had once been bogs, scattered across the glaciated area of northern Europe. Such deposits could be rather easily worked by men who had hand hammers and small furnaces of only a few pounds' capacity for smelting the ore. The bogs still exist; iron ore from them could be dug and used today. But it would not pay us to do so, for a modern exploiter would exhaust the ore in such a deposit in the course of a few weeks. A map of European iron resources available to the men of the five, six, or seven hundreds is different from that of iron resources for the present day; the bog areas were important then, while such areas as Lorraine, so important to modern man, were of very little importance, as the ore was beyond the reach of their tools and refining equipment.

Another consideration in appraising mineral resources is transportation. Until railroads and docks are built there is no more value in a mountain of rich ore in Venezuela than there would be in a similar mountain on the moon. In many parts of England and Germany, Italy and France, there were iron deposits which were used locally and very sparingly all through the period of the Roman Empire and through the time we are discussing here. But when that iron ore had been made up into good iron, there was still such a distance to carry it, over such rough roads, that there was no place for it in the general competitive market. More and better and cheaper iron came in from other sources nearer the markets, so the deposits where production cost was high and transportation difficult were not important.

Above all, iron workers need a good supply of fuel for smelting and for fabricating tools and weapons. Nowadays we use heat produced from electricity or petroleum as well as from coal converted into coke for such processing. But of course not one of those heat sources was of use to anyone working iron before the last few generations. All through the earlier history of ironworking, charcoal was the fuel relied upon. There was no value in ores which were too far from sources of charcoal.

Usable iron was quite widely available in the seventh century in Europe. Some was rock ore, as on Napoleon's famous island of Elba. The Romans had used a good deal of that iron, and of other iron in Italy and the Alps, to equip the Roman legions. There were many other small diggings north of the Alps, and there were the bogs. To be usable the ores had to be rich, and even so the technique for producing iron was a costly one. This, as we shall discuss later, made iron slow in coming into universal use as a farmer's or craftsman's tool.

The use of copper, which was fairly easy to extract and purify, was very widespread throughout Europe. The ores were found in Spain, in the Alps, and in great quantities in Bohemia, Sweden, and Hungary. Because there was enough copper, Europe enjoyed a lush Bronze Age before it began to use iron tools. Better than stone and poorer than iron for tools, its alloy with tin, bronze, remained important even after its value as a weapon and tool material declined once iron was easily available. Copper stayed in use for the same things for which we use it today —for piping, roofing, costume jewelry, and for mixing with other metals for various purposes.

There was tin in the southwest part of England, in Devonshire and Cornwall. There were also good supplies in Spain and Germany and in Bohemia and Hungary. It was plentiful enough to make bronze fairly cheap, and it was not difficult to refine the metal. Zinc, chiefly valuable as an alloy with copper to produce brass, was available in western Germany, but was to be used chiefly in modern times.

Lead was found in useful quantities in England, Germany, Spain, and elsewhere. With the Romans, lead was in tremendous demand for plumbing, *plumbum* being their name for it. The Roman demand for lead was so great that some of the emperors put their legions to work in the lead mines of Britain. Archaeologists in modern times have dug up shipments of British lead which had sunk in the Tiber River at Rome, this lead being in the form of pigs bearing the stamps of the legions which had sent them to Rome, and indicating the place of manufacture. Lead was also useful for roofing, and greatly in demand for the better types of buildings. Today the great medieval cathedrals of France have lead sheaths for roofs which in turn rest on timber frames which cover the stone vaults.

As long as the Romans were building large buildings, lead had a very considerable demand in masonry to make beds between the courses of large cut stones being built into walls. The Romans also used copper and bronze straps and bands in tying masonry together, and iron rods and pins. Since there was such a considerable amount of metal in Roman stone buildings, men later ruined many of them for the sake of the metal which could be obtained by tearing them apart.

Along with the metals just mentioned, those precious metals must be considered which have for millenniums had such great influence upon human beings and societies. Today we are not accustomed to thinking of Europe as a land producing gold and silver. Yet to some extent, and in widely spread areas, it has always produced those metals. It has both exported and imported them, and various aspects of the exchange of these metals will interest us later. What we must concern ourselves with here is the supply Europe possessed in the period with which we begin our study.

Gold-bearing veins are found in various places throughout the Alps, the mountains in Spain, and in the Balkans. They are also to be found scattered through older rocks elsewhere in Europe. Gold dust and nuggets can be found in gravel beds in streams which flow out of gold-bearing mountains. These natural supplies of gold, however, are meager. Neither in the five and six hundreds, nor since, have great mines of gold been opened except in Spain, despite the fact that traces of the metal are found so widely. However, in generations when human labor is cheap and gold is valuable, even poor gravels will be washed and thin veins worked. Some work of the sort was going on in many parts of Europe throughout the period we are studying, for Europe was short of gold, and it was gold hungry. As a matter of fact, in the early Middle Ages the supply of gold coming out of the ground was less important than the gold which had been accumulated in antiquity.

In ancient times silver was to be found widely over Europe and in good supply. Rich silver mines near the city of Athens furnished that city with its money metal during the Age of Pericles, at the time of the building of the Parthenon. Given the technology of the times, those mines had been exhausted, as had others in the Balkans which had been opened, used, and worked out. Silver combines very easily, chemically, with many other elements, so that it is not often found free. It is often found with lead or copper ores, so that many veins yielding these metals also yield silver. However, mines worked out much more quickly then than now because of the difficulties they had in getting rid of water, in taking care of ventilation, and so on. Thus diggings reached a limit, beyond which they could not be worked, much more quickly than today. Furthermore, having less effective refining techniques than ours, they had to use richer ores and from them extracted proportionately less silver.

All mining was, of course, rather primitive in the matter of tools and techniques. Poor drainage, poor ventilation, and methods which called for hand-moving of the rock and ore caused all metal to be costly in terms of man hours. The ancient Greeks and Romans had used the very poorest of slaves—slaves condemned for crimes, the most unlucky of the bought slaves—to work their mines. The idea was to work these men until they died, with little thought of taking measures which might prolong their lives. Therefore, the workers themselves were in no position to contribute any suggestions or advice for improvements in technique, the accumulation of which, over the years, can make for changes in efficiency and safety. The paucity of improvements between the first Greco-Roman mining and the last is striking. This lack of improvement continued through the seven, eight, and into the nine hundreds in Europe. But apparently once the mine workers were free men, improvements of all sorts began to appear. We can see this happening in the nine and ten hundreds, when improvements were being made constantly in the techniques of work underground.

In the period where this study begins the ancient mines had been largely well worked out and current working of silver mines was not very extensive. There was silver mining going on in Spain, some in England and Germany, but very little elsewhere. There was unknown silver in the ground in such places as Germany, Bohemia, the Carpathian Mountains, and the British Isles. But only a trickle of new silver was being produced, and this from widely scattered areas.

However, in the north silver was becoming the chief metal used for money, and in the seven hundreds the shift over to silver for coins took place officially in the empire of Charlemagne—a shift begun by his father and grandfather. Apparently a good deal of the silver used for this came from Mohammedan lands deep in Asia. New silver, coming through the Mohammedan channels of trade to both the Mediterranean and Baltic areas, gave Europe much more silver for trade purposes in the course of the seven, eight and nine hundreds than it had had for some time. In later years Europe itself was to have some great silver strikes. And during any generations when important new supplies were coming out of the ground in Europe, there was a resulting effect upon prices and the political situation.

Inherited from Roman times, Europe had an appetite for the goods of the East, notably for spices, and especially for pepper. The price of these spices, imported by routes which went around India and up through Persian and Arabian waters, was high. For them the Europeans had to pay in money, for the most part in silver, secondarily in gold. As a result there was a draining-off of money metals toward the East which was continuous across centuries of European history. There was a call in most generations for new supplies in Europe to keep even with what had been in circulation a few decades before.

Europe has salt in great quantities. We today are so accustomed to having plenty of salt that we are likely to have little realization of the lengths to which men will go where they have difficulty obtaining it for their diet. In parts of inland Africa and Asia, until the middle of the twentieth century, salt has been used for currency and its value has been very high.

Europe had important salt licks and great salt mines where the salt could be dug out quite easily by primitive men. Then there was the ocean, never too far away from any part of Europe. Of course, the drawback for both ocean and salt-lick water was that it had to be evaporated. Around the Mediterranean, in very early times as well as today, broad evaporating pans have been used. A shallow tidal flat could be diked so that when the slight tide came in it would be covered with water; the sluice gates would then be closed and the water allowed to evaporate until the pan's bottom had a crystal surface of salt. After several repetitions of this the salt could be shoveled off. In the north it was necessary to boil the ocean water. This in turn called for a supply of fuel from the forests. As a result there was much boiling of salt in coastal neighborhoods where a supply of fuel could be easily obtained.

The European was interested in salt not only for his diet but also as a preservative for his food. Except for smoking, salting was about the only method by which meat could be kept through the season of short supply, so the demand for salt was steady in the interior, a very important stimulus to trade. Even in the years of sick commerce there was always the movement of salt and salted fish, one of the "vehicles" in which salt was shipped. Later, when the use of salt was to be very great in industry, its abundance was to be another of Europe's assets.

Europe had supplies of many other minerals and metals in addition to those mentioned here. In fact, no other area of similar size has a longer list of such assets, either in forms which made them available in earlier centuries or in forms which facilitate exploitation today. Abundant enough, seldom too far from means of transportation, they were still spread far enough apart to stimulate the oganization of exchanges of raw materials and channels for distribution.

Still, little or no modification in economy or society could have come had there not been, even by 600 A.D., a population already well endowed with tools and, more importantly, curiously addicted to making improvements.

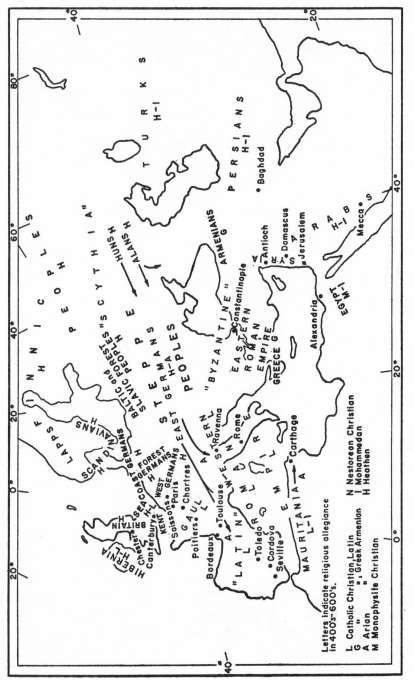

West Europe and nearby Asia and Africa: peoples and culture

CHAPTER III

Tools,
Crafts, and Processes

ABOUT 600 A.D., all Europeans had economies and societies conforming to a general pattern. Just as they had complexions and features generally similar, as against those in eastern Asia or in tropical Africa, so did they nearly all speak languages belonging to one family of human speech.

To be sure, the languages at the level of actual speaking were numerous and grouped in subfamilies, or even down to petty dialects. Complexions and features also were distributed somewhat regionally, and group resemblances were often remarked on. Similarly, regional and even very local subcultures existed, interacting upon one another and expanding, contracting, and modifying internally as European subcultures have continuously been doing since at least Neolithic times.

In Section II of this book attention will be paid to the economies and societies of all of the major subareas of Europe, both as they existed about 600 A.D. and as they were subsequently modified. All that is intended here, before discussing tools, crops, and the like, is a general sketch of the main zones of cultures as they had been shaped before the "fall" of the Roman Empire.

The discussion of climates brought out the point that bands, more or less parallel to the equator, crossed Europe, creating the zones of Mediterranean, prairie, and forest climates. Climate imposed the conditions that the general Iron Age economy had to meet in each zone; migration, conquest, and contact modified details and introduced confusion and special exceptions to confound the modern generalizer. But over-all, regardless of how language families or physical types were distributed, there were the forest band (and coastal) peoples, the prairie-steppe peoples, and the Mediterranean peoples.

We know a great deal about the culture of the Mediterranean zone, its origins, spread, varieties, and variations. It has left its own modern descendants, its archaeological and literary monuments. From near-Eastern centers it spread around the coast lands, largely through colonization by peoples from Palestine, Asia Minor, and Greece and through imitation of those colonists by tribes they touched. It was then imposed by Carthage and Rome, and in the end by Rome alone, on the lands between the Sahara and the Alps, the Euphrates and the Atlantic. So it went on broad lines.

Closer examination shows that by 500 A.D. the political division of the Empire into an East and a West really manifested a deeper division of the Mediterranean culture into two major subcultures which—anticipating further developments of the characteristics of the two in the next centuries—can be characterized anachronistically as Byzantine Greek Orthodox Christian in the East and Latin Roman Catholic Christian in the West.

But still more was to come. Between 600 and 700, in round numbers, a third powerful subculture, Saracenic Mohammedan, embracing lands and peoples never ruled by Rome (although Greece had influenced them for a thousand years), established political and religious dominance around the eastern and western ends of the sea and across the southern shores. The southern half of the Byzantine East had fallen to Islam (which will be discussed in a later Section) before it had had time to complete its modification from Late Roman to Byzantine, while the whole southern half of the Latin West was as untimely snatched from its womb.

The area dominated by the Latin Roman Catholic Christian culture was tiny. By 600 the culture had undergone generations of wrenching and crushing and tugging in every one of its aspects. It had, since Neolithic times, been continuously influenced by and been influential on both the forest and prairie lands to the north. Migrants from the north had pushed through the mountains; the Greeks and Latins themselves, and later on Gauls and Germans, had been among them. In the other direction, political conquest followed by army and administrative colonization had carried Mediterranean people to the Rhine River mouth, to northern and western Britain, and to the inner foothills of the Carpathians where Slovakia is today.

Warriors, moving in and out of the Empire as invaders; captives, hired fighters, and purchased slaves, also moving both ways; and merchants and ambassadors, traveling from center to center of wealth and power every year for centuries—all accounted for the transmission of ideas, tools, and religious and governmental principles and practices. The interflow of cultural influences had been incessant for at least two thousand years.

North of the Danube a great stretch of combined forests plus prairies had been ruled for generations by Rome and then lost before 300 A.D. to a new wave of invaders—a people in the process of being transformed from forest to steppe Germans—the Goths. Rome's way of doing things, or its total Mediterranean culture, could not be maintained in the most westerly of the important steppe expanses of Eurasia. Yet that area, while giving home to tribe after tribe of dominant steppe peoples— Sarmatians, Visigoths, Huns, Lombards, Avars, and Magyars—served at all times as a center for the schooling of such tribes to the ways of western Europeans.

It is regrettable that our records of this area are so scanty. At least we do know that it was there the Visigoths ruled subject peoples for generations before the Huns came. These subject peoples had in turn been under Rome for generations previously. It is here also that the Visigoths adopted Christian baptism, part of the Bible in their own alphabet and tongue, and had bishops and priests who spoke Greek and were familiar with Constantinople, Antioch, and Rome. They also learned from the other steppe peoples to migrate as a way of life.

As the Hungarian plains served as a hub for intermingling of steppe and Mediterranean cultures, so Gaul and Britain in the same way served to mingle the cultures of forest and coastal northerners on the one hand and Roman southerners on the other. Forest Gauls and Germans, not greatly different from one another in culture, had been in contact with peoples of Mediterranean culture for centuries before the time of Caesar and his immediate successors as rulers of Rome. Thereafter Rome's military frontiers were pushed by conquest to the Irish Sea and the mouth of the Elbe River; they held thereabouts until they began shrinking back from time to time, finally receding by the later four hundreds.

Yet the Roman way of life, centering upon walled urban towns, political affairs, economic and social organization, and everything else worth while to civilized men, never completely took hold in those northerly provinces.

All across Europe the tools with which men worked the land, made their clothes and houses, prepared their food, and made their tools themselves, were those of an Iron Age civilization. But iron was too costly to be used lavishly, so for the peasant it was an age of wood, leather, and iron, with emphasis on the wood. Even such a thing as the shield a soldier carried was made of either wood or wickerwork, with a metal center, or boss, on it to catch or deflect arrow points and blows. There was a great reliance on wood for all kinds of things, exactly as there was in similar circumstances on the American frontier. (In Abraham Lincoln's boyhood the logs of frontier buildings were fastened together with wooden pins.) During the course of the centuries, however, iron was to become cheaper and better and much more plentiful.

The metal men used by preference for their tools and weapons was iron worked into steel. Their second choice, iron, was usually quite pure, and hence rather soft, but it was tough and slow to rust and so had its own advantages. Fine steel was used above all for noblemen's swords. The best swords were literally without price, and the smiths who could make them became legendary figures. German and feudal poets included fine steel blades in the legends of the Nibelungs, of Roland, and of Arthur, and often these swords were given names. In real life the very fine sword was cherished generation after generation as the best thing a noble father could give his son. When steel was of such value as that, no peasant could be found using it to make a hoe. (Parenthetically, the best steel of that time was no better than the ordinary working steel of today, and of course far poorer than our specialty steels.)

Before the six and seven hundreds there was little change in the design of tools; few new things had been introduced since the end of the Smooth Stone Age through the Bronze Age and the period of Roman antiquity. That does not mean all tools were poor. Some beautiful ones were made in Greek, Roman, and even Egyptian antiquity. For example, some of the surgeons' kits contained fine scalpels, saws, tweezers, forceps, and so on, but such implements were most precious articles. Tools of that quality were not for the peasant out in the countryside, and he had often to be content with a thin ferrule of iron on the cutting edge of his wooden spade.

The tools which were generally available made hands rough and calloused by the time children reached their early teens and, again because of poor tools, their backs were hunched soon after. Peasants aged quickly —men ready for discard at forty, women at thirty-five—and in part their tools were responsible.

Tools for working wood are of great antiquity. Perhaps the earliest stone tools—knives and hatchets—should be classified here (although a knife or axe is as much a war weapon as a woodcutter's tool). Axes were stiff and clumsy and chisels inefficient. There were saws and files—but not many of them and owned by only the best carpenters—and gouges and such modifications of the chisel. All of them, except for the fancy kits of the cabinet makers and of the best workers in the towns in the Eastern Roman Empire, tended to be crude and of poor metal. They did not wear well and the handling of them was difficult.

There were saws and planes, but the adze was the tool chiefly used to work planks. An adze, broadly speaking, is an axe turned edgewise so that by chipping it can make a flat surface on a beam or plank. (In many old barns in the United States it can be seen that the beams were chipped with an adze or its structural relative, the broadaxe.)

Stone workers, found at first only in areas that had earlier been Roman, had a simple kit of heavy hammers of several different weights; various lengths and strengths of bars and wedges; chisels; and a few simple tools for polishing, drilling, and grinding. The very best of the stone masons were well equipped, but the very best, again, were men who had learned their craft and obtained their tools in Constantinople, Egypt, or Syria to the East, or who were sons and grandsons of migrants from the East who had come West. By the five and six hundreds the stone mason's art was generally at a low level in the west of Europe, and it came back slowly. The crudeness of their tools is reflected in the crudeness of the finish on even the most beautiful things made by Irish or English or Lombard stone workers.

In addition to tools, the stone masons inherited ideas for heavy machinery, especially cranes and winches and ramps and pulley arrangements for lifting large stone blocks into place. The medieval builder was always able to put up fairly sizable stone or brick buildings, using lifting devices like those of Imperial Rome. But during the six, seven, eight, and early nine hundreds, there was little stone building in western Europe. Even the wealthiest and most powerful man known in Europe between 500 and 1000 A.D., the Emperor Charlemagne, could not find stone masons inside his Empire who were skilled enough to quarry and to shape artistically the stone for his private imperial chapel in Germany. (Incidentally, the Moors of Cordova drew skilled workers and fine materials from Byzantium in the same period.) The workers hauled old columns and other cut stone pieces from buildings in Italy.

The ceramic crafts were at low ebb in the seventh century. Europe had had marvelously skilled and artistic potters—those who had made the beautiful Grecian vases. Some later Roman Imperial potters had also been very highly skilled. As a matter of fact, ancient potters had also been what we would call industrial organizers and had had mass-production plants for the putting out and wide distribution of pottery of good quality all over Gaul, Spain, and Britain. Some of the work was finely made. Their tools—sieves, troughs, molds, wheels, kilns, decorating devices—were of high quality and the workmen in these potteries were very skilled.

The Romans were also magnificent builders in tile and brick. They set up their kilns wherever they could get fuel and the right clay and made a fine substantial brick. However, in the late two and three and four hundreds the Roman potters and Roman tile and brick makers began going out of business, until they had practically ceased to exist.

In part their going out of business was due to the profusion of junk brick and tile available all over the old Roman territory; there was no need to buy expensive new brick when one could get all he wanted by tearing down one's great-grandfather's temple. Men built largely with junk for hundreds of years; city and monastery walls were made by quarrying deserted buildings. Sometimes junk was used over and over again—the reusing of Roman materials goes on to this day. By about 600 A.D. the fine Roman kilns, the purifying and kneading troughs, the panels, forms, mortars, and pestles, were simply not much known and the men who were skilled to use them had disappeared.

By the six and seven hundreds much of the household pottery was only half-baked; and pottery that is half-baked falls apart. Water put in such a vessel goes into the walls of the vessel, which then begin to turn back into mud. When archaeologists investigate burial and town sites of the medieval Merovingian-Ottonian period, half-baked pottery too often comes out of the ground. In that period men were not without good cooking and eating vessels, but they used horn, glass, leather, and metal to make them, and good pottery was no longer much prized. Among other things, the coming into general use of the wooden barrel, which was a much handier and tougher container for wine and oil than the old Greco-Roman jar or amphora, left the potter with a good deal of his business superseded.

During Greek and Roman times, the art of glassmaking had been carried from the lands of its origin, probably Palestine and Egypt, into Italy and Gaul. Much of the product of Western glassmakers consisted of colored glass cups and goblets, and of imitation jewelry for armor, sword hilts, necklaces, and the like. As late as the seven hundreds, some glass seems to have been made for barbarian customers even far back in the old German lands. This glass was pretty but crude, made with mediocre tools and skills. But as time went on, even that manufacture faded out, and glass objects had to be imported from Eastern and Mediterranean lands. Then, in the nine hundreds and with increasing volume in the ten and eleven hundreds, Western glassmaking for mosaic and window art gloriously revived.

The miller is needed at all levels of advancement in any grain-consuming society. The simplest milling can be done with metate stone implements such as those used by the Pueblo and Mexican women. A grinding bowl will serve, and even a hollow stump will do as a grinding bowl, with a pestle to pound and push the grain around inside. It was in this way that neolithic grinding had been done, and it was considered woman's work.

In the Roman cities large stone mills powered by animals were in use. The animals could be either four-legged animals such as donkeys, or two-legged animals, for slaves were often used. The government maintained great public mills in such cities as Rome itself for the grinding up of the flour to make the bread which it distributed to the plebes.

Ordinarily the Roman mill consisted of one fairly heavy rough stone that was cylindrical outside with an interior hole from top to bottom which fitted down on another cone-shaped stone. Enough space was left between them so that grain sliding into that space would then be ground up and either the meal or the flour and grit would come out at the bottom ready to be made into pottage or bread. (Up to the last generation or two, grinding machines of the Roman type were still to be found in Scotland, where such an implement is called a quern. The quern type of mill, either very large or small enough to be turned by two hands, was commonly in use throughout the Roman Empire.)

By the three hundreds the largest mills in the largest cities were being turned by water power. The mill would be situated beside a river or an aqueduct or it could be placed on a raft and the raft anchored firmly in a river. This last, for example, was done in the five hundreds in the Tiber River at Rome, where the current turned the mill wheel which in turn turned the stones.

By the time our study begins, flat revolving mill stones were already in use. A fixed lower stone had little cross grooves which caught and turned the grain or meal outward as an upper stone set above it went round and round. This top stone could be adjusted tight for fine grinding or more loosely for coarse grinding, and held at whatever level it was set for. It could be powered by hand, by animals, or, as later, by water or wind.

Tanning is a very old process or succession of processes. By bacterial action, all organic ingredients which are subject to quick decay must be worked out of a fresh skin of whatever kind. If leather which still contains fat and muscle cells is used to make shoes, putrefaction will set in after the shoes are made. As the first step in making leather, the tanner tries to have the decaying process completed under careful control. Until the last generation tanning has been a most noisome process—a decaying process in which fluids containing the proper bacteria were put in with the hides to eat up the fat and meat as thoroughly and as evenly as possible. At a proper point a contrariwise preserving process was begun. Its purpose was to preserve the bundles of hard fibers which make up the leather. (Under a microscope these fibers, twisted and tied together, appear in a complex of layers to form the leather.) Salt could be used as a preservative, except that salt-preserved leather is hard and brittle when dry, and turns slippery and flaccid and loses its salt when wet. Much better were the various kinds of smoke tars; leather could be smoked just as ham and bacon are. Or various acids could be used which could penetrate and partly tighten the bundles of fibers. The best acids have been called tannic acids because it is precisely for tanning that they have been used.

During the Middle Ages these acids were extracted from oak galls, oak bark, bark from various other kinds of trees to be found in Europe or not too far away, and from different sorts of leaves and twigs, such as sumac. The list is long, and a tanner skilled in making different combinations of tanning solutions could, through them, produce many different kinds of finished leathers. Alums were also used to produce leather which was excellent for such purposes as the aprons of a smith or the armor of a fighting man. Such leathers have been tawed (chemically pickled) rather than tanned.

At the time our study begins the tanners used old-style tools for cutting and scraping the hides and for stretching them. They had pits for controlled decay and vats for making tanning solutions. But by and large there had been no progress in this field since the Bronze Age and the days of the Greeks and the Roman Empire.

The fanciest leathers were imported, made by skilled workers of Mohammedan Spain, North Africa, and the East, where very fine leathers were produced and used for garments, book covers, and so on. The names which still cling to certain kinds of leathers recall their places of origin: "cordovan," made by the Moors of Cordova, Spain, and "morocco."

While the Western leathers were not so fine, leather, along with wood, did many of the things that metals do today. For example, even later on when they had good metal, leather armor continued to be used. A suit of armor was as often as not a leather garment on which rings and plates of metal had been sewn, the leather being part of the armor, not just a foundation for the metal. Furthermore, leather aprons and jerkins were used in daily life for protection against their tools by craftsmen, by peasants, and also by warriors. In addition hard leather was used for joints and bearings where today we would use metal. For instance, they would shrink a treated rawhide around a pin that was to bear something that revolved. On its drying, the bearing part would be protected; the leather would wear, not like iron, but at least relatively well, especially when kept lubricated. The use of leather was much more extensive even into the 1800's than it is today.

When discussing leather working we must take notice of an important shift which took place in writing materials during the six, seven, and eight hundreds. During this time scholars and the keepers of records changed from the use of papyrus, imported from Egypt, to the use of hides, especially vellum (which was made of calf hides) or parchment (made of sheep skins). These hides were treated very carefully and usually scraped evenly, producing sheets much thinner than the original hide. They were then treated further by scraping and polishing with fine stones and powdered talc until the surface was right for use with quill pen and ink. Vellum and parchment making became progressively important as they became the main writing materials. Largely a craft carried on by monks, the skill in making these was carefully guarded in the better monasteries and the libraries of those monasteries.

Weaving processes for cotton, wool, silk, or linen all differ from each other. However, since most of the work done in western Europe was with wool and only secondarily with linen, we shall be concerned here with the process for preparing and weaving woolen cloth.

All the work was done with very clumsy tools. Even today a sheep may be nicked when being shorn, and with the far poorer shears of the time of our study, which were neither springy nor sharp, both the animals and the cleanliness of the wool suffered. Plucking the wool by hand, although slower, was commonly done, and the fleece of butchered sheep was also used as a source of supply.

The wool of their sheep was short and kinky. The long-staple wools, used for more tightly twisted yarns, began to be available only in the later Middle Ages, as use of Spanish Merino sheep became more widespread. Since raw wool is greasy and dirty, it had to be washed in little dishes or basins, and the shortage of good soap was a handicap at this point. Although they could and did make soap, it was of uneven quality and the washing of the wool was hard work.

When the wool dried, it had to be carded with hand carders, which are wooden cards with spikes set into them and with handles to hold them by. A card was held in each hand, and the wool put between the cards and the cards rubbed against one another carefully until a kind of roll was worked up which was quite light, fluffy, and fairly thick.

After the carding the fluffy strands had to be spun into yarn for the loom. This was woman's work, the work of the spinster. Spinning was done by women of all classes; it was so characteristic an occupation that the distaff, one of the tools used, still is, in the art of armorial bearings, the symbol for a woman, and genealogists still talk of the "distaff side" —the mother's side of a family. Starting as youngsters, women spun by the hour, and they were still doing it when they were old women. They spun while they were tending sheep and while they stood out in front of their houses along the village streets. (Even in the last few years this was being done in parts of Italy, and in Irish and Scottish cottages they still make thread in this way for tweeds.) The spinning wheel, which we consider an archaic piece of equipment, was yet to be invented.

Weaving could be done either on tiny looms which made quite narrow strips of cloth which had to be sewn together or on large looms which, while they made wider strips of cloth, were so heavy and clumsy to manipulate that the use of larger ones was a man's work. Bulky wooden parts and friction in the movement had to be surmounted. Despite the clumsiness of their tools, some fine cloth was produced, but in general woolens were rough and coarse.

When the weaving had been finished, still another process was needed for woolen cloth since the threads were flimsy and the cloth fragile and, even worse, it would shrink drastically as soon as it got wet; it had to be preshrunk and strengthened by a process resembling felting. (It was not true felting, however, for there was already a pattern of crossed threads through the fabric, while true felt does not have woven threads.) The process used was called "fulling" or "walking" or "tucking." The bolt or piece of woven goods was treated in a trough which contained detergent and highly astringent liquids, and then the fuller "walked" it. Walking the cloth did not require that the fuller actually walk up and down; rather, holding to a bar, he stood with his bare feet on the cloth, and with them pressed and rubbed it about until every square inch had been evenly treated.

Walking this loose, flimsy woolen cloth produced a felted surface and resulted in the woolen fibers all clinching together and the cloth shrinking in such a way that it would never again shrink very much. By this process the cloth also became thickened, until it was more like the weight of the materials we use for warm overcoats than like the light, hard-spun cloths we use for most of our woolen clothing.

After the fulling, the cloth was not quite finished; there was still a job of restretching and shearing to be done, the former to bring it back into shape, the latter to make it smooth. After this work had been accomplished the cloth was finally ready to be dyed, unless the wool or threads had been dyed before being woven.

Not only were the tools for clothmaking clumsy, but also the making of a whole piece by one man, not skilled particularly in the use of any one tool, would go both slowly and badly. Consequently, a division of labor in the art of clothmaking took place at a very early time. In the more advanced establishments in the ancient world fullers, weavers, and dyers carried on their crafts separately. Just as soon as the medieval Western communities grew big enough to have specialists in different lines of work, the clothmakers set up separate establishments for the different processes. The fact that no man could easily own or house all the tools and equipment needed—the loom, the fulling troughs, frames and shears, dying vats and tools—was an additional incentive for this division of labor in textile making.

Brewing of a sort can be done on a small scale, as was proved all over the United States in the nineteen-twenties. But brewing is a matter not only of equipment, but also of considerable knowledge of what could be called kitchen chemistry and bacteriology. Lack of that was the great stumbling block all through the twenties; a person could get his brew to working but he couldn't be sure of what would come out because all kinds of weird, stray bacteria and yeasts got in, giving curious flavors to the mixtures. Brewing is not just a matter of having materials and tools; it is above all a matter of knowing what to do with materials which in minutes can go totally bad. A brewster (a lady brewer) or a brewer (a man, and less common) was a person with skill not only in handling equipment but also in handling the processing of the materials. Since she had to work like an old-fashioned cook, without temperature controls and without anything more than eyes, nose, taste buds for controls, she had to have real training in the craft.

The tools were fairly simple. The first requirement was a malt house where the selected barley was turned into malt, in itself a ticklish job. After the malt was ready there was the problem of mixing and controlling the brew. Brewing equipment can be fairly expensive and bulky; there must be a floor and drying apparatus for the malt and any flavoring that may be put in, vats for the cooking and clarifying, and, finally, containers—which were most often barrels.

The brewing establishment, instead of being something every home had, tended to be something every village (north of wine country) had, and as soon as the population grew to be large there would be many breweries in any one town.

The baker often lived next door to or was the husband of the brewster, a very sensible arrangement as both of them used yeasts. The proper preservation and use of yeast was something both brewster and baker had to know about. The baking of bread could of course be done in anyone's home and over even a small fire. Nevertheless, in order to save fuel and work, very commonly there would be only one bake oven in a neighborhood or even in a village. Here the baker could bake everybody's bread, although the mixing, kneading, and preparation of the loaves could be done at home. On the other hand, he would also do all of the work if the villager was willing to pay for it.

Leavened bread was really the staff of life for most Europeans. It was one of the two ways in which they consumed grain; boiled meal or pottage was the other.

In any district where olive trees could be made to grow—that is, in frost-free country—olive oil was the chief cooking and shortening ingredient in food. Olive oil, by quite a long process, is made from ripe olives. Before an olive is edible a great deal must be done to it. The work of preparing ripe olives for either eating or, more important still, pressing has always been a process calling for knowledge and for presses, containers, tanks, and so on.

Once prepared, the olives were usually put through three separate pressings. The product of the first was a very fine clear oil, almost colorless and tasteless; the second pressing produced a useful cooking and eating oil; and the third an oil used for lubricating and for burning in oil lamps. Olive oil was also used for rubdowns after games or baths. The oil had to be stored, and for this the ancient Greeks and Romans had used amphorae, great jars of baked clay which usually had pointed ends which could be sunk in the ground or sand to be held upright. But later Roman populations, primarily those living in western Europe near the barbarians, began to use the coopered barrel for shipping and storing liquids.

The presses used for production of olive oil and wine could be very similar. However, olive oil could not be produced by that most simple of all operations used in the production of grape juice—trampling in a vat by the bare feet of village youths and maidens. Grapes were not normally pressed that way either. Instead, presses were used and the development of the presses has had its effect in the whole history of mechanical inventions, for the screw piston and the lever piston used for the squeezing out of juices reached a further development in power-producing engines and in metal and printing presses. Beside the press with screw or lever pistons, other tools and processes were used at this time. For example, rollers propelled by hand or animal power could be moved around on a flat surface or trough in which the olives or grapes had been placed, squeezing them and crushing out the juice or oil. This principle was also used for grain threshing.

The development of the tools of the iron worker during the Middle Ages was a very important matter because all other advances in all other fields of tool using depended on the smith as maker of tools. The steady spreading out of mechanical know-how through all other crafts is tied, all through the history of metal working, with advances in the craft of the ironmaster and the smith. During the Greco-Roman period, their crafts had not greatly advanced. They did very little more and they did very little better than the older, early Metal Age smiths had done. It was in the so-called Dark Ages that basic advances again began in techniques and in the tool kits of the smiths.

The kit of tools of a smith is basically simple. A forge is needed in which the temperature of the metal can be raised to such a point as to change its character so that striking it will in turn change its shape. Also, in the forge the crystalline structure of the metal can be temporarily or permanently modified, either from hard to soft or from soft to hard; the heat can take impurities out, or the same heat can help put controlled amounts of impurities in. Some impurities make iron poorer, some make it better; if the proper amount of carbon in the proper way is added to pure iron, then the iron becomes steel; and so on.

A simple fire can be made in a forge, but it will hardly do for iron working. To make a better fire and a hotter one, there can be special ducts which will send a current of air up through the coals, and the effect of these special ducts can be increased by greater exposure to the winds supplied by nature, say by putting the forge on a high place where the normal winds will blow in with some force. As this is not always satisfactory, men have long worked to increase the pressure of air through the ducts by putting in bellows or pumps. In this field great advances have taken place. We today are standing at the end of thirteen hundred years of important progressive improvement in the matter of getting more air and more heat, both under better control, into the smelting furnaces and the smiths' forges. By changes in fuel—first charcoal, then more recently coke, oil, and electricity—the forges of the smiths have been enormously improved.

Over a long period the chief improvements were made in the matter of working out better bellows arrangements. The earliest bellows, pumped up and down with one hand, gave a jerky jet of air. The addition of a kind of pressure box, made with valves at both ends so that the air could not back out, produced a jet of air from the box to the flame which was relatively steady. Then two bellows were put in so that an assistant working them alternately with his hands could compress double the amount of air. When the two of them were put on the ground he could work them with his feet and increase the production of air even more. Then, by attaching the bellows to a pole or lever hooked up to a water wheel or to a wind mill, nature could supply the mechanical power. Still other devices were worked out: better linings for forges and larger, higher forges in which ore would melt were devised; and so on.

One of the places where the increased use of iron was to be most important was for shoes for oxen—the chief work animals—and for horses. If they put shoes on horses in ancient times, they did it sparingly and not very well. In the period we are studying the protection of the horse with a nailed-on iron shoe first began. So did the shoeing of the work oxen's front hooves (since it does not do any work with its rear legs and uses them chiefly for balance, it is not necessary to shoe them). Shoeing the animals brought them into much greater productivity in terms of delivered power. A horse without shoes is not able to give long, steady pulls through a workday as can a horse with shoes. This increase in animal power brought with it a great increase all over Europe in the amount of food produced and goods transported.

As the smith produced better metal, he himself was one of the craftsmen who most benefited. He got better metal for his own purposes; his tools were themselves subject to steady improvement in the matter of anvils, hammers, shears, and tongs, and of course with each improvement he could do more.

Tools for turning the soil, cutting down weeds, evening off lumps, and so on, had existed ever since men and women began putting seeds in the ground. (The western Europeans had had plows from Neolithic times.) By the five and six hundreds there were two main types of plow in use. One of these, a light plow, was essentially just a "forked stick." (A great deal of plowing is still done with a forked stick, and it is quite a good instrument for dry farming, where the object is to keep the surface powdery so as to retain the moisture and discourage the weeds, and to cover the seed.) For one thing, using simple tools a man could (and still can) make a forked stick plow, say from the fork of a tree. The heaviest point of the fork would be sharpened for contact with the ground. To one branch would be attached a rope, which in turn was attached to perhaps a wife or a donkey. Using the other branch end as a plow handle, the plowman would put the point of the fork into the ground and stir the motive force into action. With the wife or donkey (or ox or camel) pulling and the plowman steering, the plow could be moved back and forth across the land's surface. The point would go into the dirt not more than a few inches, the object being to stir up the surface. Since this was literally a scratchy job, it would be necessary to go back and forth across a field first from north to south and then from east to west, and to repeat several times.

The forked-stick type of plow still is widely used in lands with a Mediterranean climate. Those in actual use are commonly more sophisticated than the one just described, although in some backward areas an actual stick is still used. But in others it has been improved by such things as adding a small iron shoe to the point, by having two handles for the plowman instead of one, or by making the shoe adjustable so that the earth can be plowed into channels and thrown, first to one, then to the other side of the groove, the channels serving both for cultivation and for irrigation because they catch and distribute water either from ditches or from light summer showers. The forked-stick type of plow is basically a good instrument, even in the most sophisticated agriculture, and is especially handy in working small plots of land such as are found on terraces along the sides of hills and mountains.

The forked-stick plow was also in very early use north of the Alps, but it had many shortcomings in Gaul and Germany, where the sod was heavy and the rainfall generous. The point clogged with roots and grass after going only a few yards and the plowman would have to stop and clean it. He would also find that the roots down in the sod had not been harmed; after two or three days the grass would have come up again. What was needed north of the Alps was a plow that would go down under the sod and heave it up and over so that the roots of the weeds and grass would be exposed. By this means the roots of the weeds would die, and also there would be a surface of dirt on which to plant seed, giving the seed at least an even start with the weeds and grass. But such a plow was not widely used during the Roman period; hence the cultivation of the light soils on the tops of the chalk downs where the forked-stick plow could make at least some impression.

Gauls along the Rhine frontier and in Britain and some Germans farther east seem to have had a heavy plow even before Roman times. Often, and perhaps usually, this plow was mounted on wheels and was very heavy, especially in its primitive forms. The heavy wheeled plow was to be a really important agricultural tool, and was to have its effect on the whole organization of society and on government income once an agriculture based on its use had become widely spread in the North.

The heavy wheeled plow had a tongue reaching in front of it to which could be attached anywhere from two to eight oxen, thereby furnishing a powerful pulling force. The plow itself would be characterized by a sharp point of iron, or of steel when obtainable, forming a plowshare which could cut under the sod to a depth of from six to eight inches— or even more—as it was dragged along. Because the whole thing would still get clogged with roots and stems, a colter (a sharp cutter), point down, was fastened to the tongue of the plow directly in line with and just in front of the plowshare's point. This gave a kind of preliminary slicing, five or six inches deep, which the plowshare would deepen and widen while undercutting the roots. Behind the plowshare was the mold board, so placed that it would heave the cut sod up and partly over. Since its action was often incomplete, it was necessary to have people walking along behind who completed the process of turning the sod upside down, and wives and children of the men operating the plow could do this. Later improved wheeled plows had levers by which the frame could be adjusted so that the plowshare could cut a deeper or more shallow furrow as desired.

The *carruca* or "carriage" plow was mentioned by such Roman writers as Pliny, but it seems to have been very little used in the Roman Empire. Instead, its use was spread widely by those "backward" barbarians who came into the regions around the Rhine and in southern Britain as the Empire faded out—and who got more production per acre in northern lands than the Romans did. This plow was to make possible the cultivation of the very richest lands, those of the prairie grasses and of the best bottom lands. Because of the carriage plow it became well worth while to cut the timber off bottom lands which had usually been wildernesses under earlier human settlement.

A hoe can be fashioned, as the American Indians knew, by tying a clam or mussel shell crosswise on a stick and cementing it on with pitch. Such a tool is useful in cultivating growing plants and in keeping weeds down and the ground stirred up. For the purpose of patch cultivation it can be used to break sod. In Europe in the Middle Ages spade and hoe blades were of metal whenever possible. But a good many workers had to use wooden hoes and spades of which only the edge might be of metal. All of these tools had wooden handles which were poorly weighted and balanced, with the result that work with them was slow and very wearing. There was no such easy cutting as is possible with our modern steel-bladed, light-handled hoe, nor was there any easy swing when using a mattock or any other earth-breaking tools.

The process of smoothing out the land onto which seed is to be put, or into which seed has already been put, is not a complicated one. Some sort of clod-breaking apparatus must be dragged over the ground. This harrowing is important not only for breaking up clods of earth so the seed will be spread evenly, and for covering the seed, it is also important for leaving the seeded ground fairly smooth so that when harvesting is to be done there will not be unevennesses to trip and dull the scythes and sickles. In the Middle Ages harrows often consisted of briar-tree branches which were dragged across the fields, sometimes weighted down with crossbeams and with stones on top of the crossbeams. Improved diamond shaped wooden harrows with wooden teeth set in them were also used.

Archaeologists have found iron sickles going back to the times before Christ, but they also have evidence that in backward parts of Europe, as late as the period in which we are beginning our study, sickles made of wood, with sharp flint points set in pitch in grooves on the inside of the curve, were used.

Most of the reaping was done by the handful. The reaper reached over, taking as many stalks of grain as he could hold in one hand; then with his sickle he chopped off the grain heads. Or he might use shears. It took many people working hard for a long time to reap an acre of wheat or barley.

A reaping tool which was a great improvement over the sickle was the scythe. This tool had a short handle, making it necessary still to bend over when cutting. (Such a scythe was in use on the frontiers in America until only a few generations ago.) As time went by, in some parts of Europe men began using a long-handled scythe. However, the handle was straight and required a long deep swing which caused a great deal of strain on the back and hip muscles; it is still widely in use. It was not until much later that the curve-handled snath (or handle) for the scythe came into use. It greatly eased the work of the reaper, allowing him to swing his scythe from the hip instead of the back.

Reaping was begun when the grain was a little less than ripe. The workers did not dare let it get wholly ripe before starting because they harvested so slowly. If they had begun when the grain was ripe all across a field, they would have lost most of that on the far side of the field before they could get there to cut it. Because of this it was—and is— necessary in general to dry grain after harvesting. Besides shocking it, in dry climates this was done by putting it in lofts; in damp climates it could be and often is necessary to have artificially heated drying rooms.

During the Middle Ages several methods were used for threshing grain. One method, that of Biblical times, was to put the grain on a hard-packed dirt floor and drive oxen, pulling a weighted plank, around and around on the grain. The pressure of the drag and of their feet broke the husks from the kernels; then the whole would be shoveled off into piles for separation later. Another method (also used for crushing olives) was to put the grain in channels, roll heavy stone wheels around and around in the channels until it had been partly crushed, then shovel it out. The wheels of stone used for this were pulled either by animals or men.

The threshing instrument most generally in use in the north was the flail. This implement consists of two sticks, each about two or three feet long, held together by a sleeve or by thongs of soft leather. One of the sticks was the flail handle; the other, a partly flattened heavy bat, was the part with which the kernels of grain were beaten. A small pile of grain was laid out on the floor or ground and beaten until the chaff was loosened from the kernels. This was shoveled up and another pile of grain spread out. By this method it was possible to thresh a few bushels of grain in a day. Much of Europe's grain, in the north at least, was threshed in this way for a great many centuries, and flails are still in use.

Once the grain had been threshed it was necessary to separate the kernels from the chaff. A fairly strong current of air was required as well as several people to do the work. An artificial current could be obtained by use of fans worked by hand. (In the United States turkey feather fans were used until the steam threshing machine came into use.) Otherwise the grain would be taken to a high place where the wind was blowing. A whole family could work together; taking a supply of baskets and cloth sheets, they would go out to a spot where, let us say, the father could stand on a stepladder or high rock. Holding a shallow tray basket with a little grain in it, he would start tossing the grain up into the wind and catching it again in his basket. The wind would blow the chaff away and soon he would have only kernels of good grain in his basket. His children and wife would be on the ground below him, picking up any kernels which had bounced out of the basket. This process would be repeated until a good supply of pure grain had been winnowed from the chaff. With a whole family working all day, several bushels of good grain could be turned out.

It is apparent, given the tools men had during the early Middle Ages, that there was no way at all—no rearrangement of law, government, or society—to produce more than they did. The amount of food grown was just at the famine level much of the time, under it once in a while, and never significantly over it for any length of time. The cloth for a simple garment took a vastly greater number of man-hours to produce than the cloth we wear today. Production of a few hundred loaves of bread involved the use of a heavy plow, many oxen, and six or eight working men with their wives and children. So large a team as this could plow only one of their acres in a day. In reaping, whole families had to work long hours to clean off a single acre, while threshing the grain for only a single village took hundreds of hours of work. As Europeans moved toward modern industrial society, the differences between what those people had and were able to do, and what we today have and are able to do, stem very considerably from the dramatic improvements in tools. We cannot visualize western Europe's development from where men were in the six hundreds, in the earlier Middle Ages, to where we are today unless we keep very close track of their implements.

CHAPTER IV

Crops,
Foods, and Livestock

E VEN in the present day grain flours baked into breads play a much greater part in the European diet than they do in the United States or in many other parts of the world. In general the western European is a bread-eater, and throughout his history the preferred bread grain has been wheat.

The strains of wheat men grew in the Middle Ages seem to have come down from Neolithic times. Stone Age Europeans had gotten wheats, already domesticated, from Abyssinia and southwestern Asia, and these basic strains continued to be grown over most of Europe.

Various sorts of wheat were known, but all of them were what is called winter wheat. They were sown in the fall, brought to quite an advanced stage before spring, and harvested in the early summer. In the Mediterranean area this wheat had many advantages; when put in the ground in the fall it germinated and grew up during the wet winter weather, getting the maximum value from the moisture. The dry season set in at approximately the time when the plants were beyond damage from drought. In the north, however, the wheat suffered occasionally from failure to ripen because of the long damp which could come with a late spring.

The wheat was planted in the fall, allowed to grow up to a lush blanket of green, and then pastured. Rather than harming the wheat, this improved it; for the plant will normally put up only a single grain-bearing stalk, but when it is cut off, as by the teeth of animals, the roots grow deeper and stronger and send up several seed-bearing stalks. Hence a much heavier production is obtained where animals have been grazing on wheat, with an added advantage of increased fertilization of the soil by animal droppings. And of course green pasture during the winter and early spring is good for the animals.

Occasionally the wheat would go bad in the ground. Farmers could usually tell this was happening and could plow the wheat under in the spring, putting in a crop of peas or oats if they had the seed.

Three-field farming, to which we will be turning further on, was pretty largely dominated by the fact that men did their heavy plowing for wheat in the later summer and fall, and that their main harvesting took place in early summer.

In terms of modern wheat production, their yield was very low. With a harvest of about ten or twelve bushels of grain per acre, they still had to put aside two or three of those bushels for seed for the next year. It was a poor sort of wheat, no better than the mediocre neolithic wheats, barely domesticated back in the Stone Ages, from which it descended. It was no more productive, the kernels were no bigger, and there were no more kernels to a head. There was almost no selection of seed for improvement of the crop, so that if an area had poor seed, then year after year men continued to get poor crops there. The reverse, of course, was true, but it, too, was by accident, not design. This was so of all their crops; they had access only to local supplies of seed and to local supplies of breeding stock. In the later Middle Ages good farmers tried to get other than local seed and to be selective, but such refinements came late.

Fertility of the soil was challenged by the wheat, and it was through the adoption of the two-field and three-field rotation system that fertility of the soil in the Northern Plain was maintained in spite of the planting of wheat there year after year and century after century.

Much of their wheat was rough-ground into coarse meal rather than into flour; like all other grains it was, to a considerable extent, consumed in the form of pottage, or porridge. This could be of various thicknesses, from watery-thin to pudding-stiff, and with various other things added to it. Whatever was on hand that day was mixed into the pot. It might be dried fish, and it was often sour dried fruit, dried onions, various bits of meat such as salt pork or fresh rabbit, while in times of famine it could be roots and leaves.

Their impure sowings of wheat resulted in loaves or cakes likely to be a mixed-grain bread, ranging in color from just a shade brown to quite black. Only the rich could always afford flour made from the picked-over wheat which would be sure to make white bread. The dark, heavy bread was sustaining, but there was a preference for white bread when obtainable.

Of the other crops, such as oats and rye, barley was the rival great grain crop in Europe. It was the old bread grain in the Mediterranean areas where the ground was too thin and stony to carry wheat well. In neighborhoods where men could not get good wheat, they made their cakes and pottages chiefly of barley. In the Mediterranean areas, where grapes would grow and wine was the favorite drink, barley was used for such pottage and bread. But north of the Alps the basic drink was ale, made of barley malt, so barley was planted there chiefly as the basic drinking crop, except when it was also used for bread in the areas where wheat would not grow.

In Roman and early medieval times oats seem to have been generally regarded as a kind of sham grain, a grass weed which appeared as a volunteer in the wheat and barley fields. It is quite likely that at that time the wild oats had a thin seed and scanty yield. Still, oats were raised for food where better cereals could not thrive. They were not appreciated until it was noticed that grazing animals had a partiality for them.

In the eight to eleven hundreds, with care and attention, farmers began to develop oats which were more productive in terms of yield for the amount of work. The oat crop began to be important as men grew it specifically for horses. The feed which had been available earlier was not, on the whole, the best answer to the problem of nourishing a horse so he could work hard. It had been necessary either to give horses wheat and barley, which were too valuable to human beings to be given to work animals, or to give them such scanty grass and leaf feed as to leave them unable to do heavy field work. Oat feed was very satisfactory, however, and the rise in its production was closely connected with an increase in the amount of work done by the horse as a work animal.

The growing of oats was also important in the development of a rotation system for crops, the oats always being handled at different times of the work season from wheat. Wheat was planted in the fall, oats in the spring; the harvests came at different times, and oats had a different effect on the soil than wheat.

Although nutritious, men ate oats reluctantly. They were used as the most important of the adulterants, or substitutes, to be mixed in with wheat when there was not enough, or where a family or region was too poor to afford wheat. Flour supplies could be pieced out by adding oatmeal to bread flour, and oatmeal porridge was a low-grade substitute for wheat porridge. But this substitution was done commonly enough, partly as a measure taken by poverty-sticken families, partly as a famine measure when wheat was running short.

In the three-field system of crop rotation, about one third of the plow land in any one year had to be used for the provision of feed for animals instead of for food for people. One of the great revolutions in agriculture has occurred in the United States during the past generation, when it has become no longer necessary to use many acres of farm land to raise crops for the support of work animals, with the result that there has been a tremendous increase in the amount of acreage available for the production of human food.

As another substitute for wheat, rye was important in lands where the growing season was too short, cloudy, damp, and cold. Thus, rye was a major bread grain in the northern German forest and swamp lands, and in Scandinavia and in the northern Russian lands. In many ways grown and handled like wheat, it was never much grown or appreciated in western and southern Europe, though in the later Middle Ages it was shipped from the Baltic countries to be used by poverty-stricken laborers as a lower-level bread grain. Apparently there was just one temporary exception to the western European dislike for rye; a taste for rye mixed with other grains for bread was brought into Italy by the Lombards during the five and six hundreds. This was a passing taste, however, for Italians do not prefer rye today.

Other seeds, such as millet, sorghum, and buckwheat, were grown during the Middle Ages, but never extensively, unless locally there was a good reason for raising them. For example, such crops were grown in the stony semidesert soils in the heel of Italy, where there was seldom enough rainfall to make it pay to gamble with wheat. But all in all, wheat was grown for all the reasons given—and for the final and supreme reason—men had a taste for it.

In the Mediterranean areas olive oil and wine, with wheat and barley bread, cheese and dried fish, were the mainstays of the diet. Olive oil was first well known in the Greek lands and islands. During the period of Roman unification of the Mediterranean basin, olive culture spread in that area to every hillside and valley that could hold a tree. Olive trees cannot grow where killing frosts occur too often, so the borders of olive cultivation run along the frost line.

The trees will grow on very thin and inhospitable soil; they are perfectly adapted to grow on terraces on hillsides. Since the olive tree does not cast a heavy shade, men could grow grain around the bases of the trees; thus, wheat on terraces which might be no more than ten feet wide was commonplace. Once planted, the olive tree can last a long time since (except for frost) it is a durable, hardy tree. While it will produce far better when both cultivated and fertilized, still it will keep on living and producing in the face of much neglect.

Another virtue of the olive tree is that it can grow in areas where rainfall is slight or where it may be slight for a succession of years, as in the Mediterranean area. While the tree is not hard to handle as a plant, the making of oil from the olive fruit calls for skilled processing. As a result, almost any farmer in the olive country during the Middle Ages was likely to be a fair mechanic and, in effect, a fair kitchen chemist when it came to handling his olive crop. His crop could be lost or its value much reduced through poor preparation of the fruit before pressing or through having the finished oil turn rancid.

During the Middle Ages, as today, the olive was the main source of fat in the diet of men living in the Mediterranean parts of Europe. They cooked in oil, they used it as a shortening, they ate it on salads—just as has been the case ever since. The diet of poverty-stricken peasants in the olive country was normally not deficient in important constituents. Even when using oil from the third pressing—and by far the least desirable one—they were eating a nourishing food.

In most parts of the Mediterranean area the olive-growing country was not the steepest mountains, but the rougher country in the lower hills. In case of war, consequent neglect of the terraces brought on loss of olive trees, and whole areas which had been supporting a goodly population would go out of cultivation and be deserted. In the five, six, and seven hundreds the cutting down of the olive trees during wars, done as a matter of scorching the earth ahead of enemies, greatly reduced the populations and prosperity of parts of Italy, Spain, and the Balkans. Great areas reverted to forest wilderness; once the trees were gone it took a long time to re-establish them and the terraces on which they grew.

The grape vine was to be found all over Europe's temperate and Mediterranean areas. There were many different kinds, and it was possible to hybridize them or to work grafts. Wine grapes were native all along the European shores of the Mediterranean and far up into France and Germany. However, the wine grape was not provided in its best form by nature: the wine grape is in part the product of man's attention to the art of horticulture.

The Greeks and Romans had been very well informed on this subject. They knew about budding and grafting, about cultivating and trellising, and about growing wine grapes against walls or in protected terraces so that the fruit could ripen in areas much too far north for the climate to yield such a product naturally. They also knew how to turn the juice into a potable fermented beverage. Good wine has always been a product of sophisticated horticultural and bacteriological processing. Quite as demanding as producing wine is its storage and shipping.

The art of wine making, so highly developed by the Greeks and Romans, was one that men of the Middle Ages kept well alive over the centuries, never allowing the lore of their predecessors to be neglected or forgotten. All through the Middle Ages the high value set on good wine led to its production by specially trained persons. One sort of well-educated person, the monk, was likely to be interested in the growing of all fruits, including wine fruits. Through the six to ten hundreds, manuals produced by intelligent monks were widely read, and their influence was significant. Furthermore, great care was taken in the education of youths in wine-growing areas so that they would learn what to do and how to do it.

Production of wine was carried on as far north as good wine grapes could be grown and handled. Except in a few valleys like those of the Rhine and Moselle rivers in the areas of northern Europe beyond the north part of France, grapes could not be ripened to the point where wine could be made. In England, the Netherlands, and Scandinavia the local beverage was ale or mead, which is fermented honey water.

Throughout the Middle Ages, however, wine was appreciated where it could not be grown, and it was one of the staple articles for commerce wherever and whenever facilities were developed for trade between one region and another. In terms of commerce, there was always a high potential in the existence of an appetite for wine in the north and a supply of wine in the south. Shipment of wine north and of salt fish south was to become one of the important activities of traders during the later Middle Ages. Another incentive for the growth of trade was to be the great temptation, in areas where wine could be produced most successfully, to concentrate upon wine as a cash crop and to come to rely for meat and breadstuffs upon imports from other regions, though this was risky in case of wartime blockade. There are few things worse than to have tremendous stores of wine and nothing to eat. An example of this was the situation of the Rochelle Protestants in 1627 and 1628; fine wine was almost as cheap as water there when the city was under blockade, and people were dying at the rate of three or four hundred a day from lack of food.

From the point of view of social organization, wine had another effect. In wine districts there was no temptation to develop the three-field system which became so' important elsewhere. Instead of plow hands there were vine dressers—persons who spent hours cultivating, fertilizing, pruning, collecting, doing all the things that had to be done with vines and wines—and by and large these people were socially, legally, and economically free. In most wine districts there were no serfs, or if there were serfs it was not the vine dressers who were serfs. They were a privileged and highly appreciated group. This is an example of how the crops grown in a given area can determine the legal and social status of its workers.

In speaking of orchard fruits in Europe it is necessary to make a division between the citrus fruits, which grow only in the Mediterranean areas, and the temperate-zone fruits which can be grown both in the Mediterranean area and north of the Alps.

In general, cultivated varieties available were not markedly better than the wild varieties. This was especially true north of the Alps of such fruits as pears, apples, plums, and cherries.

Men depended on fruits growing wild in the forests, in clearings, and along rivers, gathering the gnarled little fruits they found and either munching them if they were sweet enough, or drying them so they could be added to puddings and pottages, especially during the winter time. Villagers did what they could to protect the fruit from birds and squirrels. These wild fruits were not so much appreciated for themselves alone as for the sour flavor they gave when added to otherwise fairly tasteless foods, while they may have been in part appreciated for their vitamins, without anyone specifically knowing about them.

There was a second great use for these sour fruits. Green grapes, apples, and pears were pressed and the juice was used, where we would use sour wine or vinegar, to add a sour flavor to a stew or to be put on leaves for a salad. The juice of ripened apples or pears could be made into cider or perry and fermented to a surprising strength before consumption. These beverages were very popular in a few districts such as southwest England and the parts of France directly across the Channel where strong ciders and perries were, and still are, made.

While even the cultivated orchards were likely to have mediocre fruit, there were at all times some specialists working on the raising of apples, pears, plums, cherries, and the citrus fruits. These men applied some of the same horticultural techniques to the growing fruits that were used in the cultivation of grapevines. Where there were monks with a skill in horticulture, or gardeners serving kings or wealthy people, the art of grafting was used to improve the quality of the fruits. Once an apple tree was found that produced a sweet apple, a branch of that tree could be taken and put in a prepared slot in the bark on the trunk of another apple tree. The grafted branch would not only attach itself to the host tree, but would produce the same good apples it had borne when still attached to its parent tree. Horticulturists had been producing fine fruit for the tables of the well-to-do in Roman times and continued to do so for the well-to-do throughout the Middle Ages. The knowledge existed, but it was not much shared with the village communities. Monks sent slips, grafts, and cuttings as presents to friends in distant monasteries.

While there were citrus fruits in the Mediterranean area, they were not nearly so variegated or so good as the citrus fruits now grown in Florida and California. Their orange, for example, was a bitter, sour-green orange which would have been good for marmalade if the people of the time had had sugar. Since they had no sugar, little attention was paid to the orange until the orange-colored orange was acquired in the later Middle Ages. There were also lemons and other citrus fruits, but reliance on them was marginal, and that reliance limited to a few areas where citrus fruits appeared on the tables of the wealthy as a special delicacy, rather than being important for the general diet.

Europe's great indebtedness to Islam should be noticed in the matter of citrus fruits. The Mohammedans were skilled horticulturists, painstaking in raising all sorts of other things as well. It is to Saracen genius that we owe the development of good varieties of lemons and oranges. The great geographical expansion of the Mohammedan Caliphate during the six and seven hundreds made possible the bringing of varieties of citrus fruits from far away in Asia to Sicily and Spain, to be of use to the populations in Europe in modern times. But their importance in the European diet came much later.

During the earlier Middle Ages sugar was unknown in Europe. There were no sugar beets or sugar cane. As a result, people were dependent for sweets on honey and any kinds of sweet fruits they could grow. Wild honey could be gathered in the forests and a considerable amount of it was obtained in this way. But men had long since learned to keep bees. Fermented honey water was popular with Germans and Slavs.

In an effort to satisfy their craving for sweets, men also tried very hard to cultivate fruits which might have more than a normal percentage of sugar. Development of grapes or plums—which would in turn become sweet raisins or sweet prunes when dried—was done whenever possible, and when varieties which would do this were found, they were carefully cultivated.

In some regions nuts were important in the diet of men, and they were everywhere important in the diet of pigs. In the mountains of Italy, where great forests of chestnuts grew, the nuts were used in place of grain for making such things as porridge or cakes. A taste for this, however, was strictly local. Hazelnuts were eaten for themselves, as nuts, or the kernels were pressed and their oil used much as olive oil. Acorns and beechnuts were eaten by men chiefly in times of famine or emergency. Otherwise they were considered pig food. Western Europeans became acquainted with walnuts during the First Crusade in the ten hundreds. Until then walnuts had been raised only in Persia and the Near East, but their cultivation spread rapidly and widely in Europe thereafter. Almonds were luxuries.

Generally in the written documents we have for the Middle Ages, the root crops are referred to simply as *radix*, the Latin word for root. (Our word radish comes from that root.) The documents tell us they grew *radices*, or roots, but we usually cannot tell whether they were growing turnips, radishes, or beets because they are seldom more specific than that in describing what was planted and what was harvested. However, we do know that they had some varieties of beets, for example, which cooked up into a dish tasty enough even for a rich man's table. But we also know they did not have anything like our variety in root crops, nor beets as sweet as ours. (The sugar beet itself is a product of the days of Napoleon Bonaparte.) Nor were any of the other root vegetables— radishes, turnips, rutabagas—nearly so good as those of modern times.

Roots were an important crop, however, especially for feeding to livestock. In the later Middle Ages roots were relied on, along with hay, to carry sheep through the season of shortest pasture. As with oats, men ate roots when forced to do so, either by the poverty of the region where they were living or because famine had come and the wheat was gone. All through the Middle Ages men ate roots unwillingly, not because they were overly particular about such things but because the roots they raised were not a pleasure to eat. The great modern "root," the potato, was not available until imported from Peru.

Development of root crops was important in the crop rotation pattern which spread during the Middle Ages. Roots made a good second or third crop. From them could be obtained a supply of fodder, and an emergency food for the people if other things had gone bad. However, in the later Middle Ages and early modern times, people in France and the Netherlands came increasingly to rely on improved root foods.

The list of legumes, of the family of locust trees, sweet peas, beans, and so on, which were available to Europeans before the days of Christopher Columbus was shorter than it has been since. (A great many of our best leguminous food plants were developed a long time before 1492 by Indian horticulturists in the Western Hemisphere, as will be noticed later.)

Still, Europeans had a number of different sorts of clovers and peas which they knew were good for the livestock. However, they did not deliberately cultivate hays in Europe until relatively modern times (the sixteen and seventeen hundreds). In some districts and in some years hays with a great deal of clover in them would grow naturally.

To a very modest extent the Romans used leguminous plants as a green manure. That is, in one season they would get a stand of legumes in a field and then plow them under, producing a soil which had had its nitrogen content greatly increased for the planting of wheat in a later season. After the six hundreds, however, this was practiced seldom, if ever, and then only in the few cases where men were reading Roman books on agriculture.

In the six hundreds, men in Europe were planting peas as their main leguminous crop. These were big chick peas, not at all so sweet as the garden peas we ourselves normally think of as peas. For the most part the peas were stored when dry, then eaten in the form of pea soup or pease porridge, hot or cold; mixed in with grains as an adulterant; and mixed into flours for bread. They were also used as a special feed for horses even after oats became much more widely used for the same purpose. Thus peas and leguminous plants served as a supplement to the diet of the people, as an animal feed, or to fertilize and rebuild the soil. Later on legumes became established as a good rotation crop to be put in every third or fourth year to build up the soil.

Beyond what they got from foraging, animals largely ate whatever the human beings did not eat—except in time of famine. Herbivorous beasts were given the chaff from the wheat, the straw from the grain mixed with something a little more nourishing, such as the root crops just mentioned, pea vines, and hay. Some of the feeding of livestock was on a starvation basis. Clipping off the tips of branches and collecting fallen leaves was pretty common practice in order to piece out the fodder supply.

Shortage of fodder in the early Middle Ages was a great handicap, producing the vicious cycle mentioned earlier, whereby men had to estimate how much fodder for the winter they had on hand at the end of the growing season. They would then kill all the livestock they thought they could not keep alive until the spring. Solution of the fodder problem was one of the steps toward developing a larger production and hence a larger human population from the eight and nine hundreds on.

The horse in different varieties was to be found in neolithic Europe. Especially in Gaul and Germany there were large, heavy horses. In the far north were little Norwegian-Icelandic ponies, to which the Shetland pony is related.

As late as the six, seven, and eight hundreds, the horse was not important as a working animal. He was primarily a war animal and the animal on which the well-to-do traveled. As a war animal the horse is superb, for he is the only animal brave and foolish enough to trust the man on his back and to plunge at his bidding into tumult and danger. Any mule or donkey would have more horse sense. The militant character of a good horse was highly prized, but not his power to pull a heavy plow or wagon. In fact, men did not have the necessary things to make the horse a good work animal: the horse collar was needed, and was just starting to be made in some neighborhoods in the epoch with which we are beginning. As we have seen, the iron shoe was an all-important invention to come into general use later on, while an oat diet was important to give the horse that extra strength needed for work.

At this time the horse was not only the animal for war, but among the barbarian Germans was appreciated as the festival food animal, associated with worship of the war god. The eating of horse meat was taken to mean adherence to Germanic paganism. This association put it beyond the Christian law, and Christian kings in the eight, nine, and ten hundreds had to enforce very stiff laws in order to stop the eating of horse flesh. Horse meat being one of the finest eating meats in the world, it was appreciated for its own quality and abolished as a part of the diet only with great difficulty. However, once the abolition was effected the habit of eating horse meat has not returned even now in many parts of the world of the Europeans.

In the steppe countries of eastern Europe the nomads milked mares. The Huns and Avars had a powerful fermented drink made from mare's milk which is still appreciated in Central Asia but has never become popular in European countries. Horse hide was fairly important in some processes of manufacture. Most of all, however, the horse was a luxury of the upper class for their hunting, their fighting, and their travel.

The donkey is quite another sort of animal. Especially in the Mediterranean areas, but also elsewhere, weight for weight he is much more useful than the horse. For carrying small weights in narrow passages in mountain country or for pulling light plows on the narrow terraces in Italy, he is a most useful little animal. He is easy to keep and gets along very well on a low-quality diet. Still, one of the donkey's greatest uses is for cross breeding with the horse in the production of mules.

The mule is the finest of animals for pulling and carrying purposes. With the toughness of the donkey and the speed and mobility of the horse, the mule can out-pull a horse of equal weight—and appetite. However, the animals must be created each generation because of the sterility of the hybrid cross between the donkey and the horse. In the Middle Ages the mule, because of the evenness of its gait, was the most appreciated of the riding animals. Later on in the Middle Ages the mule was to become associated with ecclesiastics; bishops and abbots preferred to ride on mules, for by doing so they emphasized their pacifism. Also, when roads became better, the most fashionable carriages were drawn by great teams of mules. Originally the mule was no better than the horse as a work animal, and for the same reasons—poor diet and no harness or shoes. But when a good diet, iron shoes, and horse collars came in, it became most useful for over-the-road travel, with even more endurance than the horse.

Beginning with the eight, nine, and ten hundreds, the horse, mule, and donkey gradually became of more and more importance in the work picture, and even more so in the thirteen and fourteen hundreds. The amount of work which could be done increased enormously as soon as the horse became the chief work animal on the highways and in the fields. Even today, however, he has not eliminated the ox as a work animal, for in many parts of Europe the less expensive and more steady and reliable ox (or cow) is still preferred to the horse or the tractor. But because a horse could move across a field far faster than an ox and could work longer hours, the tempo of work and amount of food produced increased rapidly wherever the horse became the chief work animal.

In any one district of Europe the horned cattle, bulls, heifers, cows, and oxen were in large measure of the same strains as those domesticated by neolithic men in that district centuries before. Thus there was great variation in strains of cattle found in different neighborhoods. In some districts the earliest taming of cattle had resulted in domestication of runty little beasts, while in others the animals were large and handsome. In some districts there were fairly good milch cows; in others the animals were better for work or meat than for milking.

In any one district there was little breeding for improvement of the strain and there was little segregation of breeding stock. However, better breeding was possible in neighborhoods where, for geographical reasons, the herds could not mix easily with animals from other neighborhoods. This was true in the Swiss valleys where improvement of the breed was possible by watching milk production and by cutting out those animals which were the least productive or which were, perhaps, troublesome to handle. On some of the islands off the shores of Europe it was also possible to breed desirable qualities because the stock could not mix with other herds. Even by the six and seven hundreds there was probably some conscious development of Swiss milking cattle and of island milking cattle, the islands of Friesland already being famous for the milk they produced. Our Holstein-Frisian cow's great-great-grandmothers were being developed on those islands. On the islands of Guernsey, Alderney, and Jersey there seems to have been conscious breeding of milking cows quite early.

These were the exceptions, however, and in England, France, Germany, and Italy we find a general picture of scrubby cattle breeding century after century with little improvement in the stock, largely because the animals wandered too much from neighborhood to neighborhood to allow control of blood lines. In only a few places were there any special breeds of cattle. One of these was to be found in the Highlands of Scotland where lived the ancestors of the present-day curly-coated Highland cattle, whose coat of woolly hair made them able to resist practically any weather. Another strain was that of the beautiful great oxen of central and northern Italy which existed there even before the Roman Empire began to grow. The Italians were justifiably proud of their great animals, which even in our times are among the handsomest of beasts, standing tall enough so that a man's eyes are about level with the tops of their shoulders, their necks and heads with their great upswung horns rising above.

The ox (and the cow, to an astonishing degree) was the chief work animal of Europe, and the pattern of work as well as the amount accomplished was directly dependent on its abilities and habits. It could work alone or better in spans, sometimes yoked by the horns, sometimes over the neck above the shoulders, with one or another of a variety of yoking apparatuses which existed across Europe.

The ox is a slow-moving animal with a steady pace. If the going is easy, it moves at a low-gear steady pace; if the going is hard, it still moves at that same low-gear steady pace. It cannot quite be said that a span will pull a plow through a white pine stump as easily as it will through a sand pile, but if it is able to pull through the stump at all, the speed will be about the same in both cases. It has the additional quality of giving a good output of work on a grass diet, which is the equivalent of a very low-cost "fuel." It is also less liable to hurt itself or to fall sick than a horse, and can be eaten without qualms when worked out.

However, an ox can be driven just so long in twenty-four hours for it must do a great deal of grazing in that period in order to eat enough to keep it going. It also has to do the same lying down and chewing of the cud which the milch cow does. As a result, an ox is available for pulling plows and wagons for only a modest number of hours in a day.

The work the oxen did was the main thing wanted from horned cattle in grain-raising regions. Next in importance came milk and milk products. In hilly, mountainous, or marsh country the milk was the product most appreciated. Without our refrigeration and other preserving equipment it was impossible to keep milk, so by and large it was used in one of its advanced stages. Sweet fresh cow's milk was rarely consumed. Sour milk was boiled in the pottage or worked up into cheese or churned into butter. Cheese or butter were very important for the winter diet.

Of course, in addition to work and milk products, horned cattle provided the most widely used hides.

Use of horned cattle for meat was normally incidental. In some neighborhoods the occupants of a village would kill a beef for a big celebration held in the fall, say on November eleventh, the date of Martinmas, the great roast-beef day. There might be occasional feasts on beef for parts of the population on other days in the year, but most people did not have much meat of this sort. Ordinarily they only ate fresh cow meat when an animal died or was ready to be cut out of the team, or was through as a milch cow. Veal was eaten when, reckoning how many animals could be fed through the lean season, they cut down the herds and left only the strongest. They did not normally eat the kind of beef with which we are familiar.

Goats did some work, but not enough to be important, and sheep and goats were chiefly grown for their fleeces or hair and for their milk.

Most of the sheep were runty little animals, not much bigger than our ordinary dogs. Nor was their wool very long. It was short-staple and usually very kinky, so that the animals were not nearly so productive per animal in pounds of wool as are the animals we have today. Wool was the thing most wanted from sheep, but their milk was also used for cheese, as is the case today in parts of Europe.

The goat was, above all, a cheese-producing animal. One of the desirable qualities of the goat is its ability to find pasture, in marsh, in brush, up in the hills, or in fairly arid areas, where a cow cannot. It still is cherished in Mediterranean dry-brush areas (called *maquis* in Corsica), which cover so large a proportion of the total area around the sea.

While the goat is the poor man's cow, he is also hard on his pasture. A goat will eat not only a blade of grass down to the ground, he may also go right on down and eat the roots. After an area has been well grazed by goats, it may become barren land, for the top soil is likely either to blow or to wash away. The decay of fertility in the soil of Greece and Italy has been attributed in part to such overgrazing, especially in dry areas, whereby the top soil was destroyed. However, at the time our study begins there was not much of this sort of damage being done, in part because the population of both men and goats was scanty.

In the time of the Greeks and Romans there were some fine, fat swine. Today we still have some pictures of great boars being brought up to altars for sacrifice. These pictures or carvings, done in the time of the Roman Republic, represent a large and heavy beast, obviously well fed and much like the hogs we have on our farms today.

However, most of the swine of the Middle Ages were not such fat animals but were razorback hogs. (The razorback hog of the breed still found in the South of the United States is just the village pig brought over from Europe in Colonial times and allowed to run semiwild.) The razorback, to exaggerate slightly, is about four inches thick, three feet high, can go like the wind, and can lick its weight in wildcats. A wildcat actually would be smart to stay away from a herd of razorbacks. They will "kill anything and eat whatever they kill." The razorback is one of the hardiest of all animals and one of the best able to care for itself.

In the Middle Ages men had learned what is also well known here— that there was no use in trying to drive razorbacks where men wanted them to go. Instead, they had to be persuaded to go in a certain direction, and then followed. Much the same techniques are used for handling the razorbacks in the South of the United States as were used in the

Middle Ages. In the South men have fun when their dogs are bringing razorback hogs in: a little dog runs up, barks around a razorback and perhaps even grabs at an ear. When the hog and the whole herd of pigs charges, the dog runs in the direction it wants the hog to go. If the dog can run fast and far enough the chase ends with the hog having run several hundred yards in the direction intended.

The razorback hog is not only quite an animal in itself, but the large, truly wild one, the great wild boar, is one of the meanest and most dangerous beasts alive. He is a razorback of especially startling proportions. In the scale of dangerous sports boar hunting ranked first in the Middle Ages, and quite rightly. One tusker weighing three or four hundred pounds could finish up a fight having killed a couple of horses, several dogs, and possibly one or two of the hunters, although the men were mounted and armed and organized in every way to put him out of business. A great wild boar brought to bay was one of the finest enemies the rabid hunting fans of the Middle Ages could think of. The razorback and the wild boar crossbreed; there is no biological distinction between the two.

The village herd of swine did not have to be coddled; there was no worry about their being attacked by wolves, for wolves stayed away from them in the forest. They could live in the forest the year around, foraging for themselves. They were able to find a very good living in the late summer and fall from nuts, acorns, roots, fungi, grubs, and plants, but even in the worst seasons of the year they could make a living for themselves; their ability to store up fat and to outlast famine also served them.

Pork had many qualities which placed it at the top of the list of foods to lay by for winter. At pigsticking time in the fall the villagers had celebrations and feasts, at the same time putting away a good part of the pork for later consumption. Like the present-day meat packers, they too used nearly everything but the squeal. The bristles were used for brushes. Pigskin was an important addition to the list of hides for tanning. Some of the meat was eaten fresh. The blood and lights were used for all sorts of sausages and puddings, smoked and salted. (Sausages could be set in lard to preserve them.) All the other parts of the animal were used for the making of bacon, ham, and chopped sausage meat. Lard was stored to use as a supplement to butter and as shortening. In the diet of the poor, smoked and salted pork was the most appreciated of the meats.

In the villages the swine were kept track of very carefully. The swine-

herd was assigned to live with the pigs. He did not take them anywhere; he just kept track of where they were, and learned their ways so
that when it came to earmarking the shoats in the spring, and bringing
the animals in to be killed in the fall, he was the expert on what to expect
from the pigs. He was in no way concerned with breeding them or
handling their feed as a farmer would be today. The swineherd was on
about the lowliest level of the specialists in a village; nearly all he had
to have was an ability to live a rough life in the woods and to like—or
at least to know—pigs.

A few piglets were often chosen to be raised in the village. Fattened
on slops and fodder and on what they found as scavengers, when the
time came they provided special feasts of fresh meat.

The poultry that Europeans had in the Middle Ages were essentially
the same that we have now, except for the guinea fowl and turkey which
have come in in modern times. They had had domesticated pigeons,
geese, and ducks for a long time—how long we do not know. Their
ducks and geese had come into domestication in the same way in which
so many wild ducks in the United States still become domesticated; they
cease migrating and stay where food is provided for them. The goose
will voluntarily domesticate itself where food is provided; all that has to
be done is to scatter grain regularly.

The well-cared-for village goose is in many ways a useful creature.
In the Middle Ages geese were important to villagers as a kind of enemy
raid alarm. Legend said the geese even saved the city of Rome at one
crucial moment; geese will set up a clamor when things sound wrong to
them, and the villagers responded immediately when their geese clat-
tered at the wrong time of day or night.

However, geese were not important just as guardians. Quills were used
to make pens for the relatively small number of people who knew how
to write. Down from both geese and ducks was of great importance for
filling cushions and quilts and their eggs were, of course, very good. Both
geese and ducks are excellent meat-producing and fat-producing birds,
and goose grease especially was considered a great delicacy to be used
in place of butter, as well as being, like lard, a good preservative for
sausages. Duck or goose meat roasted or dropped into the pot for boiling
was an important part of the diet. Goose livers, packed in goose grease,
were and still are considered a great delicacy.

The little goose girl of the village who was assigned the task of watching the geese performed a useful function for all the villagers, each household having one or several geese in the village flock.

The domesticated hen was an importation into Europe. Apparently its ancestor or ancestress was the southeast Asian jungle fowl which still exists and which can be crossbred with modern domesticated hens. By the time of the Roman Empire it appears in many beautiful mosaics, not only as the hen with its egg, but with that creature beloved by sporting Romans, the fighting cock. Romans delighted in the cocks, and "mains" (that is, fights between two roosters) were among the most popular sports not only for Roman grandees but also for their villagers. The sport is still widely promoted in many parts of the world.

By the Middle Ages domesticated chickens had spread all through western Europe. While villagers could not easily afford the luxury of game cocks, which ate but did not produce eggs or meat, the types of hen which laid plenty of eggs, forerunners of our Leghorn and Minorca and like strains, or the heavy-bodied fowl, like our Wyandottes and Plymouth Rocks, were to be found in the farmyards everywhere. The hen was largely important as an egg producer, and what chicken meat the villagers ate came chiefly from the young cockerels, when they were thinned out of the flocks in the late spring and summer, or from superannuated hens.

Only the wealthy could afford the luxury of feeding such beautiful and purely ornamental fowl as peacocks and swans. However, these elegant birds were very popular and carefully guarded so that they could stroll about the lawns or swim in the streams of the well-to-do.

The fish supply in Europe came partly from the ocean and partly from fresh water. Fresh-water fish were in good supply in the rivers and streams to the north of the Alps, while even in Mediterranean lands there were pond fish. In rivers, traps and weirs were used, while in ponds seine nets or hooks and lines were employed.

But it was the ocean waters which furnished the greatest fish supply. Caught with hook and line or in nets by fishermen in shallows or in boats, ocean fish could either be eaten fresh at the time and place where they were caught, or could be salted or smoked to be saved for other seasons or shipped inland.

In western Europe the eating of fish was common everywhere, and in fish-producing regions fish was then, and still is, the commonest and most important of all foods. But even where fish-eating was not, so to speak, native to an area, the development of the Roman Catholic Church fast system, especially from the six, seven, and eight hundreds on, with meatless Fridays and other holy days when meat could not be eaten, served as a real stimulus to the catching, salting, and shipping of fish. This became so important a part of the European economy that later in the fifteen and sixteen hundreds, when some countries turned Protestant and gave up the whole pattern of fast days, law still required the population to eat fish on the old fish days simply to keep the fisheries going. The fisheries had become important not only as an economic mechanism of the time, but also as a training ground for young sailors and mariners needed in overseas trade and navies.

The great diet staples of these times were bread, porridges, and stews. Bread was ordinarily baked at the bakers', whether prepared at home or at the bakery before it went into the oven. The porridges and stews were cooked in a single large kettle over an open fire. These could be made with a combination of various things, depending on what was available, but usually had a base of cracked grain, meal, flour, or peas boiled up with roots, berries, or dried fruit. Some were made with sour boiled milk, often mixed with meal or flour and scraps of meat or fish. Eggs and cheese formed an important part of the diet, as did fresh or salt fish. While the wealthy ate great quantities of fresh meat, especially game and beef, the poor ate small game, fowl, swine meat, some old mutton and goat meat, but in general very little meat. They depended most heavily on salt pork for their meat supply during the winter and spring. In the south, olive oil was an important part of the diet, while in the north butter, lard, and goose grease filled its place. Along the seacoasts fish oil was often used. There was much use of aromatic, sour, or bitter herbs for the flavoring of sauces and stews, while the rich preferred imported spices which the poor could not afford. Salads were widely eaten by people at all levels, especially when green things were fresh-sprouting. The beverages of rich and poor alike were wines and hopless ales and mead.

When we try to imagine what the men of the Middle Ages had to eat, it helps to remember that for all ranks of society there was no coffee, tea, chocolate, sugar, potatoes, tomatoes, navy or green or lima beans, corn, molasses syrup, hopped beer, spiritous beverages, tapioca, or sweet potatoes. There was no way of canning or preserving food in jars. There were no bananas or pineapples, and only rarely such things as tasty apples, cherries, plums, pears, oranges, lemons, or peaches.

Section II

MEDIEVAL ECONOMY AND SOCIETY

600 to 1350

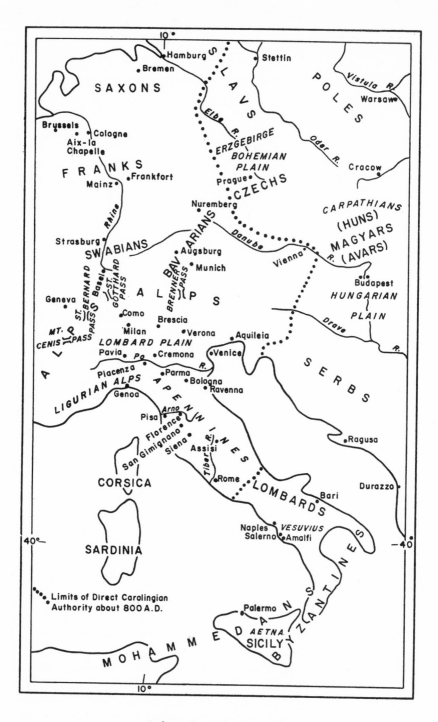

Italy and neighboring areas

CHAPTER I

Economies and Societies
in Nonmanorial Areas

IN RECENT generations so much emphasis has been given one "system"—the so-called manorial system—that it is rather assumed to have been the only medieval pattern for organizing production and distribution. Although it was an important system, it was far from being a unique one. It was fitted to its own climate and soils, its tools and human beings, just as the others were. To emphasize this point, a chapter on the economy and society of the nonmanorial areas is being presented ahead of the one on manorial patterns which follows.

One term we shall borrow from the following chapters: to a degree, references to the manorial system's *conditions precedent* will be made in this chapter. It will be described before it becomes a subject in its own right. The two chapters belong together; read together they round out the whole picture with proper emphasis.

Our survey of districts where the manorial system did not exist or where it was imposed from the outside only in partial measure will include the Scandinavian, Irish, Iberian, East European, Italian, and many other peoples and lands.

Italy

Italy was one area where the manorial pattern never became established, and where conditions made it difficult to develop.

Italy, a peninsula extending southeastward into the Mediterranean, with a wall of high mountains, the Alps, to the north and with the spine of the Apennine Mountains down its back, presents a very broken and uneven topography. In the north lies the fertile Lombard plain, the only stretch of flat land of any size in the entire peninsula. With its main ridge of mountains running from northwest to southeast broken by smaller crisscrossing ranges, Italy has only a few small plains, especially around Rome and Naples, beside the great one to the north. From the center of any one of these plains, even the largest, mountains can be seen. Only a modest proportion of the whole surface can be plowed, and for even that it was necessary to build many terraces and to drain and clear out marshes. Terraces and irrigation-drainage agriculture did not lend themselves to the manorial pattern, dependent as it was on large fields and groups of men working with heavy plows.

Nor did it work where the animals had to be off the home land for a number of months in every year. Transhumance has been practiced extensively in Italy. In most neighborhoods the long summer dry spells forced men to move their animals to higher mountain pastures for the last of the winter moisture. As was common outside Italy—in Africa and elsewhere around the Mediterranean—there had to be a period of intensive use of the animals just before the heavy rains. Then in the winter the animals pastured on the sprouted grain and in the lowland pastures, returning to the hills when those pastures began once more to dry out.

In Italy, as in all the Mediterranean area, light plows work best. This meant that the plow could be pulled by a wife or a donkey and, by not requiring coöperative organization of animals, equipment, and men, made the one-family working unit perfectly feasible. In the south most of the work was family work, making for a strong unit both socially and as a working team. Thus the community itself had no real need to be a coöperating unit.

In fact, Italy itself had no need of a manorial community, for Roman law was still deeply imbedded. Here people had, in a way, been living by the Roman law before it was invented. In the course of Rome's own development, the Roman lawyers had patterned their law upon the customs of the people then living in the Italian peninsula, and as Rome itself disappeared, the law stayed on. Roman law, or Italian customs, involved ways of handling land transfer problems at the moment of death, at the moment of sale, or at the moment of dowry which were in no way usable in a manorial organization. The Italian people were accustomed to sharecropping; they had patterns for the handling of rent and lease contracts which made the manorial pattern unnecessary and unworkable.

Although Italian cities were never fewer or smaller than they were about 600 A.D., the persistence of true cities affected the economy in important ways. In the five hundreds, Italy was devastated by the horrible

Gothic wars, followed by Lombard and Frankish invasions, famines, and epidemics. But even at the lowest point, the cities remained. They were walled cities with houses built close together, covering dozens or even scores of acres with market squares. Officials living inside these walls told the people what to do, presided at the courts, led small army forces, and controlled a good part of the neighboring countryside. Fundamentally they were like the cities of antiquity and also like the cities of modern times.

These cities kept metal money in circulation, because those living there were able to pay in part with money, thanks to their trade with other centers, and they had to be able to pay at least partly in money for food and the other things they consumed. Country people came in to trade food products and raw materials, to acquire goods made in the city or made far away and imported by city merchants. The use of money and the possibility of trading made manorialism unneeded, for the manorial pattern was initially mainly concerned with producing enough locally to fulfill almost all local needs, with limited chance of trade or substitution of goods into money.

In the five hundreds through the eight hundreds there were, of course, rural areas in Italy where the cities had little influence, as in the mountain back country. But even here, because the land was too rough for the manorial pattern to develop, Italy did not adopt this system.

At the eastern end of the Mediterranean, with Constantinople as its capital, lay the great Byzantine Empire, a cultural, economic, religious, political, military, and naval force of great strength from the five hundreds through the nine hundreds. The Greek-speaking eastern half of the Roman Empire had not died. It had never had an interruption in its series of emperors but went on, through Constantine, Theodosius, Justinian, Heraclius, through Basil the Bulgar-Killer, and the Comneni and Paleologi dynasties, until 1453 when the Empire finally came to an end. For as long as it endured, the Empire was a most important force in Italy, especially in south and central Italy, in diplomacy, politics, war, economy, art, and learning.

Not only did trade continue between the Italian cities throughout the Middle Ages, but trade with Byzantium never died. Sea-borne trade was primarily carried on by the coastal cities of Venice, Naples, and Amalfi and, later, Pisa and Genoa as well.

All through the Middle Ages the steady modification in government, economic, and social patterns of the Empire were felt in Italy. During the six, seven, and eight hundreds, for example, a sturdy fighting peasantry quite unlike the old servile country workers of the late Roman Empire developed in Byzantium and in the parts of Italy still under Byzantine control. At about the same time the status of craftsmen changed. In the late Roman Empire of the West craftsmen were tied by law to their jobs and reduced to something less than full freedom. But in the Byzantine Empire, by the eight and nine hundreds there were free craftsmen everywhere, and this influence was also strongly felt in Italy, where the Empire did not lose its last holdings until the middle of the ten hundreds.

To a marked degree, the manorial system was developed by the non-Roman element in western Europe. It was the barbarians to the north of Italy to whom the essential patterns of the system were familiar in the organization of villages, laws, and the use of tools. Few of the German barbarians came into Italy, and those who came in the four hundreds were absorbed into the population. Barbarians of the four and five hundreds—Odoacer's troops and the Ostrogoths—either were very few in number and disappeared into the general population by inter-marriage, or were exterminated. Even the Lombards were never more than a small part of the population compared with the great mass of resident Romans, and by the eight and nine hundreds had given up speaking Lombard German and become Italian. Most barbarians, such as the Lombards, came into Italy because they were interested in carrying a sword, not in pushing a plow. Later, like-minded French Normans and Angevins came, and they too Italianized quickly.

From late Roman Imperial times until less than a hundred years ago, the nobility has been of great importance in Italy. Contrary to our American idea that a count or a knight must be rich, the fact is that most nobles in Italy were and are quite poor. In Italy the poverty-stricken nobleman, of whom there have always been many, has been of enduring importance. For purposes of analysis the nobility is divisible into the very rich upper-level nobility—the wealthy nobles of Italy in Roman Imperial, medieval, and even modern times—and the rest. At any one time only a few dozen families fall into the category of nobles of great wealth, while thousands of families fall into the categories of the lesser and the poverty-stricken nobility.

Purely by historical military accident, the nobilities in Italy were subjected repeatedly to strong influences from outside Italy. These in-fluences came in a succession of waves through medieval and early modern times, and touched the nobles more than any of the other

Italians. One such wave came in the seven hundreds during the time of the powerful Carolingian Empire. About 750 to 770, that great state, created in Gaul (or France) by Charlemagne's grandfather and father and passed on by him to his sons and grandsons, absorbed northern and central Italy. It was necessary for the Italian nobles in that area to fit themselves to the ideas and ways of their Frankish conquerors, while many Franks (or Frenchmen) came down and set themselves up as Italian nobles, taking land and positions in Italy.

The process of tying the Italian nobility to northern Frankland was carried another step further when Saxons and other Germans took top-level control of northern and central Italy in the nine hundreds, the period of Otto the Great and his successors. German influence was very strong in the upper-rank nobility in the period that followed. Another wave came in the ten hundreds when free-lance Norman adventurers came from northern France, where they had lived along the shores of the English Channel, and carved out for themselves a kingdom which included about the bottom third of Italy's mainland and the island of Sicily. These Normans organized their pattern of life in that neighborhood according to the north French ideas of the ten hundreds, and imposed this on the local Italian nobility. There were other such waves of invasion in Italy during the Middle Ages, but these are good examples of the sort of thing that happened.

Hence the nobility in Italy was not only once but repeatedly subjected to influences from northern France, from Germany, or from both. For centuries in many areas of Italy Germanic languages or French were in use among the aristocracy, while the common people spoke either Italian or Greek.

In the five and six hundreds the wealthy noble families in Italy were like the uppermost families in Gaul, in Spain, and in North Africa, holding under their sway tremendous amounts of landed and human property. At this time the rank of an upper-class noble was still symbolized by admittance to the senate at Rome, which still existed, and the class is often designated by writers today as the "senatorial aristocracy." By the five and six hundreds the true, legal senatorial aristocracy was fading out quite fast in Gaul, Spain, and Africa, and the term "senator" was coming to be loosely used for important persons in general. However, in Italy it faded more slowly. In the seven and eight hundreds the land in many parts of Italy was still in the hands of a few very rich families, with ancestry going back to late Roman Empire senatorial families.

The properties of such a senatorial family bulked very great. Their chief holdings were dozens of square miles of forest, plow land, and pasture; one senatorial family often not only owned many country villages but also controlled towns of good size. Such a family also owned many human beings, working slaves who produced for one another and for their owner. More than that, a senatorial family had strong influence over the lives and property of a great many dependents who were not slaves, but were hereditary attachés or protégés of the family. Many of these were arms-bearing men who provided the senatorial family with its own private army, which could be used either for keeping order or for private warfare against other senatorial families. While extensive, most of the holdings might be widely scattered, even some in small parcels. Rational management was difficult.

But management there was, with a long history behind it. Men of business served senatorial families; others served the colleges controlling pagan temple properties which subsequently became Christian church endowments with that of the bishop of Rome (the pope) outstripping all in extent; the largest staffs of all managed the central, provincial, and lesser groups of the emperor's own income-producing estates which, with their managements, became subsequently royal or ducal under such as Chilperich the Frank, Gundobald the Burgundian, or Grimoald the Lombard. All the men of business had to draw into funnels the wealth flowing from scattered holdings toward the purses of the great beneficiaries. Monasteries, too, after they became well established, had large fraternal holdings whose returns had to be channeled into the abbot's hands.

A central court (*corte*), with subsidiary centers below it if necessary, was headquarters, treasury, collection and storage center, fabricating and shipping center, and even fortress and governmental stronghold. These *corti* could serve—as did similar centers in northern feudal Europe in the eleven hundreds and on into much later centuries—as heads or *chiefs* of *honours*.

These great nobles suffered a serious setback in the wars and troubles of the five hundreds. Many of the families were exterminated by hard treatment, and in any case great estates were often reduced to little value by the destruction of the countryside and the killing of the people. (The ownership of three or four hundred square miles of land does not amount to much if there is nobody on it.) The disruption of the senatorial families in the course of the five hundreds was marked, but not overwhelming. There were senatorial families to be found until they came to lose their old name, and we begin to call them by our modern phrase, "the higher feudal aristocracy." There may have been a change in actual family from time to time, but the class evolved without too much trouble into the aristocracy of dukes, counts, and marquises of the eighth, ninth, and later centuries with their tremendous properties, armies, and governmental power over the areas under their control.

In addition to the great nobles there were the lesser aristocrats, the lesser nobles. Each one of these had, or hoped to have, a small holding of several hundred acres by the time he was a person of middle age. This may sound as if they had rather large ambitions, but we must remember that an estate made up of hundreds of scattered parcels of land in Italy is not necessarily a rich estate. Even today a man may own considerable acreage and still not have much of an income from it. And of course it was income, not just acreage, that such a noble wanted. Specifically he wanted sufficient returns to allow his family to live on a level of respectability according to his lights.

This included owning a house inside the city walls of the city state in which lay the landed property. For the nobles in Italy, unlike nobles elsewhere in Europe, a city house inside city walls was normally deemed necessary. It was not always much of a house and might have only three or four rooms, or, typically, it might have only one room on the first floor, one on the second, one on the third (and perhaps even more floors). These houses were fortified, and the noble considered himself part of the city's army for its defense or for its wars against some other city.

In addition to his "town house" (we can call it that, although it is rather a fancy name for most of them) the noble also owned a country villa. The word "villa" in Italian does not mean a house that has forty rooms and a hundred servants. It means a detached house; a villa may be a very small country place. Their villas were their country houses, and the average noble in Italy had a country house which could not be reckoned a great rural mansion or manor house at all. However, it was likely to be fortified. If the noble had a feud with his neighbors, it was sure to be fortified—and he was more than likely to have feuds with several neighbors.

These nobles did no manual labor; they especially did not work at producing food. If their properties were worth anything they had shepherds, goatherds, and villagers who did the farm labor and who either paid rent to them or sharecropped. Neither did they put in much time and energy supervising the work of their villagers, even of their unfree villagers. The work was more or less cut and dried, and the nobles normally preferred to take rent in kind, in work, or in money instead of insisting upon managing the productive activities of the persons who were on their property. Income came from produce, in cash, and in services. The noble sometimes enjoyed an income from the delegation to him of the collection of public tolls or of church tithes and could use the money thus collected more or less as private property, although much the greater share remained under the control of the greater aristocrats.

These lesser nobles, during the six, seven, and eight hundreds, came to be more and more in what was later known as a vassalage relationship to the greater nobles. Increasingly over the years the lesser noble, or at least the able-bodied lesser noble, came to be a sworn follower of some great noble, in turn perhaps enlisting supporters as his own sworn followers.

It was perfectly possible to have this essentially military organization of vassalage without also having the manorial pattern of agriculture with which it is so often associated. A man did not have to have his acreage divided into strips of land plowed with a heavy plow in order to be in a relationship of vassalage to an overlord and to have others serving as vassals under him. Vassalage was a matter of income. If he had an income, that made him a fit vassal for someone with more money than he; or he in turn gave incomes down to other men, which made them vassals to him. The pattern of vassalage was used very early in Italy; the word "vassal" itself was used there about as early as anywhere else in Europe, and it is in Italy that some of the first changes and developments in the history of vassalage were to take place.

In the peninsula of Italy the lesser nobles always tended to be more interested in their cities than in the general affairs of their country. A man wanting justice or a career placed much greater reliance on, say, the city of Parma than he would upon the Italian kingdom. Rural nobles were city nobles too, in a degree not known elsewhere in Europe, this being one of the reasons why the cities survived in Italy. Nobles were not hostile to the cities as they were in some other parts of Europe. What is more, in spite of the fact that by the seven and eight hundreds they were also becoming armed vassals of greater feudal lords, the nobles, especially the lesser ones, behaved like city men, even economically. For example, these lesser nobles went into business; they traded overland and they built ships and ran them for a profit; and they went into banking and finance as soon as there was any way of making a profit doing so. In short, these lesser nobles of Italy, inside their city walls, behaved as French and German nobles never did. An attitude of complete snobbishness toward trade, or of dislike of city people, never developed among them as it did in other parts of Europe.

Furthermore, when the Italian cities began later to grow in strength and size, they did not have to fight with rural nobles for their freedom as did some of the towns in northern Europe. Instead, they were led away from central governmental control toward autonomy by these very city nobles we have been discussing. Inside the walls of an Italian city there were always citizens who knew how to handle weapons and who were fighting men by profession. By the nine, ten, and eleven hundreds they were also the leading citizens of the cities. The important military power of Italian cities in the ten and eleven hundreds was not something developed against the nobles; on the contrary, it was something developed by the nobles who were also the leading citizens.

There was no such division as that to be found later in the north of France, where the nobles centered their lives on the countryside and the townsmen centered theirs on the town. In some of the cities in Italy of which we know a great deal, such as Venice, there was always a class of noble seafaring merchants, pirates, slave dealers, and diplomats. These men were the dominant element in the commune or municipal republic of Venice.

In Italy fairly easy entrance from the class next below up into the nobility was possible, for the strata of society were not sharply defined, one from the other, by social and economic barriers. As the Italian cities began to grow in the ten, eleven, and twelve hundreds, it was rather a common thing for a person to start in business in a modest way and to have his family reach the highest grades in the nobility of his town either during his own lifetime or within the course of one or two generations. Wealth could do it—wealth and a few good marriages of sons and daughters into families which were already noble.

Immediately below the nobles, but not sharply set off from them, was the class which in general carried on business inside a city. These persons did the over-the-counter business, and the making of goods for consumption either inside the town or in the neighborhood, or for sale to the nobles to ship abroad, whereas the nobles carried on the larger businesses, reaching out into foreign trade, finance, and so on. Most of these non-noble businessmen ran shops which they owned, or at least rented, and had anywhere from one employee to a good many. As merchants they either handled merchandise bought from the country-side—wholesale fish, or grain, and so on—or as artisans they ran some sort of business which produced goods for a wider market, wholesale or retail iron manufacture, wholesale or retail woodworking, and so on. These men were on the whole prosperous and had their ranks in the city's politics and business world.

They, too, frequently had some sort of foothold in the country, and once again we find that here a complete separation of town from country was not something that city walls made imperative. To hold one or many modest pieces of land in the country was always a family ambition of the city merchant and artisan.

In the tracing of the rise of city families, we find their origins were usually in small country villages. But the original migration to the city had not meant a sharp cutting of all rural ties. When a man moved to the city and set himself up in the cloth business, he still sent his children back and went back himself to the village in the summer. He would be likely to have part of his supplies brought in from a brother's place, or from a place he still owned but which he had let for sharecropping in the village neighborhood. Strong ties with villages which were not too far away from the city walls (within ten, twenty, or thirty miles) remained a fact of real importance in Italian life, and were another factor making very difficult any development of the manorial pattern. Instead, the ownership of parcels of land by city dwellers which called for share-cropping or rental arrangements produced a pattern which ran strongly counter to the manorial system.

And at all times in Italy there were urban wage earners, persons who were paid on Saturday night, who were hired by the week or even for only a day or so at a time, and then were on the streets, waiting to pick up another job. In the Italian cities some of the hired labor was fairly well-to-do and respectable, always able to hold steady jobs calling for special skills. There were also many other laborers who were migratory, low-grade employees with no "position."

The migratory laborers were villagers, sometimes from scores of miles away, who came in for certain seasonal jobs in the towns and then left to take other seasonal jobs in the country. In the country they would appear when wheat was being harvested or threshed. Then they would appear in the cities, digging ditches or laying pavement or working on the city walls. They would then go on elsewhere. Such a worker usually had his real home somewhere in a village, or his wife did. In hard times they would go to live with relatives, not necessarily in a city. Of course, some of them lived in the cities, and would go into the country for seasonal work, but to think of the city laboring class in Italy during the

Middle Ages as being always resident within the city walls is to overlook important facts.

The conditions in Italy which induced laborers to move about during a fair part of each year, and indeed made many laborers cyclically move within a certain set pattern from one region and one sort of work to another region and another type of work, made it nearly impossible for a manorial pattern of agriculture to become established. The manorial pattern was based upon residents who stayed in one place the year around, doing all the different kinds of work there were to be done on the home place, and nothing else. In Italy there was not that much work to be done by the residents in any one area: plowing was not so heavy and did not require big teams of men; many other rural activities were much lighter; the units of land used were so small that there was no use for large groups of people except during certain seasons, as at the harvest.

In the rural areas in Italy serfdom existed, mostly in the regions of the good-sized plains where a better quality of soil called for a larger number of people to work than were needed in the hillier areas. Periodically, wars and hard times would wreck the lives of poorer persons, causing them to seek food and protection under almost any conditions which might be offered, even serfdom. But the more fortunate rural poor were likely to become either migratory workers, as described above, or to find a small holding which could be worked on a sharecropper basis with the owner, or even on a rent-paying hereditary-tenant basis.

Although the greater part of the total population of Italy was rural, there was always access to city markets where city products could be purchased, and farm produce or time as a laborer could be sold. Within this framework, the upper class of the villages was of considerable importance. These men were likely to be the rent collectors and managers of country estates, the village priest and the notary public who were dependents of the nearest castle, the tavern keepers and loan sharks, the drovers and the grain buyers, the local craftsmen of standing, and the peasants who owned outright some good acres of productive land. They could have two-room or three-room houses, stores of wine, grain, and meat, could dress comfortably, and be important in village and parish business. Their children intermarried with dowries as carefully arranged as those of noble families.

In Italy there were always boys from the country who drifted toward the cities in search of an arms-bearing and fighting career. These men served as the *bravi*, or armed followers, of the lesser nobles, or even of the great nobles. They also served as mercenary soldiers in larger armies. In a few romantic instances such men became great nobles in the span of a single lifetime, but such cases were extremely rare.

Iberian Peninsula

Spain and Portugal, in the Iberian peninsula, were in some ways quite like Italy, and the same factors which in Italy militated against the rise or the maintenance of the manorial pattern existed in Spain too. This peninsula (which for brevity's sake shall be called Spain) is much larger than the Italian peninsula, and in it there are some regions where the manorial pattern could work—and was made to work. But such regions were not extensive.

In most areas, as in Italy, the topography is too uneven for use of the great plow. In many places the land has had to be terraced. Even more than Italy, Spain has great areas where irrigation projects and horticultural activity are worth while and are pursued as the main type of agricultural work. For centuries water has been brought down from mountain reservoirs in these areas and put into irrigation channels, to be distributed almost cupful by cupful around the roots of precious fruit trees and other plants which require hand cultivation. No one has ever been interested in ripping all this out and trying to substitute for it the three-field manorial system. Instead, there has always been an intensive gardening activity where irrigation is carried on.

Away from the irrigation areas, much of Spain has always had a pasturing economy. In Algeria and Morocco, where today we find much the same kind of people and the same set of conditions as existed in Spain in the Middle Ages, transhumance is still practiced. In Spain in the Middle Ages the coming of the season of the high pasture meant moving the flocks and the herds a long way, sometimes over mountain ranges and across difficult stretches of limited pasture and water. Such movement of the animals called for organization, control, and planning. And of course the movement of them back to low pasture was just as complicated.

The result of this was that many areas had a full population for only part of a year. During the late fall and winter, the families and their animals would be in their villages in the lowlands. Here they would put in some patches of barley and wheat. Later on those same areas would be partly deserted, save for old persons and some of the women and children too tender to travel, and with most of the able-bodied persons a long way off with the animals. The crops had either to be cared for by those left at home or to be harvested in late March or April before the long trek with the animals was to begin.

This pattern of existence, calling for organization in order to take care of water and grazing rights, was of great importance to a large part of the population in Spain in the later Middle Ages and on into early modern generations when the modern state of Spain had come into being. Since the kings of Castile came to rule much of the dry steppe lands on the central plateaus only during the early and middle twelve hundreds, a control system with full organization of pastures and herds came later than the period with which we are beginning our study. Nevertheless, during these earlier times, there still was transhumance on a smaller scale; during the twelve and thirteen hundreds began the earliest development of what was later to be called the *mesta*. This organization, which set the laws for man and beast and land all across the great sheep ranges of Spain, was constantly being perfected and expanded. With a concentration upon breeding sheep which produced a fine grade of wool—the Merino sheep, which were a Spanish breed, or an African Berber breed brought into Spain—the *mesta* was to be one of the most remarkable organizations that we have in the history of European social, economic, and political life. One of the great achievements of the Spanish population, it was a dominant influence on their economy in the fourteen and fifteen hundreds and on up to the eighteen hundreds, when it faded out.

Moorish Spain.—A lastingly important development took place in the year 711 (one of the easiest dates in history to remember) when Mohammedan forces, crossing from North Africa, overran almost all of the Iberian peninsula in a single campaign, with a mopping up of only a few years' duration to follow. These forces represented the forefront skirmishers of the Caliph, head of all Mohammedans, whose residence was then at Damascus.

Culturally, the Mohammedans from North Africa represented a blending of many important and originally quite dissimilar civilizations. Islam had originated among both desert and city Arabs. Then, by 711, all Islam had been drawing heavily upon the civilizatons of the ancient Persians and of the Hindus. Furthermore, by that time Mohammedans had overrun and were in the process of absorbing whole great provinces of the Roman or Byzantine Empire, and in that process were taking over all there was of Greek science. They came into Spain definitely

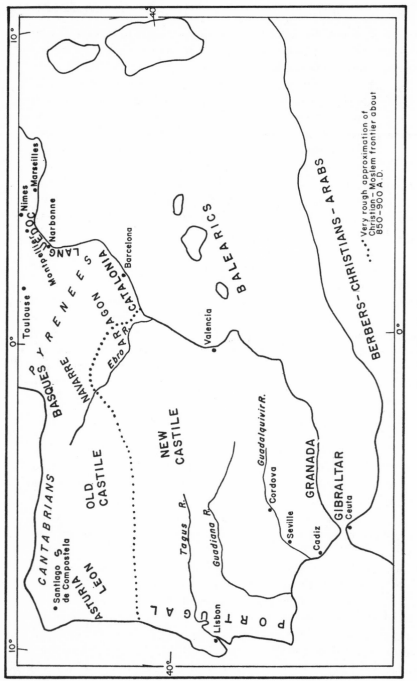

Iberian Peninsula

Very rough approximation of
Christian–Moslem frontier about
850–900 A.D.

BERBERS—CHRISTIANS—ARABS

more civilized, better organized, and in matters of economy much more advanced than the contemporary western Europeans. This was quite clearly an instance of those from an advanced area conquering those in a backward area. The cultural advantages and superiorities of the Islamic peoples over the Europeans lasted from the early seven hundreds until at least into the late eleven and early twelve hundreds.

This overrunning of southern and central Spain had several immediate effects upon its economy and society. For one thing, all of the leading people were the conquerors, and were Mohammedans. Personally, mentally, and spiritually, and in matters of taste, appetites, and business connections, they were from Africa, Egypt, and even the Middle East. They wanted to trade with Cairo, with Mecca, with India, for it was easier for them to trade with India through channels controlled by the Caliph than to trade with the Rhineland, England, or Scandinavia up the coast to the north in Europe. It also was far safer to go to Baghdad or into Central Asia or down into India when starting out from Mohammedan Spain. The upper classes craved the products of their old home countries—such as the good oranges, sugar cane, and other products— which could be brought into Spain through trade or which could be acclimatized and cultivated.

Added to this was the fact that Mohammedan Spain was faced on the north by a very hostile people. The relations between the Christians to the north and the Mohammedans, especially in the earlier periods, were violent. As a result, the cutting away of Mohammedan Spain from Europe was a very sharp thing in matters artistic, social, and economic as well as political and religious.

Another factor in the separation of southern Spain from northern Europe was the fact that the Mohammedans imported their own law in matters of business, commerce, manufacture, organization of guilds, and so on. While it had some kinship to Roman and Greek law, it was nevertheless different and distinctive enough so that the Mohammedans did not feel at home when doing business in Italy or Gaul near at hand, while they felt very much at home when doing business in Persia, Turkestan, or the Indus Valley.

For all these reasons Mohammedan Spain became a part of a world which had its center in Syria and Mesopotamia. Nor was it a backward part of that Islamic world. During the eight through the eleven hundreds, this part of Islam produced some of the most important of the Saracen scientists and poets, and some of the most prosperous communities, finest manufactures, and ablest, richest merchants. It was a world quite remote in every way from the northern Europeans.

Inside Mohammedan Spain there were, of course, social patterns which were important in shaping life in Spain itself and which fashioned conditions and ways of doing things which have made modern Spain what it is today. There were persons whose importance in the Spanish population came largely from the fact that they were Mohammedans, and many others whose lack of importance came largely from the fact that they were Christians. Any Mohammedans outranked any Christians of whatsoever rank, with Jews as a third element of considerable importance in the whole medieval history of Moorish Spain; inside the Spanish world each society had its own gradations of rank within its own orbit.

The Spanish Mohammedans were largely of two sorts. One consisted of aristocratic, educated, cultivated men whose lives centered on rural villas and palaces in the towns and who imposed their culture upon the cities. The other was the rest of the Mohammedans, who were tribal Arabs and Berbers from North Africa. The Berbers were not Arabs; they did not speak the same language or have the same history, law, or background, but like the Arabs they were Mohammedans. The Berbers and many of the Arabs brought with them the animals and the way of life they had known back in the semideserts of Africa and even of Arabia, and imposed them on the local populations. They also brought their feuds with them—the fighting from clan to clan and family to family which they had started back home and did not give up when they found themselves in a new country. In general the Mohammedans who came into Spain with either of these backgrounds were completely incapable of—and not the least bit interested in—settling down and tilling the soil with great teams of oxen or working the soil in the manorial pattern. If anything, there was a strengthening of social and ethnic factors which went against manorialism.

The Christian North.—In northern Spain, on the other hand, in the Cantabrian-Pyreneean ranges and along the coasts of the Bay of Biscay and the Mediterranean, there were persons who were in touch with the north. The population of that part of Spain was made up of persons who had always lived in those mountains, of people who had come down from farther north, and of people who had come north to take refuge when Islam overran southern Spain.

Among the population in this part of Spain, the outside ties were entirely with Rome, where the pope was, or with southern France where reinforcements could be found and rallied under the Cross to bring Christian assistance to those resisting the Crescent (Islam). In general the people of northern Spain were further away in mind and heart from the people in the Islamic south than they were from Paris, London, or Rome.

However, northern Spain was not very strong for a number of reasons. The population was not large, nor was the economic base for the population very broad. The valleys were not wide, nor were they rich. There was pasturing and patch farming, as in most mountain country. In addition to this kind of agriculture there was considerable transhumance. However, during the entire period we are studying, this northern area was to attract settlers from the north whenever there was an advance of the frontier toward the south. As a matter of fact, some of the urge to advance that frontier was to come later on from north of the Alps. Adventurers from Burgundy or Normandy (to name areas in France which sent contingents south) were to participate in the reconquest of southern Spain. A younger son of a Duke of Burgundy in France was one such adventurer, and he eventually founded the Kingdom of Portugal as a kind of splinter off the older Kingdom of León. He was the most successful; but lesser enterprisers did the same sort of thing.

In addition to the fighting men who came over the mountains to fight, there were plow-handle peasants who moved into the conquered areas. Where the land and rainfall together made it possible to use the great ox teams and heavy plow, these people brought in manorialism. The system seems to have made its home sporadically in the northeast corner of Spain. After eight hundred, these immigrants from just north of the Pyrenees and from central France itself began to set up communities modeled more or less on what they had known back at home. However, once in Spain they quite soon plowed along other lines, so that manorialism in Spain did not quite duplicate manorialism proper. To this day the population in northeast Spain does not speak Spanish, but Catalan (an offshoot of south French), and this language use extends along the Mediterranean coast as far as Valencia—a city where immigrating Catalans developed the growing of olives and all sorts of other fruits, but manifested no interest in manorial economy.

In this study we are in general more interested in the Christian communities huddled in the north of Spain during the seven hundreds than we are in the Islamic communities farther to the south. In that Christian area there were noblemen who, like those of Italy, were of two general levels. The sort known later on in Spain as the grandee had existed from a long time back. Great Roman and Visigothic families which owned hundreds of square miles of property, with thousands of dependents, had continued to exist until 711. The events of the year 711 shattered a good many of those families. Some of the most important went over to Islam almost immediately and became Mohammedan nobles, so that indeed there were Mohammedans with Visigothic ancestors still holding great tracts of land in the eight, nine, and ten hundreds. But the great nobles who retired to the north in 711 ended up as poverty-stricken refugees in the northern mountains of Spain, and above all in the north-west corner toward the Atlantic Ocean. For a long time this element, which had before represented great wealth and power in Spanish life and which was to do so again, was weak and unimportant.

That did not mean that the nobles in the seven and eight hundreds were not ever important. When reconquest began, some of them obtained great stretches of land, and the class of the grandees was to come back again. But most of the men in the north who reckoned themselves as nobles began to call themselves "hidalgos." (The meaning of this word is in dispute among the etymologists.) During this period the class of stiff-necked fighting nobles who called themselves hidalgos made its appearance—or perhaps had never been lost—in the northern mountains.

The hidalgos were not at first very rich. They were men priding themselves on valiant ancestors and personal worth, not on any bank account or even on broad acres. The hidalgo was a fighting man from birth to death if he lived up to the code and general attitude of his class. Although he disliked hard work, he might have to do some, simply because he did not have houses full of serfs or lands full of peasants who would do the work for him. So the fighting nobles of northern Spain were, in a measure, self-supporting in economic matters. They did at least supervise their herds and what little agriculture was carried on. In other words, it was difficult to distinguish them from the tougher, better-off peasants. Except in law, the nobles and peasants were not too obviously divided, and even there it was hard to be very specific.

After the reconquest of Moorish Spain began, a fairly considerable number of recruits kept coming from the north, moving in to join the ranks of the upper nobility. These recruits from the north apparently brought with them attitudes and ideas about the life and correct points of view of aristocrats which had not previously been strong in Christian Spain. Examples of these are an attitude of contempt toward merchants and mercantile life; an attitude of daredevilishness when it came to field actions and personal bravery; and also a great love of tournaments and spectacles.

In Spain the municipalities suffered during the first years of the Mohammedan conquest, with the exception of those municipalities which were quickly overrun. The latter were mostly in the south where such cities as Seville, Cordova, Valencia, and Cadiz immediately went under Mohammedan control. It just happened that in the Christian northwest there were no big municipalities in any case. The small Roman and Visigothic municipalities there had never been important and did not become so even after a number of refugees had come north. Playing parts in the development of municipal life in Christian Spain there were to be refugees from the Mohammedan areas, and persons who came down from the north, as well as natives.

The settlement of a new municipality often began with the stationing of frontier warriors around a block house as a fighting garrison. Such a population of any newly founded city was a population of castle dwellers, or *castilla* men. The central plateau land of Spain, Castile, takes its name from them. The land of the small castles became the land of the small municipalities when still larger populations began to huddle around those castles. These people began either to make things as craftsmen or to trade. Some could enjoy the fruits of income from landed property and from flocks in the country around about—rentier aristocrats, at least on a small scale. Most of the people who moved into the earliest of these northern Spanish municipalities were peasants who were free, or noblemen who served in the garrisons, or runaways from the south who were mostly craftsmen and traders. The latter often were Christians whose ancestors had never stopped being Christians, but had gone over to use of Arabic, whose costumes were Arabic, and whose art, music, and customs had been Arabicized. So, while the business population in these Spanish towns was Christian, it had a broad Islamic streak in its culture. The southerners brought their Arabic names for town officers, such as *alcaldes*.

Each municipality in Spain, partly because it contained a number of fighting men, built up political liberties—and important ones—at an early time. Since in the long run the Italian cities developed even greater liberties than did these Spanish cities, becoming practically independent states, the attention of modern scholarship has been heavily turned toward the history of the Italian communes. There has been a tendency to overlook the Spanish communes because they lost their liberties and had little influence upon later democratic republican history. But the northern Spanish cities, perhaps as early as the Italian cities, became quite strong municipalities, with small armies and with self-government; for centuries the king and the nobles were largely excluded from their affairs.

In the mountainous north in the seven and eight hundreds, as has been indicated, most of the nobles could not easily be distinguished from well-off peasants; and it was also true that it was hard to distinguish, in turn, the well-off peasant from the nobles. While in the manorial areas of Europe serfdom had disarmed a great part of the population and made field workers very different from nobles, danger armed the rural peasant class in Spain and drew them closer to the nobles. The man at the handle of the plow had to have his sword and spear ready and know how to use them, or he would not be plowing long in a land where border raids and guerrilla warfare with the Mohammedans went on endlessly. It might be added that guerrilla warfare between Christians went on endlessly, too. The peasant in Spain was more or less a frontiersman, needing to use his own weapons and his own skill and requiring the backing of his neighbors to keep from being wiped out. Consequently, in many parts of the north the peasants, since they bore arms, were recognized in law to be free (though unfree dependents were also armed). Because they did not seem to be either less brave or less well-to-do than the nobles, there was a tendency for the free peasant to take on, in law, many of the attributes of nobility.

There was another northern group, the Basque people, who were not then, and are not now, Spanish in either language or background. By the eleven and twelve hundreds the Basques had gained an advantage which they maintained as long as there was special privilege in Spain: any Basque, no matter how poor, no matter what his occupation, was entitled to the privileges of a nobleman, before the law, in any court. The same recognition, but not so complete, was given Cantabrian, Navarrese, and some other mountain peasants. They were brave, free men, and there was no king or noble who could push them under legally either in this earlier period or in later history. Their descendants were to be the rank-and-file troopers who later rewon the center and then the south of Spain from the Mohammedans, and were to be the population of free peasants in Spain down to the twentieth century.

There were always slaves in Spain, both in the Christian north and in the Mohammedan south. The never-ending raids and counterraids produced captives, and all healthy captives, unless wealthy enough to be ransomed, were enslaved. At first the north had little use in its economy for such slaves; they were sold off to Christian masters farther away. On the other hand, in the Islamic south the rich garden agriculture and town trades which flourished gave employment to slaves, while Islamic households and military formations were largely staffed by them. Rural slaves might be scarcely distinguishable from serfs bound to their work, but there was a difference; unlike serfs, they or their daughters and sons could be sold away. The lot of the lowest pre-Mohammedan rural peasants had been a hard one, but after the change of masters, unless Islam was embraced, it grew worse.

Later on, as much of the east and south were won back in the reconquest, the opposite was true. Mohammedan peasants fell nearly or completely into slavery; their sale in southern France and Italy, or farther away still, was a profitable business for Christian merchants from the Catalan ports. These slaves were often skilled in gardening and in many sorts of craft work.

The Eastern Part of Europe

In the eastern part of Europe (to use modern geographical terms for the sake of clarity), in the lands of the Baltic States, Poland, Lithuania, Hungary, and European Russia, there were many conditions which seemed to make the introduction of the manorial pattern a reasonable way by which to increase production and populations, as it did in western Europe.

There was some difference in climate from that of Europe farther west, but not much, while vegetation, animals, fish and birds, and the human populations differed only slightly. But by the six and seven hundreds its peoples had not reached the density and skill levels necessary for the introduction of a manorial pattern.

There were some centers where people were gathered about forts and on advantageous agricultural locations, but over-all settlement was spread much more thinly than in western Europe in any areas where the manorial pattern could otherwise have taken hold. One condition necessary for the manorial system was a population of at least enough density for the division of labor and carrying out of a fixed annual routine of work to be properly managed on a community basis. In too small a community it would not work.

In addition to being thinly settled, the communities were subject to raids and extortion by neighbors who were, in military matters, much more powerful. The native populations across the belt of land with which we are dealing, from the Baltic to the Black Sea, were persons of Slavic

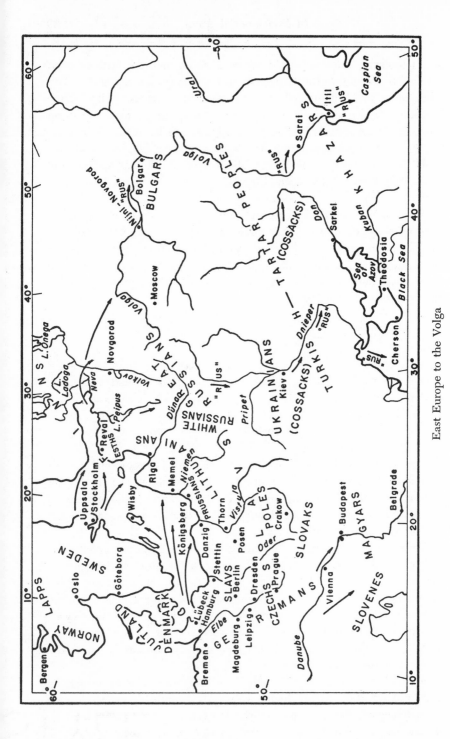

East Europe to the Volga

or Lithuanian-Prussian or Finnish speech. The nomads who harassed them spoke alien tongues; they were mostly of Mongol-Turkish affiliation linguistically, such as the Huns, the Avars, or, later, the Mongols.

These nomads were organized for rapid movement in cavalry warfare. They had a tradition of military accomplishment and of living by raiding instead of by planting. They had contacts with the more civilized states of Persia, Byzantium, and China, and hence had much better fighting equipment than the local villagers and cottagers native to that part of the world. The latter were forced to give up slaves, linen, grain, honey, furs, and amber, which the nomads used for themselves or in trade with the more civilized areas. In return for giving up a good part of their annual produce, the natives of the country got nothing, save that they were not butchered as the nomads might butcher cattle they did not wish to carry through the winter. Subjected to exploitation without return, it was very nearly impossible for the settled agriculturalists to make improvements which would allow their population level to rise.

The fierce nomad raiders from the steppes played their part in this eastern European area until as late as the fourteen hundreds. The last great wave of the Mongols had an influence on south and southeastern Russia until roughly the time of the Plymouth Colony and the settlements of the French and Spanish in the New World.

The steppe nomads were not themselves temperamentally or technically equipped for installing and supervising a manorial production. They could not have introduced it, and the natives did not have the techniques themselves. Doing only occasionally what agricultural work they could, using simple spades and mattocks and plows, the natives in Poland and Lithuania were not in possession of the tools necessary to carry on full-fledged manorial agriculture, nor did they have the social, political, or legal institutions which, we shall see, were needed to make the introduction and operation of the manorial pattern a simple thing to achieve.

While in eastern Europe there was broad land good enough for growing grain just as it stood, there was also a great deal of land under forest and swamp. In the swamp lands was a population of fresh-water fishermen who supplemented their fishing with a little agriculture on the dry spots, and who gathered honey and furs to give to their lords, the steppe riders. In such lands there were never to be any manors save where they were introduced from outside after the expenditure of a great effort to make the land productive and to bring in from western Europe people who could work such a system.

Another factor which seems to have retarded the development of a native advanced agriculture was the rather precocious and high development of commerce in this region. For a long while it was a commerce which was not under the control or leadership of the people of the neighborhood and, save perhaps for fine linens, it was not a commerce based upon articles manufactured in the forest lands. It was a commerce which little profited the people who lived as natives on that wide plain from the Baltic to the Black Sea across the eastern lands of Europe. Instead, this commerce was carried on past them.

The rivers which cross the plains are so interlocked at their headwaters that they invite river travel from the Baltic to the Black Sea, from Norway to Constantinople, or by the Volga to the Caspian Sea and Persia. The result was that Norwegians, Danes, and Swedes from one side, and Bulgars, Khazars, and Arabs from the other, were devoted to trading across the eastern European lands whenever political conditions allowed it. For their own purposes these alien traders built forts at strategic points along the rivers, just as fur traders did when they went into the American West to trade with the Indians. Those forts were manned by fighting men who were merchants—or by merchants who were fighting men—whose interest in the local country people was purely exploitive. They cared nothing about the local area so long as they could keep the natives from raiding their boat caravans and warehouses.

Russia.—The alien merchants were inveterate slave traders, and they found that their greatest use for the natives was that they could be turned into merchandise—slaves. This is the pattern we particularly find in the six through the nine hundreds in the whole of eastern Europe, and especially in the land now known as Russia. During that period the Swedes dominated trade in the area. They penetrated from the Baltic, and at strategic points built blockhouse forts or *gorods*. The greatest of these in the north was "New Gorod" or "Novgorod," which was an old town dominated by these Swedish adventurer-merchant-warriors. Toward the south at the other end of Russia was Kiev, with many other towns existing between it and Novgorod.

The Swedish merchants were known by some of their neighbors as "Varangians" and also as "Rus" or "Ros." They were the first "Russians." Coming from Sweden, they were not natives, not Slavs, nor Finns, nor Lithuanians in speech. They finally Slavicized or Russified; about 1000 A.D. they gave their name to the Slavs and in return took the latter's language. Until they themselves became natives, these aliens were as completely outside the country in which they traded and resided as would have been utter aliens from much farther away in western Europe.

These traders used money in their commerce—great quantities of silver and gold from Islamic countries, from far off Turkestan, from Baghdad, and from Byzantium. They were not trained to be, or interested in becoming, promoters of improved agriculture. Their trading outlets were hundreds and even thousands of miles apart, between such places as Iceland and Constantinople. They were precociously advanced in matters of commerce but far behind in matters of agriculture.

The steppe nomads exploited the native villagers. So did these alien merchants with their advanced money economy. When the poor villagers were not giving slaves—that meant their sons and daughters—to the steppe nomads, they were losing them to the alien merchants from Scandinavia who were just as rapacious, at least to start with.

The nobles took the tributes or rents from their villagers by going out and, practically speaking, raiding them. It was much the same thing as looting. There was little concern for raising production in order to bring in better returns. Later these nobles themselves became tributary to the steppe nomads and were cruelly under the nomads' heels. This happened in the second half of the twelve hundreds when the great Mongol Empire of Genghis Khan, stretching all the way from the end of Korea into Hungary, and from the Arctic down to Burma, put the principalities of the Russians and their nobles under tribute and kept them there until the later fourteen hundreds.

Society and economy were held back after the great Mongol invasion in southern and eastern Russia since these were no longer connected with western Europe. Instead, they were tied to Karakorum, far off in Mongolia, and with Peking in China. Mongol-exploited Russia was behind an Iron Curtain, for the Mongols cut the Russians off quite as sharply from the Western world as anything we know today.

Poland, Lithuania, Hungary.—On the other hand, the Mongol overlordship did not extend to Poland, Lithuania (including westernmost Russia), and Hungary. There the nobles lived lives along a somewhat different pattern, and leading chieftains among the peoples began to feel the influence of Western ways and ideas in the eight and nine hundreds. The first Polish princes to take Christian baptism lived in this period, and it was just about the year one thousand that the first Hungarian (or Magyar) king accepted baptism. With Western influence in the Church came Western influence in politics. Under the Ottos, both the Magyars and the Poles suffered from German military pressure. In an indefinite way the kings of Poland and Hungary became vassals of the German kings who had a higher title: Holy Roman Emperor. These German and Roman Catholic influences worked especially on the upper-rank and middle-rank nobility as intermarriage came about. From the eight and nine hundreds on there was a strong tendency for the Hungarian and Polish kings to use German as their language in their families and their courts. While it was a tendency which was far from triumphant, still nobles were likely to be bilingual.

Monks, bishops, and priests came from the West to set up monasteries, bishoprics, and parishes. As young Magyar and Polish boys began to seek education, they tended to go to Germany, to Italy, and even to France. This was especially true from the mid-eleven hundreds on, when Paris and Bologna became great centers for learning. Westernization of the church personnel was also considerable. Even where a Magyar or Polish priest did not go West for an education, he nevertheless learned Latin and read the books of the West—ancient Roman and medieval Western Christian books, all of them overwhelmingly Western in orientation.

Monasteries and bishoprics set up in the East were very often sister monasteries (or daughter monasteries) and daughter bishoprics of church establishments in France or in Germany where the manorial pattern of crop cultivation was by then well known. When the nobility of the Eastern countries, both lay and church, visited the West and saw with their own eyes how much greater was the yield of the Western system of production as compared to their own, they were likely to think in terms of establishing such methods in their own holdings. Hoping to raise the level of their own incomes, they considered it worth while to take the steps necessary to bring the manorial system over to the East. In addition they also saw feudalism in operation in France and Germany, and it was through them that it was introduced into their governmental and legal patterns. Feudalism and manorialism were not identical and did not necessarily exist together, but they were likely to do so; and in the period in western Europe which we are discussing now, they did. Hence the introduction to the East of Western ways included the adoption in many respects of the legal pattern of feudalism along with the social, legal, and economic patterns of manorialism. But in the East neither was completely adopted.

As in Russia, most of the men who lived in the blockhouses and palisaded forts of Poland, Lithuania, and Hungary were aliens. This was a phenomenon enduring through the history in these areas. Before 1000 there may have been Swedes (Varangians) trading south of the Baltic and into the Carpathian region, living there as they then did in Russia. If they were, they were superseded quite rapidly by Germans who came in as specialists in town making. These Germans were interested in the development of new towns which they hoped to attach commercially to the Western trading centers. After about 1000 A.D., the Germans became more and more numerous in the towns of this region as the natives, especially the nobility, were taking Roman Catholic baptism and becoming politically tied to the Holy Roman Empire.

The new townsmen were neither Magyars in their interests in Hungary, nor Poles in Poland. The Germans remained German, never particularly interested in the welfare or politics of the natives in the countryside. As a rule, these alien burghers were brought in on the invitation of the rulers to set up trade and to hold the towns for the latter. Where they settled, they made little Germanys surrounded by city walls. A hundred, two hundred, four hundred years later those town populations remained the same. They were set apart from the nobles outside even where the latter were also under German influence. They also stayed just as apart from the peasants, who had great dislike for their foreign ways and language.

It might be added that the Germanization of the towns in this whole part of Europe was supplemented and strengthened by the introduction of a German Jewish element along with the German Roman Catholic element. In every town there came to be a German Catholic element and a German Jewish element. The latter group was known in the German language as "Judisch," which in its own dialect became "Yiddish." The Yiddish settlers who moved to towns all over central and eastern Europe came largely from the middle Rhineland, and carried its dialect with them.

Practically all manufacture was concentrated inside the towns. There was not a lively development of diversified crafts out in the country such as went along with the manorial pattern in western Europe. As a result, when manors came to be introduced in this part of the world, they were not oriented toward self-sufficiency. Instead they were primarily designed to produce a merchandisable surplus for sale in the towns, and through the towns to still more distant places. The manor, when it came into eastern Europe, came in as a big agricultural producing unit designed to make a surplus profit for some landlord instead of being designed primarily to give a balanced, rounded-out life to its own community. The people on such manors did not have to make their own craft goods. The towns were there to do that for them.

From the six into the ten hundreds the peasants in this part of the world did not in general fall into a category which meets our definition of a slave, nor into a category which meets our definition of a free man. They were not ruled by men of their own stock who might have been bound to them by customs and tradition as masters were bound to true serfs. Instead, they were ruled by outsiders whose attitude toward their peasants was a good deal like the attitude of a·wolf toward neighboring flocks of sheep.

The peasants in that part of the world were not governed from above in such matters as taxes or laws and the other things we think of as government, for their lords did not care how they arranged such matters among themselves. Consequently they had a very considerable amount of autonomy in their handling of local affairs, and within their own communities there was much social and legal difference in rank.

Consequently, peasants in the villages across Poland and Hungary, and even in Russia, had much real freedom, with election processes established, and so on. On the other hand, overnight the lord (who might be a Varangian or a steppe nomad chieftain) could come by and many villagers might be dead within a few minutes and the rest of them walking away as animal slaves to be shipped to markets at Baghdad or Constantinople. Such a lord considered them his slaves to gather at his convenience. If the thing happened more peacefully, the results were just about the same. In his expeditions around his tributary provinces, the lord, say, of Kiev could collect those young men and women whom the villagers had elected to be given as tribute. The villagers were subject to slavery at the drop of a hat: they could not be called free.

In the matter of food production and techniques the native peasants were behind the western Europeans. Here the slow rise of technology is something to be comprehended partly by looking at the map. In general it was by a process of radiation, of culture diffusion, that manorialism spread. The nearer a community in Poland or Hungary was to the West, the nearer it was to areas with advanced technology, and the sooner it picked up that technology. The farther away from the West it was, the less and the slower the influence of Western technology was to be.

By the year 1000 the peasant populations in the Rhineland, the nearby parts of Lorraine, and the Low Countries had come to operate estates which were generally of the manorial pattern, modified locally as the lay of the land caused differences from one place to another. These peasants had the tools and the animals; they were familiar with the organization of work; and they had institutions and customs of the manorial pattern.

The Westerners and Easterners were quite distinct from one another culturally. By and large the German was proud of himself and of his ways, the German peasant feeling quite as superior to the Hungarian or Polish peasants as any German noble felt superior to the Eastern nobles. For all that, large numbers of German or Dutch (we can call them Dutch; many were Flemings) peasants were induced, especially during the eleven and twelve hundreds, to move eastward, bag and baggage, into new lands. Later on we shall see how that movement eventually swamped out the Slavic population east of the Elbe as far as the Oder River, and made all classes in society in that great belt of land Germanic in speech and in every way. But in the lands of which we are speaking here, there was never to be a swamping-out of the native Czech-Polish-Croat-Magyar peasant.

In their home districts these western Europeans had either been subject to servile dues which made them somewhat less than free or, if legally free, they had nevertheless paid heavy rents in produce and money to landlords. But the men striving to induce them to leave their homes for the East bid high; these peasants were given a kind of pioneer's privilege of bargaining for what they would have to pay and what burdens they would have to bear in their new homes. They went East carrying with them the knowledge of how to set up and operate manorial communities. They also carried with them the promise that once the hard pioneering days in the East were past they would be much freer and wealthier than they had ever been in their Western homes.

This transplanting of Westerners, primarily of Germans, into Eastern lands began in the nine hundreds, but continued down to the generation which saw the American Revolution. Once the Czars of Russia came in close contact with western Europe during the seventeen hundreds, they followed the very pattern here described to induce Saxons and other Germans to form peasant communities as far away as the Volga River region. Until 1941 there was a "republic" of people who were German in speech and cultural background far over in the Volga River region. (This was a republic, incidentally, which sent migrants to the United States, notably to Nebraska, in considerable numbers late in the eighteen and early in the nineteen hundreds.)

The Westerners, transplanted into Poland or Hungary or Czechoslovakia, and later on into Russia, were legally, physically, and financially free men. The obligations they paid the lords were in every way at a minimum, although the lords did obtain some income from their lands. The peasants from western Europe were given villages, often prebuilt for them or built by advance parties which had been given special inducement to undergo camping-out hardships for the first few years; they were given churches and organization as complete in every way as that of the villages they had left.

Such a village was often built rather alone in the midst of other villages, where the original native peasants still lived by the older productive techniques which they themselves had developed.

In many ways the two kinds of villages had little in common and were not very friendly toward one another. It was one of the problems of the Czech or Hungarian magnate who was lord of all the land to keep them from physical violence. In this he was not always successful. In some cases two villages existed quite close. There could even be a German end of a village and a Polish, Slovak, or Hungarian opposite end of the same village.

Contact between two nearby villages or the two ends of one village was, however, inevitable, especially when the natives embraced Christianity and all the villagers went to the same church, or at least recognized the same church authorities and the sanctity of the same sacraments. Many of the Magyars, Slavs, and other natives in such positions began to take on the ways of Germans. Such individuals among them as learned German also learned the crafts and field techniques of the Germans at the other end of the village.

At first, when the native population had begun to Germanize slightly, it came to be in a position where it did the heavy work and the poorer work in the general community. Many of the Germans got the hard work done on their lands simply by hiring the native peasants to do what called for strong backs but not much general skill with tools. The subordinate part of the village and the better part remained separate, even when the lesser part was itself partly Germanized. Many of the peasants in the poor part were unable to get any land, or at least any of the good land, in the neighborhood. Even when they were independent of direct German control in their households or were free of the need to seek employment from their German neighbors, they were little able to match in income, in mode of life, in housing, the Germans at the other end of the village or in the nearby village which had become German.

Still, by the later part of the Middle Ages, native peasants in areas in

Poland, Czechoslovakia, and Hungary where the manorial pattern of grain production had made a good establishment had slowly come to absorb the pattern which the western German immigants had introduced. Once natives had assimilated the new ways, many villages were founded with "German law" but with inhabitants of native stock. They had also maintained their own identity and languages. By the beginning of modern history most of the Polish land and much of the Hungarian (save where the nobles were running what amounted to large cattle ranches) had taken on a manorial pattern. But it was one designed to furnish a salable surplus for export rather than a pattern of production for community self-maintenance, as had originally been the case in western Europe.

Lands Between the Elbe and the Oder, and East Prussia

Between the Elbe River on the West and the Oder River to the East there was a land which, in soil and climate, was very much like the lands just considered. About the year 800, when Charlemagne was Emperor, those lands were inhabited mostly by Slavic peoples closely related in language to the Slavic peoples of modern Poland and Czechoslovakia. There are people near Berlin and in Saxony near Bohemia who to this day maintain the dialect inherited from those Slavic ancestors.

The western Slavs were fairly numerous and certainly dangerous to the frontier populations in Charlemagne's Empire. As long as Charlemagne and his immediate successor reigned, these people were kept in a position of inferiority, paying tribute to the German lords. But later in the eight hundreds these western Slavs became aggressive, adding greatly to the problems of the Germans, who were already having troubles with internal wars and dissensions of every sort as well as with invasions by Vikings and Magyars.

During the middle nine hundreds, the German Emperor Otto the Great had a considerable influence over many of these Slavs. Some of their leaders went to his court and became his men. Others resisted and were persecuted by flying columns of German raiders who went through their lands, carrying off women and children to be sold into slavery, largely to Mohammedan Spain, and systematically harassing the Slavs so as to make them weak and impotent.

Along the eastern marches, or frontiers, of Germany, Otto and his successors established military lords whose powers were very extensive, including what practically amounted to the powers of perpetual martial

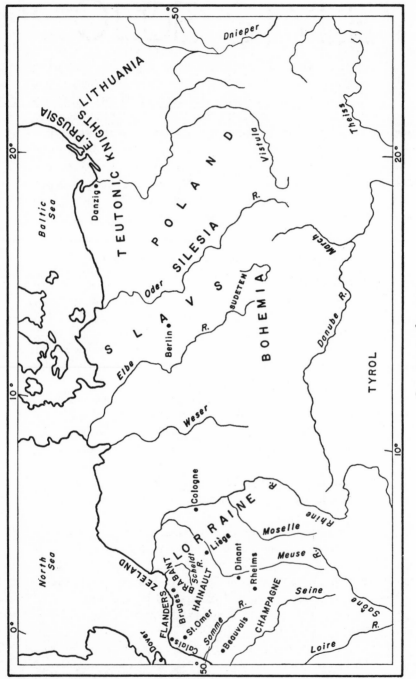

Germany in the west

law over the frontier Germans. Some of the time the frontier Germans, a fighting aggressive people, under such marcher lords, were the ones who did the harassing of the Slavs; in other years the Slavs did the harassing. When Germany was strong, the marcher lords pushed expeditions eastward. When Germany was plunged in civil war, as it frequently was, or some border lord had hard luck, the Slavs came over the frontier to burn and raid in their turn.

In addition to the fighting lords along these frontiers there were also important church lords, bishops whose city sees were farther back in Germany and who sent missionaries to evangelize the Slavs. Many of the Slavic chieftains became baptized and imposed baptism upon the little tribes under them. In general the Slavs never made a united front against either German fighting forces or German religious teaching.

The Slavs living between the Elbe and the Oder faced a complication which grew on their own eastern frontier when the equally Slavic princes of both the Czechs and the Poles became Christian and formed alliances with the German kings. They found themselves in a giant nutcracker with Slavic Christians to their east, Germans to their south, Germans to their west, all working in concert to subjugate them. The Catholic Danes, attacking by sea along the Baltic coast, closed the circle about 1000 A.D.

The greatest pressure came from the west when the Germans seriously began to colonize the lands east of the Elbe, during the eleven hundreds. Various of the marcher lords, from the Baltic Sea down to the Bohemian mountains, began to establish strongly fortified permanent posts garrisoned by troopers. Soon these were surrounded by settled, protected German peasants who were apt at arms and ready to repel any local Slavic attempt upon them or the fortress or burgh which they had established. (It was all in the pattern taking place in Spain in the same generations.)

By this means the German lords came to dominate the Slavic peasants, and in the twelve hundreds succeeded in forcing all the Slavs to accept German taxes, Catholic baptism at the hands of German priests, parochial organization in the German church, and in economic matters gradually to accept a rather harsh and vigorous German exploitation. The native peasants were forced to pay heavily for the right to use lands their ancestors had always held. Slavic lords themselves Germanized quite quickly and took just as much a part in forcing the local Slavs into German ways as did any immigrant German lords or bishops from west of the Elbe.

The over-all result was that rather rapidly German peasants from farther west, and local Slavs who were being forced to become German by all sorts of pressures, started a process of absorption, of Slav into German. There were some reservations, curiously like the reservations set up for the American Indians, established for the Slavs who were either too difficult to Germanize or who lived in lands which were not worth Germanizing. In these unfavorable spots, in the hills and the marshes, Slavic communities were subjected to tribute, forced to keep the peace, but allowed to remain, in language, agriculture, and other ways, just about what they had been before.

In the areas of Slavic lands east of the Elbe where the lands were not at once perfectly adapted to the manorial system, the Westerners brought in persons of more than ordinary talent and education in the management of large estates. Good engineers, notably Cistercian monks whose home monastery was in eastern France, were brought in to plan and achieve great ditching and draining operations which got rid of marsh vegetation and the waterlogging of the land. They turned whole areas into rich meadows for sheep, or into good rye and pasture lands for the production of commodities for export. Other Germans who moved in cut down the forests and established village communities like those they had known farther to the west. Slavs who came over to the German way of life cleared lands as well and, having Germanized their speech and names, became villagers like the rest.

East Prussia had a special history; a religious order of fighting German monks played a notable role there in the introduction of Western ways, including the introduction of the manorial pattern to lands which in the process became German.

To the east of the Slavs of whom we have just been talking, and between the Poles on the plains of the Vistula and nearby streams and the Baltic Sea, lay the lands of the Prussians, or "Borussians," whose language was close to Lithuanian rather than to the Slavic or Germanic groups of languages. The Borussians, or Prussians, remained stubbornly heathen during a great many generations after Poland, Russia, and Scandinavia had all become Christian. Like their own brothers the Lithuanians, just to the east of them, these last European heathen proved to be very stubborn fighting men.

In the course of the twelve and thirteen hundreds one of the projects which interested Germans, Frenchmen, Popes, and Englishmen alike was that of bringing the Prussians under the Christian banner. In the greatest number of cases it had to be by military action. Crusaders who had joined a special order known as the Teutonic Knights moved armies from Germany proper into Prussian land, where they followed the technique just described as successful earlier between the Elbe and the Oder. They built strongholds and settled Germans around them who could be relied upon and who would furnish the necessary supplies for permanent settlements under the swords of the Teutonic Knights.

Peasants were brought in. So were German merchants, who were induced to found towns which were completely German at the mouths of rivers or at important strategic points inland, especially along river courses. German towns, German forts, German religious knights, and German peasants moved in and imposed themselves upon the native Prussian population. This population was put through the same kind of Germanization process under the direction of the Teutonic Knights as has just been described for the native Slavs who had inhabited the lands between the Elbe and the Oder.

By the early fifteen hundreds this process had produced a population which was German from top to bottom: lords, bishops, townsmen, and peasants. The ancestors of these German peasants were some of them truly German, but most of them were descendants of Prussian ancestors. Bad luck in war in the early fourteen hundreds chopped East and West Prussia apart. Curiously, West Prussia, the land nearer Germany, fell under the direct control of the king of Poland, and the population there, although it was manorialized, became in large measure Polish. East Prussia, the segment farther from Germany, remained directly under the rule of the Teutonic knights and became a broken-off, outlying Germany far to the east of the Germany between the Elbe and Oder, or the still older original medieval Germany which lay west of the Elbe.

In the eastern part of Europe the activities of promoters were so important that they call for some attention on their own account. In American history we have had promoters of new towns, "boomers" who went out West, bought up great sections of land, and then tried to attract settlers by "boosting" their properties to prospective purchasers. It is a little surprising to find that in the eleven, twelve, and thirteen hundreds there were just such promoters in frontier Germany. They were speculators, immigrant recruiters, and community planners.

When the new society had settled down, it had its own pattern. At the top there was a nobility which was itself separated into at least two quite distinctive layers. The margraves, the great counts, the great bishops and abbots who ranked with the highest nobility of the Empire, constituted an upper nobility. Many of them had royal blood, or were of families which were later on to become the swarming petty royalty of the German world. In the twelve hundreds, the grand master of the Teutonic Order, as head of the Order but not in his own name, became lord of Prussia. The few score full-rank knights under him, themselves men of high family in Germany (a few did come from England and France), formed a monastic warrior brotherhood which ruled the region. Much later, when the Protestant Reformation began, the leaders of the group at that moment, the grand master and the knights, went over to the Lutheran Protestant camp and divided Prussia among themselves, the then grand master becoming the duke and the rest of the knights becoming counts with private estates and families, the ancestors of the haughty East Prussian nobility of modern German history.

However, there were a great many nobles of more humble position. The title "knight" was seldom taken by them; much more common was the title "Junker," equivalent to the English word "squire," signifying literally "young man." The title indicated that they were gentlemen but not full knights and that they held lands but did not carry on their lives in the grand manner. They had peasants and villages under them; they were well-to-do and solid, but they were not swank. These Junkers, habituated to arms, were also closely connected with the management and life on their estates. Many of them were descendants of land promoters and speculators; they sometimes had peasant ancestry, but long generations of holding estates in the new lands made them noble, or nearly so.

Below the Junkers in social rank, or rather to one side in most matters of government and society, were the townsmen who, in this region, turned out to be agents of a total Germanization rather than aliens left in little islands in the middle of a non-German population. The population inside Prussian towns started like that inside those towns farther east, as imported German and Yiddish settlers who for a while remained aliens in the midst of Slavs and Prussians. But the Germanization of the country brought them into close religious, social, and cultural contact with the open country, and after a few generations they were no longer aliens. At the same time they did not mix very much with the nobility, either with the great nobles or with the Junker class, nor did they tie up closely with the German peasants next below in social rank. Instead they maintained their identity as townsmen who were craftsmen and merchants.

The peasants started out as two distinct groups, sharply different from each other. There were the imported or immigrant German peasants, far superior to the natives in their neighborhoods in every way. These immigrant Germans were not only privileged, they were more privileged than peasants back in the older parts of western Europe. They had good holdings, paid small fees, or paid in money and did no work on the lord's land, and so on. They also had most of the craft skills; smiths, bakers, brewers, and the rest were in this group. In any village which was primarily German, the very privileged Germans were key figures in managing the newly imposed or newly brought in manorial pattern whenever or wherever it was first introduced.

At the same time, and perhaps in the same village but at the other end, or in a little cluster of huts only a half mile from the German village, lived the natives who were almost completely without good economic, political, or social position. Many lived as hired hands who worked for the German peasants; others fished, gathered honey, or transported freight. In the course of time, however, instead of staying different from the Germans, most of these peasants became Germanized in language, clothing, and so on, although their names were still in a great many cases non-German in origin.

In the course of the fourteen and fifteen hundreds these people came to exercise a strong influence in the communities where they existed, and as they rose in importance the German immigrant peasant families fell. Competition for land, competition for jobs, forced the Germans to undercut their old going rates because these native workers, who by becoming Germanic were no longer outsiders, began to bid against the Germans proper for all the kinds of jobs, privileges, and incomes that a peasant could hope to get. Over the centuries which bring us down to about the Protestant Reformation in the fifteen and early sixteen hundreds, the privileged German peasant of the Prussian area was becoming an underprivileged German peasant. No longer were the native peasants outsiders deserving no particular attention. They were Germans, and Lutherans after the Reformation, and they had a reasonably decent fixed position at the lower end of the social scale.

The thirteen, fourteen, and fifteen hundreds saw the peasants in all eastern Europe increasingly subjected to restrictions on their movements and restrictions on their political or village rights. In other words, there was a movement toward serfdom. So we have the curious paradox that while serfdom was dying out in England at just about the time of the settlement at Plymouth Rock (the Pilgrim Fathers left an England in which serfdom had just evaporated), the Russian and other Eastern European peasants were being made into serfs; there was a downgrade development in eastern Europe at the time of a correspondingly upgrade development in the social and legal position of the peasantry in western Europe. The process was not everywhere uniform or complete, however. Wars, and the policies of rulers who needed much military service from their nobles, contributed to this enserfment of villagers for the benefit of the lords.

To return to the area east of the Elbe River. In the older mountains, as earlier noted, there were good mineral resources, especially copper, iron, and silver. In the nine hundreds lucrative silver mines began to be exploited in and near Saxony. The Saxon miners who knew how then began to go as prospectors farther and farther into the Bohemian, the Carpathian, and the Balkan mountains. The prospectors made "strikes," and when it was clear that there was a promising development in a region, there would be a rush of miners to stake out claims and do all the things that are always done when a mining rush begins, be it the United States, Australia, Africa, or Canada.

Since at first nearly everyone who knew how to handle mining tools and do mining engineering and smelting was a Saxon German, the mining settlements were German even when the country around was Slavic, Roumanian (Vlach), or Hungarian. For this reason mining towns which were German to the very core grew up in what are now modern Hungary, Roumania, and even western Russia. An ethnological, political, and cultural tension was introduced into the mining areas by mining prospectors, smelters, developers of mineral resources in general (glass workers did the same thing), who very seldom turned Hungarian, Slavic, or Roumanian, but remained German. This tension continued into modern times.

The Celtic Fringe

In about 600 A.D. the western edges of Europe were occupied by peoples who spoke Celtic languages, and the whole district, comprising Ireland, Wales, Scottish Highlands, and Brittany, has been called the "Celtic Fringe" by modern writers. There were various sorts of Celts.

The Bretons in Brittany and the Welsh in Wales spoke dialects descended from the language of the ancient Britons Caesar had found in Britain. The Irish and Highland Scots spoke languages which in the year six hundred were called "Scottish." The Scots had lived in Ireland, and when some of them moved to Scotland they carried the name "Scot" to its highlands. For some time these peoples had about the same social,

economic, and governmental patterns, and nearly the same basic laws.
The whole of Celtic Europe has a wet climate. The Scottish Highlands,
the Welsh and Irish mountains, and the rougher country of the peninsula
of Brittany are fairly elevated, though not high enough to interfere very
much with the prevailing westerly winds which swept on into Europe
after passing over them. Still, they increased precipitation. In general the
soil was thin, there were bogs where the drainage was poor, but cattle
grazing was possible nearly everywhere. Because of the slope of the
ground and the thinness as well as the poverty of much of the soil, it
was difficult to make cereals ripen.

In Highland Scotland, for instance, it was possible to grow some of
the cereals, such as oats, in little patches where there happened to be
enough level ground and enough depth to the soil. But wheat was hardly
worth risking the labor in great parts of this whole fringe area. Later on,
with improved techniques, it became possible to grow good grain in the
best parts of Ireland, but nowhere was it so easy to grow grains as it was
on the less damp, more level, deep-soil lands of northern France or southeastern England.

The coastal villagers, beaching little boats in the coves, were able to
net and hook fish all along the coasts. They did not have good ships, but
the little skin-covered coracles of the Welsh and Irish were used for
fairly long voyages even though they were tricky and uncertain craft
and could not support a large overseas shipping trade. We do have
records of voyages from Ireland to Brittany, down the coasts of France,
and into the English Channel; it is not, however, at all certain that all
of the shipping in those parts was Irish. There may have been seafarers
from the French-Dutch coasts engaged in the maintenance of seagoing
communications between the continent and the Isles—men with better
ships.

The raising of cattle was the chief occupation of most of the population
in the mountains of Scotland, Wales, and Ireland, and even on the plains
of Ireland and Brittany. Soured milk (clabbered) made into stews or
into porridges with some grain or vegetables added, or milk mixed with
meat or fish, with poor cakes, was basic in the diet of most of the people.
The herding and milking of horned cattle and the making of cheese
and butter took up most of the attention of most of the people. The
cattle drive, the deeds of heroes engaged in rustling or pursuing cattle
raiders, all bulked large in Irish epics. It is quite clear on the face of it
that a manorial pattern of production with an emphasis on grain raising
could not have had much chance in any of the Celtic fringe countries.

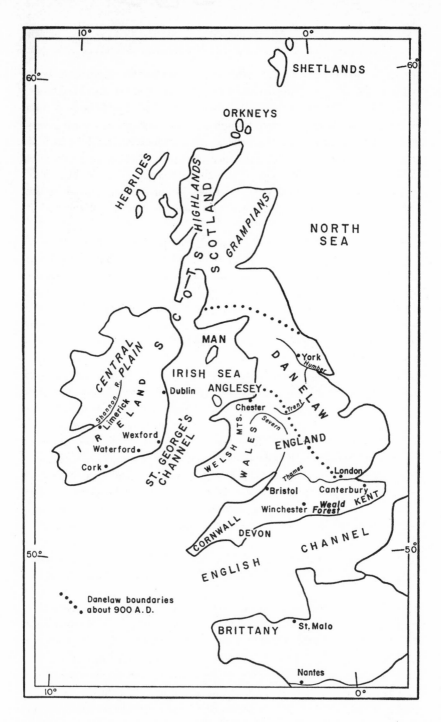

Celtic fringe

Even when persons migrated to those areas, carrying the skills with them, it still was difficult to make the manorial pattern operate.

But there were still other factors. For one thing the chieftains, the middle-class people, and the lower-class people lived in rather scattered hamlets, little clusters of houses, with no strong inclination to live in good-sized, settled villages. The necessities of cattle raising in part explained the scattering of their dwellings. For another, the people in all the fringe areas who were closest to the soil were barred by language barriers from close communication with English, French, German, and other western Europeans who might have taught them how to use the tools and to set up the organization of manorial villages.

In some places such as on the eastern shores of Ireland and in western Wales, where Englishmen and Flemings in the eleven and twelve hundreds made establishments, they did, with moderate success, operate manorial grain-producing units. But there was never any consistent effort at colonization, and even where outsiders came in, the tendency was strong for them to go over to the native cattle culture or in other ways to modify the manorial pattern they brought with them into something that was nearer the native (and, on the whole, more successful there) way of producing goods for everyone's consumption.

Not only was there a difficulty in the matter of languages, but also there was a schism or chasm for many generations between the Roman Catholics of Gaul and England on one hand and the Catholics of Wales, Scotland, and Brittany on the other. The church in one area and the same church in the other had misunderstandings. Irish bishops were at odds with the Pope and the English and French bishops. English and Welsh Catholic bishops would sometimes refuse to sit down together. Other matters, but especially a disagreement over the dates of Easter and Lent and the organizational obedience of bishops, embittered the contestants. These disputes ultimately faded out, but they hindered the communication of economic, legal and social ideas between people of the Celtic fringe and the rest of the people of western Europe.

The society of these people, above all of the Highlanders and the Irish, was based on the clan, the unit into which every man, woman, and child in Ireland and Highland Scotland, and to a lesser degree in Wales and Brittany, was born.

In the thinking of early Scots and Irish the clans were graded from top to bottom. The gradations usually reflected ancient, or not too ancient, historical events. When one clan had defeated another in war, the defeated clan became subject to the victorious clan; or a remnant of a clan might have gone in flight from its old home and been given shelter but low rank in the territory by some other clan. There was a royal clan, and one or two others near to it in rank, which disputed the overlordship of everything and everybody. All the members of such clans were in a sense able to think of themselves as royal and to get something like royal honors from ordinary people. The royal clan had its enemies, and it might be displaced. A clan could stand high for a long while, and then tumble down and become really quite poor and humble. The MacGregors did this in Scotland; to a degree the MacDonalds lorded it in western Scotland until they broke into subsections and fell from power, at which point the Campbells began to rise. That sort of thing took generations and sometimes centuries to work itself out.

Every king and every pretender had in his court anywhere from one to a hundred or so skilled professional singers and poets who sang of kings and the royal clan. In their songs, which were tales of heroic deeds, the kings fight one another, raid, steal cattle, and then are finally cut down, dying in kingly fashion. The common clansmen whose cattle were stolen and whose daughters and young sons became slaves to be sold to the Vikings by the victors were left out of the poems.

These common people were themselves organized in clans which in turn owed allegiance to the lordly clans by whom they were granted range areas for their cattle. There were even slave clans, all members of which were unfree, at least with respect to some royal or noble clan under which they were forced to serve.

Inside any clan there was rank as well. It was either historically true, or assumed to be true, that everyone in a clan was descended from a common ancestor. Other things being equal, position in the clan depended on distance from the main trunk of the clan tree. A person who was the chieftain's brother or nephew was in a high position, while a person whose great-grandfather had been a chieftain's brother might not be nearly so high in rank. Individual bravery and skill in leadership, or notable piety and learning, might modify the pattern so that an individual far from the main trunk in birth might rank high because he had made his way in his own lifetime. Rank within the clan was important, person to person, but even the most humble person in an important clan was above the highest person in a humble clan.

Beginning in the late seven hundreds, the peoples in the fringe lands suffered some very severe invasions from another group of people also living on Europe's fringes but of Germanic affiliation in language and customs. The great invasions of the Danes and Norwegians into Scotland,

Ireland, Wales, and Brittany did not wreck those lands completely, but it hurt them, especially Ireland. Through those invasions, settlers from Norway and Denmark were introduced into each of the Celtic lands, and their assimilation by the Irish, Scotch, Welsh, or Breton natives took some generations.

The natives found these people from overseas difficult to withstand because of their superior weapons and organization; their hit-and-run tactics, used at first, made them hard to catch. But later the invaders settled down in towns which they raised out of fortified war and trading camps along the coasts. The Danes and Norwegians settled along the coasts of Brittany, and to a degree along the coasts of Scotland and Wales—but above all they settled in Ireland.

These invading Danes and Norwegians spoke the same language as the Swedish-Varangian town founders already observed on the Russian rivers. In Ireland they lorded it over the native Irish near their towns, they raided them for slaves, and traded with the chieftains. In a little while they began to intermarry with the families of native chieftains so that an Irish-Norse upper-class developed. Just as happened with the Scandinavian invaders who turned Russian in Kiev and Novgorod, so the Scandinavians in Ireland, Wales, and elsewhere turned native. The towns around the edges of Ireland, notably such towns as Dublin and Cork, Wexford and Waterford, were not Irish at first. They were founded as Norwegian or Danish towns, and they kept that character for a long while, losing it slowly to become English, not Irish, during the eleven and twelve hundreds.

So the Irish townsmen, beginning in the eight hundreds, were aliens, just as townsmen were in central and eastern Europe at the same time. While the native Irish continued to be cattle raisers, the Norse townsmen imported goods and exported cattle products and slaves. Townsmen were not integrated into the country any better than they were in the East. Towns, except for English forts, never did develop in Wales or Highland Scotland until modern times.

Scandinavia: The Norse

The Scandinavians might be called fringe Germans. They lived far enough off the continental mass to become a separate kind of German, but in many ways in the eight and nine hundreds they were still more or less like the Germans of an earlier period.

Nearly everything said about the Celtic fringe also applies to this

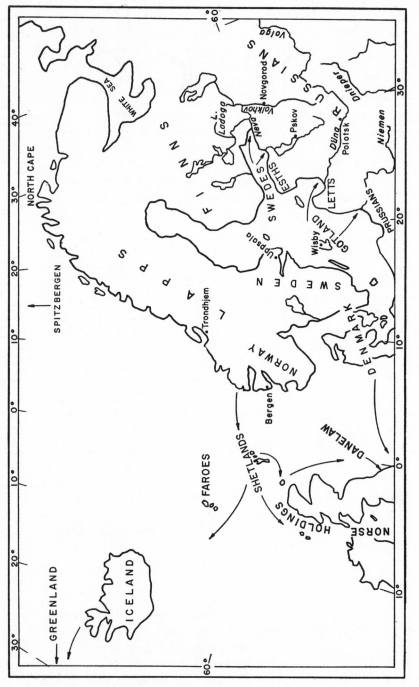

Norse areas

German fringe. The lands front on the Atlantic where winds come in from the ocean. Winters are not bitterly cold. Although it gets colder and colder as one goes north, nevertheless even around the northernmost part of Norway the sea is ice-free.

The land of Norway is mountainous, as is that of Iceland, whereas in Denmark the land is generally low. Sweden has been heavily glaciated and is inadequately drained; on its new surface the river valleys have not fully formed, so great parts of the land lie under bogs, tidal shallows, or fresh-water and salt-water lakes. In general there is heavy forest wherever the land is good. Many of the coastal areas are covered with sand dunes.

The early Scandinavians grew grain wherever possible, even where it was difficult to grow and a crop uncertain. Rye grew better than wheat and so did some kinds of barley. But it was not a land which rewarded grain culture generously.

Most of the people lived close to the sea. In Norway even now most of the people live within ten miles of salt water. A farmer might drive his cattle up to the mountain valleys for a while in the summer, but his home was lower, toward the coast. In most cases the Swedes lived within a few miles of the Baltic or near the big fresh-water lakes in the interior. In Denmark, because it penetrated so deeply between the islands and the peninsula, it was not possible to get away from salt water. Since at the same time the waters around Denmark and Norway have always been among the world's very richest in herring, cod, and other fine salt-water fish, these peoples have always fished. Fish traps, fishing lines, and nets have received the attention of most of these populations.

Raising of horned cattle and horses was considerable. These could be pastured on wet grass flats, and the making of hay and its storage were at all times important. Swine roamed oak and beech forests and were fed on scraps around farmsteads.

The resources of their own lands were never ample enough to please the Norse. Trade was necessary if the cravings of the nobles were to be satisfied. Embroidered and dyed silks from China or Constantinople, steel and fine woolens from France and England, and wine from the Carolingian Empire were known and desired. As far as we can tell from the sources (which are poor) in the five, six, and seven hundreds, such goods were brought to the Norse by Frisians, whose boats plied the English Channel and the North Sea. The Frisians, we know, had trading posts at the base of Denmark, and at various points along the coast of the Baltic and of Norway. At least until the late seven hundreds they were superior to the Norse in ship building and operation.

It is not quite right to think of the Norse trading places as towns (although eventually some became real settlements); they were often deserted for months on end, but they were fortified with palisades and had huts in them which could be repaired and made usable for a few weeks in the trading season when the Frisian merchants would bring their goods by sea. The Norse would bring walrus ivory, walrus hide, furs, and other products to trade with the foreigners. There was a special peace around such places for the duration of the trading season.

After about 790 the Norseman began to take the lead, venturing over the Baltic Sea into the Russian river lands as described earlier, or down the coasts of the North Sea and around the British Isles. Yet peaceful trade could, at any moment, be converted into raiding and warfare. It was when the Norse trader became the Viking raider that the harrying began in Germany, France, Brittany, England, Ireland, and Scotland. The beginning of these raids is fairly easy to date—they started along the coasts of England just before 800. Only a little while after that we hear of their operations on the Continent and in Russia.

The Viking raider was a merchant turned pirate and brigand, but he turned back into a merchant almost the moment the shedding of blood had ceased. The loot in most instances was not what he wanted back at home. The poor natives who were swept into slavery could not, home in Norway, Denmark, or Sweden, be of much use to him, but, traded to Constantinople or Moslem Spain as a commodity, they could be converted into wine, silks, weapons, adornments, gold, and silver.

The Norse merchant, then, was the raider, and vice versa, depending on the circumstances of the moment.

The Norsemen, as revealed by the oldest evidence concerning them, seem to have been more or less one people in language, customs, law, weapons, food, and housing. They had no political over-all government but were, instead, divided into many little "folks." Our English word "folk" no longer means what it did. It meant then a tribe—although even that is not a very good term—a community of a few hundred or a few thousand fighting men with their women and children, living fairly near one another in a recognized folk land, with perhaps one or several strongholds to which the women and children and movable goods could be sent in case of an invasion by another folk. There were various folks around the coast of Sweden, in the Danish Isles, and around the coasts of Norway when we first find those peoples mentioned in surviving records.

Norse nobles loved to fight. They enjoyed fighting between themselves even more than fighting utter strangers. (In the entire history of Norse warfare and Viking piracy it is apparent that most of the victims were other Norsemen.) Danes fought Norwegians, Norwegians fought Norwegians, and so on around the Norselands. However, in the course of the eight and nine hundreds, successful leaders in the homelands drove away or exterminated their rivals. Gradually the states or kingdoms of the Swedes, Danes, and Norwegians were consolidated. It was through this process that the differentiation into those modern peoples came about.

In Norse society and government the kings were members of families which were recognized as royal. The mode of life of the ordinary king did not particularly differ from that of any other important lord in the folk over which the king ruled; he was simply the lord of other kings or chieftains who had recognized him as overlord. There was little in the way of formal government, of a central capital, or of a bureau in charge of making and keeping records. There was no formal tax or judicial system. Most of the trappings of a government were missing.

A king was a member of a royal family; in one sense he was born king, while in another he was not king at all until he had proven himself one. Very frequently history shows us a member of a royal family who, usually in his late teens or early twenties, was given the opportunity to succeed his father, an uncle, a cousin, or some other relative who had been on the throne of the folk before him. Very often on such occasions near relatives, such as his own brothers or cousins, were candidates in competition with him. The successful king was the one who eliminated such rivals, normally by a battle which would end in the death of the rival, or in his flight or disgrace. Often enough, however, a composition would be worked out, and it was not at all abnormal for a Norse folk to have two kings at once who were either brothers, or cousins, or an uncle-nephew combination. Such a situation was usually temporary, for one of the two kings was quite likely to eliminate the other by treachery or by open warfare after not too long a time.

The cohesion of a given folk was considerable. Members of a folk normally claimed a common descent from some ancestor, a real one or one invented by the folk's poets. But in any case a folk had other elements of unity, notably a common custom in matters of land inheritance, the settlements of disputes, and so on (custom, in their language and in ours, is "a law"). Usually an area was known as an area of such and such a law, the word "law" coming to have a geographical connotation. To cite a famous example, the northeasterly part of England, from the late eight hundreds on, was the "Danelaw." In all cases of warfare with other folks, a folk rallied around its current king, except, of course, when disputes within the royal family split a folk into factions.

Normally a folk had its subleaders, who were nobles personally in attendance upon the king in peace and war. They fought next to him in battle, leading their subcontingents on campaigns, and hunted and caroused with him in moments of peace. All of those who normally lived with or near the king were noble. Such families of nobles perpetuated themselves for generations. In general the nobles had lives and establishments considerably like those of the king himself.

In the English language the king was known as the "lord" of such nobles, his wife as the "lady." Quite commonly the man who was a noble follower to a lord king was himself the lord earl of lesser but still noble fighting men. The group of men who surrounded a lord were known (again using an English term) as his "thanes." The lord, in the original sense of the word "lord," was the provider of food and all other needful things to his followers. Originally the word actually meant "the giver of loaves," while the original meaning of the word "lady" was "the maker, the kneader of bread," for the lord her husband to give to his thanes. It was perfectly possible for a lord to have lords under him who were in turn lords of other thanes, and for that pattern to go down a second and even a third step from the king.

The Norse nobles devoted their lives to leading their followers in battle, and their way of life is the one we identify primarily with that of the Viking raiders. To the rank-and-file Vikings they gave leadership and a pattern for behavior. The Norse nobles with their group of fighting men were usually clustered around a still greater leader, and together they lived for glory, for war, and for trade.

As just noted, the follower of a lord of importance was, in English, called a thane, and the thanes took gifts of bread and entertainment from the lord and lady to whom they were attached. The gifts were frequently in the form of steady incomes, usually associated with lordship over villages, people, or production, or with customary renders inside the lands and holdings of the greater lord. In the early days in which we start our study this was a pattern which had not yet taken full shape, but it is one of the important factors leading toward feudalism later on. The great lord with his vast holdings could entertain his thanes at his table and keep them well content. He could also provide for thanes of note who had been responsible followers of his by assigning them holdings within his own lands. While a young thane would be happy enough to stay on at the lord's table, a middle-aged thane wanted a wife, family, and a settled home, and would be happier if given an establishment of his own somewhere in the lord's properties.

Such a thane would of course still come to the lord's table frequently, and would follow the lord in battle or in the hunt. He would spend much time with his lord, yet would also spend a good deal of each year at his own homestead with his wife, children, and his own followers in turn. In a famous Anglo-Saxon poem, Beowulf, himself of royal blood, with his own following, attached himself and that following to a still greater man, the King of the Danes—Hrothgar, or Roger—at Heriot, which was a great palace, or rather a great drinking hall.

While great lords could be persons of importance, receiving the spotlight in literature and historical writings, the people who formed the largest element in Scandinavian society were the free peasants. They were freeholders who had rights as full citizens and normally owned productive land, although it might not have been so productive as land in better climates. These persons, to give the English of a Scandinavian word, were the *bonder.*

Although simple free men, they were not at all humble. They carried spear, sword and shield, battle-axe, and bow and arrow. On raids they filled the benches on the rowing galleys, or "snakes," as the Norse liked to call them. The noble leader commanded, but the bonder were the fighting men.

At home the bonder filled the assemblies of a folk. Because the territories of a folk were not large, on certain days of a month, or in certain seasons or years, the free men of the folk could all gather to decide important questions of general policy, to act as a court of law settling the quarrels which were common enough among both nobles and bonder, and to take notice of inheritances and transfers of property.

In Norway the bonder usually lived scattered across the country. Except for a few places where trade could flourish, there were no tightly settled villages. Normally the bonder lived in a separate homestead close to his pastures, his animals, and the landing where the boat was kept. In Sweden and Denmark the bonder might live in this same way, but frequently they lived in small villages. This was partly for protection, partly because there was kinship between the different heads of the families within small groups, and partly because in those areas they did some plowing where coöperation was of importance (and where conditions were a little better for the introduction later on of the manorial pattern of agriculture).

Norse society knew slaves, and the name for slave, "thrall," has come down to us—a young lady can *enthrall* a young man. Thralls either had been captured in war or were unlucky bonder or nobles who had gambled their freedom away. Thralls might also be criminals, or the descendants of criminals or of people who had been enthralled even generations earlier. They were frequently freed, especially the husky, able-bodied young men who were taken along on war expeditions and who might move up into the class of free men by becoming warriors. Other thralls, managing the properties of rich nobles, could also be freed and even establish respected families.

Once the great raids began, a good part of the thralls were foreigners: Irish, English, French or German-speaking captives from the Continent, or Lapps or Finns or others from the north and east. However, the thralls were of little economic importance in Scandinavia. There were no shops into which to put them, as the ancient Athenians had done with their abler slaves, and there were no great fields for them to cultivate, as did the rural slaves of the Romans. A thrall simply dwelt inside the household, or in an outbuilding near the master, and lived like the master, only with no elegance and abundance. Since the master himself lived with little elegance, that meant a low living standard.

But still, a noble liked to have thralls, partly because it was a sign of importance to own captives, especially captives from his own raids, and partly because the young ones were the best sort of export commodity. Normally thralls were traded toward the East, toward Baghdad and Constantinople; in large measure they were simply merchandise, on its way through Scandinavia, waiting for shipment to market.

At all times the Norse peoples were in touch with Roman Catholic Christian countries. The raids into Ireland, Scotland, England, France, and Germany brought back to Scandinavia thralls who were Christian clergymen, nobles, or peasants from the countries raided. They were not all treated roughly; many of them made their mark in the families and communities where they came to live.

Trade also played its part in the penetration of Christianity in Scandinavia. As noted above, the Norse were traders as well as raiders. The normal pattern of a raiding party was to raid one area and then quite quickly, not far away, set up a market where booty could be sold or rich captives exchanged for ransom. An example of this is western France in the eight and nine hundreds. The feudal territories there were so hostile to one another that it was possible to raid Brittany and sell to Anjou, or to raid Burgundy and sell to Champagne, the rise of feudal "states" making it possible to be friendly to some and at the same time hostile to others nearby.

It has been observed that the gorods on the Russian river routes turned into settled capitals of principalities with the Norse inside and the Slavs outside, but with the Norse turning Slavic as the nine hundreds drew to a close. We have also seen how they fortified towns such as Dublin, Limerick, and Cork in Ireland, and how those towns turned into the main trading centers of Ireland. The Norse also helped build up the prosperity of London (although it had existed before they came), of York, and of other towns. Wherever the Norse went they built up inter-communicating trading centers.

Although without an emperor, they had a great trading empire. The units within it were politically independent of one another, but the language and customs the traders used were the same from Greenland to Constantinople. The contacts and lines of communication their trading empire sustained served to introduce Byzantine culture into Russia, and the whole complex of western European Roman Catholic (and Germanic-Celtic) culture into all the rest of the Norse world.

For in addition to being traded with by the Norse, in the middle eight hundreds the Westerners began sending Christian missionaries from Frankish lands and England to Denmark and Sweden. But most important of all was the lodgment in Christian lands of Norsemen who, while in those lands, became Christian Roman Catholics. The Danes, who took over about half of England in the later eight hundreds, became completely English except that they still kept in touch with Denmark. They turned Roman Catholic so quickly that within the second generation after King Alfred—the English king who stopped the Danish advance and began the English reconquest of England—the archbishops of both Canterbury and York were believed to be descended from Danes. By the middle nine hundreds the Danes and Norwegians in Ireland were intermarrying with the Irish and were being baptized. Around the mouth of the Seine River in France the "Northmen" were becoming "Normans." (In English usage a Northman was a Dane or a Norwegian, perhaps lodged along the French coast as a pirate settler, but his grandson was a French speaking Norman—French except that he had a Danish or Norwegian grandfather.)

The outpost Scandinavian settlements did at first keep up close relationships with the home countries. In the later nine hundreds the kings of Denmark and Norway, and then a few generations later the kings of Sweden, worked to draw their peoples into western Europe religiously and politically. Danish control of England was won by King Sven Forkbeard, whose son, Knut Svenson, was one of England's greatest kings. Knut (or Canute in England) was a devout and very powerful Roman Catholic ruler. But he was also king of Denmark, and his reign just about the year 1000 can be taken as indicating the time when Denmark became as Roman Catholic as Germany, France, or England.

At about the same time Olaf Tryggwasson, and then his cousin St. Olaf, became reigning kings, first over homeless Vikings in England and France, then in Norway. As kings of Norway they saw to it that all the Norwegians were baptized—in some cases rather violently.

The assimilation of the Norsemen was not just skin deep; it was not a matter of only a little sprinkle of water making a man a western European. Under strong kings the Norse peoples had to accept Roman Catholic Church organization, with bishop and parish, with monk and monastery, with church land and endowment. Managing all this were English and German priests and monks and bishops, or Norsemen who were themselves trained as ecclesiastics in Frankish or German or English monasteries.

The church helped bring the whole Western pattern of culture to the Norse. The Western feudal system, as it went on developing, was introduced into Denmark to a degree, and in lesser measure into Norway and Sweden. Then, too, the Western economic patterns were introduced wherever the people and the land could change over to them. Where the manorial pattern could work it was brought into parts of Denmark and Sweden, with some modifications.

All this was tied up with introduction of Latin as the learned language, of the philosophy of the Roman Catholic Church and of its music, art, and architecture. During the generations right after 1000 A.D., the Norse in general became part of the Western world.

This was true for all the Norse with the exception of those who had settled along the Russian rivers. Until Christianity triumphed, the Swedes in Russia had stood fast in their national identity. By 1000, however, the Slavs were absorbing the Swedes in Russia in language, family patterns, and the rest. More than that, the Norse in the Russian river lands were in the closest trading connections with Constantinople. In Constantinople the language of civilization was Greek, not Latin. In

Constantinople the church organization was that of the Greek Orthodox Church, headed by the patriarch of Constantinople, and the architecture and music were Greek-Byzantine. It was in Constantinople that those who lived by the Russian rivers learned about civilization, and it was from Constantinople that they were evangelized. This started about the year 1000 (as had the great Roman Catholic movement into Scandinavia in western Europe) when Saint Vladimir and his ruling princely family accepted baptism in the Greek church and began the Byzantinization of the Russian lands. This fact has had its effect in keeping Russia different from western Europe ever since. (A glance at a Russian postage stamp will show one difference; their Slavic alphabet is based on the Greek, not on the Roman one. Or listening to Russian church music in the Lenten season will quickly show how different it is from the Western church music for the same season.) The Russians hark back to St. Basil and St. Nicholas, the Westerners to St. Augustine and St. Benedict. The fact that the Slavicized Norse in that area turned Greek Orthodox has had its important effects on those of us alive today.

In Scandinavia itself, as the Viking epoch ended, stronger and stronger central government developed. Royal estates, tolls, and officials appeared. But as the Norse who lived in the western European trading posts became part of the local populations, those trading posts lost their strong affiliation with the home countries; the Norse lost some of their pre-eminence of trade. More importantly, the growing superiority of the north German traders, with better ships, greater numbers of traders, and wider varieties of goods for sale, led to German control of Scandinavia's own exports and best fisheries. As the power of the north German Hanseatic League waxed during the thirteen hundreds, the power of the Norse waned.

CHAPTER II

The

Manorial System

FOR all the stress put upon the nonmanorial economies and societies in the foregoing chapter, we shall see in this chapter that the manorial system was highly important. Between the seven and eleven hundreds there were probably more Europeans living by it than were living under all the other patterns combined; the richest lands and most dense populations were to be found in manorialized France, nearby Germany, the Low Countries, and England. This was due partly to climate and the figuration of the land, and partly to the fact that this system, when operated successfully, fostered greater agrarian production and hence greater population growth. If the land and the climate were right to support it, it was a good system, and men lived better where they could make it work.

The word "system" keeps insinuating itself. However, manorialism was not rigidly systematic. We must not think of it as a system which worked the same way from one century to another or from one area to another. No one estate or manor was identical with any other. One would have more wet land, and another more sandy land; one would be big and another small; there were all the variations that there are from one farm to another today.

Next, and this is more subtle, there was no over-all systematic regulation of the rights, duties, or patterns of behavior of those who lived on the manors. In any area each manor had its own recognized custom, and customs were law. Furthermore, in no manor did the customs of a hundred years before remain unchanged; they were modified as each decade went by. Causes for change could be such things as enemy raids, famine, or plague. The raid of an enemy could come overnight, causing a permanent reshuffling of the lives of the survivors. Survivors might return, but they could not completely restore what they had had before. A famine, a plague among the people, or an epizootic among the cattle could permanently change the arrangements of great sections of manorial Europe. And if new people came in, filling the gaps in the ranks which had been left by raids, famine, or plague, they would bring different customs with them, and old customs were then modified.

Yet despite such changes, the manorial system in its general features could be maintained, for it allowed for latitude, both in the arrangements from place to place and from time to time in any one place.

Imitators seldom duplicate exactly. When imitation of the complex of North French, Belgian, English, and West German "manorial system" was tried east of the Elbe, it was so modified, as was noted in the last chapter, as to become a nonmanorial system. The object there of those who held the big estates or manors was to make money by producing a surplus to be sold away, and this was the fundamental difference in aim from that which earlier governed the manors in western Europe. Serious modification also occurred when the Norman nobles, in the ten hundreds, obtained great holdings in southern Italy where the manorial pattern as a producing system could not possibly work. Yet they granted and held what they called "manors." In that land their manors covered arid sheep-land, forested mountains, and marshes. Actually those manors were rent-collecting and governing units. When their Norman cousins went into Wales and Ireland, they too set up "manors," although on many such a manor there was neither a big heavy plow nor a village. To such nobles a manor was a unit of local finance and government, carried with them as a concept to strange lands. It was not a system for working the soil and arranging the life routines of men and animals.

To contradict further any preconception that in the manorial system there was static uniformity, we see that in some areas the manorial system was being discarded just when it was being expanded into others. For example, even as early as the eleven hundreds, the manorial pattern tended to disintegrate around almost any growing town of importance. It did this in Belgium, where apparently the big plow and other features of manorial production were found earliest. In the county of Flanders the rise of industrial cities, and the production of cloth and other goods for a world market, made it difficult to hold serfs to their work on the manor when jobs could be found in town. It also seemed foolish to work to produce grain when grain, produced more cheaply in other areas, came in through trade. It seemed equally foolish not to go into the production of vegetables, butter, cheese, and meat for the city market, which paid well. So we find the manors fading out around the big cities in Flanders and practically gone by the twelve hundreds, while they were hardly established as yet in any countries east of the Elbe River.

Requirements for a Manorial System

Ideally the manorial system aimed at solving basic problems of production and consumption, keeping these in balance, and arranging the work of everyone who lived on the manor. It assumed the complete management of the people who lived there. On the manor (or estate or villa) every person, old, middle-aged, or young, had a part in doing the job of keeping the community going. It is no accident that our word "team," used in sports, comes straight from the manor. A team meant more than animals hitched together; it meant experienced animals and men working in unison to get the most done. A smoothly operating manor was itself an all-inclusive team of smaller teams working coöperatively in a social and legal pattern which took care of everybody and governed everybody.

The team organization was imposed or controlled from above only to a limited extent. Of course there was direction from above, but everybody had to do his part for his own sake too, and had to know ordinarily what he was to do next without specific instructions. It was a system of social and legal controls, of training of replacements, imposed by everybody on everybody.

In order for the manor to rise and flourish, quite specific circumstances were required. The soil had to be rich enough to sustain a fair crop decade after decade, and to maintain continuously the people settled upon it. But if the soil was too rich, the people living on it were tempted to operate it with a system other than manorialism. If the soil was not rich enough, the population would dwindle away as the fertility dropped. So to maintain the system, it was necessary to have a certain level of soil fertility.

It was equally necessary that the manor be in an area of temperate rainfall climate such as that of the Great Plain of Western Europe. Men who tried the manorial system under other climates sometimes found some of its features usable, but not necessarily all. That particular climate, it has been mentioned, was found extensively only in western Europe's Great Plain.

It was also necessary that a manor be located where fertility of the soil could be (and had to be) maintained by intention and by system, rather than by act of nature, as in Egypt where the lands are kept fertile by the Nile River. In order to keep the acres of a village in western

Europe in production decade after decade, it was necessary endlessly to return to the soil as much as was taken out. This the manorial pattern did more efficiently than any that preceded it. The key to its success was the way animal manure and animal power were used. The climate was generally temperate enough so that livestock could be carried through all twelve months, with weatherproof shelter needed during bad spells only for a few weeks or for a few days. If the animals were culled out carefully in the autumn, some fodder, but no great amount, was necessary, there being sufficient grazing to maintain them much of the time.

To be sure, a manor required a considerable amount of half-usable land, perhaps potentially good for plowing, but not so used. It had to have waste land, and commons for grazing, and woodland where the animals could find rough foraging in the brush. There was also need for extensive meadows for raising hay. As soon as men began to clear off the brush land and to fertilize and plow it, the manor began to evolve into something else. What followed was still more efficient, and in recent generations it has been commonplace to look down on manorialism in retrospect. However, its introduction and its replacement later were both, in their times, big advances.

The manorial system (having commented on the phrase, we can revert to its use) called for a development of tools, crops, and livestock which was neither too backward nor too advanced. Stone Age man, for instance, would not have had the kind of plowshare necessary; it had to be an Iron Age system of production to make the system work, and to work at its best it had also to be an Ox Age system, operating where the horse was not yet the work animal for the field. As soon as lighter plows and horses harnessed and shod for plowing with oats for feed appeared, the great plow with its gangs of men and oxen could disappear. Then more people could be kept well-fed with increased production by shifting to the present system—which is now being abandoned in its turn.

Trade also had to be in correct balance for manorial patterns to work properly. There had to be some of it, but too much destroyed the system.

Through the Middle Ages there was always some trade in salt, iron, millstones, and luxuries. But the manorial system flourished best when and where there was not enough to tempt men to produce a surplus to sell to city and foreign markets. As such opportunities appeared, men embraced them and started to think of ways to produce more surplus in order to make money.

Finding, furthermore, that city markets furnished better goods cheaper than villagers could make them—goods often from far away—they had a real inducement to turn to newer economic patterns; the division of labor between town and country began in a modest but significant way. As for the lord, he too could use money for his expenses at distant courts or as a crusader in the far-off Holy Land. (It is easy to push this argument—that production aiming to produce a surplus would break up manors so operated—too far. We have only a few pages above stressed the point that adapted manorial types of systems were in fact worked with that objective in much of the continent east of the Oder. Pressure heavily applied from above to enserf the peasants in those lands, an overbalance of the share of the lord, and the fact that in the German-language towns immigrating Baltic or Slavic villagers were not welcomed, all seem to have weakened the forces which operated to dissolve manors in western Europe.)

The manorial system also presented one way of feeding and maintaining a population in an epoch when there was very little money. As soon as metal money could be obtained, villagers were tempted to start saving it, which for this economic system was a bad thing. When money had been saved, some serfs bought their freedom and went away. Others bought land for themselves, maneuvered neighbors off, and set up their own private establishments; the manorial pattern broke up.

Another prerequisite for the successful development of the manorial pattern was a system of holding land, of arranging work, and of law and social customs, which would make many men dependent upon and subordinate to others—a group of seigneurs or lords under whose will and direction was a group, in turn, of slaves, clients, or working peasants. Such preconditions had already existed on a very large scale in the western provinces of the later Roman Empire.

To be sure, there remained individuals everywhere who were free, and who had small plots of land which they themselves worked with the help of their wives and children. For example, there were the quite wild people who continued to live independently in the islands of Sardinia and Corsica. Elsewhere in mountain valleys there were people who lived by herding their animals or by cultivating their own small plots of ground, and did so without either lords over them or dependents under them. Such people remained outside the pattern of lord-dependent relationship.

Roman Influence on Manorialism

In tracing the growth of manorialism, we can see some of its beginnings in much of the Roman Empire. Where the land was good, there had been lords who possessed great holdings which, in size, would dwarf many of our present-day Texas ranches; the holdings of some of the greatest Roman senatorial families were scattered from Gaul out to Syria, from the German Danubian lands over to Morocco. Such great persons had had their lands worked either by true slaves or by persons who were somewhat between slaves and freemen, and who in the Middle Ages were to come to be known as "serfs." Whatever the local arrangements were, the work on big villas was done on the fields by persons whose freedom to go away was either somewhat or entirely limited, and whose ability to direct the work they were to do was not in their own hands. This was done either by the petty lord, or by the great noble's business managers.

Great Roman nobles were not resident on their estates, overseeing their field hands. They were in Rome or in a provincial metropolis or at the Imperial palace or at pleasure resorts or on other properties they owned —and these establishments were especially designed for unremittingly fine living, not for grubbing. There had to be a controlling central mechanism, of course—the confidential slave or freedman whose hands touched all the strings that moved all the producing puppets down below.

This chief domestic had his headquarters staff and the regional agents needed for the conduct of business. Managers of the regions in their turn supervised each estate manager, resident in a chief house or grouping of buildings (some of them little industrial establishments) near the huts of the villagers. Each of these villas contributed its thin skimming of economic cream up the pipeline to the household purse of the great one; thinner distributing pipes supplied relatives, managers, and even fighting retainers. But over-all, most of the nourishment below the cream level had to be used to sustain the villagers themselves.

While the Roman system did not call for all of the tools, rotation of crops, and such technological devices as were characteristic of the Middle Ages, still there was the pattern of an owner (with or without a manager under him) and a great many dependents. It was by modifying that only a bit here and there that the system grew into the medieval system. In fact, the word "villa" came down from the Roman antecedent, when it meant the villa of the great Roman noble; the usage is still to be seen in the words "village" and "villagers."

Among the barbarians there were two patterns of lord-dependent relationship. One of these was the relationship between the lord and his fighting men, which was described when discussing the Norse. The barbarians had been long acquainted with the lord and his fighting followers who in turn might have followers. When we turn to the working population, we find that the barbarians also had slaves who could be modified into village serfs without too much change. Even among the barbarians, the lord of fighting men could also be lord of lands, worked by peasants for his benefit. The serfs or slaves of rich Roman nobles were easily made into the serfs or slaves of barbarians who took over Roman villas, managers and all. Franks in Gaul or Lombards in Italy fitted perfectly into this system of lords and dependents.

It should also be noticed here that in Gaul and Italy, and probably also in Spain and North Africa, long before Rome came to rule the land, large holdings by wealthy nobles had been familiar. Many great senatorial collections of estates in Roman western Europe had their origins before Caesar in the holdings, say, of a Gallic Haeduan or Arvernian chieftain, cultivated by his subfree Haeduan or Arvernian villagers, and inherited in direct line by his Romano-Gallic successors.

In areas over the world where such a background had not been preestablished, the manorial pattern has never appeared. Certainly free men have not quickly become village serfs when any attempt was made to impose the pattern on them. Nor have gang slaves ever been transformed smoothly into manorial serfs.

Background of Manorialism

In the four and five hundreds large numbers of barbarian warriors took their families along with them in true folk migrations. There were other than just purely economic reasons for such movements of whole peoples. The urge to gain booty and glory was always sufficient to make barbarian men go on the war path, but this time there was pressure on them from still stronger tribes behind. To the east, the Huns, true steppe nomads, had been uprooted, possibly by changes in the climate and pasturage in the high country of Asia. The barbarians who came in over the Danube and Rhine were fierce as they moved forward and were terrorized by the Huns from behind.

Yet the economic reasons for the migrations were important; one important reason was that with barbarian methods there was a limit to what a tribe could get out of its lands. Overpopulation is a completely relative term, since the amount of living that can be obtained from the soil of any one region will depend on the methods used. A given territory in the United States could support far fewer Indians than it can people of high agricultural skill in present days.

Since the neolithic revolution, European barbarians had been using slash-and-burn methods for clearing land. Individual families or village groups would cut a great hole in the forest, plant crops on the ashes from the burned brush, and do well for a few years in that clearing. The fertility of the soil would soon dwindle, and they would have to slash and burn another section of land. Within a quite short time—only a few generations—production would not be sufficient to keep the inhabitants comfortable, and that particular group of barbarians would grow restless. Or starvation would set in and then there would be a real need to move; they would begin to attack their neighbors and to hunt for new lands and better resources. A good part of the upset which Europe saw in the four and five hundreds came from this source.

Politically, another great change took place during the five hundreds in a good part of western Europe. The unrest and movement and fermentation of tribes suddenly slowed down when one tribe, that of the Salic Franks led by Clovis and his heirs, subjugated everyone for a great distance around the Frankish homeland (the modern Netherlands and Belgium and northern France). The Franks themselves stopped moving, and in turn stopped the Saxons, Thuringians, Alemans, Bavarians, and tribes still farther away. Thereafter groups had to stay put, as in the game of musical chairs—and the peoples have stopped for century after century nor have they as groups moved since, after fifteen hundred years. Slash and burn and other neolithic agricultural methods which depleted the fertility of the soil could no longer serve. (There was just one last movement, that of the Lombards into Italy in 568.) After about 570, there was growing pressure on the people in every community to learn to make their own local resources continue to support them, and their low-grade techniques began in fact to be displaced by something more efficient.

Another thing which seems to be closely associated with the development of the manorial pattern, and which is closely tied up with a system of lords and dependents, was the development of a specialized and privileged arms-bearing class generally quite separate in mode of life and position from the plow-handle laboring workers in the villages. During the barbarian invasions, a considerable modification in military techniques was under way, tending in this direction.

It has been habitual to maintain that the Romans, who were used to fighting on foot in ranks as legionary soldiers, lost the art of fighting, lost their bravery, and, rich and sinful, began to hire barbarians to do their fighting for them. It does not seem to have been so simple or such a clear-cut case of virtue triumphing over vice. Romans still fought efficiently and bravely; there were not so many of them any more and there were more barbarians. But also, in the four and five hundreds, the kind of barbarians who lived to the north began to ride roughshod over the Roman legions. The Romans had been falling behind in military technical advance. In the earlier generations the German barbarians themselves had largely fought Romans on foot, and generally with inferior weapons, discipline, and leadership. But the new barbarians were equipped differently. They were a heavily armed mailed cavalry; the old Roman cavalry had not been heavily mailed and mounted, and the riders had no stirrups. The cavalry had not been relied on to face the main strength of enemy battle lines.

The barbarian cavalrymen of the four and five hundreds were mounted on war chargers, with stirrups and deep nomad saddles which were like our Western saddles with their high pommel and deep seat. With these a man could settle into his saddle and become very hard to knock out. They also had good protection for their horses. Most important of all, the horses and riders were trained from early youth to work as fighting units, horse and man, so that each horse was as well trained as any highly trained horse today, able to respond to a slight pressure from the left knee, a turning in of the right toe, the man and horse maneuvering as one unit—the horse, incidentally, himself fighting the other horse and the other rider too.

These men fought either with their chief weapons, the bow and arrow —probably the short but very strong Tartar bow with which they could send clouds of arrows into the Roman legionary ranks—and their spear, thrusting it and charging into stationary troops and riding them down.

The Romans had always used cavalry and nearly always had hired the best. Allies and foreigners brought their special weapons and tactics— often very useful specialties—to serve in cavalry auxiliaries even in the armies of Julius Caesar and Augustus. Instead of breeding and training horses and horse-warriors, it was better, they felt, to hire some barbarians to fight others, in foreign wars and even in civil wars. This was not very risky, for the barbarians had very little political loyalty or unity, and one group would fight another if the Roman paid. These barbarians, more than the Roman soldiers, were to be the predecessors (if not the physical ancestors) of the armed knights of the Middle Ages. They came to be popular because they won battles.

As time went by, a social, political, and taxation system had to be worked out to support the squadrons and the individual units of this new heavy cavalry. The Franks went over to the heavy cavalry; during the course of the seven and eight hundreds they came to be quite well equipped in this fashion, while many other peoples, either a little earlier (for example, the Goths) or a little later (for example, the Norse), did the same thing. The professional arms-bearing class was to become the class which received the top margin of the production of the big estate units. The lord of the estate was to be a heavily armed cavalry man, with his own small troop of fighting squires, while the rest of the people lived on what was left of what they produced in the fields and villages. And this production system was to be the one by which the ordinary village or community managed its affairs.

The Functioning of the System

Let us imagine a manorial production system that has been fully put together with all the main factors combined, and is in proper operation in the region of Paris, say, or up northward in the region of modern Brussels, or in Germany in the region of Cologne, or (somewhat later) in England in the regions nearest the Channel. The first sight of one of these estates, as a traveler approached, gave a striking view of great open fields. There were no hedges, no fences, perhaps a small shelter here or a tree or two there, and the great fields with their hundreds of acres lying open. On closer examination, if in the spring when the crops were up, the traveler could see that the great open expanse of arable land was divided into two or three subsections or fields and very exceptionally (but there were a few of them) into four. In one of the fields wheat would be growing, in another some spring crops. If there were three fields, animals might be grazing on the third. The fields were being culti- vated in a three-field crop-rotation pattern. In the wheat belt one of these would always be planted with wheat, or with barley or rye beyond the edges of the wheat belt. The other might bear a secondary grain—oats or barley or a root crop or peas—while the third would be lying fallow that particular season, cropped by animals but not being plowed for seeding, though good practice called for plowing to keep the weeds down.

It was these great open fields which gave a characteristic look to the villages and communities. Because of the crop-rotation system, modern historians have called the whole system the "two-field system" or the "three-field system" of the Middle Ages. It is just as possible to use the three-field system on a farm in modern times, and it is not necessary to have a feudal government or the great medieval plow in order to keep one of these three-field communities operating once it gets started. In England at Laxton, Nottinghamshire, there is a village which even today operates the three-field system. It is the last one of its kind. No one would think of putting such a system into operation nowadays, but it can survive even when most of the conditions which caused the system to be set up in the first place have disappeared.

Until the traveler came right up to them, he would not be aware that the great open fields were subdivided into sections of considerable size, which in turn were subdivided into long acre-strips. The strips were in blocks, and a block of ten or a dozen strips in some localities was called a shot. Every area (or even every village!) seems to have had its own name for these units, and no kind of uniform nomenclature can be worked out.

The acre-strips were the working units within the shots. A strip was the amount of land which the oxen—two, four, six, or eight of them— and the men (and even some of the women and young children, in the families concerned) could plow in a single morning, the working day of the oxen. That meant that on a gentle sandy slope where the plow moved fairly easily, the strip, or "acre," might be relatively large. In a wet-soil bottom, the acre might be relatively small. The acre was the size of the work unit, not an artificially fixed measurable area. The modern American and English acre is just an officially established approximate average of those acres. The medieval acre was a long thin one, "one furrow long" or furlong. (The furlong, used in our track events today, is 220 yards long.) Those furrow-long acres were separated from one another by narrow strips of unplowed sod, both at the ends and along the sides. In fact the ends had quite a wide spread, being large enough for the ox teams to walk out onto and turn around on; the grass on them was used for hay.

It was very rare and only by chance that any one person ever had two strips next to each other. Normally the strip of one person in a field had the strips of persons also in the same plow team on either side; the team would plow the strip of villager A on Monday, the strip of villager B on Tuesday, and it was a good thing to have A's and B's acres right next to each other, so they could unhitch the beasts on Monday and leave all the equipment right there, only a few feet from the place where they could start plowing B's acre on Tuesday. Then C's acre came next, and so on.

A shot might have contained just the same number of acres as there were men in its plow team. There might be eight men, eight oxen, and eight strips. However, it did not actually work out this way, for there were always some outsiders to insert in the series of acres in a shot. For one thing there could be one or several strips held directly by the lord, and not parceled out to any of the villagers. Such strips had to be plowed by the villagers—and as a matter of fact they had to be plowed first. Then there could be a strip, perhaps several, assigned to the priest. The priest was not personally a member of the team of plowmen, though he might frequently be out with them. There could well be an acre strip held by the village miller, another by the baker, and so on. Specialists whose time was taken up inside the village had their acres plowed for them by the plow teams, and would compensate in one way or another for the work done for them on their strips. In a given series of acres there should always have been at least one strip for the owner of each ox of the plow team and for each of those outsiders who also had interests. The shot was a series of such acres blocked together, the long sides touching one another.

The plow team would progress from one acre to another, taking care of them from one end of the shot to the next, then move on and start another shot somewhere else in the great open field. This shot would contain the same sequence of owners, or nearly the same. (Right through the plowing season the team would be plowing A's acre in one shot, and then a week or two later in some other shot they would be plowing another acre for A. B's acre would lie next to A's as it had in the first shot, then the miller's, then C's, etc., these shots being twinned with others as much as half a mile away across the open field from one another.)

Normally one ox was equated with about five acres in the wheat field, acres which were scattered all across the great open field planted to wheat that year. In addition to his five wheat acres the same peasant A would have five more acres, similarly scattered over the field, which was planted to peas or barley or some other secondary crop that same year. In the three-field system he would also have five more acres in the field where the animals were grazing that season, the fallow acres. Thus there would be fifteen acres attached to an average peasant, having the normal quota of one ox to be yoked up in the plow team. Some villagers would be more important people and have twice the quota. They would be two-ox men, with ten acres in each of the three fields, a total of thirty acres in all.

Some villagers had much smaller holdings, perhaps only an acre or two, and they did not have enough to live on unless they could be hired part time by a man with a larger supply of oxen and acres. In order to get his plowing done, the man with an oversupply of acreage hired these men to work for him when the plowing was being done. Although himself a serf, he was an employer also. Beside these, there were some persons in any village who had no strips of land at all and had to work for someone else or live on charity. There was no absolute uniformity; in fact there was very great lack of uniformity in this matter of holding strips in a village. Every death or marriage could effect a change of some sort in the holdings of one or more families. To confuse us even more, acres were divided lengthwise into halves and quarters by sales, gifts, and dowries, or brought into groups held by one person.

The work on the strips of land in the wheat field which were retained directly by the lord for his own exploitation was done by the peasants in the village. They did the plowing, sowing, harrowing, reaping, threshing, and storing away—the lord did none of it. Those acres were considered to be part of the lord's *demesne* land (to use the English word), but his demesne included much more than just those scattered acres. Commonly there was a block of land near a main house where no strips were held by villagers, all of them being held directly by the lord; and in that sense a demesne was a close block of holding right around the main hall or castle or whatever it was the lord or his bailiff lived in. (The demesne included a good many other things too, which will be discussed later.)

In addition to the lord having some of his demesne scattered around in the strips, it was fairly normal to have enough acres to furnish a good living for the priest of the village also scattered through the shots. The land attached to the parish house was called the *glebe* land (once again to use an English term). The glebe included other rights beyond those to crops from these strips.

There also, as mentioned, might be those acres attached to the miller, the brewer, the baker—persons who labored in the village and did little in the fields, but who also needed wheat and all other necessaries for their support, and who got the work done on their plots by other villagers either through custom or by pay.

In addition to the persons discussed so far, there were individuals connected with the lord's own household and family and with military service. There could be strips assigned to his squire, to his huntsman, to his steward. This is not a specific list; all of these could have holdings but did not necessarily have to.

The rotation of crops through a cycle of three years and three big fields conserved fertility and provided a wider range of products. It also made for more rational use of animal and human time and energy than one-crop cultivation or simple pasturing. All the acres that the village could devote to wheat were put into wheat. Plowing had to be done within dates set by the climate; tight calendar limits governed the beginning and completion of reaping. Only by hiring seasonal labor from outside could more acres be plowed or harvested, and the pattern was quite as much one designed to operate effectively where there was no supply of such hirable outside hands at harvest time as one designed to keep up soil fertility or to get along with a slight amount of buying and selling outside.

While there was no use trying to handle more wheat acreage (and less would be painful), the force of men and animals would have been too lightly employed for long stretches of time between the periods of peak labor had wheat been the only crop. And the animals would have had to consume some of that precious grain in the seasons of scant pasture. But an oat field, planted where there was no wheat, could be tended through its seasons of plowing and harvesting without demanding attention when the wheat needed care. So the oats in a second field were pure profit. Finally, the pasturing of the fallow on the third big field and its plowing to keep down weeds, the working in of manure to render the soil richer, all used tools, men, and animals when the other two fields presented no urgent demands. Even special group or individual tasks not having to do directly with field work could be fitted into such a routine.

On a manor, working at its best, the village had its acreage, its manpower, its animals, its goods and services, and its food, housing, fuel, tools, and clothing roughly in balance when the times and the climate were fairly good. Disasters, or the inflowing of labor, fertilizers, food, clothing, or tools, with the outflowing of crop surpluses, would crack or destroy the pattern.

The People under the Manorial System

In addition to the plowing, there were community jobs such as ditching and draining, hedging, fishing out the fish ponds, and cleaning out the fish weirs if they had traps in the rivers. Some community jobs were a cross between community picnics and work jobs. One of these might be the big nutting day in the autumn when the villagers went out to try to get what nuts the squirrels and pigs had left. Since that was fun, the villagers would pick a good day for it and all go out and have a celebration along with work. Another such day was pigsticking time in the fall when they could eat their fill of fresh meat, blood sausage, and other dainties which they did not have during most of the year. At this time they had games, which are discussed at the end of this chapter; we today still have a reminder of them in the chasing of greased pigs and the kicking of "pigskins."

Mass jobs were done, as at thatching time. Everybody plaited straw, cleaned it, got ties ready, worked on repairing the slats in the roofs the thatch was to be tied to, and so on. Then the villagers would put on the thatch, with everybody helping for quite some time. Expeditions to cart harvest to the lord's grain storage places could be fun. A string of carts would form up and a straggle of the villagers would traipse off with them. When the lord lived quite a distance from his working fields, the peasants on those fields had to cart the harvest, when it was finished, to where the lord wanted to consume it. Bishops, abbots, and monasteries were especially likely to need their harvest carted a good distance, and a great many persons participated in such jobs. At the lord's residence people of many villages could meet and enjoy the assemblage.

In addition to these group jobs there was a good deal of private work. Time off from community jobs could be spent cultivating a small garden patch, and normally even the householder who had no acreage at all still had a garden patch and perhaps one cow to run with the village herd (being just the sort of person Jack's mother was in the story of Jack and the Beanstalk). A little patch of ground around the house belonged to the householder. It was here that the housewife fed her chickens; in the Middle Ages, just as today, the "egg money" was hers. There was also private family work with threshing out the grain. In many families wheat was threshed in small quantities when needed, instead of being done as group work.

Usually the gathering of fuel was private work, although whole families might go together to pick up twigs, bundle them together, and carry them home. These, however, might be deposited in a village fagot pile rather than in a wood pile by the cottage. There was also a considerable amount of private work cutting turf in districts where peat was an important fuel. Most storing and cooking was done in their houses. People in manorial villages did not live in gangs with chains around their legs, nor did they live in servile barracks. They did not live as forced labor. They lived in villages where a good deal of the work done between dawn and dark was for themselves, and done by them privately in their own homes without anyone bossing them in the doing.

Many of the tasks done by the villagers as a group called for the oversight of specialists. Such a specialist directed the work while his particular talents were needed, then rejoined the rest of the villagers as an ordinary member of the team of workers for other activities. Such things as ditching, maintaining the chief hedges, or thatching called for management by men who might come to be called Mr. Ditcher, Mr. Hedger, or Mr. Thatcher in recognition of their roles. The butcher functioned in a particular job at pigsticking time or at Martinmas, when one great ox was roasted for the whole village, and so on.

There were other specialists whose jobs called for less team work and perhaps higher skill. These men were likely to work almost full time at their trades. Family names are descriptive of the list: Smith, Cooper, Miller, Wright, Carpenter, Baker, Brewster.

The highest of these specialists' jobs was that of the chief local man of the whole village, the "reeve" (Mr. Reeve, as he was called in England, and in France or Germany he might be called Lemaire or Meyer or Schultz). Throughout the year it was the reeve who was in charge of the whole organized teamwork effort of the village. Above him could be Mr. Bailey or Mr. Steward who functioned in the lord's name, but out in the fields it was the reeve who saw that the work was done; he was the chief man in any village.

The reeve was a proper villager; he lived among the villagers and not in or by the great house separate from all the rest. He might well have the best of the village houses, say two rooms instead of one, and keep his animals in a separate building instead of under his own roof, and he was usually much better off than the other villagers. He was, however, related by blood or marriage to most of the persons who worked in the fields with him. He had to go out in the fields to see that the work was being done properly, he supervised the cartage, he made sure the thatchers did their work right, the ditchers theirs, and so on.

It is very difficult today for us to see how persons can be put into office in an undefined way; we think they should either be elected, should inherit their jobs, or should somehow or other be appointed in clear-cut fashion. Men in the Middle Ages were not at all clear and sure about such things; and it is an interesting point that kings obtained their positions, as did dukes and lords and other nobles, by much the same means as did the reeves.

Although methods varied from manor to manor, in general the reeve was an elected hereditary appointed official. It worked. He usually held his office for a year, three years, five years, or for life. That also sounds indefinite. It was. He held his office because most of the leading villagers were reconciled to having him as boss. When he lost the confidence of too many of them, he lost his job. A village could not function with a reeve who was not wanted by the majority of the other villagers. In that sense he was elected, and especially when he first took office the villagers agreed at a meeting that he was to be the reeve.

The position was hereditary in that most often the reeve was the son or younger brother or nephew or son-in-law of the last reeve. There was no definite line of descent along which authority passed, and if there was a choice between near relatives of the old reeve, the villagers might have quite a bit of leeway in picking one as against another from the family. Yet they could also choose a reeve from an entirely different family than that of the last reeve.

The position was appointive in that above the wishes of the whole village was the lord (or the lords of the village; more often plural than singular), and the lords' steward or bailiff had to approve the new reeve. When all these various angles had been fitted together, the man was the elective, hereditary, appointive reeve. Of course in some places and times the position was strictly appointive, in others strictly hereditary, and so on, but generally it was a mixture. (This was not so different from the way in which even kings and popes were put into office. In the Middle Ages there was a great deal of uncertainty as to how to make officials. Clarity on such matters is modern, and in many cases very modern.)

The reeve, then, was the equivalent of the foreman, with strawbosses such as the thatcher, miller, and so on under him. He was supposed to see to it that all the work was done and done properly; to bring to the attention of the bailiff or steward any person who shirked his work and deserved punishment or who was rough or (we might say today) was criminal in his attitudes toward other villagers; and to take care of filling all of the vacancies, shifting personnel as death or illness made changes necessary.

The Lord's Household in Manorial Society

What of the lord and his place on a manorial estate? Usually the picture we have in our minds is one with the lord physically present on the place. In plain fact that was a fairly rare occasion. The lord was normally an absentee and, even when a particular place was his home, he was away a good part of every year. In the case of nearly all estates belonging to secular church officials, the lord lived in a distant city and came to his estates only as a visitor. An abbot lived at his abbey. A monastery which was possessed of only one estate could house very few monks; most monasteries possessed many estates and were absentee collective and corporate landlords. That also held true for a king, who had dozens and scores of estates and never visited most of them at all, and for the great dukes and counts whose numerous estates were scattered widely.

When we come down to the simple knight who owned just one estate, which would of course be his home, we have only to examine his routine of annual activities to see that during most of each summer he was away fighting in the train of his own lord or serving in the castle garrison, while during much of the winter he was at the court of his immediate lord or of his lord's lord, hunting, helping maintain the court, politicking, and living courteously. He came around to his small hall only occasionally in the course of each twelve months and might be absent for years.

Through divisions of inheritances, and because part interests in them were used to make up daughters' dowries and the like, there were many villages in which more than one lord had an interest. In fact the one lord–one village combination was relatively rare. Every lord had as many estates or villas as he could, and was perfectly happy to take in addition quarter, eighth, or even smaller interests in any others that brought in an income. From the point of view of the lord, the villa was an income-producing unit, and it was the small surplus off the top of the economic return which interested him. Consequently, divided interests were commonplace, which meant, since there was unified management, that the bailiff or steward had to account to a number of different individuals when the year's returns were in. It was the bailiff or steward who did what we would call today the declaring of dividends for a year's operations to the different persons —nobles, women, monks—who might have an interest in returns from a given single manor. Perhaps a better statement would be that each interest was taken care of by custom.

Work for the lord was looked upon by the villagers as work on or for the lord's demesne. The word demesne has both a broader and a narrower meaning. In the narrower sense described above, a piece of land which was retained by the lord in his own hands and not granted out to villagers formed part of the demesne. Commonly it was that good piece of un-broken acreage in the near neighborhood of the lord's house (even when he did not reside in it there was usually a big house in which the steward in fact lived) consisting of some fifty, a hundred, or a hundred-and-fifty acres, which was the lord's demesne in the narrowest sense. In addition to this single piece of land, there could be those strips out in the open fields which were also part of the lord's demesne.

Then we come to some of the less tangible assets of the lord's demesne. In addition to solid acreage the lord had rights in the produce of the villagers. He had rights in the hay which the villagers cut and brought in from the meadow when they were haying for the village in general. When the hay was divided, the lord got whatever was his customary share. The lord had demesne rights in the running of cattle in the village herd; so many of the cattle would be his, so many sheep, so many pigs, and again custom fixed the numbers. His pigs had the lord's ear mark so they could be recognized when the roundup came.

The lord's demesne also usually included the forest and the wild animals therein. At least it included the good building timber in the forest, and the game animals which it was his delight to hunt. It also included the tolls on the mill, on the bridge, on any of the other income-producing things. Finally, and very important, for it really was lucrative, the lord's demesne included the fines levied when court was held for the villagers. Fines for crimes and misdemeanors, and fines (they were called that, too) for transfers of land, ratification of agreements among the villagers, and special permissions, were a real source of income, as will be seen below.

In many parts of Europe the lords had serfs who did nothing but work on the lord's demesne. They handled the big land around his house, and the strips which were his out in the fields. Outright attachment to the demesne was the lot of many villagers in many villages, but not in all of them by any means. There was great variation, for some estates had no demesne acreage, some had little, while some were all demesne. There were usually not enough serfs to do all the necessary work on the demesne, so that other villagers were held to payment in work, being required to labor one or three or five days a week on the demesne, as custom might direct. Such work, if regular, was known as "week work." At special seasons when there was heavy pressure to get plowing or harvesting done "boon work" or extra work was required. These things were usually understood on a given estate.

In addition there would be some rather irregular jobs such as cartage, when the serfs or free villagers brought in their own ox carts and wagons to carry the hay, grain, and other produce from the estate to the place where the lord was to receive it. In the case of a bishop, this would be to the bishop's city, or to the home buildings in the case of a monastery. For a king or a count it would be to that place in the neighborhood where he stored up food for his visits when on his itineraries around his dominions. In addition there was the need for the lord's animals to receive normal care at such times as lambing or when the pigs were being rounded up. Such work was done according to rules customary in any particular village.

In addition there was all the work that had to be done in the big house of the lord and that work which went with his being head of the estate. In the lord's own household there had to be servants, and since there was no modern labor-saving machinery, everything had to be done by them. Usually there was also a kind of sun and moon relationship between the lord's household and the lady's household. There had to be two persons with much the same titles to serve the queen or the lady and to serve the king or the knight, almost a complete double organization. Among such servitors there was frequently cross marriage, so the treasurer of the lord might have as his wife the treasurer of the lady. In every household of a dignified person—an emperor, a pope, bishop, duke, or simple knight—about the same hierarchy of servants was to be found.

These household officers or servants were, speaking generally, those who did ministries or services in a noble's behalf, and they were members of higher or lower society depending on the position of the person they served. The chancellor of a great German emperor was an archbishop himself, with his own household; the chancellor of a petty knight was the local village priest, very different from the chancellor of an empire. The chamberlain of a king of England was one of England's greatest earls; the chamberlain of a petty knight was a barefooted villager who worked in the great house and was no different in the way he looked and dressed and acted and talked from the rest of the villagers.

These persons who ministered to the lord, *ministeriales,* could be and in the lesser ranks usually were personages of servile rank in law. The *ministeriales* of a house of nobles which grew in importance rose with that house. There was, for example, the house of Hohenstaufen which came up from simple knights to counts, from counts to dukes of Swabia, from dukes of Swabia to kings of Germany and emperors. Rising with them came their household servants. By the 1190's the *ministeriales* of the Hohenstaufen family were still serfs in law, but in fact were lords of tremendous territories as delegated rulers, on the nod of the Hohenstaufen family. The man who ran all the south half of Italy from 1193 to 1195 was a serf, a ministerial of the Hohenstaufen family. In Germany a whole class of such noble serfs eventually moved into the nobility proper, but most were not so lucky.

In wartime those servants who were largely occupied with military business around the lord's person were called *servientes* in the documents which were in Latin, and *sergeants* or *serjeants* in the Norman French of England. These fellows have given their name to the highest rank of non-commissioned officers in our own army. (The lowest knight in any feudal army was a commissioned officer, a second lieutènant, so to speak, and hence a gentleman, and vice versa.) In theory the common fellows who followed along corresponded to our privates and noncoms. The *servientes* or sergeants who were attached to the hunting and fighting occupations of a lesser lord were, in most cases, villagers. They often were villagers who had come into the young lord's service and become attached to him instead of to the handle of a plow. Many of these sergeants came to have modest assignments in land and to be given duties in war which put them into the lowest-grade nobility. Even when the grandfather or father had been a serf, or when the sergeant himself might have been a serf originally, he still could end up as a sergeant with a fixed holding and a position in the lowest level of feudal society if he rode a horse like a cavalier.

Stratification of Manorial Society

The villagers were stratified in position, and here again it may be better to confuse than to oversimplify. In the Middle Ages men were not the least bit clear in their minds about social or legal stratification—not nearly so clear as we are today. It was not at all easy to make a distinction between a slave and a serf, between a serf and a free man, and they usually did not care to make this distinction. Instead of having general, abstract concepts of slavery and freedom serve in this matter, men of the Middle Ages preferred to be very particular and concrete. At a given moment they did not ask "Are the serfs free?" but "Is so-and-so free?" (or even, "Is he free of this specific burden?"). And they expected him to prove that he was, or expected someone who claimed to be his lord to prove that he was not. They had no general rules. They never freed the serfs. They freed individual serfs from specific obligations.

They did not have a category of free men, with all the attributes of freedom, and another category of unfree with attributes of unfreedom. What they had were many freedoms, and the word for a single freedom was "franchise." A man could have a great many different items in his list of franchises, or freedoms, or liberties—plural, always plural, no abstract franchise, no abstract freedom, no abstract liberty. A man could lose or sell or gain or buy an item in the list of franchises without disturbing any of the others which might apply to him. A full-fledged slave or a full-fledged serf was hard to find anywhere exactly. In any village some individuals were subject to this, and others to that, and some to so little that they were reckoned free. There was no clear-cut stratification.

We can look back and, using our modern ideas on things like this, envision two great socio-legal strata and in effect project them back on people now six or eight hundred years dead. But that does not mean that they had them. We can theorize about status in regard to the law, and status in matters of economic and social position. When we do, astonishingly to us, we can find that in the Middle Ages they did not coincide as we think they should have.

We have the rough idea that the slave can always be found at the bottom of any social heap; a real slave does deserve that sort of reckoning. He is lowest in law, lowest in wealth, lowest in social rank. There were true slaves in the Middle Ages. True slaves had been known to the Romans and to the Germans at all times before the Middle Ages began, as we have seen.

In the Middle Ages there were plenty of slaves who had usually begun their slavery (or family slavery) as war captives. For an illustration of this we can turn to the Anglo-Saxon language of the conquerors from Germany who had moved into Angleland (or England) by the five hundreds. In their language the word for the person who had no freedom was "Welshman"; in other words, he was one of the descendants of one of the enslaved native Britons, or Welshmen. The word "Welsh" meant slave and the word for slave was "Welsh." The same thing roughly accounts for the development later on of the word "slave" itself. Originally this meant a Slav, a heathen Slavic captive possessed by a German, Moslem, or Italian owner.

Usually, however, when slaves were left in a rural community where hands were at a premium, their sons and grandsons melted into the general run of villagers. That would be notably forwarded the moment they became Roman Catholic baptized Christians. Such a slave turned Christian was well on the way toward turning into a serf instead of being a slave. The slave was not worth much as such unless he could be sold away as a commodity. Down until 1066 the English were noted for selling their children and their neighbors' children into slavery. It is noteworthy that, until the time of William the Conqueror, England was one of the chief producers of raw slave material for the markets of Europe and even farther afield. William the Conqueror restricted, not slavery, but the selling beyond the seas of English slaves. While the slave as a commodity had some value until into the ten hundreds, the whole slave trade was already fading out in the nine and ten hundreds, and by the eleven and twelve hundreds we can say that there were no true slaves in areas where the manorial pattern was well established. We can go even further and say there were seldom any true slaves in the manorial areas at any time. It was not a system that needed true slaves to make it operate well. (In the Mediterranean areas, where the manorial system was never in operation, true slavery lasted until only a few generations before our own time.)

While the manorial system was becoming established, there were what we today call displaced persons. Troubles uprooted people. Famines, plagues, animal diseases, and war drove men, women, and children onto the highways to hunt whatever kind of shelter they could find. Many of the persons cut adrift had been well-established, respectable villagers back home, but they were not home any more. Along with the honest refugees there were also the dishonest ones who had become outlaws from their own villages, and who were far enough away so that the story of their misdeeds did not follow. If he was lucky, the person on the road could be cared for by monasteries, by the private charity of the church if it had any resources, or by the charity or tolerance of the villagers in a neighborhood to which he might come. But on the whole, throughout the history of this period, the villages were very unfriendly toward wandering persons of any sort.

Displaced persons, when they came to a village, were utterly free and the most miserable of all the people there, perhaps far more miserable than the one or two slaves who might be working in the lord's house. They lived completely by charity. Week in, week out, they were free to go; no one cared where they lived or died; they were as free as any stray dog. These people were quite happy to exchange their lowest-level, most precarious economic status for a very low-level servile status—to take any kind of holding however small or poor, as long as they could become fixed in a village. Persons could go from homeless freedom into the lowest level serfdom, not only with their eyes open, but hungry for the change. We cannot look upon serfdom in itself as the lowest a man could go.

The Romans had a word for slave—*servus*. The *servus* was the legal slave in the Roman law, and there were many of them. At most moments in Roman history there were more slaves than Romans in the city of Rome itself. According to the Roman law the slave was a buyable and salable commodity. We have some management books, written by able Roman nobles, on how to make money from estates. Their attitude toward the field hands was like that of some persons today toward automobiles: buy a new one, drive it hard until it is about to fall apart, then junk it. That was the way they recommended handling field slaves. It was not wise to have "slave jalopies" on hand because, like a car when it has been overdriven, a sick or an old slave had to have expensive repairs, and he continued to consume.

In the course of the one, two, and three hundreds A.D. there was increasing generosity toward slaves. This was in part due to Stoicism and other philosophies which recommended treating slaves as brothers. Under the influence of these philosophies the law began to give *servi* some protection. Aside from the philosophies and laws, however, was the very important fact that there were not nearly so many serfs or *servi* available any more. The supply earlier had been kept up by great victories and the capture of great masses of barbarians. By the three hundreds it was the barbarians who were capturing Romans, and there was not much of an open, easy slave market. When the lords lost their slaves, for whatever reason, their stewards could no longer order a new lot. The next crop had to be bred.

It was this which made it necessary to be generous to slaves. Human beings will not reproduce themselves unless their situation is more tolerable than that of slaves who work in chain gangs. In order to have enough people to do the work on the estates, generation after generation, it was necessary to give the slaves enough of a stake in their world to make their lives bearable. The process of doing this can be summed up in our word "husband." The slave was given an opportunity to be a husband. The slave, or *servus,* was encouraged to have a mate. She might not legally be his wife, but she was there all the time; they had children of whom they were fond, and the children grew up in the family's hut in the village. By the time the manorial system began to take shape in northern France, villages were full of hutted *servi* rather than of gang slaves. The word *servus* still applied to these people, only by this time we can call them by its variant, "serfs."

After these developments took place, over a period of some four hundred years, the serf had evolved into quite a different individual from the *servus* of earlier times. To start with, the *servus* could be bought and sold into distant lands, while the serf was fixed where he was born. The family could not be broken up, for the church had recognized the union of baptized serfs as holy marriage. This was sacramentally established and the principle "let no man put asunder" was being applied. Once married, the village serf and his wife were really husband and wife, and their children were recognized as belonging to them, although they also belonged to the lord. The hut the serf occupied could be passed on to his oldest son, to his youngest son, or to his son-in-law, as though it were the property of his family. Actually it belonged to the lord (as did the whole serf family) but it could be passed on according to the serf's wishes because the custom of the place agreed that that was the right thing to do when an old serf died.

In addition to his hut and family, he had his work in the fields and his allotted land which made him perhaps a five-acre, or fifteen-acre, or thirty-acre serf. He had a position which was recognized by custom. The support of all the serfs for one another guaranteed that the customs would work; if the lord did not follow the custom the serfs would not produce well for him.

In the law there was one remnant from slavery, namely, that a serf could not sue his lord (save for life and limb, under Roman law—if crude circumstances made it worth while!) any more than a man's dog can sue him. But there were some benefits; for no one outside could sue the serf. Instead, outsiders could sue his lord for the things a serf did, and it was only through his lord that he could be held responsible.

In addition there were other matters. A serf might pay money to his lord in order to obtain some small favor or exemption, for one occasion or in perpetuity. For example, one of the burdens of the serf was that he could not marry an outsider nor could his daughter. For a fee, however, the lord would let him do it. The lord did not prohibit marriages between serfs from one village and those from another, he merely took a little more money in the form of a fee out of his village court when he allowed such a step to be taken.

As another example, the successor of a dead serf owed the lord that serf's best ox, best pig, best sheep, and so on. The lord might either take those things, or take money as a substitute. All such things furnished income for the lord. And herein lay many of the burdens of the serf— payments (fines) to the lord on top of week and boon work.

In many parts of the manorial world the serf was the commonest sort of villager. In southern and western England many of the great estates about 1050 were entirely servile, while in the north and east the servile estates were less usual. Like variations obtained on the Continent.

The serfs themselves were not at all a uniform sort of group. Serfs in a village ran all the way from the serf who was reeve down to the lowest servile cottager, with great differences in economic and social positions within the one village community. There were always serfs who were moving up, individually, into the privileged classes of society by becoming *servientes*, or sergeants, or *ministeriales* in the lord's house. As the serfs at the top faded into the lowest nobility, so at the bottom they were recruited from the displaced persons who came wandering into the villages.

The free man was not at all an unusual figure in the village. In addition to the free man who was a displaced person and had no position at all, there still were many established villagers who were free. Often they were very heavily burdened with work and money payments. A free man was often required to do a heavy stint of week work and boon work, to pay eggs or wine and the like as rent in kind. But he was free. There might be serfs who led an easier life than he, but although he worked hard to pay his rent, still he could (and had to) bear arms and that pretty generally meant that he was free.

Here we find an attitude which was widely considered a sensible one during the Middle Ages. If a man bore arms he was free; if he did not bear arms, he was not free. If he was subject to the militia call, to the sheriff's posse, to the *ban* or draft, to attendance in the king's court, he was free. There were bad periods in the Middle Ages, as in the eight hundreds, when men were giving up their freedom in order to escape the burdens of military service, and in so doing binding themselves and their descendants to serfdom. Then there were better periods in later times when men were breaking away from their serfdom by assuming arms.

The old, normal criterion applying to freedom or nonfreedom in the villages associated arms-bearing and freedom with one another. But in England and also in other lands, a second criterion also evolved slowly: the fixity of a man's burden. When a man had a fixed obligation to his lord, then he was free; if not, he was a serf. Thus a man might work very hard for his lord, but if it was a fixed amount of work, to be done according to his own plan and whim, then he was free; on the other hand, another man might do relatively little work for his lord but, if the work he did was at the lord's command, then he was a serf.

For historical reasons, due to local developments, still other criteria as to what constituted freedom and what serfdom developed in other countries in western Europe, but are too varied and uneven to warrant discussion here. It is to be remembered that at all times some men, usually young men, escaped from serfdom by simply going away. Such men made up a fair part of the lowest-level fighting forces. Maidens' charms sometimes were as useful; at least two French queens were slaves when they met their future husbands.

Recreation and Sports

The working day for the lower classes was wearyingly long when weather allowed, and idleness was a serious problem for all classes when the weather was bad. Wrangling and fighting, and even feuding and war-fare, had at least some of their roots in boredom.

For all except townsmen, "going to town," when towns grew up, was a major outlet for country folk, as it was in all rural American society only two generations ago. Markets and fairs, in town, at crossroads, or on porches and in the yards of churches, served the same purpose.

Castles and monasteries, when the great were celebrating personal or religious occasions, gave their own inmates and the able-bodied of all classes from many miles around appreciated opportunities to foregather, eat, drink, court, and do the other things persons like so much to do. Spectator and participant pleasures were afforded in all degrees at weddings, christenings, buryings, on holy days, and at parties just for funmaking. If the great were not taking the lead, the rustics could take it themselves—and enjoy (or put up with) the company of gentle gate-crashers of all ages.

Frolic aside, there was still solemn appreciation of inspirational serv-ices indoors and out in honor of the saints, in propitiation or in jubilation, or in the mass.

Music by voice or instruments, within the limits set by the availability of talent, was in demand for jollification or marching, for church or tavern, harvest festival or funeral, rope-walking or rowing—through the whole list of activities known to our own grandparents. Solo and group singing, highly sacred or lowly, was universal, and either was cultivated assiduously and professionally, or was completely untutored. The drift of the spoken languages towards patterns of stress made song of all sorts increasingly like those commonly preferred for a thousand years since by most west-ern Europeans.

Wind instruments, from simple pipes through bagpipes to organs, and through a considerable variety of wooden or brazen horns, were every-where known. So were stringed instruments of the harp, lyre, zither, guitar class, all appreciated for the way they could be used to fit a tune and a beat to the recited poetry of lay or epic, ballad or lyric. Little bells and jangles for the trapping of harness or carriage, or for belle or beau, were always in order and so were the great bronze bells of the major buildings, both secular and religious, in the towns, when these appeared, and in the clock bells and chimes of large and small communities from the later Middle Ages on. Only gongs, drums, cymbals, and their like seem to have been cultivated less in western Europe than by most other peoples of the world, though percussion instruments were known and used.

Indoor games and other pastimes for the well-to-do were established in the pattern which held until very recently. Toys and tag, hide and seek, and all their variants were known to the young. Group dancing, amateur and semiprofessional plays and recitations at banquets or after them, were commonplace. The villagers had barns which were about as comfortable and commodious as the halls of kings—and vice versa—for larger entertainments.

Dice and bones pleased the richest and the poorest. These could be combined with board-and-counter games of the backgammon-parchesi family to bring in an element of skill or judgement. Chess and checkers were games for gentlemen from the eleven hundreds on. Playing cards came into use only two or three generations before Columbus was born.

Outdoor play for nobles was hardly a step removed from war games on an individual or a small-group basis. Sword, spear, shield, hook and club, bow and arrow, and even shield and armor were needed. A large part of the waking hours of youths and young men, in the good seasons, went into weapon-handling that was more or less serious—the thrusts and slashes being directed at two-legged or four-legged opponents. Stag and boar and, where they still survived, the wild bulls and aurochs were fought to the death with hand weapons on fairly even terms through all the centuries which interest us here.

Afoot or ahorse, against dummies or targets, in single combat or in squads, young warriors practiced fighting. The fancy tournament with damsels dropping handkerchiefs for gallants in fantastic get-ups was a late development by the very rich. Even at such perfumed jousting, men were killed—even princes and kings. Hard brutal fighting was a commonplace everywhere until about 1200, and long after among nobles who liked it that way—but under rules and with umpires and judges.

Hawking on foot but usually on horse was everywhere practiced by those who could afford it. Trained hawks and even eagles brought down edible and inedible birds while their masters pelted across field and marsh to watch the sport and to gather in the downed game.

All of these sports, incidentally, were greatly beloved by the warriors in Islam and most of Asia as well as in western Europe. Indeed, they still survive more vigorously in some parts of those regions than in Europe.

Noble sports called for wealth, just as, in general, the sports monopolized by the rich today require full purses—deep-sea yachting, sports-car racing, or squash, as examples. But the poor men's sports were widely appreciated. In recent generations the expensive noble sports have faded as real-life applicability of their skills has disappeared, as the animals hunted have been exterminated, or as the rich have themselves transferred their affections to track and field, ball and bat, hook and line, and weaponless strugglings, which the villagers had enjoyed all the time—but which they had also had to share with nobles, even in the heyday of jousting.

All kinds of animal races, with or without wagers, with or without jockeys or drivers, delighted emperors and serfs as participants or as spectators. They may not have matched jumping frogs, but the principle of such a competition was universally understood in all generations before and since a ringside reporter described one of those meets.

Amphitheatrical fights between animals or between men and animals went out by the later five hundreds, but it must be seriously doubted that Christian preaching scotched the amusement; rather, it was a dwindling population and the high costs which were undoubtedly responsible. For, in fact, these games as such never were eliminated. The pitting of cock against cock, of bull against bear, of dogs against bulls or bears or badgers or rats or dogs, and of daredevil men against all sort of things, went on and in ways continues still.

Racing on a track, during the work breaks or after a day of plowing or harvesting, was easily arranged by manorial villagers. The grassy paths or balks along acre-strips were ready-made sprinters' lanes for fast youths. The paths were closely alike in grade and equal in length: a furlong, or 220 yards; down and back was the 440. The shepherd's fold was made of movable sections of fencing called hurdles. Used as obstacles for sprinters, they were ideal. The hurdles were at hand in the open field where these track and field athletes were having fun.

The pitching of stones, of wagon tongues, and of logs, and the throwing of the sledge hammer were natural avenues for competition. So were wrestling, yanking, jerking, tripping, cuffing, clubbing, and other pastimes. More or less formalized and carried on under accepted rules, they are represented today by most of our ring sports.

Balls of wood, of leather-bound hanks of wool, hay, or weeds, or balls fashioned from inflated bladders of freshly slaughtered animals, invited throwing, kicking, butting, and batting. Europeans, from remote times on, had inherited ball-playing of all sorts, and women and nobles played ball games in Roman society. What the object was—who won and why, what sort of sides and strategy and rules were followed—are matters our sources conceal. But we inherit accounts of what came close to rural warfare, as the whole north end of the village, say, played at harvest time against the whole south end, kicking an inflated pig's bladder up and down the north-south single street, the weather brisk, the supply of beer ample, the girls screaming from the windows and doors, the youngsters peeking around the corners from side lanes or alleyways or pressing in from behind hoping for a swipe at the ball themselves or a chance to trip a player from the other side or to get into a fight with a boy from the wrong end of town. Respectable persons disapproved; the pulpit spoke and laws were passed. But the gentry looked on and placed wagers, drank heavily, and cheered; and their younger brothers and cousins joined the sport. Later, especially in England, these same younger boys were to be going to boarding school and to universities, and by the mid-eighteen hundreds the village sports had most of them gone to school with young English gentlemen. Modern sport was taking its shape.

Management and Government in Manorial Society

In modern society, when we think of management, we have quite a definite idea of what it means. And when we think of government, we think of rules and regulations that are quite different from those of management. But when we turn back to the Middle Ages and the manorial system, we find almost a turning upside down of our concepts of management and government.

For example, we think of management in a modern factory or business as having to do with telling employees what to do and when to do it, with planning the work, making changes in the program, and so on. We think of government as something which has its operation in most cases outside the factory, as having to do with the police, with the courts, with the officials of the state, with the handling of broad national and state problems, municipal and local problems, and so on.

It would seem perfectly sensible to us to think of a manager as ordering the hands to do various jobs on various days, as having enough foresight and authority to plan what should be planted, when and where, and by whom. In the Middle Ages, had the ordinary reeve or bailiff or steward, or even the lord, gone to the villagers and, for example, told them that this year they were to turn the three-field system around, that instead of planting wheat it would be barley, there would have been a look of complete incomprehension on the faces of all who heard him. That was not what they were going to do. What they were going to do was what they had done the previous year (having moved the dial of field rotation around one notch, of course), what they had done the year before that, what their grandfathers and great-grandfathers had done, time out of mind. Changing the routine of work would have been no function of management; such

matters were handled on the basis of custom, of the old rules and regulations, and it was not within the power of the lord or his officials to change
what we would think of today as the most important things connected with
management.

On the other hand, it would not seem at all necessary to us for the head
of a modern factory to concern himself with such things as the holdings
in land and goods of those who were employed by him. Neither would we
think it necessary for him to see that those who had started fights in a
tavern on Saturday night were brought into his office and fined; we would
not think it needful for him to approve marriages, protect widows and
orphans, and do many other things which might interest government
nowadays. In the Middle Ages, in matters assigned management today,
we find that custom controlled, and where we think primarily of government as functioning, we find management was again operating under
custom.

We have thin evidence for earlier centuries, but in manuals written
during the twelfth, thirteenth, and some later centuries for the direction
of managers, we find that civil and police fines were a primary source of
revenue to the lord (or the lords) of an estate. Of course, the writers of
the manuals had a good deal to say about income from crops and livestock, but also a good deal to say about such things as fees, fines, and other
revenue which came from the manor court.

Much of the work of managing a single estate fell on the shoulders of
the reeve and of the bailiff, who might at the same time be the lord's
steward if the estate happened to be the only one held by the lord. Whether
the lord personally occupied the large hall or not, his officials had to
be there, waiting his coming and keeping various managerial jobs going
in his absence. In the big house, or in houses near it, were those whom we
might call the lord's managerial staff, or his governmental staff, the two
things being run together. This staff consisted of several different persons,
their numbers and dignity depending on the size and wealth of the establishment.

In the first place there would have to be at least one person on the place
who could read and write. The parish priest might serve, of course. If the
lord did not have very much more in the way of assets than a single village,
the parish priest would likewise be a familiar person in the big house,
acting as chaplain for the lord, his family, and the immediate household
dependents. But the priest would probably also be records keeper, and so
he would function as the chancellor. Later on the court would usually come
to have a reader and writer regularly employed, who was only by con-

vention reckoned to be a churchman or *cleric*. He was in actual fact the court's clerk.

Along with the clerk there would have to be a steward, if it happened that a steward held that particular manor house in the lord's absence, or at least a bailiff. The name for the bailiff or steward of a great man might be that noble word "seneschal"—"oldest servant." For a king of France or a ruler of great lands, the hereditary seneschal would himself be a noble-man of the highest rank. However, the seneschal or steward of a single village was not a particularly formidable person. He might even be bare-footed, or, if he rode a horse, it could be a nag, not a war horse.

In addition to these persons there would be a man who had charge of the lord's table when he was in residence, the butler. Great kings and dukes had butlers, and simple knights also had butlers who were in charge of the food when it was out in the kitchen or on its way to the table, and of the drink. The butler had his wife and children, and his wife might serve the lord's lady just as he served the lord.

Then there was a person who functioned as constable, in charge of the barns, of the grooms, and of the lord's animals, and also a marshal who was in charge of the active field operations of the lord's army, which might consist of only two or three men, and which might well be no more than a small police force. In case news came to the great house that there was fighting in the village, that women were quarreling, or that there was danger from wolves or bandits, it would be the duty of the marshal or the constable of a village to assemble the lord's small army, the huntsmen, sergeants, and others who could ride and fight, and rush to take care of things.

This staff of persons at the big house or in its near neighborhood was made up of persons whom we have seen reckoned as *ministeriales* or sergeants in the service of the lord. Under ordinary circumstances they had nothing to do with the actual plow-handle work of the villagers. In-stead, they occupied themselves with administering the lord's buildings and demesne, with his warring and hunting, and with his social activities. How well they carried out their work affected the profit a lord could realize from his estate. If the villagers were given too much leeway, the income of the lord would suffer; if they were abused and down-trodden, the income of the lord would also suffer, for they would either become hopeless and unwilling or incapable of good work, or they would become disgruntled and deliberately not put forth the amount of effort of which they were capable. As there is variation in personalities, so there was variation in the ways in which the lord's demesne was administered by his subordinates, throughout Europe, ranging from enlightened administration (according to the standards of the time) to the utmost abuse of human beings.

In addition to the problems which went with management and overlordship we must consider the village, or manor, court. According to the custom of any particular village, the village would meet, often in the courtyard of the great house, at stated intervals. This might be once a week, or perhaps once every three weeks or every month, while bigger meetings for special or difficult police cases, inheritance cases, and so on might be held about twice a year.

In a great many ways the meeting of the court at the village level was like the meeting of a king's court. Three great high meetings of the court of the king of England took place each year, while in the meantime there were lesser meetings where the king's legal, diplomatic, and financial affairs were carried on, often by underlings rather than by the king himself. Down at the village level the same thing obtained; the lord was often or always absent. He might, at the same time his village court was meeting, be attending as courtier the meetings of his own great lord's court. But if he was not at court, his bailiff was, and the court was held in the lord's name.

A session of the court was the high moment in the functioning of both management and government, melted together as they were, with more government than management. Much of the interest of the lord in the court lay in seeing to it that things were keeping on an even keel in the village with respect to work that had to be done for him, and to returns of sheaves of grain, oxen, and what not that were due him. The lord was interested in the court both as something which produced income directly from those who had to attend, and as the lever or instrument for maintaining tranquility and continuous production inside the community on whose productivity he in turn depended.

The lord's bailiff, or the lord, if he was there (or often enough, his lady), presided but did not run the court in an arbitrary or authoritarian fashion. Instead, he was there with the marshal, constable, and huntsmen to keep order and to see that things were conducted in a decent and respectable manner, and of course to make sure that the lord's income was taken care of at all points in the court's operations. Also present were such persons as were charged with specific duties, above all the reeve.

Forming the real body of the court were half a dozen or more of the responsible, substantial, well-regarded villagers. Some of these would be free men, some serfs, but they all functioned as what were called "suitors" in the English courts; suitors were those who had to be at court because their holdings and status obligated them to function there.

Before these men the reeve would come to complain that such and such misdemeanors and crimes had taken place, the marshal having picked up the defendants or having ascertained so far as possible the facts with respect to such persons as had run away from the community in fear of being tried. A series of what we would call criminal cases would be brought up, the lord's immediate interest being in the confiscations and penalties exacted. Older villagers could be asked what was the custom of the place with respect to this or that particular charge. This having been determined, and the facts having been established, either from witnesses or by ordeal, a person who was found guilty of what we today would call a crime might lose his holding, be outlawed from the village, in some cases be subjected to serious physical punishment; in any case he would be given a fine which might be severe enough to beggar him and his. For a misdemeanor or small crime the whole thing might be taken care of with just a few whip lashes, or by a fine in money or cattle or goods, imposed by the bailiff in the name of the court, in the name of the lord.

Much more important than the criminal business of the court was that of changing holdings for one reason or another, or taking notice of exemptions which villagers might be asking. There might be need to shift the holding from old A, who had died, to his son, young A, who was fit and able to take over. At that point a payment which was called the "heriot" in England would have to be made—payment of, say, the best ox of the dead holder, while the young new holder had to find himself a new beast to put into the plow team where it belonged for that holding. There could be other incomes to the lord as such a transfer was made. The court would notice any changes in status of holdings or men and, from the twelve hundreds on, the court roll (the rolled-up long parchment record of court actions) was made to show that the changes had taken place properly in open court. There would be ratification of transfers, of dowries, and of any acquisitions of franchises which individual villagers had arranged with the bailiff acting for the lord. Such agreements would be completed and made firm in the court and recorded on the court roll.

In addition to these things, all of which brought income to the lord, shirking in the field or failure to do a proper share of the community work were matters brought up against villagers at the court. The reeve and other villagers would be the first to make complaints against the person who had neglected to do his proper share of the ditching, of the lord's haying, and so on, or who had encroached on his neighbor's hay or had cut into his neighbor's wheat. These matters might be brought up either individually or collectively by the villagers who felt aggrieved, or by the reeve, who considered that the individual culprit had been infringing upon the lord. In any case, after determination of the facts and custom in the matter, there might be more fines, and payments made into the bailiff's pocket, the bailiff's money in turn being held for the lord, minus what the bailiff held out as proper (or improper) fees.

In addition to all such matters the court might take care of things which we would consider managerial. There might be a real managerial decision concerning the clearing of a new field, "assarting" in the forest around the village; there might be discussion of building important improvements such as a new mill, bridge, dam, and so forth, with great argument and debate as to who was to have what burdens and interest in whatever was to be constructed or cleared. They might—and later on this would be a matter of real importance—make decisions on the changing of the crops and the handling of field routine. That was to be more and more the case as the twelve hundreds passed and men came into a time when many other things were changing in the manors themselves in the more prosperous parts of western Europe—in other words as the manorial pattern so far described was beginning to break up and to change into other sorts of patterns for the conduct of village life and agriculture. But in the earlier times of the manorial ages, such occasions would be rare.

With an increase in production, as manors came to flourish, there was a steady increase in the wealth and population of those parts of Europe where the manorial system first and most completely established itself. By the ten and eleven hundreds there were more people per square mile in the north of France, in the neighboring parts of Alsace and Lorraine, in the Low Countries and nearby parts of England, than anywhere else in the west of Europe. In that sense the manorial system was a tremendous success. On the average it kept producing more each year than any other system before known in those parts.

The population responded by increasing, and at the same time there was a steady raising of the living standard, not from high to higher, but from very low to less low. Just the same, it was a step up for everybody, and for some of the greatest personages it was a notable step up, for they were to draw off more and more of a surplus (even though not an increasing proportion) as the twelve hundreds came along. Through its success in providing surplus, this same area became the home of the most advanced learning, the best armies, the most advanced literature, the most active commerce and industry in western Europe. The things it could support could not have been maintained by earlier systems of agriculture, but could be by the manorial system. Through its success in building up towns and industry, the manorial system opened the door to the still more generous economy which superseded it.

Even at its best the manorial system provided only a narrow margin of comfort for the villagers. But it supported them, and above them it managed to support the small clerical and noble society which concerned itself with religion, government, war, the arts, and learning.

CHAPTER III

Feudalism:
Government and War,
Land and Law

TERMS like feudalism, or the feudal system, are extremely hard to deal with. No one at the time knew they were living under feudalism, and it never was a system. It is only for our own convenience that we call it the feudal system; in its own day it had no name. Feudalism had to do with those who received the surplus income that came from the work of the villagers in the manorial world—and from the work of other producers in those parts of Europe which did not follow the manorial pattern. Feudalism concerned the military and governmental, the property and social relationships, among only the elite in the society with which we are dealing.

Feudalism had to do with a class in which all of the men who were at all fit for battle were warriors. They themselves (and everyone else) assumed that they were the persons who alone should govern. No serf, no villager, was really a member of the feudal system of society. Feudalism could take from him what it needed to survive; it could give him protection, direction, and leadership; but he was not a part of it. Nor were the lords of the feudal system part of the manorial pattern. They were the personages in whose name the bailiff conducted the estate's business; they were not the men who held the handles of the plow and goaded the oxen. They did not even have to have manors where manors did not exist. A regular stipend paid from the royal treasury in return for homage and fealty served as a satisfactory fief to any English noble in a position to get one. These became rather important, in fact, in the twelve hundreds and thereafter.

First of all we must consider how and why feudalism came to be, what it was, and its outstanding characteristics.

In western European history feudalism had its origins in some earlier patterns which were not feudal themselves, but which under certain conditions lent themselves to being remolded into the feudalism of the ten, eleven, and twelve hundreds.

To begin with, there were ways in the Roman pattern of law whereby lesser men were brought into contact with great men. The system by which a wealthy Roman noble drew around him or drew into his service a great many hundreds, sometimes many thousands, of free Roman citizens was known as patronage. The Latin word *pater* means "father"; the word *patron* (our English word "patron" comes from it, but is not the same thing) means a "father" in a higher and not in an intimate way.

The person who came under such a patron was his client. In Roman law a client owed a great deal to his patron, and the patron owed a great deal to his client. At first, in about the time of Julius Caesar, the client could be expected to follow, to cheer, and to vote for his patron, and, incidentally, to help get hold of the polling places in the city in order to keep the clients of rival candidates from defeating by votes his own patron. Patrons (through their business managers) in turn saw to it that needy clients got at least food and shelter, that good clients obtained lesser jobs in the political machinery (which is something we ourselves call patronage); saw to it as well that clients who were caught in the toils of the law were given the best legal advice and defense possible, and so on. Once in a while, in the Roman civil wars, great men armed their clients. But most of the time, when the government was stable and the emperors were strong, such an act was considered criminal and was, in fact, very dangerous for the rich man who tried it.

However, during the course of the two hundreds, there were bad civil wars in the Roman Empire. Brigandage and foreign invasions ripped up many areas in western Europe. In that century many a rich senator was arming his clients and ranging them against bandits and rebels to protect his goods and serfs and all the other clients who were under him. In the course of the four hundreds this became a regular pattern, especially after the last of the Roman emperors in the West no longer had authority. Great senators in Gaul, Spain, and Italy made private armies. They bought equipment, furnished the clients with commanders, furnished strategic and tactical direction and so forth, exactly as the owners of private armies were to do in other parts of the world at other times. By the four and five hundreds the great Roman with his private army had become a fixture.

When the barbarian Franks and Burgundians went into Gaul, and the Visigoths into Spain, in general the great Roman nobles with their wide estates, their thousands of clients, and their hundreds of armed men were not particularly disturbed. Individuals were, but the group as a class was not. These wealthy men became the predecessors of feudal lords whose great estates and private armies were for long to be a feature of the political and military landscape.

We must now turn to the barbarians and see what they were like before they came into the Roman Empire. When discussing the Norse, mention was made of the important nobles who had big halls where meat and drink were served to the lord's followers, or thanes, who sat around tables and drank and caroused, and who of course hunted and fought in the train of such a lord. Thanes were fighting men and themselves of noble blood. For the most part they were young men, sons of thanes who had served the father of the current lord, or the younger brothers of other lords. Sometimes they were strangers, but they were always noble warriors. They lived for glory and for gold, ready and willing to fight to the death in the train of their lord. After success in battle they would expect to be nobly treated with great gifts of captives, weapons, and gold and with drink and song in the lord's court.

However, it was not easy for a lord to take care of thanes when such individuals became a bit older than our high-school and college students are today. As we have seen, as a young man passed the age of twenty-five or thirty, he was likely to want to have a wife and home. He wanted to keep his connection with his lord and his lord's table, but also to spend at least a few weeks or months of each year with his wife and children at some place removed from the lord's court. It was considered appropriate that the lord should give such a middling-aged thane an estate which normally furnished food for the lord's table. The thane would establish himself on the estate, where others did the plow-handle work, and would feed himself, his wife, and children from the proceeds of the estate. It would still be a pleasure and duty for him to go to his lord's hall and take his part in the activities there several times during a year. But permanent physical presence at the lord's court was not a career which appealed equally to the boy of sixteen and the man of from thirty to sixty years of age.

The handing out of holdings to thanes apparently went far back in barbarian society. When, however, some of the barbarian kings established themselves as rulers over much wider tracts of land than the early barbarian kings had ever ruled—when, for example, the kings of the Franks became rulers of more land than that which comprises modern France—it became difficult for such a king to feed all of his thanes at his own table.

Indeed, he had hard work for his thanes to do, and needed many more thanes than had been necessary to an earlier king whose territories stretched for only a few miles in each direction. Consequently, the king of the Franks found it necessary, in fact if not in theory, to send scores of his thanes away from his table to take charge of the different things the king wanted done in distant parts of Gaul, far from Paris or Soissons, where the king lived. Thanes who were of the lord's table companion group, but in fact resident far from that table, became commonplace. For their support when they were away great sections of royal land, usually directly inherited from the Roman emperors who preceded these Frankish kings, were assigned to favorite thanes who were busy on the king's business far away from the king's own court. While they did go back to court, and spent much time in the company of the king, still they also spent a good deal of time away from it.

The king at all times wanted to make sure that from his thanes he was given loyal military service. Each year, when his fighting forces were mustered, the king expected his thanes from far and near to be standing around him. With him at all times he had as a core of his army the younger thanes who were of prime fighting age. These younger men formed the body guard and shock force which fought shoulder to shoulder with the king and was likely to decide the issue in pitched battles. But the king of the Franks had to have many more soldiers available to him than just those who could be close to him at all times; there had to be contingents which were available from the far corners of his realm. By and large the commanders of these contingents were the trusted older thanes who had come to reside much of the year away from the king's court. It was their duty, above all, to make sure those contingents came when the king called the army together, with all their supplies and equipment, with good morale, and with great loyalty to the king.

The services of these thanes were paid for by the king's assigning them holdings in land and tolls and fees in the neighborhoods where they were temporarily or permanently placed by his order. They had their own practically private armies, for their followers swarmed around their small courts just as they themselves had swarmed around the king's court. As neighbors these men had the great Roman senatorial proprietors in the same areas. The thanes had their armies, the Romans had their armies; the thanes had their incomes, the Romans had their incomes. All were Roman Catholics. There was a general tendency for the nobility everywhere, above all in northern Gaul, to fuse into one class which was both Roman and barbarian in background, but similar in way of life.

This combination of Roman and barbarian antecedents, already modified by fusion with government in the six and seven hundreds, did not have to result in feudalism. But feudalism did come, above all in the northern parts of modern France and the nearby parts of the Low Countries and Germany, as the result of some very severe pressures put on the inhabitants of all those areas in the course of the eight and nine hundreds, pressures which were most of them from the outside. Given the Roman and barbarian patterns described, the collapse of the royal dynasty and severe invasions from the outside at the same time, feudalism proper developed.

This part of the world suffered great blows when the barbarian Vikings, the Magyars of Hungary, the Slavs from east of the Elbe, and the Moors of Spain and Africa invaded. The people found that the older ways of putting an army together, of commanding it, and of making it work were simply no longer effective. The Frankish armies down to and past the time of Charlemagne (d. 814) had been large, fine armies. They had conquered half of Europe, far down into Italy and deep into the east of Europe, but the new wars which came after were not the kind that that army could win.

The Magyars, fast-moving horsemen from the plains of Asia, came in what we can call "blitz raids." They rode fast across the country, hit, and ran. As they ran, they drove along unfortunate people whom they had taken as slaves and forced them to carry the other loot. The Vikings administered perhaps the worst blows of all. They came in ships and, since western Europe was easily accessible by water, could penetrate deep into the interior. The Vikings would come up over the horizon, go far up the estuary of some river, and disembark at dawn. Within a few hours they were scouring the country in wide arcs from the point where they had left their boats. In a few more days the boys and girls whom they had swept into slavery were carrying the loot down to the Vikings' boats, and long before the great Carolingian army of the neighborhood could be mustered and march to the defense of the affected area, they had gone over the horizon to hunt for new victims a hundred or two hundred miles up the coast.

The western European defenses were not at all arranged to take care of hit-and-run raids. But in the course of some very severe suffering, gradually one area after another learned how this problem could be met. The solution lay in having, in any one district, a system of fortified strongholds whose garrisons, even if the Vikings and Magyars could take them, could at least delay the raiders; or, if the invaders bypassed the forts, could certainly make the raiders' return costly. The problem of stopping the raids had to be solved also by having local commanders charged with the immediate mobilization of an ever-ready, ever-armed, ever-organized local fighting force. The force to stop the Vikings did not have to be large, but it did have to be brave, well equipped, well supplied, and able to be marshaled at a fortified stronghold at once when raiders struck a locality.

Where the outside raids were the greatest problem, the building of forts here and there across the European countryside began first of all. One expedient was to fortify a bridge over or under which raiders would have to pass. While the bridge would not have a large resident garrison, still it would have one; and, as the garrison was beating off the first attacks, the country around could rally quickly to come to its garrison's aid. In case they bypassed such a place, raiders found themselves increasingly vulnerable as their successes multiplied. A Viking force of several hundred men, compacted together, full of verve and fighting spirit, was a very tough thing to tackle. But a week or so later when the same raiders returned, strung along a road in order to drive slaves back to the ships, they were vulnerable. At that point the defenders of a garrison could really damage them by taking their loot away from them and inflicting severe harm on the raiders themselves so that a few days later the remnants of the raiders, after all their trouble and having shed a great deal of their own blood, would be back on their boats empty handed.

Such defenses required men who were prepared in every way for any military emergency. They had to have been trained, from the time they were small boys until they were grown men, in the arts of war. They had to be free of all duties connected with farm work, so they had to be supported by the villagers to whom they gave protection. The building of the forts and the building of this professional fighting class had to be accompanied by the assignment of absolute command to local officers who had to have the allegiance and support of those who made up their small armies.

This arrangement was strengthened and emphasized by the development of many civil wars all across western Europe, as the different descendants of Charlemagne wrangled and fought for the imperial and other thrones, and as the leaders among themselves began to develop what we know as "feudal warfare."

First of all came need for protection from outsiders. Civil wars brought, in addition, need for protection from hostile neighbors up and down the coast or across country only a few miles. All of this contributed to the development of governmental-military command units on a fairly small scale. The men who made up those units were the nobles of the feudal system.

When a man became a full-fledged unit in the military force of his over-lord, such as a commander of a subsection of the lord's army or a ruler of an area in the lord's territory, his income, assigned to support him, was his *feudum,* or fief, or fee. We still use the word "fee" and it retains for us somewhat the sound of a gentlemanly thing when we speak of lawyers' fees or doctors' fees for services rendered. That is one of the original meanings of the word. (The oldest meaning of the word is cow, and we still have that word in German, *vieh,* meaning "cow"; in the most primitive society a fee was paid in cattle.) But a fee by the time of Charlemagne's successors was a piece of property which would produce an income of the most varied sort, from which the holder received the benefits. In fact, fees were at first called "benefits," which then came to be benefits lasting "for three lives," and finally became hereditary. By the nine hundreds a heredi-tary assigned holding was coming to be called a fee or *feudum* in the usage of northern France.

We are likely to think of a fief as acreage, and to think of the chief in-come from the fee as rent paid a landlord in kind or money from the peasants who worked the fee. But the men who gave a fief or who received one thought in terms of military pay, political rewards, family honors, and duties of government. From a single villa-village-estate-manor a petty lord got about enough to equip and supply himself, a squire and a sergeant or two, and a small troop of cavalry men ready during the spring, summer, and fall campaigns to serve his lord further up the feudal chain. From one village just about enough would come in the way of income to take care of such a heavily armored knight with his small following. As prices rose, such fee-holders, whose estates were not yielding enough, were ter-ribly pinched for money and worked to get their obligations fixed at low minimums, to get the legal power to rent out or to mortgage their holdings, and so forth. Landlordism did begin to manifest itself.

A fee did not have to be one of those bottom-most units such as a villa or manor. A lord's fee depended on his rank. Generally one good estate or village took care of one knight; but the kind of income that came to one knight was not nearly enough to support one duke. A duke needed the income produced by scores of such holdings. He needed it not only for himself but also for his following. By subinfeudation, the greatest and great lords took care of building up the small armies they needed, of building the castles which were the strong points they needed, and of supporting garrisons for such strong points.

The way in which one man could go to another and become his man became more or less fixed in the course of the eight and nine hundreds; even earlier it had been something men recognized and knew about. By the eight and nine hundreds the ceremony through which they both went was known as the "man ceremony" which is the meaning of the word "homage." (The Latin word *homo*, the French word *homme*, are both there in this word which, however, is English enough.) The ceremony resembled in considerable measure ceremonies we know about today, such as the wedding ceremony or the ritual by which a man is made an officer in the United States Army.

The ceremony was a very dignified one, intended to make an impression in the memories of the two who participated in it and on those who stood around when it took place. It was to symbolize the entering into of a lifelong contract—and beyond, through the following generations. Tied up with the ceremony, but not an integral part of it, was the taking of an oath of fealty to the greater man. Ceremony and oath were normally done together, but could be and were sometimes separated. (Fealty is an English word which comes from the Latin word *fidelitas*. This means the same thing as the English "fidelity.")

Generally in the homage ceremony the lesser man approached the greater one who in a few minutes was to be his lord. Symbolically he was supposed to be a poor man with nothing or with very little, though actually he might be a duke and the son of a duke and well off in worldly goods. However, he came into the ceremony symbolically poor, needing a lord to help protect and endow him. He knelt, and the lord-to-be asked his other "men" there if they would accept this newcomer as a member of their companionship. Upon their acquiescence he took the hand of the kneeling man, and they repeated a formula in which the lesser promised to be faithful forever and the greater promised to give protection and love and affection forever. The lesser was to counsel the greater; the greater was to protect the lesser; and they were to protect one another's dear ones, honors, and property. The lord was to protect the widow of the new vassal and his infant children. The vassal was to rally round and fight to the death for his lord, to protect the lord's widow and children, and so on.

Accepted at this point, the new man, or *vassal*, would rise. From the ranks of the group around the lord someone would step forward and hand him a twig (this varied from place to place) symbolizing the fact that the vassal now had hold of the forest of the fief which was being given him;

someone else would give him a flask of water from some mill pond on the property, showing he held the waters; a piece of turf would also be given him. They might even go out to the very place where the main part of the fief was and take a piece of turf from the soil to confer it on the vassal at that point. All these, the woods, the water, and the land, were given along with the homage ceremony. It was the endowment, by an officer, of one of his followers, with sufficient wherewithal to be worthy and able to perform the duties of a follower. The land, and of course jurisdiction over the human beings who happened to be on those lands, all went together.

The vassal was given these things, of course, from out of what the lord had to give. On a given manor the demesne was what the lord of that village had. But a great lord, such as a duke or count, would have in his demesne great areas of direct jurisdiction to give away, and it was from what was his demesne originally that he gave to his subvassals in the homage ceremonies.

Every lord at every level had to have a demesne. From part of it he could reward his followers. Chiefly from it he obtained the bread, butter, bacon, and other foods for his own table and for the very large sumptuous table which he had to set for the persons living in his company, his visitors, superiors, servants, and all his kin. In this process the vassal received some part of his lord's demesne. By subinfeudation this process of giving could go down four, five, or six steps. A king from his regal holdings could grant a county but retain a royal demesne. The count could grant several viscounties and still hold some demesne in his own hands for his own table; each of the viscounts in turn could grant part of what was given him to various knights and still hold some of his own demesne, and so on down until some village lord granted several sergeanties out of his demesne in the village to those sergeants who followed him in war and hunting.

In this process nobody owned what he was given. Fiefs were not owned outright; instead each fief was "held." Later they even talked in terms of the king of France or the king of England "holding his kingdom of God." He held it, and the Latin word *tenere* ("to hold") comes over into the English legal term "tenement." Those who held duchies or earldoms in England, in France, or elsewhere were called "tenants." Those who held straight from the king as the king's vassals were tenants in chief—head tenants ("chief" meaning "head"). Those to whom they had subinfeudated parts of their holdings were "rear tenants." The rear tenants and the chief tenants did not own, they held, and the king held from God. That was the theory finally elaborated by the twelve hundreds.

There were ways in which a holding could be lost by its holder. One was for the line of holders to die out. A tenement might be passed from father to son for a number of generations, but when the male line ran out, or when there were no daughters' husbands fitted to take the tenement, the property reverted to the lord next above to be granted to some new holder who would found a new line of tenants.

A major reason for the loss of a holding was the awful crime of treachery, either in battle or in council, which was known as felony. A felony was the unforgivable crime, and when the felon was convicted of it, his holding went straight back to his lord. The felon himself was killed, usually as roughly as possible, and the blood of his family line was considered "attainted," which meant that his descendants were ineligible in the future, forever, to hold a fief, at least in that area. While we still have the word attaint in English law, we no longer consider a felon's descendants attainted. But in the Middle Ages people might be reduced to the displaced-persons class, below the lowest serfs, by a conviction of a relative for felony. So the felon did not just suffer alone, he attainted his whole family. Sometimes it was forced on his brothers and cousins too, and a whole clan would go down, thanks to the attainder or attainting of one of its important members.

In the fashion described, a lord could create a new fief and acquire a new vassal to found a hereditary line of such vassals holding that fief. Or an heir of the first vassal could move into the tenement and into the relationships held by his ancestors. These situations characterized the system when it was already well constituted.

The system grew up even where at first most men of property did not "hold" from anybody and had no lords. Subsequently, great holders could and did parcel out pieces in the manner outlined, and by itself this largely brought the pattern into being.

But also, in dangerous times many a lesser man, to win shelter, put himself under the wing of a greater one by going through the formality of passing title to his properties over to that great man and receiving them back as a fief. Great lords and even kings and popes, after military or diplomatic victories over others of their own rank, forced the losers to become vassals. By this device, around the year 1200, the pope came to be lord of the kings of a very large share of Europe, including England.

On the other hand, a surprisingly large proportion of Europe's lands were never turned into fiefs at any level. In England by 1100 *all* land was held from a lord, who was the king himself if no in-between lord (or *mesne* lord) existed. At the other extreme were great parts of Europe where free unfeudalized holdings of all sizes were commonplace. Germany stood rather between, with the additional peculiarity that large owners commonly had vassals below them holding fiefs, but had no feudal relationships to any lords next above themselves, so that the state and its army were not uniformly of feudal character. In Italy, especially as town authorities developed the power of their city-states, they made their cities lords over neighboring vassals; cities themselves might become collective vassals or lords of outside men or other cities.

Subinfeudation was fundamentally a way for making up an army; this shows in the likeness between the homage ceremony and that of making an officer today. After making his oath to his lord, the vassal was invested, meaning he was "clothed" with insignia which symbolized his new position. Since a fief or *feudum* was a military office, at the proper moment during the feudal ceremony he had a sword belted at his hips, the symbol of his function as a fighting man. If he were a church officer, he could receive the symbols of ecclesiastical authority.

A duke was about the same as our lieutenant general, a viscount was like a brigadier general, a baron about the same as a colonel, and the lowest knight the equivalent to a commissioned officer of the rank of lieutenant in our modern armies. We must note that feudalism was a system for providing officers of the fighting classes, and hardly concerned the non-coms, let alone any rank and file. The earlier feudal army was essentially an army of officers.

These officers were expected and required to be in all ways, in their attitude and conduct, fit to be officers. The members of the feudal class were trained from boyhood in the handling of fighting tools—horse, sword, battle-axe, lance, and shield. They were taught simple tactical operations. Warfare had been simplified considerably, and the main object of a knight in battle was to ride into the enemy full charge, with companions at each side. If a unit happened to ride through the enemy, it formed again and rode back through. It was not very technical, but they had to learn how to do it and it called for skill in handling the tools of war. Since ordinarily the enemy was similarly trained, a ride-through was rare. Individual combatants paired off and fought with sword, axe, mace, and dagger, standing in their stirrups, fencing and even wrestling, their horses fighting as well, and a man-to-man combat could go on with both men dismounted. The simple group tactics could dissolve into protracted fighting of individuals even in large battles. The greatest lords were as personally involved as their simplest knights.

These men in their army of officers had a very definite code of behavior. There were things which were done and things which were not done. At least at first there were no laws about it, but everyone was expected to abide by the code. Once their system became well organized these men were recognized as the horse-riding nobility. The Latin word for fighting horseman came to be extended to cover them. The old Latin word for a horse, the one the student of Cicero learns, was *eques*. The fighting soldiers of the Roman army had also a soldier's word for horse. They called it a nag, a *caballus*. By the period we are studying the word *cheval* or *caballo* had come to mean horse in French, Spanish, and Italian, and a man who rode one was a *caballero* or *chevalier,* and the whole mass of them were the *chivalry*—and all these words come from the idea of an officer who rides a horse. Strangely enough, in English there was no translation or adaptation of the word. Instead, an Anglo-Saxon word for servant, "knight," came to mean a fighting man who rode a horse.

Chivalrous behavior came to be the custom of this class at a time when custom was law. No legislation was passed setting up chivalric behavior; instead the chevaliers did things certain ways, and these ways became a pattern whereby men lived. Unchivalric behavior came to be considered disloyalty. Conduct unbecoming an officer (as we would call it today) could lead to the loss of a man's tenement. The felon was not only a criminal, he was also the sort of person one would not associate with; he had declassed himself. In fact, the concept of felony began that way, and only afterward, as this code of behavior came to be dominant in chivalric society, did it become a crime. The homeland for all of this was northern France which set the tone, gave the leadership, and in general contributed most of the words in the vocabulary of feudalism and of feudal law. Perhaps it is legitimate to insist that poets and romancers did most—far more than any law—to determine those things a chivalrous man should or should not do; a given act was cultured or uncultured.

When this whole pattern had become well elaborated, the church came to be thoroughly entangled in it. The system was one not only for maintaining fighting men, but also for providing income to other persons who had something better to do than plowing, reaping, and watching cattle; this, of course, covered the whole ecclesiastical hierarchy from the priests up to the popes. If a bishopric was to be maintained, it had to have broad lands and incomes such as those a lay lord received, fines, forests, and all the rest. A bishopric needed an endowment with a fixed income from holdings accumulated through the years.

No one thought in terms of the bishops' doing military service, for they thought of one class as differentiated from another by function. They thought of the great class of nobles as serving all the rest as fighting men and governors; they thought of the ecclesiastics as serving too, through prayer. In many ages it has been considered that a man beats his enemies partly by swords and battle-axes, and partly because his cause is just and the prayers of those on his side have been efficacious. So the endowment of ecclesiastical holdings was justified on the grounds that that was a way to provide for prayers for the welfare of the community. Such endowment also provided for charitable work, in which men were interested, and such decent activities as the support of scholars and other work among the poor.

The means for endowing a church were the same as those whereby a fighting man was endowed, so that a great archbishop would receive about the same tremendous great holdings as a duke, the lower bishops and deans about those of viscounts and simple knights.

The endowment of religious units with fiefs brought great trouble to all of Europe in the ten hundreds, when it created tremendous social, political, economic, and jurisdictional problems which in turn generated long wars and wrangles known as the Investiture Conflict. (These coincided with the fighting of the First Crusade.) The investiture struggle concerned the right to invest a new subvassal with the symbols of his office if that subvassal were a churchman. Put crudely: Who could make a bishop? Was it to be the pope who would invest a new bishop with the symbols of episcopal power? Or was it to be the king or emperor who, after granting him a fief, should also have the right to invest him with the symbols of his episcopal office, including such churchly symbols as the crosier and the ring? They did not manage to get allegiances untangled, but fought to a kind of draw and then left it there to be a problem in most countries in Europe even through the fifteen, sixteen, and seventeen hundreds.

The feudal lords and kings could not simply hand over their endowments to churchmen with no strings attached, thus ridding themselves of the problem, for the churchmen served them not only by prayer but also by providing them with large parts of their military contingents, under command of a lay delegate or lay lieutenant. He was the man who could get blood on his battle-axe while leading the bishop's forces, the bishop himself not being allowed to shed blood. (Some bishops who loved battle got around that by using war clubs with which they could bash in a helmet without shedding blood.) But in any case, most kings and dukes could not afford to let their church vassals slip away from under their control because of the difficulty they would then have in raising enough of an army without contingents from episcopal and other ecclesiastical lands.

In the handing down of a fief at any level, jurisdiction over human beings was passed from the upper to the lower. Normally, when a king passed out duchies and counties (the largest units), he passed "high justice," as they later came to call it, to the new vassal. The right to hang a man was perhaps the most notable of the elements in the right of high justice. The right to control lesser bad behavior such as misdemeanors, and civil matters such as violation of contract, the passage of property, and so forth, was known as "low justice." These are the terms found more commonly in France than elsewhere, but essentially they were found everywhere in one form or another. On the whole, high justice meant jurisdiction over capital crime, the really serious things, and fiefs which were only a little lower than those of duke or count did not include it. In England high justice was never given out by the kings, who continued to control it everywhere save on the Scottish and Welsh frontiers where there was a kind of perpetual martial law, and where the highest local lords held the high justice.

What a lord had when he was given high justice, or low justice, or both, was power, of course, but he was also given income. One reason the king of England remained so powerful, though a ruler of a feudal country, was that he had a leverage on all his subjects which came from having the courts that could hang a man. But also the very large income from those courts enabled him to build better and more castles and to keep soldiers in them. The matter of justice was important from the point of view of income—and with this queer little twist: such fine, useful devices as the jury system, the circuit court system, and other things cherished by English-American populations everywhere over the globe, were originally put into use as revenue-producing devices. The king allowed persons who wanted to have the benefits of his good law service to pay him a special fee to get such a thing as jury trial. This is an attitude toward the doing of justice which we have forgotten, but it is not forgotten everywhere around the globe; there are places where appointment to be a judge is still eagerly sought after as one of the best ways to get rich.

Under the feudal system a lord's fief(s) in general returned the kind of income his small state required (for he ran something very much like a modern state) and the word "state" at that time was fused with another word which comes from it, "estate," which could mean not only his properties but his way of living. A person who maintains a grand state today will have a fine house, elegant cars, and so on, all showing what his "estate" is. In the Middle Ages the noble who had a duchy or county considered it his estate or state, and it supported him in a state appropriate to his status.

The feudal system, then, provided what has been known by some writers as the "iron men." This was an army of officers who had a fighting code of chivalric valor and behavior, fine equipment, tough physiques, and skills sharpened by endless practice with weapons and horses. By about 1090 there were no peoples with whom the western Europeans were in contact whom they could not commonly beat. At that time the western Europeans were driving into the center and the south of Spain. They were driving out the Moors and dominating the Greeks of southern Italy and Sicily. They were forcing the peoples of the middle Danube River valley to accept Western Catholic civilization and lordship. They were pushing in the same way against the peoples in the northern Slavic belt, and in part to protect themselves the Czechs and Poles had turned western European. Finally, they were just about ready to start a great series of military invasions and conquests in the eastern Mediterranean known as the Crusades, which were to begin in 1095. Feudalism was producing a powerful military establishment.

Later on, in the twelve hundreds, when the feudal pattern had been partly modified by further developments, the middle European feudal armies stood up to and took the starch out of the Mongol armies. These Mongol armies swept everything from the Straits of Korea to Hungary, from the Arctic Circle down to Burma, but when they came into feudal Europe they ran into its castles and fighters, and the costs of conquest rose. They found that while they could overrun the western European armies, the Europeans fought so fiercely as to push the costs up. The Mongols seem to have decided that the returns from so backward a land would not be worth the waste of much good Mongol blood. The western Europeans fought mulishly, they fought to victory in a considerable number of their aggressive attempts, and they had the spirit to make it costly to defeat them.

It was this spirit and morale which produced a European push on the military front which has not been lost even today. There have been a few times through history when it did not work so well, but in large measure the European morale and attitude toward war is, to this day, governed by the feudal pattern, especially in the concept of conduct becoming an officer, which is the essence of the military system that the feudal society left us. Nearly everything else feudal is gone.

The whole system also provided local government, at a time when kings and higher officials were not very good at keeping records, nor able to make decisions at headquarters which could be practicably enforceable at a distance. In a world of poor communications and poor records, government had to be localized. Feudalism provided a chain of command down which authority could be passed, and up through which authority could be certified and supported. In that day this was an extremely useful arrangement, even down to the kind of government provided on a given estate by the manorial court. When a bureaucracy and better communications were established, some of these features of feudalism became superannuated.

Along with a chain of command and authority went a chain of loyalty. The king had lords as his vassals who were supposed to be loyal, these in turn had vassals who were loyal to them, and so on down to the lowliest knight. One of the results of this was not only the localization of governments, but also the localization of loyalties, with the court of the great lord of a neighborhood constituting the center of life for its countryside. Such a court was likely to become the most important place for all those who lived near by, and to influence strongly the customs, costumes, dialects and habits of those living within its sphere, through which it would be differentiated from other courts in other parts of a kingdom. It was also likely to be a center for loyalties, with attachment to the local count or duke running far ahead of loyalty to a king or to an emperor. Such local loyalties could often make a king's or emperor's crown sit very uneasily upon his head, and one of a ruler's chief concerns had to be to keep his powerful vassals loyal to him, for failure in this respect could be disastrous.

As soon as there was enough money in circulation, the feudal army, through the introduction of the mercenary soldier to do the fighting, lost its importance. The vital battle-winning man came to be the fellow who was paid a shilling a day (the shilling is the *solidus* or *soldo,* and a man who fights for a shilling is a *soldier*). It is redundant to call him a mercenary soldier, for a mercenary is, or was at first, a soldier, and a soldier a mercenary. When a few of the kings began to hire good armies of soldiers, the feudal lords' local armies lost their importance. The soldiers were themselves feudal knights in training, equipment, and attitude of mind, but they were to become the private knights of the king as against those' lords who had vassal forces.

The feudal system provided a whole system of local governmental fortified centers. Local castles were timber and earth fortifications to begin with, but from the ten and eleven hundreds their construction was steadily improved. They served not only as strong points but also as centers for the protection of men who made things with their hands or traded in goods. In other words, they could be the nuclei or cores around which towns were to grow up. Strangely enough, by providing the safety which made it possible for towns to grow, the feudal castles provided the means

by which feudalism was eventually to be bypassed. A population of craftsmen and merchants was not easily feudalized, for such men had no background or interest which tied them to the feudal system, and their activities were bound to carry them around and beyond feudalism.

At its best feudalism was a workable system for the provision of schools,
hospitals, charity work, refugee aid, and the whole hierarchy and staff
of the religious organization. It regulated social rank, providing inside
the feudal class the various gradations between emperor and simple squire,
and separated the feudal class from the classes immediately below. It
provided a system of recreation for the upper classes, giving them occupation and social life. Finally, it was a system for the holding of land which
in essentials comes down to Englishmen and Americans today. It is also
true that while parts of the system were eliminated and other parts retained, this was done little by little, and a few fragments have never disappeared. Modifications by 1750 will be noted later

CHAPTER IV

Developing Trading Patterns, to about 1350

WHEN we come to the nine and ten hundreds, we will find that there were beginning to be economic activities of importance other than agriculture. During the nine hundreds, there began to be a rather steady stepping up of the volume of production and of trade in the area which interests us most—western Europe. At first there was not enough to make much difference to the agricultural, rural communities, but there was an increasing effect on the older styles of economic activity as trade and industry increased in volume.

Of course, there was never a sudden displacement of one economy by another. When we consider the dates, we can see that rising trading activity in the nine hundreds was beginning at a time when the manorial system also was still establishing and strengthening itself, and was still destined to be the dominant pattern where it was well established for some hundreds of years more. The plowmen did not stop raising grain and go into trade. Trade began to be important, and so did towns and townsmen, guilds, manufacture by guildsmen, long before there was a cracking up of the manorial system.

Local and Interregional Commerce to 900

As an introduction to the history of the rising trade of the nine and ten hundreds and thereafter, we must first look at the earlier trade of the five, six, seven, and eight hundreds in western Europe to see what it was that men could trade in while the economy was still backward.

At all times there was an active local trade, even in the period when, by modern theories, everyone was living on the "self-sufficient manor." The notion that there was no trade between one manor and another, since they all raised beets, cows, and everything they needed, is contrary to rural facts: sometimes one manor would have a surplus of heifers, another of young bulls, while another had a surplus of sheep, and so on. There were bound to be shortages of one kind or another in any locality. The net result of shortages and surpluses was rural trading from place to place, from villager to villager, and from village to village.

Such trading in a village or neighborhood would normally take place at whatever spot was a gathering place used for other purposes, such as the church. Games and sociability and trade all centered on the parish church of a village (when these were built) or on some more important church for several villages together. As a result, some religious festival, such as Sunday for a village, or a saint's day for a neighborhood, would also be market day. Trade at such a spot would be fairly active for at least a few hours every week, or every month or season, depending on local custom. For sheer volume alone, that kind of trade was of much greater importance than trade between regions and trade with foreign areas outside western Europe. There was also a trade between the uplands and the lowlands in an area which had the two situated fairly near each other. Goats' meat and cheese could be brought down to the market, and grain from the valleys taken up to the hills.

There was also regional trade in addition to the local trade. Men from quite a distance away went to the markets which served the local trade for the purpose of buying and selling. Because of the distance involved, they were likely to come to the local markets only occasionally, and to try to do all the business they had there in two or three days' time. Since they had to travel thirty, fifty, or a hundred miles to reach the market, they did not wish to make such a trip every week, but preferred to come a few times in a year or season. Such a large, more specialized market was usually given the name which was also the name of a religious festival, a "fair." The medieval fairs, which were pre-eminently regional exchange places, will be described below.

Despite the relatively small volume of production going into inter-regional trade to begin with, the relatively few people involved, and the relatively small value of the goods, we must pay attention to it for this reason: local trade and regional trade did not have much in them which could lead to still further developments; the methods and commodities could remain the same for centuries. It was at the top of the economic pyramid that the possibility of change and growth was to be found.

Using that figure of the pyramid, agriculture, the great economic base, has had our attention; most people were involved in agriculture in the eight through the eleven hundreds. (As a matter of fact, most of the people were still involved in agriculture in western Europe as late as about 1850, and beyond that in many countries.) Above agriculture in the pyramid came local and regional trade. At the very top, involving very few people directly, was interregional trade. Yet it was here that changes started, and the influences generated here were to modify importantly the economic activities lower down.

For this reason it is important that interregional, or international, trade be evaluated. (The word "international" is an anachronism when applied to medieval times, for there were no nations. But it is a far more familiar word in its connotations than "interregional"; so it will be used here with that understanding.) So far as medieval western Europe was concerned, the international trade that went on until about the nine hundreds was largely the sort of trade in which western Europe was the backward area to which came traders from more civilized areas. Many other parts of the globe have played this role, as we shall see. Trade in backward areas is likely to be carried on by visiting merchants from important and active regions. The great centers of trade and of economic activity were to the east and to the south of western Europe during the five through the nine hundreds and into the ten and twelve hundreds. In terms of political geography the areas of the Byzantine Empire and of the Moslems were both of them far in advance of western Europe. They were actually in advance of western Europe in every way—in art and literature, in all cultural activities, in political and military and naval power.

Western Europe had gone backward a long way since about the year 200 A.D. when the Roman world of Gaul, Spain, Britain, nearer Germany, and Italy had flourished economically. Since then its manufacture and trade had slumped until most of it was carried on by strangers who came from the more advanced parts of the world to work or to buy what they wanted, and then went away again. The foreigners conducted their trade for their own benefit, without much regard for local interests, or at least with regard only for those persons and powers who had to be reckoned with locally, such as the lords and ladies.

In the list of commodities traded in, we can judge the character of the western European economy of the time. Until only a little over a hundred years ago, in the nineteenth century, most backward areas were looked upon as slave-hunting grounds by merchants from more advanced areas. In just that fashion slaves were important in the trade between western Europe and Moslem North Africa and Byzantium. The slaves were sold by their parents or as captives of war, and sent off toward Baghdad, Alex-

andria, and Constantinople, or down into Seville, Cordova, and Fez in Morocco. The routes leading to the great slave markets were the most important of the trade routes. In the fifteen, sixteen, and seventeen hundreds
Europeans were picking up slaves in the most backward areas and sending them where Europeans most wanted slave labor at the moment, handling African slaves in the same way the Byzantines and Moslems had
handled European slaves in the Middle Ages.

Another commodity sold from Europe during the Middle Ages was
unprocessed raw materials such as furs. Furs moved from the north of
Europe, largely by the Russian river system, toward Byzantium and Baghdad in considerable quantities. So did such things as walrus ivory, amber
from the Baltic Sea coasts, honey from the forest—unprocessed commodities of rather high value.

It was in Byzantium and Islam that the dynamic part of the commercial
economy was to be found. Their traders did most of the work, especially
if we add to the list of Byzantine-Greek traders and Moslem-Arab traders
the Jewish traders from both Byzantium and Islam. All of these came into
western and eastern Europe loaded with the sort of goods which advanced
areas always send to backward areas. They brought gewgaws, trade goods,
eye-catchers, dazzlers, gaudy clothes which would catch rather barbarous
fancies, jewelry, and a little very elegant, fine art work. On the whole they
were goods designed to delight the rich barbarian chieftain, or his rich
and not too delicately esthetic lady. They were intended for a very small
market—only the very rich, who could afford carved ivory work, carved
jewelry or woodwork of different sorts, elegant and very gaudy silks,
and the like.

Besides these there were things which could please rich men's palates,
such as pepper, cinnamon, and other spices, as well as incense and per-
fume. The Easterners had had these brought through channels all the
way from India, China, and the Spice Isles. Another characteristic of
these trade goods should be noted—the great concentration of value in a
very small bulk and weight. A ruby would be much better to take on a
long trip through dangerous pirate-infested waters and over bandit-
infested roads than an equivalent value in wheat or olive oil. There
was very little trade in necessaries coming up the channels from the advanced parts of the world to Europe. It did not pay, was too risky, called
for ships which would be too large and for port facilities and storage
warehouses which did not exist, to handle such things. So the trade was in
luxuries intended for rich bishops, dukes, counts, and their like. In-

cidentally, for the bishops and abbots there were, of course, such things as church furniture—reliquaries, crosiers, and other elegant articles, either jeweled or semiprecious, for church services and ornamentation of church buildings.

As to the traders, our few sources mention Syrians in Gaul and Spain, and even up in Britain. Archaeological findings show that articles were indeed moving from Syria and Egypt to the far ends of Europe—not in great volume, but moving. The Syrian label seems to have meant the Byzantine citizen in general, not necessarily a Syrian from Syria, the term being used loosely in the same way that Europeans today call all Americans "Yankees." The Syrian trader, or the Jewish trader, might sometimes have a home in Italy or southern Gaul rather than in Antioch or Alexandria. These traders came through the Mediterranean or through the Russian river system to the Baltic region. After about 650 there were also Arabs, such as the emissary who went far up the Volga, where he encountered some Swedes, and who has left us a hair-raising description of a party of merchant-Vikings as they were when he met them on the Volga River headwater.

There were some places in western Europe, above all in Italy, toward which traders in all generations between 500 and 1000 steered their boats, and from which they set out, and among those places were such south Italian ports as Naples. Other ports in that neighborhood, such as Amalfi or Salerno, were like Naples in putting a person on a good Roman road toward Rome. Rome itself was a good market place. There was no industry there, and very little prosperity in the country around, for that was a malarial swamp during much of the period we are covering. But in Rome were not only the resident church men from the pope on down, men of great wealth, but also pilgrims—kings of the Anglo-Saxons, dukes of the Bohemians and Poles, messengers of the Christian kings of Spain, and so on. When they were at Rome, they bought elegant gifts to take home with them, either for churches in the far corners of Europe or for princes and princesses far away.

This brings us to the Venetians, who looked like Italians, talked like Italians, and were Roman Catholics like Italians, but who were politically tied to the Byzantine Empire at this time, and whom we must count as Byzantines for practical purposes. Venice provided another port at which western Europe touched the Byzantine-Moslem trading areas. During the eight and nine hundreds, Venetians went up the Po Valley to other Italian towns, and over the Alps into Germany and Hungary. However, until the ten hundreds we cannot count the Venetian as having been a true western European.

We would say that the Frisians were natives, because they lived on the western and northwestern fringe of Europe, but in an important way they were not properly western Europeans until about 750 to 800. This is in part due to an arbitrary definition made here; for us a proper western European of those times must have been a Roman Catholic. In this sense, Scandinavians were not western Europeans until around 1000. By and large the Frisians did not turn Christian until at least 750, and in part not before 800. Then they were very careful about it, and when they were away from home in the heathen North they were likely to conceal the fact they had turned Christian.

The Frisians were a special sort of Germans, living on a long strip of marshy islands and swamps off the main coast of the North Sea, roughly between the mouth of the Rhine River and the peninsula of Denmark. They lived on mounds which they built up on the low islands or salt marshes. Their language was almost English; they were close brothers of the Anglo-Saxons, speaking what was merely another dialect of the English-Frisian family of languages. They needed no interpreters when they went to London or York. They had the same type of law, the same kind of ornaments and organization, so they were not foreigners in England. Nor was their language so different that they had trouble talking with the Franks and Saxons and Scandinavians who were all near them. As a language, Frisian stands near the center of the group of dialects just mentioned, so it was very easy for a Frieslander to get around.

The Frieslander was not of a numerous breed, but he was hungry. Except for fish and the milk which he could get from the Holstein cows he was beginning to develop in his salt marshes, he was short of food. Furthermore, since he was a fisherman—he had to be—he learned to go great distances by water, up the Rhine, Maas, and Scheldt rivers, along the coast into the Baltic Sea, across the Channel to the English; and as he went he sold fish and cheese and bought meat and grain, especially grain, of which his own area was short.

He also saw that the Scandinavians were short of millstones, and that in the central part of the Rhine River valley there were good ones. So he began to transport millstones from the Rhineland quarries to Denmark. Modern archaeologists are finding such stones and there can be no doubt as to their source; they came from one district south in Germany, and they are being found in Denmark along with other things the Frisians traded in.

Frisians found that the Flemish were making very fine cloth at a rather early time, and that that cloth was not only prized on the Continent, but was good enough for Charlemagne to send some along with other royal presents to Haroun al Raschid (or Aaron the Just), the caliph at Baghdad about whom so many of the Arabian Nights stories are turned. The Frisians distributed them from the north down into Italy, or over into the Baltic region. In the north country it was possible to find ivory tusks and walrus-skin ropes, both things which were much in use at that time. The Frisians distributed those. They became the middlemen, collectors and distributors of merchandise, with trade channels flung out all the way from the region of modern Finland and Russia to the narrows of the English Channel, and up all the rivers, the Rhine to Switzerland, the Elbe into Bohemia (Czechoslovakia). They may have gone as far as Marseilles, for many Frisian coins have been found there.

The Frisians were forced to join the Carolingian Empire, not because they were conquered, but because their business required them to do it. They could not be hold-out heathen, still worshiping Thor and Wotan, when the people with whom they had to trade on the mainland had made it a point that Frisians had to be baptized. So they were baptized. But it did not hurt their approach to business; they went on as they had before.

Stimulated into existence by the Frieslanders was the trade of the Norse world. The Norsemen were so close to the sea that seafaring was the main activity of a good many Norwegians, Danes, and Swedes, and nearly all could be interested in seaborne trade, if not actively, then as investors or traders bringing goods to the seafaring merchants and taking goods back in return. We have noticed that the position of the trading man in Scandinavia was always high. The kings of Denmark, Norway, and Sweden and their rich earls were great merchants. The Swedes who branched into Russia were themselves trading princes. When they set up or took over control of their gorods (such as Novgorod and Kiev), the biggest trader was always the richest prince, or vice versa. Then, also, trade was very important to the Norwegians and Danes who came to control Rouen on the Seine estuary in France, and to control London and York in England, Dublin, Waterford, and other places in Ireland.

We know that either they themselves went as far as Turkestan, or that they were in immediate contact with the Turkestani merchants, for Swedish museums today have large collections of coins from Turkestan with their Arabic inscriptions, amounting to thousands and thousands of such

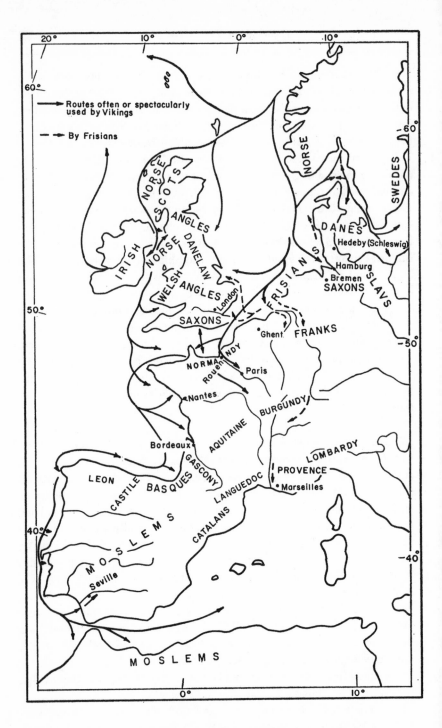

Frisians and Norse trade

coins brought back and buried or lost by Swedes in Sweden. They went down the Volga River to northern Persia, along the Caspian Sea, and crossed the Black Sea to Constantinople. In all the places mentioned the Norse language could suffice a trader, for the markets were generally under Norse control, or there were special quarters reserved for them, as at Constantinople.

The Norse trading world, as we have seen, received partial political consolidation in the last of the nine hundreds and the very first part of the ten hundreds, when Canute, as King of Denmark, became overlord of Norway, the terror of the Swedes, the conqueror of England and much of Scotland, and overlord of nearly all the Norsemen elsewhere except those in south Russia. He nearly translated the great northern linguistic, cultural, and economic area into a political empire. It fell apart when various sons, nephews, and other kinsmen began to fight among themselves. As a result the English and Norwegians pulled away from the Danes, and the empire fell apart. It was all gone by 1050. But for a while, around the year 1000, it had looked as if it might really form into a great state.

In the course of the eight hundreds the Norse had pretty badly wrecked Frisia in their raids, seizing one important place after another, burning and looting them, and rendering the travel of Frisian ships precarious. But the Frisians held out, and they came back in the nine hundreds to a considerable degree, being themselves responsible for much of the drawing-in of the Norse world. Frisians who were Christian, going to Denmark and Norway, or Norsemen who had gone to Frisia and returned, having turned Christian in the process, were important in the Christianizing of the Norse world.

So far all the trade we have been discussing has been essentially non-European—if we keep to our definition.

Rise of North European and Italian Commerce about 950 to 1350

Within western Europe proper, in part a result of being stimulated by the trade outsiders brought along, but also a result of simply growing up, was a native trade. It began to expand noticeably in the nine hundreds, and from then on steadily increased in volume and in scope of activities both geographically and in varieties of goods, and it steadily grew more advanced or sophisticated.

It can be recalled that as the nine hundreds went along the feudal lords created a relative stability and security in the lands of western Europe.

They continued to have feudal wars and skirmishes, but compared to what it had been western Europe was stable and secure. Among other things, the Emperor Otto the Great and his immediate successors made secure trade between Italy and Germany as well as trade within Italy and Germany. Dukes and counts in France also created considerable stability within their small states. The king of England headed a strong government and a strong army and navy; except briefly late in the century there were no invasions or civil wars. The worst creators of chaos and confusion—the Mohammedan and Viking pirates and the Slavs and Magyars —were being whipped or Europeanized.

In addition to relative security there was the stepping up in the production of food, above all where and as manors developed, for it was in the home of manorialism that we find the greatest evidences of increases in population, in buying power, and in standard of living.

Besides increasing productivity, there is evidence of increasing dependence of one area on another, not for gewgaws and jewelry but for staples. In the ten hundreds (a little later than the period we are actually discussing here) documents mention shipment of bacon and butter from England into Flanders. Butter and bacon are gross staple goods. But the new Flemish industrial towns of the times, which we shall be discussing later on, were already unable to feed themselves on local production alone. At the same time manufacturing areas began to depend on raw materials produced elsewhere.

Another kind of interdependence came when the wine growing regions of southern France, the neighborhoods of Bordeaux and Burgundy, began to emphasize wine production while turning to other areas for their supplies of grain and meat. The dependence of the wine centers on the grain centers, and of the grain centers on the wine centers, was to become increasingly characteristic of their economies from the ten hundreds on.

Mining in Europe, in the course of the six, seven, and eight hundreds, had been rather inconsequential. There was not much coming out of the ground—only a small amount of lead and silver, some gold washed from rivers, and local mining of iron ores to satisfy local needs. On the other hand, in the nine hundreds a different sort of mining industry began to make its appearance, and mining steadily improved and expanded as the next centuries went along.

We have already mentioned in connection with German expansion how local prospectors in central Germany began to get silver out of the ground in one of the old mountain regions known as the Hartz. This silver was found in veins, which they began to follow into the ground with mining shafts. The men who did the work were local Saxons, and the land on which the mines began to be developed was the land of the duke of the Saxons and of some of his chief monasteries in that part of Germany. Very quickly the Saxons learned better ways for propping tunnels, for moving air in and out, for getting water out, and for processing the ore. In general the Saxons began to accumulate the experience about the below-ground world which has been important to miners ever since.

It is no accident that the duke of the Saxons soon became the leading political and military figure in Germany, in the 930's and 940's. In 962 the Duke of the Saxons, who was already King of Germany, became Otto the First, the Holy Roman Emperor by papal coronation in Rome. The development of his silver mines was not the only reason why the duke of the Saxons rose to paramountcy in the politics of central Europe, but wealth in silver pennies was one of the things he needed.

The fresh Saxon silver, flowing into the arteries of commerce, provided much more money for the doing of business than had been available earlier, and as the Hartz Mountain mines began to play out, other mines were brought into production. Miners and prospectors, the greater part of whom were Saxons in background, continued to draw silver out of the Bohemian, Tyrolean, and Hungarian mountains into modern times.

At the same time that they were putting effort into silver mining, western Europeans increased the vigor with which tin was mined in England. Saxon miners were brought from Germany to teach the Cornishmen to mine tin underground. Ever since there have been Cornishmen wherever English-speaking men have dug mines. The Cornishmen themselves became great mining teachers, as they are to this day in Australia, New Zealand, and the United States.

In addition to the mining of tin there was, of course, the mining of iron —always the most important of mining operations. More efficient work underground was coupled with steadily improved working of the ore. With each generation since there have been improvements made in the breaking up and refining of iron ore. (This is a developing process from about the 950's on through the 1950's.) From 950 on, the economic effect of having more metals, cheaper metals, better metals—because they did this with copper and lesser metals also—was increasingly felt.

As we go from 950 on, there was also growing manufacturing of textiles, pottery, leather goods, and many other things. The list of articles manufactured gets longer and longer; in general the products get better and better. Prices go up in terms of money but down in terms of man hours because of more efficient management, the application of mechanical power, improvement in tools and machinery, and better transport and distribution.

The development of manufacturing was important for local markets since, through this development, the list of articles available in those markets became longer, quality better, and prices more reasonable. Trade within regions was also stimulated by the development of manufacture. But for our purpose it is needful that we keep an eye on the international trade, including the trade of Europeans with non-European peoples, recalling that whereas earlier they exported low-grade, backward-area products such as slaves and furs, by the ten hundreds they began to export textiles and manufactured metal goods to Africa, the Near East, and into Asia. Not all at once, and never completely, but more and more the European line of goods became basically a line of manufactured goods.

By about 1200 A.D. cargoes going from Italy toward Byzantium and Islam were remarkably like those of ships leaving Europe in the nineteen hundreds. Above all the Europeans were sending high-grade woolen textiles to customers in Alexandria, Constantinople, and farther east, but they were also sending high-grade metal objects—good bar iron and ingots of copper, but much more importantly, manufactured kitchen wares, military goods, and the like. Moreover, much the same thing can be said of the import invoices, for the returning ships brought grain to take care of the extra mouths of those who had come to work in such cities as Pisa, Florence, Milan, and Genoa. Europe was still pretty well self-supplying, but some grain was needed from Sicily and North Africa. By 1300, when the king of England fought the Scotch (the great war against Robert the Bruce), he had Italian businessmen buy grain in Morocco for him and ship it to the English-held ports in Scotland to be consumed by the English armies. Centers in Europe were coming to depend on outside food supplies, at least in emergencies and on special occasions, and in the case of some of the Italian cities it had become a lasting dependence by the twelve and thirteen hundreds.

By thirteen hundred, western European areas in which there was an active manufacture were drawing foodstuffs from a good distance away in the more backward parts of Europe itself. Examples of this are rye from the region of Prussia and Poland, and from Russia considerable quantities of what are known as naval stores—hemp and pitch and ships' timbers.

Another pattern which was modern was the importation from the non-European world of industrial raw materials. Above all, Europe began importing quantities of chemicals. The most important of the chemicals was alum—various forms of aluminum salts that have astringent properties which in turn were needed in the dying of woolen goods in the big textile centers of Europe. Alum came from Africa, Turkey, and the Byzantine Empire in great quantities.

To anticipate a bit, the first great vertical and horizontal and international cartel of which we have a record was in the alum business, erected by a man who was at one and the same time a Genoese businessman and a Byzantine noble. This was done between 1280 and 1290, and lasted a long time. It was an airtight cartel; one could not get out, prices were fixed, production was fixed, distribution was controlled. Everything to maintain it was done just as beautifully as any modern cartel has ever succeeded in doing.

Another important import was raw leather to be used in tanning and manufacturing. Quantities of dyestuffs, some from far-off India, were coming in by 1200.

It is hard to define what it takes to make a good merchant, for a good merchant must know and be able to do so many things. But one of the things a merchant must have is knowledge of who is who in his own town and in all the other towns where he does business. For he is largely dependent for his success upon those who supply him and those who buy from him, their reliability and availability, their credit, and all such things.

Beginning in the nine hundreds and increasingly in the ten hundreds, businessmen in the European world became familiar with other businessmen across Europe, until a great network of persons who knew each other existed all the way from Iceland to the Holy Land. By following lines of business contacts, goods and money and credit could move profitably for those concerned; individuals or groups did fail in business here and there, but on the whole business profits swelled. The period we are covering saw the rise of this class of traders who knew who was who elsewhere, how to ship goods, how to analyse purchases or to appraise them, where to go to get money when it was needed quickly, where to invest money. Such a class grew up, steadily increasing in numbers and know-how and in goods on hand—in short, capitalists. It was this class that made the whole economic world move along.

Closely tied to this was the development of a well understood merchant law. Western Europeans, and especially Italians and southern Frenchmen, were lucky that there was literally on the books—the Greek-Roman law books—a merchant law usable in a fairly advanced society. It had more or less vegetated. Between the three and four hundreds and the period we have reached, no one had been doing much business and those merchant-law sections of the Roman law were not much studied or applied.

But now men were beginning to do things which that law could regulate and control. So they turned to it once more, a great center for the study of Roman law growing at Bologna in the course of the ten hundreds.

Interest in the Roman law was broad, covering more than just an interest in its merchant law. But the general interest was greatly stimulated by the fact that a graduate who had a good law degree might go to any busy Italian town and find clients, make a profitable career, and end up a rich man. Rich merchants intentionally sent their sons to study law and the notarial profession—the drawing of sound legal documents—so that those boys could be better businessmen. In the business world everyone who had any responsibility had to know how to read and write. As a result, literacy was becoming universal among this trading class. What is more, high competence in law and legal documents as well as in languages was becoming necessary to the successful direction of big business, of a family business, of a bank, or of a government's finances.

In addition to the development of knowledge of merchant law there was development of merchant mathematics, or accounting. By about twelve hundred at the latest every intelligent Italian merchant knew how to keep books. In doing this he had not invented anything, for the Roman law required all Roman merchants to keep books. But by the thirteen hundreds in Italy, merchants were keeping books in double entry, with posting to ledgers and the possibility of analysis of results of any individual enterprise or investment which had been hazarded.

In mentioning law we have spoken first of Italy. In northern France, Belgium, England, and Germany they did not have the Roman law. However, Northerners were in touch with the Italians and greatly influenced by them, since the Italians came up to middle France, to the Rhineland, and to England to do business. But although the Italians influenced them, still they lived by and were ruled by custom, as emphasized when describing the life of villagers in the manorial system and of the noblemen in the feudal. Custom ruled the relations of merchants with one another too.

As trade increased in volume and importance, the development of merchant custom in the North was deeply influenced by direct contact with the Italian merchant law, but it was also steadily amplified, clarified, and expanded as practical problems came up and had to be settled. This was done under the direction of the merchants themselves, for when a case came up, the government (either local city or national government) would set up a panel of merchants to bring in a verdict as to what the law was on the disputed matter, and through this means the merchants developed their own custom. By this method the Law Merchant (to use the English name for the law of the merchants) took shape quite quickly in the North in the course of the eleven and twelve hundreds. It was not something legislated into existence by parliaments or decreed by kings. The medieval Law Merchant is the foundation of the law of business as carried on in the United States.

Expansion: Trading Penetration, Conquest, and Empire

In addition to the rise of the trading class and the improvement in education and law, there was, beginning in the 900's, a very rapid development of European naval supremacy over all accessible waters.

As the Norse turned West-European about the year one thousand, the Baltic, the North Sea, and their neaby shores became European, not alien, shores (save that still-heathen Slavs and Balts built pirate fleets and harried the shipping and shores of the Danes and Swedes). The northern Germans began to send their ships out of the estuaries of the rivers and to the harbors of the British Isles and Scandinavia. The kings in Germany made treaties with the kings of England; the latter had treaties with the kings of Norway, and so on around the circle of northwest European Catholic Christian lands. Trade and treaties to regulate it and make it possible took on a modern aspect.

In Mediterranean lands there was more violence. Through the eight and nine hundreds the populations in the little fishing villages and trading ports along the coasts of southern France, all around Italy, and around Spain both on the Atlantic and Mediterranean sides, suffered from the terror of Mohammedan raids, some of the raids taking place rather late in the nine hundreds. Occasionally Byzantine cruisers would come by and shake off the raiders for an area round about. But in the nine hundreds, free-booting Mohammedan pirates from Crete, from Spain, from North Africa, were seizing forts around the islands of Sardinia and Corsica, and on the Balearic Islands between Spain and Sardinia. From these bases they made hit-and-run raids all along the Christian coasts of Italy, Spain, and France. They raided the Mohammedan coasts too, for they were true pirates.

But about the year 1000, quite a different picture begins to be seen. Fleets of the small ships of the Pisans and Genoese began to harry the Moslem pirates in Corsica and Sardinia. Along the coast of Spain, when a raid by Mohammedans near the great Christian shrine of Santiago (St. James) of Compostella had terrified the local people, a Genoese pilgrim asked "Why do you tolerate this? Why don't you chase them away?" They

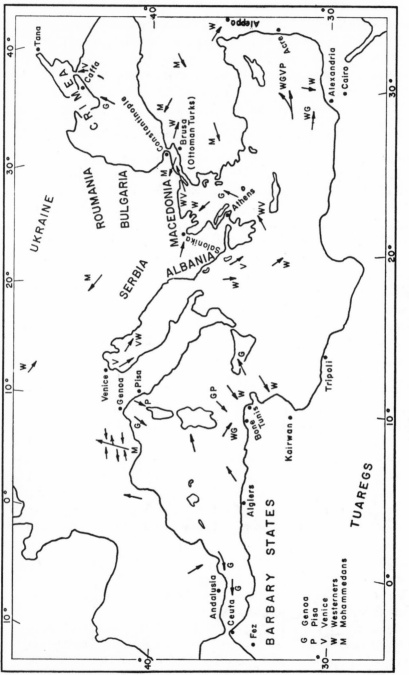

Mediterranean expansion of Europeans

answered, "We don't know how to make the proper ships or use them." He said "I'll show you how." So they worked hard for some time at building the ships and learning how to handle them; they then chased the Mohammedans along the coast, having taken them by surprise.

The Christians also began to make great raids on the coasts of Africa. A considerable part of the expense of building the beautiful Christian edifices in Pisa was met by selling the loot from raids upon the Saracens of North Africa.

In the ten hundreds Normans from Normandy began to take control of southern Italy and then of Sicily. By 1100 they had a kind of kingdom set up, composed of the southern third of Italy and of Sicily. They built a fleet, and within a short time, in the early eleven hundreds, had taken control of the middle of the Mediterranean.

In the period of the Great Crusades, the western Europeans were able to send great armies by land, but supported by sea, all the way to the Holy Land. The Italians had bigger and faster ships, better captains and admirals, far better weapons and organization in every way than did the Mohammedans. Control of the Mediterranean also became control of the Black Sea, after the Westerners won much of the Byzantine Empire in 1204 by a great amphibious siege of Constantinople.

It was not long before the Europeans were sending ships along the coasts of Africa toward the Guinea region. Almost exactly two hundred years before 1492, a group of Genoese proposed to reach India by way of the Straits of Gibraltar in a ship which sailed out into the Atlantic and probably turned south. Genoese long dreamed the same dreams as those of Christopher Columbus.

This naval power was tremendously important, and was tied with the feudal military superiority already described. In the course of the late ten and the eleven hundreds the western Europeans had achieved military superiority over the Mohammedans and Greeks. At first they relied heavily on pure spirit and on the great proficiency in handling weapons which was possessed by each individual Western warrior. Then, in the course of the eleven and twelve hundreds, Europeans tremendously increased their knowledge of how to build castles, how to build and use siege machinery, and how to use some strategy in warfare, thereby adding sagacity to their tremendous morale and individual proficiency.

By means of their naval power, in the course of the eleven hundreds the western Europeans came to dominate militarily most of the ports of North Africa, the coasts all around the eastern Mediterranean with the exception of the city port of Alexandria, and soon after all of the Black Sea. On land they drove the Mohammedans almost entirely out of Spain, leaving only a small satellite sultanate around Granada which survived until the days of Christopher Columbus, militarily and politically under the thumb of the king of Castile.

All this was tied up with an equally vigorous commercial imperialism. The extension of German trading centers into the lands between the Oder and the Elbe was part of this. We have seen that towns which lived by trade were closely involved in the political, religious, and economic assimilation of eastern lands by Germans.

Italian colonies were established around the Mediterranean. The Italian colonies had the same sort of relationship with the local world where they were established as did the European foreign settlements in such places as China and Turkey in the seventeen, eighteen, and early nineteen hundreds; they were like little Shanghais.

In one Moslem or Greek city after another, for instance, the Genoese would secure a walled city to themselves inside the native city, with control over the best landings and warehouses, and sharing the international trade of the city with other Italian colonists similarly established there. (This made things very hectic when, for example, Venice was at war with Genoa, for the Genoese and Venetians would both be in their fortified inner cities in Acre, or Africa, or Constantinople. The mother cities of Genoa and Venice would be fighting on the sea, and their native sons, living in rival communities in the midst of Mohammedans or Greeks, would be catapulting great stones at one another's settlements, burning each other's ships in port, and paralyzing the trade of the natives. A very difficult military and political situation usually developed.) After the middle and late eleven hundreds no Mohammedan could freely trade at wholesale between Syria and Baghdad in the East and Morocco in the West, for all the sea routes were under the control of Pisans, Genoese, and Venetians.

By the middle twelve hundreds these Westerners were putting out their tentacles all the way to Peking and Burma, and toward Timbuktu.

In Asia the opportunity for wide expansion was given by a great political-military development which had taken place during the 1220's, 1230's, and 1240's—the rise of the Mongol Empire of Genghis Khan.

The Mongol Empire, stretching from Poland and Silesia across to Korea (as mentioned in another connection), was stabilized and then firmly governed. Its ruler was the Khan of Khans, who was whatever brother, cousin, or second cousin in direct descent from Genghis Khan his family chose to be its head.

The Mongol Empire was not a wild steppe barbarian state without sophistication. Almost from the first moments of Mongol conquest, very highly civilized and able Chinese were absorbed into the Mongol government, contributing to it all the valuable knowledge of government possessed by them. Also, before Genghis Khan died, highly educated Mohammedans from Turkestan and Persia had been absorbed, bringing with them their governmental and military knowledge.

A considerable draft was even made on western European skills. By the middle twelve hundreds there was a jeweler from Paris, manufacturing metallic jeweled fountains at the Great Khan's court for his amusement and in order to beautify the place. There were western Europeans trading, and serving the Great Khan at the same time, in China by 1250 and 1260. We know all this from written accounts of literate western Europeans who were sent to Peking and North China as ambassadors of the pope or of the king of France, and who on their return to western Europe wrote of such things.

From the point of view of traders the most striking thing about the Mongol Empire was its development of policed land routes from the Black Sea, where the Great Khan's territories came down to the Crimea, to Korea, and all the way from northern Siberia to the Indus Valley or to Burma. Garrisons of Mongol cavalry were posted at strategic points, ready to keep bandits down and to protect travelers and their goods. Along the routes, only one day's march from one another, were good hostels. These were caravansaries where from two or three men and their animals up to a caravan of several hundred men and their animals could be taken care of. There were supplies of remounts, water, and food. It was possible to go on business from Rome, Bordeaux, or London all the way to Canton or India and to send a letter to an associate at the other end of the route (reference to some of these letters still exists).

Things had become so easy and regular that by the early thirteen hundreds an experienced banker-merchant who was writing a book on how to be a businessman started with a perfectly matter-of-fact explanation of how to go from Florence to Peking. He simply included it as one of the routes, tracing it out the way a modern travel folder would trace a trip to Australia or Bali. However, after around 1340, the Mongol central government lost its hold on its subunits, and the whole thing tended to fall into chaos as the Khan's descendants fought each other for control, with no one actually achieving it.

Any factor which can start trade is also likely to be influential in continuing and building it up. Then, as one factor has built trade up a bit, another one begins to have more and more influence. It cannot be said

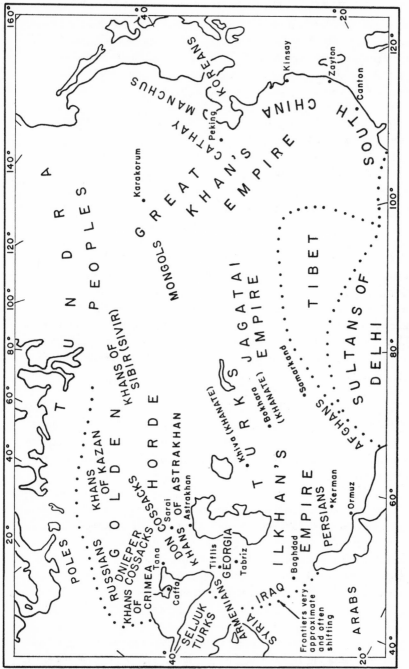

Mongol Empire

that any one of these factors has priority over the others either in time or influence. Nor can it be said that any one of them necessarily made for the rise of commerce. We just know it rose. The things mentioned here seem to have played parts in bringing about that rise and, once it got under way, in accelerating it.

General Organization of Towns and Fairs

We must now turn to the organization of trade as it underwent a continuing rapid rise in its volume and scope during the nine through the early thirteen hundreds. (By the mid-thirteen hundreds, as will be seen, western European trade suffered a major depression which lasted roughly about a hundred years.)

Throughout the whole epoch the bulk of the trade was carried on in small towns. Small towns serving their immediate neighborhoods began to take shape as the nine and ten hundreds went along. To be sure, as in modern America, a town could grow, then as trade currents shifted a little might shrink back and not be so important, having been replaced, perhaps in its own neighborhood, by another town which had been a bit luckier in attracting customers, or perhaps in having survived warfare. In the Middle Ages every now and then towns died as a result of warfare as well as from a shift in trade channels.

In the ten hundreds towns were rapidly becoming the trading centers for the surplus manufactures and goods of the areas around them. While some manufacturing was done in the towns themselves, the greater part of the activity in the towns was in handling the things brought to them for sale—from the country that was within a day's walk or a wagon trip away. The merchandise for sale might be materials which were chance surplus, or which had been consciously raised or made for sale in the town. By putting a circle around a town market at the distance of a day's travel it is possible to ascertain fairly accurately the area which that market served.

It happens that a very large part of the original research work done in the nineteen hundreds on the history, economics, and institutions of medieval towns was concentrated on study of small towns of France and Germany. As a result, the great trading centers were overlooked, and the popular modern picture of the medieval town came to be that of a small place of from fifteen hundred to two or three thousand inhabitants, serving a fairly restricted local market. This is the kind of place that is still likely to be described as the typical medieval town in ordinary text books and in most of the books of scholars who are specialists in other fields than medieval history. Even all the historians have not as yet become fully aware of the great difference between the small medieval town with its service to a geographically modest market and the role played by such places as medieval Paris or Florence.

Local towns were always important, for more people, over-all, lived in them than in the larger urban centers. But the local town, like the local agriculture, did not have much to offer in the way of growth-stimulating practices and ideas. Its importance rested on its role as the place where local products were gathered together to be channeled toward the regional center, to go from the regional center toward the international center, and thence to other international trade centers far away. The local town also served as a distributing center. It was the final place where spice was sold in the channel of trade which had started far away on the Spice Islands. And of course this was true of all the other articles of trade which went through the great channels.

Shop keepers and provisioners and nearby estate managers were the "big" figures in these little towns. The customers were the peasants and the lord's family and so on, folk who went into town to pick up things they would need in the next week or month or so for consumption; or they might be persons who drove in some cattle for sale, or who brought in some baskets made in the neighborhood, or butter or cheese to be put in kegs or tubs, all these being things to be sent on along the channels of trade to the regional or international centers.

Activities in the regional centers were of course very much like this, except that while they served their own neighborhoods, they also at the same time served a great many lesser towns. In the regional centers the volume was greater, the deals were larger, the "big" figures were richer, and a good part of the trade of the dealers was in buying and selling wholesale. ("Retail" is a word which comes from the cloth trade. *Tagliare* means "to cut" in Italian. In French the word "to cut" is *tailler,* and the word tailor comes from it. In the cloth trade, when pieces of cloth were sold which were small enough—cut off—to make clothes of, then the merchant was "retailing"; while when he sold a whole bolt of cloth, many yards long, he was a "wholesaler," for he sold it "whole.")

In the regional towns a good deal of the trading was wholesale, not just in cloth, but in many other lines of goods, and the wholesaler was the person who sold to the men who would later sell retail at home in their small towns or even in their shops in the same regional town.

But we are most interested here in the great metropolitan centers which served a large part of western Europe—a London, which served all of

England, or a Paris which came to concentrate a great deal of the whole-sale trade for northern France, and so on. For we are especially interested in the interregional, international trade.

Metropolitan centers rise and fall. Through the history of the last thousand years in Europe, there has been a succession of chief cities, and there have come to be many cities that could be considered finished. For example, Venice was a great metropolis as far back as the eight hundreds when men began settling on the main islands, the Rialto, which *is* Venice to American tourists and to the Venetians who live there too. Until the seventeen hundreds Venice was a metropolis. In the later centuries it may perhaps have come to be not so great as it had been in the thirteen and fourten hundreds, but it still was an important town. Then it became a museum. A town with a like history is the town of Bruges, in Flanders. Bruges was a great town, and is now a perfect example of what a great town was in the thirteen and fourteen hundreds. Today it is a tourist's delight, but not a lively center of commerce.

The important towns changed, but there were always some in any one region. One can take a compass and put its point on the map at about the Straits of Dover, then draw a circle about one hundred and fifty miles across, and within that circle will be the territory wherein, at all times, has been the greatest city in northern and western Europe. It has not always been the same city, but it has lain within that circle. First Bruges, then Antwerp, then Amsterdam, then London—which has been larger than most cities in the world ever since the sixteen hundreds—there had always to be a big city within this circle, though local conditions might move the center of trade from one to another.

Looking at Europe as commerce began to grow in the nine, ten, and eleven hundreds, we will see that there were some areas which had an especially quick growth of towns, while others did not have much. Then as now there was no important town in the central part of France, for it is rough and poor. But in the region of Paris there have been rich towns for many centuries, for this is rich land with important trade routes centering on it.

Towns grew up in Italy, and especially in Italy north of Rome—in Tuscany and Lombardy. In considering the list of towns in the north and central parts of Italy such names as Pisa, Venice, and Genoa come to mind immediately. Venice began to be a great center during the nine hundreds, followed in the ten hundreds by Pisa and Genoa. In the ten hundreds these all came to have fleets with trading connections all over the Mediter-ranean. They were starting points for the Crusaders going by sea, and bases for supplies to sustain the Crusaders in the eleven hundreds. They were the places to which the ships brought spices from Egypt and the Black Sea. After awhile they began to develop lively manufactures as well, and they traded actively with the inland parts of Europe.

In addition to these cities, which were primarily great ports, were the inland cities in Italy. There is a long list, but the two which are most notable are Florence (which had a slow start and only reached the top in the late twelve hundreds, but stayed there once it arrived) and Milan, which had been a great Roman city and which rose fast again in the nine and ten hundreds to become the wealthiest and most populous north Italian city. It was Milan which took the lead in north Italy in developing its communal form of government and its independence from the Holy Roman Emperors. But its size and importance in politics both went back to its leadership in trade with Germany over the Alps. Goods coming from either Venice or Genoa and other places went to Milan for redistribution and re-routing up into Germany. Above all else it acted as a point toward which German and North European goods went on the way toward consumers in Italy, or to export ports for shipment to Egypt and elsewhere across the Mediterranean. Milan also soon became a great manufacturing center, the armaments and arsenal center for southern Europe, basing that industry on the steady flow of German metals over the Alps into the city—copper, iron, and steel, especially.

Once we leave Italy we find that Italian activity was paralleled on not quite such a grand scale in southern France and nearby Spain early in the eleven hundreds. There was a very precocious flowering of literature in southern France, the literature of the troubadours. It was the literature of an enlightened and commercially active people with a very strong Roman background and a pretty thin barbarian admixture. Such towns as Nîmes and Montpellier (which became the home of a great University especially strong in medical work in the twelve hundreds) and Marseilles on the coast were like the Italian cities not only in their commerce, but also in their institutions, developing very similar political organizations. Barcelona, south of the Pyrenees in Catalonia on the Spanish coast, was in the forefront in the same sort of development.

Quite a bit later, in the twelve hundreds, such towns as Cadiz and Seville and Lisbon began to come up fast in this development of commercial activity on a metropolitan basis. Seville rose partly because it became a second Genoa to the Genoese, who settled there in large numbers and laid the base for the activities of such men as Christopher Columbus, who found himself, practically speaking, still in Genoa when he went to Seville and Cadiz in his negotiations with Queen Isabella. He was talking with and among Genoese as he promoted his project.

In the north, important centers existed elsewhere, but there was a precocious development of active metropolitan trade in the Rhine River valley. The most notable of all these towns was Cologne; it not only controlled the traffic up and down the river, but also was located at the point where east-west travel in north central Germany passed the river, and where a Roman main road furnished the best route from the Rhineland to the English Channel.

In the course of the eleven and twelve hundreds many Cologne merchants moved to other likely spots to set up new towns. It was the moving of men from Cologne to such towns as Bremen, Hamburg, and Lübeck, and then on along the southern coast of the Baltic, which more than anything else created the great Hanseatic League of merchants which had its family ties spread from city to city—ties which preceded and helped create the League itself. Towns stemmed from this Rhineland center, and then stemmed out from all centers as newer towns were built up in the east and north. In the twelve hundreds the town of Lübeck became more important than Cologne, the grandmother city of the German trading centers, and it was the main town of the Hanseatic League. Lübeck was never formally set up as the League's capital, for no such thing existed, but it was the chief center.

These towns in the north were matched by London and by Paris, which in the course of the nine, ten, and eleven hundreds began slowly to be cities instead of primarily river crossings and strongholds where the kings stopped. Rivaling those in Tuscany and Lombardy were the towns in the small county of Flanders (modern coastal Belgium) and in the neighboring counties of Brabant, Hainault, and Zeeland, which are in the region of modern Belgium. In that area the "great trading town" was at first Arras. It is from the name of this town that came the word we find in Shakespeare for a large beautiful wall hanging—an "arras"—and it was also from its region that artesian wells came, "artesian" meaning wells of the Arras sort. However, Arras was surpassed in the early twelve hundreds by Bruges, a town on a river estuary. It was the London of its day, holding supremacy over all the commercial cities of the north through the twelve and thirteen and most of the fourteen hundreds, until Antwerp, just over the horizon a few miles away, took primacy.

Some large towns in the north were primarily manufacturing centers. Inland from Bruges, and not commercial in primary activity, were such towns as Ghent (or in older English, "Gaunt," which gave its name to gauntlets), which was a great manufacturing town, above all for woolen textiles. It stood for woolen goods as Detroit today stands for automobiles. Also near at hand was the Flemish city of Ypres, which was another of the main industrial towns until it became a dead city in the thirteen and fourteen hundreds when the competition of other kinds of cloth, made more cheaply elsewhere, put it out of business.

These towns were the places into which and out of which large-volume trade flowed. These towns, north and south, were the centers for innovation.

The wholesale businessman, who financed and managed wholesale business, was primary in those towns. We can notice today that the rich wholesalers, importers, and exporters of Manhattan Island are absolutely essential to the economy of New York, even though all of them could probably be assembled in a good-sized auditorium; they make New York a great working center. The same was true in the cities of the Middle Ages; there were not a great many wealthy wholesale businessmen in a metropolis, but they were essential to the conduct of its business.

Then there were the persons who did the heavy work—dockers, stevedores, handlers of merchandise at different stages of being moved about inside such a town. Other persons necessary for such a busy town would be innkeepers, the police and weighing officials and other town officers who handled the trade and the problems created by the population, all of the clergy who had to take care of the spiritual needs of such a population, all of the entertainers who took care of other needs of the same population, especially the visiting buyers. (That was, and still is, another attraction of a big town—to have it be a place where a merchant not only could obtain the goods he wanted but also could go to shows and entertainments. The largest wholesale center is also at the same time a chief entertainment center.) All of these people were there, together with the little local retailers and sellers of services—the barbers, hairdressers, and so forth needed to take care of the whole population, visitors and home people alike.

A few of those towns had more than 50,000 inhabitants, with a very few growing to have 100,000 or better. We are talking of a world in which "big" meant something quite different from what it means today. The very biggest and best of these, Florence, London, and Paris, went beyond 100,000 population rather late in the development of this period. Before 1150 or perhaps 1200 there was no town as large as 100,000. To give an example of what the "big" towns were like: in the mid eleven hundreds the Crown Prince of France was thrown from his rearing horse, which was shying from a sow rising up out of a street in Paris, and he broke his neck. (It was only about 1880 that foraging sows were gotten off the streets of Mid-western towns.)

Towns might have been larger had they not had important substitute centers and rivals, the fairs, for the conduct of local and international trade. When the great fairs faded, the towns finally took over altogether, or vice versa; we cannot tell which. The great period of fairs in western Europe was the eleven and twelve hundreds, and they steadily faded in importance thereafter save around the geographic and economic fringes of western Europe.

A fair develops where there is a desire for an active regional or inter-regional trade, but not enough year-around volume to maintain a town for handling it. The medieval fair was a very lively regional or interna-tional trading "city" while it lasted. But it lasted only a few weeks or per-haps a month and a half; then its traders pulled out and no important activity centered in that spot until the fair reopened a year later.

Fairs usually took place alongside little towns, and even the greatest fairs took place near only medium-sized towns. For a few weeks, when the Bos-ton fair was going on at the doors of Boston in England, there was a great concourse of merchants, retailers, entertainers, and the rest. For a few weeks Boston would do a metropolitan business, then the town would slump back to its normal state of being a modest market-supply center for its part of England. And in Champagne in France, to which we will come, some towns, which in their own right were only of four or five or eight thousand population, became for a month and a half or so, while one of the great Champagne fairs was held at their gates, cities of twenty-five, thirty, or fifty thousand souls.

Fairs tended to be arranged in cycles of successive related fairs. Mer-chants would congregate at a given fair in January and February, then move from it directly to another not too far away. Then a third fair would open by late spring and early summer, and so on through the year. In England a cycle came to function at Winchester, St. Ives, Boston, St. Bartholomew's, and so on. In our nursery jingles there is still a recall of the time when the fairs were important, for Simple Simon met a pieman, going to the fair; and also there is that riddle starting "As I was going to St. Ives." There was a German cycle of fairs developed, the last vestige of which is now under Soviet management at Leipzig; the fur and rye trade during the twelve and thirteen hundreds was centered there. There were fairs in a cycle in Flanders and, finally, the most important cycle, that of the fairs of Champagne.

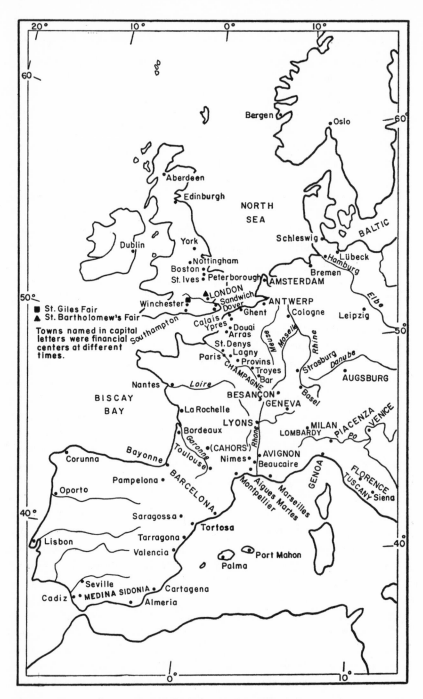

Towns, fairs, and finance centers

Champagne is known today as the region from which comes a bubbly wine, but in the Middle Ages the Champagne region did not produce a wine that anyone thought worth drinking except the peasants who lived there; our modern champagne wine is a more recent invention. In the course of the eleven hundreds Champagne became even more famous as a center for international trading at its great fairs.

Six fairs came to be arranged in a cycle within the county of Champagne, each fair lasting between a month and a month and three quarters. A fair was going on somewhere in the county practically right through the year. There was one in January-February, another in March-April, another in May-June, and so on, alongside the towns of Lagny, Bar, Provins, Troyes, Provins again, and finally Troyes also for the second time. We still have two systems of weights in the United States and England, one a system of ounces and pounds for weighing such things as flour and meat, the other a parallel system for weighing jewelry. The name of the latter, troy weight, goes back to Troyes, a center for trade in precious items in the Middle Ages.

Champagne was a sizable county a little southward and eastward of the city of Paris, along the Seine River and its tributaries. The Seine runs mostly from the southeast in an arc going northwest toward the English Channel, providing a valley along which traffic can move from the south toward Paris, the Channel, and Flanders, or from England toward Rome. Champagne lies within easy reach of the main routes from northern France into the Rhineland and beyond, or from Germany on down to Spain. Champagne made a first-rate hub for all the spokes of a great wheel of trade covering north and western Europe. Its lower side, to the south, connected easily with the trade of Italy and the Mediterranean.

Not only was Champagne well situated, it was also lucky in having early in its history a very strong count in charge of the whole area, and the Counts of Champagne in turn showed themselves to be enlightened patrons of trade. They policed their county tightly, and generously. They gave special privileges to the fairs which began to develop in their region and, instead of charging all the traffic would bear, they tried to give a maximum of security for as low a charge as possible. This attracted merchants from Germany and Italy, from Spain, southern France, England, and the Low Countries, until by the later eleven hundreds the fairs of Champagne had become the hubs for all of Europe's commerce. While whole regions traded with one another through their own metropolitan towns and through regional cycles of big fairs, when we come to the highest point, where all of Europe traded with everyone else in Europe, we find the fairs of Champagne. They were the New York and London of their day.

As a Champagne fair opened, there was normally first of all a period of entry, during which merchants got their goods and themselves installed. Then began a rapid sale of cloth. Unlike the medieval merchants pictured in scholarly thought only a generation ago, sitting around dumbly while the interest on their investment ate up their profits and capital, the great merchants in fact sold by sample the way any able large-volume merchant would do today. After inspection the buyers took possession and shipped their purchases right on out of the fair. The goods did not sit around week after week in booths and stalls. Cloth came in primarily from the north, chiefly the product of England and Flanders, and only a few days later was on the roads to Italy and southern France for use or for further shipment overseas.

Professional transport men conducted pack trains between Italian cities and the fairs over the Alpine passes. The shipments were sent off, winter and summer, with clocklike regularity. In transporting over more level routes, wheeled carts were normally used, as between Marseilles and Champagne. Special couriers rode "pony express" with business documents and letters along the most used routes, and by the middle twelve hundreds we find evidence that Italian cities whose merchants had large interests in banking had their own municipally paid and managed postal services.

The buyers did not pay with coined money; they paid with written promises backed by their credit. Records have survived in Italy amply revealing this practice by Italian merchants. We have no record of such activities on the part of merchants in other countries for these earliest days, for no records have survived, but know it was normal practice a while later.

At a fair, as soon as the cloth sale was over, there began a rapid sale of leathers which came mostly from the south, especially fine moroccan and cordovan leathers from Mohammedan lands. Those were bought by merchants and shipped north for distribution all over northern France.

Then came the sale of spices and other goods high in value but low in bulk. Again the sales were wholesale. They calculated in ounces, but they sold large lots by the pound and the hundred-pound bale or sack, whatever the container. Leathers and spices were bought mostly by northerners for transshipment to the Baltic (the Hansa region), the British Isles, or even Iceland—wherever the retail market for pepper, cinnamon, or ginger was good. All along, sales were on credit.

When the selling was over, there came a period which lasted about a month in each fair during which bankers (who were also rich wholesale merchants) took up the work of closing out and balancing accounts. Since most of the buying and selling had been with notes, there was need for the balancing of accounts of merchants against merchants, cities against cities, and regions against regions. It was basically the process carried on by our modern clearing houses. A check written in a small town in the Middle West may have to clear through banks in the town where written, in Chicago, then in New York. Certain clearing work may progress through London to still further cities. So at the fairs of Champagne accounts were cleared, by bookkeeping work, between merchants who were at the fairs; but they also balanced out the accounts owed by all Italy to all England, and vice versa, and so on. Men could get goods on promises-to-pay based on moneys and assets anywhere in Europe, and both merchandise and credit instruments could move then into the trade channels. Eventually, functioning as general value, the latter would pass through the fairs of Champagne for clearance each four or five or six weeks. Things moved more slowly than they do today, but the pattern was basically that which has operated ever since.

This is the top achievement of the merchants and financiers of the eleven hundreds, and was operating by the year 1200. Richard the Lion Hearted or Robin Hood could have paid a debt in the Holy Land by going to a banker-merchant in Nottingham and having that banker run the transaction through to Jerusalem via Champagne and Genoa. Saint Louis, around 1250, actually did meet his tremendous obligations in Egypt and in the Holy Land by taking merchant-banker advances; his "paper" was used in turn for buying, selling, and money deals at the fairs of Champagne, being highly valued since his promises were payable eventually at the royal treasury in Paris and Louis and his mother Blanche, heading the government, were conspicuously honest.

Italian primacy in all financial developments is manifested by the modern European terms for all sorts of such affairs. *Endorse* stems from *in dorso,* "on the back"—the signature on the back of a money-document which adds the obligation of the endorser, and of his assets, to those of the man who first promised to make payment of so much at such a place at such a time. *Credit* (Latin-Italian, Latin being the official written language of business as it then was of theology and law) means "he believes" —he believes a promiser's promise is going to be carried out. *Debit* means the opposite, "he owes." (Since the twelve hundreds, the man on the street has been puzzled by what seems to him at first glance to be the up-side down usage of these terms by double-entry bookkeepers, though the usage is logical and necessary.) Bank and bankrupt are equally Latinate Italian: the *banca* or *bancum* was the banker's bench on which he sat, behind the table on which he counted (*contare*) money when he was open for business, and kept his accounts (*conti*). There he could also conduct exchanges (*cambia*). In case he could not meet due obligations (*obligationes*), police officials could be called by his distressed creditors. Then his bench was physically broken by husky policemen, across his counter (broken or *ruptum; banco rotto* in Italian). He was thereafter publicly bankrupt.

Men had all these things by 1200. They existed and were used to take care of the ransom debts of Richard the Lion Hearted and to swing the great ransom deal for Saint Louis, King of France. Documents growing out of his ransom deals still exist in the State Archives at Genoa. Hundreds of thousands of pennies had to be raised; the king's men had to produce in Egypt, out of revenues in France, cart load after cart load after cart load of silver pennies for the ransom.

Banking came to be at the service of all the rest of the community, but it started and primarily served as the tool of the wholesale international and metropolitan businessmen. Then, as now, banks would have starved if they had relied solely on the business which Crusaders and students and tourists gave them. Of course, since they were already in business, they made an appreciated extra income by taking care of the accounts of such persons.

But to return to the towns and the fairs. It was in the course of the early thirteen hundreds that Bruges finally outstripped the Champagne fairs. Soon thereafter the fairs died. There were other than just good business reasons for this. One of the good reasons was a shift of trade routes more and more to the Gibraltar route for the trade between Italy, the Low Countries, and England. Galleys, first of the Genoese and then of the Venetians, began to carry goods around by sea instead of their being taken overland. This, of course, took business away from the fairs which straddled the overland routes. The king of France began to manipulate his money (he was also, by 1300, Count of Champagne), debasing it, changing it arbitrarily, until bankers lost confidence in the fairs of Champagne, or rather in financial dealings there. For political reasons there were blockades against first the Flemings and then the Italians. So the fairs died and Bruges took their place.

In the days of Christopher Columbus, during the fourteen hundreds, Bruges ran into competition from Antwerp in the Duchy of Brabant, and Antwerp began to pull ahead of Bruges because of special privileges and other reasons. Finally, in the course of the wars of the Protestant Reformation, Antwerp was horribly cut to pieces by fighting men, and the center of commercial and financial gravity shifted again, to Amsterdam. Then, in the later sixteen hundreds, London began taking the lead away from Amsterdam; the two cities were about even for a while, with London pulling ahead by 1700 to a leadership which she was to maintain until 1914 without much challenge. During the past thirty and forty years New York has made the first real challenge ever made to the supremacy of the area near the English Channel for leadership in financial business. Nor should we forget to mention that there was considerable financial activity in Genoa also and in fairs devoted to financial dealings, primarily in Lyons, Avignon, and Piacenza, and in southern Spain in various later generations.

CHAPTER V

Business
and Finance

ONE of the things which had greatly handicapped trade, mentioned when discussing precious metals and money, was the shortage of money which a man could carry with him and use for purchases. The shortage of gold and silver coined into money made gold and silver valuable; it kept prices very low in terms of these two metals. For a good many generations right after Charlemagne about the only money to be minted was the silver penny. In size somewhat like but smaller than our quarter, it took twelve of them to have the calculated worth of one shilling, twenty of the theoretical uncoined shillings to make a theoretical pound. (This is, of course, still the English system of reckoning money; all western Europe used it then.) At first there were not many business deals which called for so many pieces of silver that they could not be counted out; to take care of smaller transactions they cut pennies in half or into little pie-shaped quarters with a chisel.

Credit can do much of the work of coined money. As the men of the Italian trading centers and of the other parts of Europe began more and more to trust one another and to keep a record of sales on trust and purchases on trust in their books, they were accomplishing the very same thing for which they had earlier needed to use cash money, transferring goods on and on from merchant to merchant, without using many coins. Credit, used more and more extensively, began to cheapen minted money as there was relatively less call for it. Compared to anything we know today, there was still a high demand, but by and large there was a cheapening of money, which is another way of saying there was a rise in prices. The cheapening of money is often called by another name—inflation—so, as the development of credit went on, there was an inflationary effect slowly but steadily operative.

At the same time more actual money began to appear, for men were digging more and more silver out of the ground in the new and improved mines in eastern Europe; and in the middle 1200's leading republics and kings also began to mint coins made of gold. So there came to be a large-value coin made of gold, and a small-value coin made of silver. They had also begun to mint silver coins which were between the silver penny and the gold piece in value. The gold piece minted in Florence was called the "florin." The gold piece minted in Venice came to be called the "ducat." Other places also minted them, but florins and ducats and the others were all about the same; they were the valuable moneys. With the introduction in addition of a great deal of locally current small-change money made of bronze, copper, silver, and lead, there came to be roughly the kind of spread between high value and lowest value coins with which we are familiar today.

More and more quantity and flexibility in money, and more and more credit, combined to create an inflationary effect on prices. As a result, anyone who had an invested income suffered from inflation just as such persons do today. By and large the persons with the largest such incomes were landed lords whose lands and villages, with their fixed rents and fees, kept yielding less and less in terms of purchasing power. By and large those who benefited by inflation were the businessmen and the peasants, both free and servile, who were able to put the difference in their own pockets as prices rose.

Credit could not operate unless it came to be better and better organized. Basic in the operation of a credit system is a credit law. An indispensable part of the Law Merchant has to do with credit. We have already noticed that during this period there was a rapid and beautifully intellectual development of the merchant law in general. In the schools the professors and the debating law students were helping perfect the credit system by working out its law. Simultaneously in the merchants' own shops the merchants and their pen pushers, who had had a little "church training" and were therefore called clerics or clerks, were working out the principles of bookkeeping so that it would be possible to keep track of everybody's money going in and out. Some of the merchants were beginning to specialize, either very heavily or even completely, in just buying and selling credits and currencies.

By about 1200 to 1250 such money-credit business had become of major interest to many persons. It had become so well defined that we can even see three main levels of credit and currency business operating from then on.

Banking and Houses and Government Financing

At the lowest but very important level were the pawnbrokers or loan sharks. There has been a curious misunderstanding, especially in recent generations, that lending was a Jewish business, but this was true in the Middle Ages only in part—a very modest part. The usurer, pawnbroker, or loan shark was almost everywhere a fellow-Christian who was taking his risks on the next life for the sake of, say, forty percent in this. Italians from Lombardy were so overwhelmingly important in the business that the word "Lombard" actually ended up in the North by meaning a pawnbroker usurer even when the man was not an Italian by nation; Belgians would call another Belgian a "Lombard" if he went into this business.

The Lombard needed around forty or fifty percent return in order just to break even. Again, it is commonly thought a noxious thing to charge such rates of interest. But even today pawnbroking loans need to bring in a very high percent or the person making such loans will slowly go out of business. Expenses are so high—the keeping of the shop, storing of the pawns, precariousness of collections, risk of loss in sales of pawns—that it can be a poor business at ten or even twenty or thirty percent interest per annum. By the twelve hundreds the pawnbroker was an absolute necessity, given the precariousness of jobs in the medieval industrial and trading centers, and the necessity nobles and soldiers faced in raising quick cash for court expenses, gambling and ransom debts, and fighting equipment.

A good part of employment was seasonal. Layoffs could come without warning on a Saturday night and last for months on end in the textile and metal towns. Without some source of cash money the working people would have starved very shortly. Every so often there was a great agitation, and rulers were persuaded to put the unchristian diabolical loan sharks and pawnbrokers out of business. When this had been done, everything was fine until about a week from the following Saturday when a whole segment of the population in a town could not find any money whatsoever with which to buy bread; this could lead to discomfort. These situations would sometimes last for months.

The pawnbroker was hated, and necessary. He was run after and chivied by the church and the state. But whenever they got rid of him they had to allow him back quite soon, disturbing as it might be to their consciences.

There was another specialist in the money world who was much more important than the pawnbroker from the point of view of credit as a substitute for coined money. This was the professional who changed one kind of coin to another at his bench. It was this man who was the banker above all others. He sat at a bench, on a *bancum* or *banco,* and changed moneys—English coins into French coins, French into Italian coins— whatever the customer wanted. He would buy at one level, making a little money on the purchase, then sell at another level, making a little on the sale, and the real value was somewhere in between. But he was selling a service which was indispensable to persons who were going on a trip or who wanted to change coins which had been brought from away into money which would be good locally.

As their business increased, these men needed to have strong boxes in which they could place the bags full of different kinds of coins for safe-keeping during the night. Soon they began to receive articles of value to be kept in their strongboxes for other persons. For the service of safe-guarding valuables they could charge a little money.

Before long, or at the same time, these men began getting still another kind of business. This was the business which came when they entered drawing accounts on their books, accounts which might have originated either as loans or as deposits.

There were two ways by which such a banker would open a drawing account. A hundred could be given him and he would stand good for that hundred; the money could be drawn out until it was used up and he would even pay a bit of interest on parts of it left with him long enough, especially on any amounts promised for fixed terms. Or, although he was given nothing, for the client's convenience he would open an account for a hundred on his behalf. Withdrawals could be made from it, and it was paid back with extra money for the convenience. The business of accepting deposits (or the same thing upside down, as a bookkeeping transaction) created accounts in banks which are recognizable as working like checking accounts. In the Middle Ages they were not yet true checking accounts, but that was what they were to develop into in later centuries.

To be sure, so bald a statement that money would be charged for the use of money, as in the two transactions just outlined, would not have been made in working business life. While Roman law would have protected a money dealer in these instances, the canon law would have operated to annul the loan itself and to have put the money dealer in serious danger in the court of the diocese. In practice the results were achieved by various devices which worked out as indicated above. Returns (interest paid) could be confounded with profits on a joint venture; interest received could be confounded with legitimate recompense for the creditor's suffering from delay in repayment or his assumption of some risk the borrower was facing. There could be shadier presents or favors or outright under-the-counter blackmarket fringes decorating secretly transactions which were valid on their face. Church courts searched behind deed and facts into the consciences of those examined, but men in business rarely tried to evade obligations by bringing charges of usury in them. One who did it once would not have a chance to do it again.

By 1200 in a busy Italian port, a man with his account in one bank could have a sum he owed transferred to the account his creditor maintained in another bank. Banks were all bunched in a city square of modest size, and their customers were in business only a few minutes' walk away, towns being so closely built. Word-of-mouth instructions could work adequately and the written order and the clearing-house organization were not yet called for.

This business of accepting or making loans, of allowing depositors to withdraw or to order withdrawals or to order transfers, tremendously expanded the whole credit structure. But it was a rare money-changing and deposit banker who did business outside his own town. This leads us to banking at the highest level, which was international.

There were persons who wished to transfer funds from town to town without carrying or sending cash. The men who stepped into this profitable business were the great wholesale merchants. They were already engaged in shipping goods back and forth from one place to another, and they normally had relatives, agents, partners, or fellow townsmen, who knew them and their credit, scattered across the map at important business centers. These merchants began to lend money within the world of merchants on the promise of being paid back elsewhere, in another kind of money, and later. Not only did they lend, but also they borrowed, whichever way promised to be profitable.

There are other important ways in which currencies can be regarded, but there is one characteristic of any currency which governs both parties right at the sharp point in time and place when they close a deal involving that currency: it is another commodity, like all other items then and there being bought and sold, in price competition with all the rest of the merchandise at the moment available. The great merchant, with a wide knowledge of demands and supplies of all sorts of merchandise over a wide arc of possible markets, with men at other key markets who could handle his merchandise as though he himself was at hand to do it, knowing as much as was possible of freight charges, future demands and supplies, here, there, and everywhere, of risks and insurance rates, of the metal and of the exchanging values of other currencies, and of many other things, would-be buyer or seller of lard or ginger, of oranges or rawhides, of government securities or slaves, of cloth or of a currency, at the moment of each individual transaction—if he felt there was more advantage in buying a ton of currants to send to London than in buying a promise of someone to pay him ten ducats in Venice, he chose the venture in currants. If he needed those ducats to be available to him in Venice, he would be one of those bidding up ducats and passing by possible ventures in currants and all other commodities whose prices would therefore in some measure be pressed down. The point is that general markets open to all goods and merchants, and including the markets for all currencies in all places which Western international traders visited, had come to exist by 1200 A.D. and all international merchants were operating in that highest form of banking, which is foreign exchange.

The growth of international exchange banking brought about still other consequences. Local currency famines or gluts had been troublesome; they became fewer and less acute. As the exchanges came to be transacted generally in only a few reliable currencies, the multiplicity of local coinages had only minor effects in general. Since news of every sort was of value in making business decisions, trading towns, families, and individuals developed systems of couriers and letter pouches which brought Genoa, for example, into close contact before 1200 with the successive steps in the trade of each Champagne fair. Exchange documents, reports on quantities and qualities and prices of merchandise, and general news moved from market to market as fast as means allowed. The mercantile world had in its exchange mechanisms another big supplement to its capital funds, with still further effects upon the general price level; money was less tight when exchanges were flowing freely and rapidly. On the other hand, all corners of Europe could feel the depression which followed a serious dislocation and contraction of the mechanism.

Exchange bankers could finance any merchants without risking a charge of usury. Since, in any market on a given day, promises to pay later in some other place in another currency had a going price, including a markup (or even a noticeable markdown) from its metal and official prices at home, and since prices for that currency would go up or down while the promise was running, buyer and seller alike hazarded something when making a deal. Returns on hazarded capital were not usurious by law. So money could be raised by asking a banker merchant for funds here and now to be returned there and later. Arrangements could be made to have agents of both parties, then and there, negotiate a reverse promise, at rates holding, then and there, payable once more at the bank which originated the first deal, still later on. With good judgment and luck, the original seller (or borrower) had to settle up at his own home without suffering a crushing cost for the use of the funds for some weeks or months. The original buyer (or lender) got back his funds with a worth-while return—if prices for the two currencies had not changed sharply to his disadvantage in the interval. Many variations on this basic pattern were of practical use; this only sketches the main theme.

Deposits could also be accepted, to be held in custody for a charge; they could in fact be pledges (if not cash themselves) for credits in the bankers' books. Or outsiders could hand sizable sums (international bankers were not interested in petty accounts) to a banker as investment in his affairs. Direct payment of money at a guaranteed rate for the use of money of this sort was prohibited usury, but dividends on such sums, risked with the banker, were allowable. A bank, which year after year paid regular dividends, drew deposits from clients about as certainly as though interest had been stipulated.

At first these persons had obtained their assets from the wholesale international trade. But very soon they began to supplement that sort of income, when they were successful, by taking commissions for the transfer of the funds of church and government officials—the popes, the cardinals, the great bishops, and the kings. For example, during the Middle Ages the pope always had good income coming to him each year from England, which during the Middle Ages was one of the most devoutly Roman Catholic countries in all Europe. Gifts and other incomes yielded pennies which no one was anxious to cart all the way to Rome. Neither did the pope necessarily want them at Rome; he might wish to influence politics in Germany, to take care of expenses in Portugal, and so on. So he was happy to allow Roman or Sienese or other Italian bankers to assume the business of picking up that money in England, for which they were willing to pay him a profit on the total amount. They in turn promised to pay him back the total amount plus the extra amount agreed upon either at Rome or in Portugal, or wherever he asked them to pay the money out of his account. The bankers could then use the money in England, where it was given them, to buy wool. As a result the money did not leave England, but stayed there as silver coins, and what left England was wool being sent toward the great textile towns in Flanders. From Flanders it went toward the fairs of Champagne, and from Champagne on through the channels of trade as described. The pope had his money paid out to him in the places he had chosen, and with a profit in addition. Meanwhile the Italians had obtained cash for purchases in England, which was to their advantage.

Credit purchases and sales at the fairs of Champagne and the clearing of accounts at the end of each of the six successive fairs have been described. In a big, perpetually open market such as Bruges or Venice, there was no periodicity imposed by regulations. All operations went on continuously although seasonal variations in volume and in products handled were normal. This observation applies also, of course, to dealings in currencies and credits.

Merchants added merchandise to their stocks in trade by drawing investments from relatives, neighbors, and those with whom they dealt. Buying on credit on ten, fifteen, thirty, or ninety day terms, they sold on the same basis. Very little cash beyond current living expenses and pocket money was kept on a merchant's person or in his home. At any moment all but a small fraction of the capital he had in business was involved in ventures in which either he chanced risks and gains but on which he owed something or much for purchase price, insurance, shipping costs, or in other merchandise sold by him on credit to other merchants and not yet completely paid for. Sums owed by or to bankers, by or to governments (as sketched above), and sums risked insuring the ventures of others were all carried on his books.

In politics, the house or dynasty was a dominant factor everywhere by 1100 in local quite as much as in royal affairs. It dominated the economic and social activities of sergeants and reeves, of bailiffs and seneschals, and in small towns and markets it conditioned the affairs of petty dealers and craftsmen; in a Rome or Lübeck, a Genoa or London, large operations in affairs were centered on the business houses.

Later, in the thirteen hundreds, long after other Florentine merchant-banking houses had risen and fallen or become merely noble, some branches of the Medici clan began to rise. Giovanni, then Cosimo, and then the latter's grandson, Lorenzo the Magnifico, rose first in the Florentine business world, and then in Europe's foreign trade and banking, politics, art, literature, and learning, up to the time of America's discovery. In actual time they come later than our period, but they walked grandly along a well-worn path in all respects.

In the last one hundred and fifty years there have been famous financial houses—the House of Morgan, the House of Kuhn-Loeb, the House of Baring, the House of Rothschild, and so on. They are still important. A house is a family, in our sense of the word, plus picked near relatives—sons-in-law, nephews, cousins, and brothers-in-law, who take part in the house's operation. In addition there will be a few reliable men who have grown up in the business and are likely to marry someone in the family. It is a sort of instrument for raising and sustaining the position of all its members.

The house as a key instrument for carrying on big business goes back to the first of the houses of which we have some record, in the time of Pope Gregory VII, whose connections with that house were important in building up medieval papal power. In the 1070's he was intimately associated with a Jewish banking family which had turned Christian—the Pierleoni House of Rome, which itself furnished cardinals and a candidate for the papacy in the next generation. Apparently their operations went as far as central France, and we know they had contact with the Mohammedan world.

Roman financial houses flourished long, but other towns had such houses too, for example, the bankers in what is now a small town full of beautiful art objects, Piacenza, to the north of Genoa. In the middle eleven hundreds these financed a whole crusading foray by the Genoese into Mohammedan Spain. It took Genoa a decade of austerity to pay off the losses. Men of Piacenza and of Siena occupied a leading place in the banking business of the eleven to twelve hundreds, with ten or fifteen major houses in Piacenza and another couple of dozen in Siena. But every Italian city had such houses.

Genoa calls for a curious amount of special attention. It was always an important banking center and has remained so until the present day. Until the time of the French Revolution, Genoa was the bankers' bank for western Europe, a role which was overlooked by students until quite recently. A great deal of research and writing has been done about the German and Dutch bankers of the fifteen and sixteen hundreds, or the Geneva Swiss still later, but we find that they themselves relied on Genoese help. Until modern times Genoa was, in a very quiet way, a center where the largest deals were swung, while lesser deals were handled in other towns.

The development of a trade in all the other things was paralleled by the development of buying and selling government securities. As early as the middle eleven hundreds there was anticipation of future incomes by government entities, to whom borrowing today and promising to pay with later revenues was very tempting. They were especially drawn into this because of the pressure to win wars. It did a lord no good to operate on his day-to-day income, going along in a quiet unaggressive way, if an enemy lord had decided to borrow heavily on his income for the next ten years in order to build up a large army with which he could at a blow take away the holdings of the careful lord. The result would be that the enemy lord could then pay off his debts with the looted money of the careful lord, who in turn would have nothing left. This actually happened in the Middle Ages. Governments which anticipated by borrowing and going into the red won wars. This was very risky, for it was possible to borrow and not win. A lord might borrow ahead for his own lifetime and that of his sons and grandsons, only to be beaten or stalemated by an enemy who had gone equally into debt.

Bankers who lent money came at times to have more and more of a particular government's promises to pay in their possession. This opened other ways for the finance men to profit, for such government promises commonly arranged for the banker to collect a given tax or income for a certain length of time. In such an arrangement a banker could lend one hundred thousand florins and obtain the right to collect a specified toll or tax yielding annually ten thousand florins over a period of twenty years. During the first ten years he would regain his capital; after that it could be profit—if all went well.

Something more could be done with government securities. The first person (or persons) who bought the promises could form a corporation for the collection of the supporting tax, and divide risks as well as profits. With good luck and good management he could create a market for his company's securities, so that everybody could buy and sell these shares in the collection of such and such a debt. Soon it became possible for a person to buy into a tax-farming company and then to sell back out of the company, all in a few days or months, or else to hold the securities permanently. By the late twelve and early thirteen hundreds cities in Italy began to set up central government-controlled administrations for all their debts, dividing the debts into shares which had begun to be more and more like our bonds. So we find there were government "bonds" on the market, and a market price for bonds which would fluctuate depending on luck, the war situation, and money rates in trade. With the development of the government "bond," which in turn was the main item of security held by the banks, there was of course a still greater increase in the amount of paper which was nearly as good as money, and which could begin to be used as capital. By the early thirteen hundreds, in the more advanced Italian cities there was, practically speaking, a regulated government-controlled public debt administration handling these "bonds," paying fixed interest regularly and managing the market for such securities. Bankers' reserves, trust funds, and rich men's final reserves were invested in them.

We should note that north of the Alps, in France and England and other countries, there was not anything like such an early development of "government securities" and of borrowing. Instead, in northern countries loans were treated practically as private personal loans to the kings involved. And they were extremely risky. They were not divided into shares with a market value and so on, as in Italy.

Then disaster struck. In the early thirteen hundreds the great Florentine banking houses found themselves heavily loaded with the promises of kings who were unable or unwilling to pay their debts. One such king was the French ruler of southern Italy, the Angevin king of Naples-Sicily. Another was the king of England. These, and a series of lesser defaulters, all combined to break the great Florentine banking houses, which began to go down like a house of cards in the 1320's and 1330's. Their difficulties were compounded by a very serious spread of famine across northern Europe, and by heavy burdens growing out of Florence's own wars.

In addition there were several bad epidemics. But worst of all, an experiment was made in the Crimea in bacteriological warfare. A Mongol-Tartar khanlet threw the corpses of persons who had died of the plague into a beleaguered city. Refugees from the plague there fled West and the plague took hold and spread everywhere, to become known as the Black Death. After 1347 and 1348 the great Black Death began to sweep across all of Europe. We do not know today just what this disease was, and some think it was actually two different diseases running riot simultaneously, but it swept across Europe, in some places killing perhaps half of the entire population in just a few weeks. Several districts escaped, but on the whole it spread everywhere from Constantinople to Iceland, and from the Arctic Sea down to Sicily. (It spread even to such places as China, Persia, and North Africa, but we are chiefly concerned with Europe.)

Bank failures, famine, and then the Black Death on top of them all, stopped the population from growing and ended the great era of boom prosperity which had been spreading across Europe, dominating its economy since the nine hundreds. These macabre conditions obtained until well into the fourteen hundreds, when recovery began.

The Towns as Business Units

We can now turn to the way in which merchants organized themselves inside their communities or groups for the purpose of carrying on the trade described above.

The core of any merchant's activities was his family or house. But around the family there were other entities to help, such as the town in which the merchant had his citizenship, the company of other merchants with whom he did business, and, finally, the nation. But the nation as an instrument for the helping of its merchants to do business was rather slow in becoming important.

Taking the family for granted, we will start with the town itself. At first the town was the most important unit in trade regulation everywhere. In a very real sense, a town which was involved in trade was like a modern corporation—like a General Motors or any other large business. There were several reasons why that was so. The whole town prospered or the whole town failed, more or less as a unit. Individuals inside the town might thrive, and others fail, but the entire town could be involved in such disasters as war, or being surpassed by rivals in obtaining special advantages or markets, and so on. Outsiders looked on the residents of towns as we nowadays look on the students of a large university—as a unit. There was a rivalry between towns, and everybody in a given town had a chance to prosper if a rival town could be done in and its trade taken over.

This in part explains the very great bitterness of the wars between Italian cities. City patriots did fight just for the fun of it. But they also fought for business.

It is to be emphasized that the town was also one of the most important units for the organization of men who wished to trade away from home, as well as for those who of course wished to trade within their own walls. The responsibility of all the merchants of a town for one another, anywhere away from home, was simply part of international law. Reprisals against one for the act of another were taken for granted. For example, if a man from Arras sold shoddy cloth or misbehaved, and got away without being apprehended, then his victim would take action against any other Arras merchant he could find. As a result, men of a town policed each other, not for the love of policing, but to keep themselves from getting into trouble because a fellow townsman had done something wrong. Inside the town's own walls there were regulations for disputes and officials charged with taking care of these disputes among the men in the town, and also taking care of reprisals, in order to catch up with the local townsman who had brought trouble to his fellow townsmen elsewhere by his behavior.

The town was likely, as time went on, either to become absorbed within one of the larger kingdoms or to become itself more like one of the national states of today than like a town of today. When it came to dealing with outside people, the towns in England, France, Spain, and most of the other countries did not become so powerful that they could operate without the over-government and protection of the king. Each was part of a royal government, and inside that kingdom there would be many towns with the king acting as referee and controller of the relations between one town and another. With other towns outside his kingdom the king dealt king to king, making treaties which would give all his townsmen privileges or whatever they needed in order to trade with the towns of the other individual kingdoms. Towns never came to operate independently, for the royal government was the final authority in handling not only trade within but also trade with all other kingdoms or all other states.

This meant that the royal governments had to organize themselves in such a way as to control exports, imports, merchant law, and so on, while they also extended themselves to make the trade as profitable as possible so as to strengthen themselves. At this time their theory was that protectionist measures which would make a given kingdom richer and another poorer were to their advantage, so that the king of England would concede bonuses and privileges to his merchants which were designed to give them advantages over the French and others. A king's court system had to include a place for merchant law, and in England the Law Merchant was taken under the royal wing and made a part of the whole English law system.

In addition, of course, any king wanted to make himself as rich as possible from this trade. As a result, a large part of trade regulation consisted of taxes, customs, and fees which the king could skim off for his own use out of the flow of export and import trade. Therefore, that particular part of the general organization was directly under the king. All of this caused dissension, argument, and debate on taxation matters which, in most of the countries in the course of the twelve hundreds, and in most of the countries where the king was strong, forced the royal government in one way or another to admit the merchants into governmental bodies.

In England the deliberative body which was ultimately to become the statute-making body was, of course, the Parliament. It was the regulation and organization of trade which drew the merchants into the house of communes—now known as the House of Commons—which developed in the course of the twelve hundreds within the Parliament already there. In France and other countries this introduction of the town class into the parliaments came at about the same time and was also tied up with regulating, organizing, and taxing of trade. (However, few other townsmen came to have as much to say as those of England.) The communes began to have a voice in obtaining for themselves as traders advantages against other classes in the society and against other towns outside the kingdom, and so on.

But in Germany and Italy the process was very different. In Italy during the ten and eleven hundreds, in Germany during the twelve hundreds, the central government rather rapidly lost its hold. By the middle and late eleven hundreds the Holy Roman Emperors, after a series of military attempts to govern Italy, lost all direct control over its cities. Nominally these stayed within the Holy Roman Empire, but actually from about 1190 on the stronger Italian cities had practically all the powers that we call sovereign—the power to coin money, to tax themselves, to make war with one another, and so on. In other words, small as they were, they became miniature nations within themselves, or very much like modern independent nation states. In the twelve hundreds much the same thing happened in Germany, although not to the same degree. In Germany the great feudal lords remained strong whereas in northern and central Italy most of them were swallowed up by the towns.

In northern and central Italy the class which earliest dominated the politics in any town was that of well-to-do merchants who also, we have seen, had country estates, who bore arms, and who thought of themselves as noble. These leading citizens in the practically independent towns not only had fought off the Holy Roman Emperors and achieved independence, but had begun to fight each other, town against town, faction against faction, the moment they had their independence. In the process weaker towns kept being swallowed up by stronger towns.

By about thirteen hundred a dozen or so really strong towns were left. The others had become satellites around the more successful towns. The town city of Milan was becoming a duchy containing a whole group of cities which Milan had swallowed. These cities had no international trade, for Milan blocked them from trade with the outside world, keeping it all for the Milanese merchants. Genoa had taken most of the coast of Liguria. Venice was just beginning to build a state on the mainland. And so it went. These were not national states, for they were all Italian, nor were they anything like so big as the leading modern states or such then-existing kingdoms as Castile, France, or England.

But they were precociously well organized. Italian leadership in political organization was pronounced in this period. Compared to other political entities, Italy's city-states were well governed and tightly organized, and their leaders were primarily interested in promoting their trade in order either to acquire enough wealth to beat their neighbors in war or to choke off their neighbors by the use of protectionist and other trade policies.

As a result of all this, well before the Middle Ages were over and even before thirteen hundred, we find that the organizational basis for trade was on a national basis in such kingdoms as stayed strong or, in Italy and Germany, on the basis of the near-national city-states existing there. The drift was well away from the towns alone as a basis for organization of trade, toward direction by the rulers of larger states.

Companies and Trading Guilds

To return to the merchant group itself, by twelve hundred the Italians had greatly developed the law and practice of business partnerships. Partnerships between two or three or four men, and even larger partnerships in which shares were handled, had come into existence by twelve hundred and went on spreading, especially partnerships for the handling of public-debt operations and ship owners' business.

In addition to these companies other organizations were being established. These were groups which had been given (or had assumed) special monopoly over all the trade of a given sort. In Genoa the city came to regulate all the trade with the Black Sea, or all the trade with Flanders. Merchants joined or were admitted to what resembled clubs (for applicants could be blackballed) which operated under special charters. Men and their partnerships operated inside their club self-sufficiently in all their buying and selling, much as is done on our stock exchanges today. An individual could go broke or could make a fortune without in any way affecting the club. But he had to operate according to the club's charter and bylaws, he took part in voting for its officers, and participated in its frolics and fines. This was very like the specially chartered guilds to which we shall return a little later.

Among companies which were regulated under the terms of charter and bylaws, the English Merchants of the Staple were famous, although there were similar groups in other countries. Staplers were those merchants involved in exporting wool from England through one or more staples. A staple town was the town in which wool had to be bought and sold, under close supervision. Sometimes it was a town in England, sometimes it was Calais across the Strait on the Continent, sometimes it was elsewhere—wherever the king said it should be, usually after talking with his merchants in Parliament.

Later came the Merchant Adventurers of England and other groups in other kingdoms. The Adventurers were merchants who, in the thirteen, fourteen, and fifteen hundreds sold abroad, not raw wool, for that export had begun to fade out, but manufactured English cloth. This product had begun to rise fast as an export for England in the thirteen and fourteen hundreds. The Merchant Adventurers continued as an organization until the nineteenth century, but were not very important after about 1600, the days of Queen Elizabeth.

In chronology the last of the companies in England to develop (but they had had them in Italy long before) were the joint stock companies in which everybody put in money at a fixed subscription rate, five pounds' worth, a hundred pounds' worth, taking up one or twenty shares if par for each stock was at five. These men could no longer trade as they pleased as could (or can) the members of a club; there was a director who took all the stock of assets under his direction as a general manager, and who bought and sold, the over-all profit, when there was one, being divided up by him and the other directors at annual and other meetings. Dividends were declared; this is the sort of company we are nowadays most familiar with.

These companies were to be very important in the period of overseas expansion and exploration, and in the development of European commerce in the fifteen, sixteen, and seventeen hundreds (we shall return to them in a later chapter); they were much older than the period of the great development of European activity overseas.

Guilds, too, were clubs. Fraternal and such features of the guilds were strong in most cases when they first appeared. Economic interests were always strong, to be sure, and were dominant in the later Middle Ages. We do not think of the shareholders of General Motors as caring much of anything about each other or taking much trouble when one of the fellow shareholders dies and needs an expensive funeral, but the members of a guild thought a fellow member should receive such attention.

The oldest guild records we have show that by the time those very records came into existence guilds were already functioning; we deduce that guilds already existed in the late nine and early ten hundreds.

Among the guilds with an economic slant, the earliest of which we have record were those with interests in trade away from the home town of the members, the so-called merchant guilds.

Merchant guilds under various names existed all across Europe. In England they were the organizations for trade away from home which were to be found in every town of any importance. In Germany and the Low Countries one of the names for guild was "hansa," and the hansa was the organization, in any town, of men who traded far away. In Flanders and the north of Germany, along the estuaries of the North and Baltic seas, the various hansas were, in the ten and eleven hundreds, becoming primarily interested in the trade from one city in a neighborhood with another, and a general understanding between the hansas of the north came to take charge of all trade—such as all of the trade of the hansa merchants between London and Flanders on the one side and Novgorod on the other, between Bergen in the north in Norway and Bohemia to the south.

It was here that a league of trading guilds grew into what modern historians call the Hanseatic League. It took final form in the thirteen hundreds, toward the end of the period to which we are giving special attention here. But it had been growing up ever since the nine hundreds. The Hanseatic League was an uncommon sort of League of leagues, sustaining reciprocal rights and privileges throughout its trading area. Nothing like it developed in the Mediterranean area. In Italy the cities engaged in distant trade always preferred to fight, and any truce they made was just a sort of settlement between fights. In the north in Germany there was practically no fighting of city with city, and instead this mutually profitable league organization was worked out.

Manfactures

Manufacture was the activity which in the course of our period came to provide a good part of the material which the merchants could sell abroad, from one region to another in Europe itself, and from Europe to the outside world. As Europe's manufactures grew in quantity and quality, the number of items manufactured for export also grew, and Europeans were able to trade more and more profitably with the people of Asia or the people of the Mohammedan and Greek worlds, their neighbors to the southeast and south.

The manufactures of Europe tended, as manufactures do today in the United States or anywhere else, to localize, with a given product more important in one area and less so in another. Just as in American history the automobile industry has come to center heavily on the Detroit-Flint area in the last fifty years, so manufacture of pots and pans in northern Europe tended to settle down in one town in Belgium named Dinant, and so on.

The tendency for one area to draw ahead of others is marked in the whole history of manufacturing; within limits its advantages tend to be cumulative. In a particular area either a special raw material or some special advantage from the point of view of distribution may exist before anything starts, but the development of a population with the necessary skill in manufacture and skill in the management of manufacture is absolutely necessary before such advantages can be exploited. Just a concentration of high-grade mechanics around Detroit would not have made the Ford organization possible. But once a given area has a concentration of skills, both craft and managerial, then its development tends to give that area greater and greater leadership for at least a long stretch of time after the first advantage has been acquired. Areas which have fallen behind in competition tend to lose their workmen and their skills to an area where things are going swimmingly. For a while at least other areas will lose in comparison with a district which has gotten a good head start.

Turning to northern Europe's manufacture during the nine, ten, and eleven hundreds, we find that one area had an advantage over the others very early, and that it steadily maintained that advantage. This was Flanders and its neighborhood.

Flanders is a quite small district along the English Channel. A good part of it was swamp land; during the Middle Ages a fair share of what is land today was under tidewater. Other counties and duchies nearby followed Flanders chronologically in their rise in the world of manufacturing. By the middle of the ten hundreds in Flanders there was already the beginning of a concentration of men who could make good cloth and of others who knew how to organize production and distribution.

From about 1000 and a little after we have evidence which shows us the development in Flanders of a manufacturing population. There are documents showing that that area imported wool and food from England during the early ten hundreds, which again is evidence of a manufacturing area, for Flanders and some of the countries near at hand were fairly rich agriculturally and would not have had to import bacon, lard, and butter unless the local food supplies were already insufficient. Then, by the early eleven hundreds, we find documents in Italy showing that Flemish merchants were there selling textiles, and that their line of goods was already a fairly extensive one; they had cloths for sale that were of different qualities and measurements. Altogether we have evidence that there was early a vigorous manufacture of textiles in Flanders and its neighborhood.

We also find that in the course of the early eleven hundreds the manufacturing towns were asking for practically complete local internal government from their lord, the count of Flanders, who was a nearly sovereign independent ruler, although technically he was a vassal of the king of France. In other words, self-government was developing before eleven hundred in this same area; it was not the same fully independent self-government for which the Italian cities were striving, but a good local autonomy with control over internal affairs. The count of Flanders gave charters to Arras, Saint-Omer, Ghent, Ypres, and other towns.

Also, well before twelve hundred, we find that at the fairs of Champagne a whole key section of each fair's time table was devoted to the selling of northern cloth, above all to Italians. And the cloths are mentioned by name in the documents; they were predominantly cloths manufactured in Flanders.

There were other manufactures in the region in addition to that of cloth. Not politically in it, but near Flanders, was the town of Dinant, mentioned just above, where traders could easily bring in copper and other metals from the German mines. Here is a case where special know-how definitely played a part, for many other good trading towns could have developed a pots and pans industry, but Dinant did it. Scores of little craft shops existed in the town, where the masters with their apprentices and journeymen made pots, pans, and kettles—*dinanderie*. (In the United States men used to speak of "Connecticut notions," meaning the kind of things Connecticut Yankees brought around on their carts and sold to housewives in New York and Ohio.) There were other products to which the Flemish towns gave their names. In addition to the general manufacture of cloth at Ghent there was also the manufacture of "hand-shoes" or mittens, known as *ghentlets* or gauntlets (which we have already mentioned). From Cambrai came *cambric*—the list of specialties developed in one town and another is a long one.

In Italy at about the same time another district was growing up which knew intense activity. The Lombard Plain, and the rolling country south of the Apennines toward Rome, the two areas known as Lombardy and Tuscany, began to grow almost simultaneously, with quite a number of good-sized towns rising—and fighting one another.

The most vigorous of all these towns was the city which first pulled ahead in making iron goods, which of course above all else meant the munitions industry. This was Milan. Brescia and some other towns also competed, the way Toledo and Cleveland compete with Detroit in automobile manufacture, but it was Milan which went far ahead. By the late eleven hundreds it was a kind of general arsenal town, manufacturing in large quantities for the over-all market such things as spear heads, arrow heads, horseshoes and horseshoe nails—all the equipment needed for fighting. They manufactured nails by the barrel, crossbow bolts by the keg, and so on. They then put them into the general channels of trade. In fighting the Holy Roman Emperors Milan could serve as the arsenal of Italian rebellion. It was Milan's wealth plus the line of goods the Milanese produced which in part enabled the Milanese armies to whip the German armies so thoroughly in the eleven hundreds.

Glassworking came to settle in Venice; how early we are not sure, but it was a great center for the specialty by the later Middle Ages. Venice was so thoroughly dedicated to the making of glass that its glassmakers were treated almost as the Strasburgers treat their forced-fed geese in the making of *foie gras*. The glassworkers were given the very best sort of treatment, life was made enjoyable on the glassmakers' island of Murano which is not far from the Rialto, but they were kept rather like birds in a gilded cage, for it was a matter of death for a glassmaker to leave Venice (if the Venetians could catch him) or to betray any of his glassmaking secrets to foreigners.

There were other towns which had specialties. Lucca, a beautiful little town rather near Florence, was already specializing heavily in the trade in silk by the late eleven hundreds, and soon after that began to manufacture silk. First the Italians had traded in silk from China, Syria, and the Byzantine Empire; then they imported silk worms, plantations of mulberries were made, and Italy began to be what it still is, a silk-producing country.

There were also many towns in Italy which centered on either the making of good cloth or on the remaking or fancy finishing of northern cloth. This latter was an additional reason for the development of the very lively trade between Flanders and Italy, first via the fairs of Champagne and then by sea. The Italians with their business connections across the Mediterranean discovered that the cloths made in England and Flanders were not always quite what the market wanted in Egypt and Asia Minor. So the Italians began to develop a cloth-refinishing industry, above all in the city of Florence. While some other towns also went into this work, in the city of Florence in the later twelve and thirteen hundreds literally tens of thousands were employed in the refinishing of northern cloths, giving them special qualities as to surface and color and so forth, for export elsewhere.

Political troubles and famines in Flanders during the thirteen hundreds sent floods of northern workers down to Italy (some northern workers had migrated there even in the middle twelve hundreds). With them they carried textile know-how, especially to Florence, where not only the refinishing industry was developed but also a cloth weaving manufacture of great importance. Milan, Genoa, and Venice then not only traded in northern cloth but also produced lines of their own, sometimes in direct imitation of leading northern cloths.

Two other areas developed as important manufacturing districts later than either Flanders or Italy. South Germany and the Rhineland did not assume much importance until the later fourteen hundreds and into the fifteen hundreds. The south and east of England were always of some importance but did not reach a period of greatest expansion until after 1500.

Meanwhile, in many parts of Europe special products of a given neighborhood stimulated local finishing industries. For example, at Bourdeaux in France everything connected with the raising, storing, and shipping of wine became highly developed. Thus, at Bordeaux there was to be found not only wine-growing work, but also a cooperage industry for making the kegs needed for its storage and shipping. Likewise, smelting and metalworking industries were to be found near iron mines, and so on.

The Craft Guilds

With the development of manufacture which was going on throughout this period, with never a settled situation at any time, but always change, there was also going on the development of two different sorts of organizations intimately connected with manufacturing.

One of these was the founding and elaboration of organizations within the groups of people making the actual articles. The other development was the creation of mechanisms within the groups of people handling production—the capitalist, the investor, the merchant-director of making and selling.

Each nation in Europe had its name or names for organizations of persons for coöperation—for work, social activities, and so on. In England they were called guilds or misteries—the latter name coming from the French name for such organizations. So in France they were *mestiers* or *métiers*, in Germany *zunfte* or *hansa;* in Italy they were arts or the *arti*. In Latin (for they needed a Latin word too for everything they had, since they wrote so much in Latin) these groups were called *universitates. Universitas* translates approximately as "a many" or "the totality." It was possible to speak of the *universitas* of Englishmen, the *universitas* of Christians, the *universitas* of cobblers in a town, or the *universitas* of students and masters and professors of Paris (the only use for the word *universitas* which has lasted on to the present day). The guilds or hansas of men trading with centers at a distance from the home town have already been noticed.

Most guilds were fairly small organizations of the fairly small total number of persons who were interested in conducting the same sort of business in a single town. A dozen members of a given craft would be all there were in many towns. In most parts of Europe the majority of guilds of this trade or craft sort were small clubby organizations. As a matter of fact, the club aspect was there from the start, and was always significant in the guilds, which were never simply organizations for handling economic interests, however important this aspect of their activities became as time went on.

The very earliest records we have of guilds show them to have been at the start primarily a mixture of religious, fraternal, and public service organizations and, to judge by our first information, even without special trading or manufacturing interest; and they were never to lose their aspect as fraternal and religious-social organizations. Indeed guilds existed everywhere solely for the purpose of promoting literature and good fellowship; the members composed poetry and songs, recited and sang to one another at meetings, drank a good deal, and went home. Guilds also existed for mutual aid in time of trouble, being in effect coöperative insurance organizations, the members paying dues and assessments and the widows and orphans and the sick being cared for out of the treasury. They were also burying societies.

There were guilds for every sort of public, social, and human interest and many guilds never developed any economic interests whatsoever. Actually, most guilds combined several or all the aspects here mentioned. The word guild and the other terms used for it in other countries were general words, being more or less equivalent to what we in America call "organizations." And of course we have organizations for all sorts of purposes, including political, social, and religious ones, as well as ones for business.

The guilds were building up fast during the eleven and twelve hundreds in western Europe, but we are not sure to what degree they were new and to what degree they were a revival of old Roman institutions or were borrowings from Byzantine and Islamic institutions.

We know that craftsmen in the later Roman Empire were organized in *collegia,* or "colleges"—that word having as its original meaning "a group of those associated for some purpose," religious or governmental or what not. Some evidence exists to prove that these *collegia* continued in Italy through the six, seven, and eight hundreds. Scholars guess—but it can be no more than a good guess—that some of the guilds in Rome, Naples, and other towns were such surviving colleges when the records begin to indicate their existence once more. Another related scholarly hypothesis is that colleges continued in the Byzantine Empire and in those towns in Italy which were connected with the Byzantine Empire. Venice and Naples, for example, were closely tied to the Byzantine Empire until the ten hundreds, and the guess has been made that Byzantium was able to influence Italian institutions of this sort.

Still, guilds were quite clearly a new thing in most parts of Europe in the nine or ten or eleven hundreds, whatever ties there may have been on the part of some areas with ancient Rome or Byzantium. Certainly they were new in the way they functioned, in their numbers, and in their importance.

Guilds never grew up all by themselves with no relation to the community in which the guildsmen lived. The guild was a unit within a town or an area, and should always be regarded that way. But as is true of some units within our own society, in some places and times guilds tended to dominate; in most others the community dominated the guilds.

We cannot generalize and say that guilds created a community, or vice versa. In some towns, for example in Florence in Italy in the thirteen hundreds, or in the great Belgian town of Liège in the thirteen and fourteen hundreds, the guilds swallowed up the whole government for stretches of time. In such a situation a man, if he wished to make a way for himself in politics, had to be a member of a guild. An example of this is the great poet Dante who was of noble ancestry and had no particular skill as a craftsman, yet with his family sought membership in a guild in Florence in order to obtain citizenship.

In some other towns, guilds were never of such importance, having been started very late or never having reached an important development. An example for this is to be found in Genoa, which became a large and powerful city with enormous fleets and important manufactures. There came to be guilds in Genoa, but they came in rather late, in the twelve hundreds, and were never highly significant. There were great differences from town to town, even between towns which were quite near one another.

During the nine, ten, and eleven hundreds there was very little restriction on craft guild membership, very little control over the guilds, and they tended on the whole to be unimportant in city government. In later time entrance requirements tended to become tighter and tighter and, as guilds grew stronger, so their importance increased. Within most communities the government dominated the guilds, yet the guilds collectively were a big factor in the community's government. Such was the case in London, where the guilds were not the government, which was a chartered corporation under the king with its own aldermen, mayor, and councilmen; yet the organized guilds in London became strong enough to have a great deal to say about what the aldermen, mayor, and council did.

There were exceptions to all the rules about the organization of guilds, but the internal organization of a typical guild rested above all on the masters who had been admitted to full voting membership. In the typical guild a master was a man of mature years, usually in his late twenties or older, who had an establishment in which a given process of manufacture was carried on, or a given product was bought and sold—for example, fish. The master in the typical guild owned his business outright. He might own or he might rent his establishment, which could be a little shop with a frontage of five or ten feet on the street, with rooms in back and upstairs for the storage of goods and with living quarters for himself and his dependents. He might own much of his own machinery and tools, which would be a considerable investment, or he might rent them. His greatest asset lay in his knowledge and skill in the making or the handling of his special line of goods, which had been acquired during his years of apprenticeship and work as a journeyman.

A journeyman was a trained worker who, when he became well-to-do enough and had married the boss's daughter or taken some such important step, could present a masterpiece to the guild to which he already belonged and be accepted into the inner circle as a master. Until he accomplished this he was just a young man working for daily wages: that is what the word "journeyman" meant. The French word for the passage of a day is a *journée*, and a man who worked for daily wages was a journeyman. (The other idea of a journey, a trip, came from the sensible process of reckoning trips across country by the number of days they took.) Although the journeyman was skilled, he was still in the process of learning, and he often learned by working under different masters in his home town and in other towns. Characteristic of the career of journeymen in most trades was what the Germans called the "wander years"—the years of going from town to town and hiring out to masters in different places. Since most masters liked to keep their trade secrets, this was a way in which to pick up different special techniques. In theory the journeyman was going to be a master when he was old and skilled enough and well enough off to settle down.

However, in some industries there came to be crowds of journeymen who never could become masters. The lifelong journeyman became an important factor in many of the guilds, notably in those that were manufacturing for the export market in the largest towns. In some of these the journeymen were permitted to form clubs of their own. In London, for example, there were some junior organizations of journeymen that were under the strict control of the masters of the respective guilds to which these journeymen belonged. In a few towns the journeymen seized the government, at least for a short time, and came the closest to establishing labor governments of anything to be found during the Middle Ages. The journeyman was a skilled working man who had no shop of his own, his nearest counterpart being the skilled employee of our modern labor force.

The apprentice was a boy or girl of about late grammar-school or high-school age (according to our educational system of today) who had been set to work to learn a given craft or business by a contract between his parents or guardians and a master, with a set number of years to work included in the contract. Later, in England, it came to be common to consider an apprenticeship a matter of seven years' work, but there were guilds which required only three or four years of such work, while there were others which required ten to twelve years of work before the apprenticeship had been completed. There were some guilds in which the parents paid a master a large sum of money in order to have their son started on a very valuable craft, such as that of banker. There were other guilds in which a master actually hired, at very low wages, a varlet to work around the place, ending up by giving the youth a small fee, tools, and board and room for the two to six or seven years of apprenticeship. There was no set pattern, although in most of the crafts the normal apprenticeship was for seven years, with bed and board as well as a small pittance being paid.

The apprentice was in effect a learner or pupil, with unimportant things to do in the craft at first; as time went on he was given more and more materials to work on under the eyes of a journeyman or of the master of the establishment. He was also in effect a young boy being brought up in a foster family, and was just as much a hewer of wood and drawer of water and market-basket carrier for the mistress as any child who was being brought up in his own home. The master whipped him when he was bad— there was usually a rule that the boy could not be whipped with anything larger around than the master's thumb, which allowed for considerable variation in the severity of punishment, depending as it did on the size of the master. There was another rule that the boy should not be whipped or treated worse than the neighbors thought decent. The contract often read that in case of trouble between the boy's own parents and the master over the treatment of the boy, a kind of neighborhood jury would settle the matter as to respectability or disgrace. The boy was learning the craft, and that learning was mainly what he got out of it.

The craft guild was made up of from a handful to hundreds of masters, and each master had one to four or five journeymen and a limited number of apprentices, depending on the rules of the guild and on how many he could afford.

Our present-day universities are the only surviving relic of the medieval guild system, with our students going through the series of gradations of learning which were required by the guilds. In the Middle Ages the words "bachelor" and "journeyman" meant exactly the same thing: a young man who was working and was not married. Ultimately the word journeyman came to apply to young men from the point of view of their guild position, while in English the word bachelor came to mean only "not married." (Modern students are in the position of being apprentices working to become bachelors or journeymen. On receiving their bachelor degree they can then go out and teach elementary subjects. But if a journeyman, or bachelor of arts, continues to study, he may then become a member of the guild and be made a master, and as a master of arts can teach even more complicated subjects. And added to these old names we have the additional degree, the doctorate.)

What happened to the guilds in the course of the later Middle Ages and in modern times is of considerable interest. The earlier guilds were usually easy to get into, and exercised light or moderate controls over the conduct of their members and the business in their towns. Entry into a mastership was not expensive, fees were not high or were not even required. Generally any citizen could be admitted if he had the necessary skill, and the examinations looked mostly toward skill in the craft and that was all, with presentation of a masterpiece almost the only thing called for. In general there was little setting of prices, little control over the number admitted, little control of working hours, wages, and so on.

During the twelve and thirteen hundreds there was, broadly speaking, a steady unbroken development everywhere of ever-tightening controls, as well as a great ramification of these controls. This went on until, in the fifteen, sixteen, and seventeen hundreds, the tightness of the guild controls became most exaggerated.

Here we have come out of the Middle Ages entirely, into the days of George Washington and the steam engine, but one hears even well-informed economists as well as others speak of the medieval restrictions and medieval tightness of controls of guilds. The tightness of control which became unbearable in the guilds was the tightness of the sixteen and seventeen hundreds—in modern times.

It should also be mentioned that there was a vast difference between those centuries when the controls were beginning to tighten, and the earlier ones, during which the Crusades began and guild controls were either absent or light. The word medieval is not broad enough, really, to cover these two unlike periods.

What were the controls which became tighter and tighter as time went on? First of all, the guilds began to try hard to have an utter monopoly on the buying, selling, and processing of whatever commodities they specialized in. Each tried, by its regulations, to push its own prices as high as possible, while in turn it tried to force other guilds and workers to take as low prices as possible. Each guild tried hard to restrict entry, making it hereditary, so that an applicant had to have a father or an uncle with a guild right, or else had to marry someone who did. Each guild pushed entrance fees higher and higher, but waived the high price for a son or a nephew or a son-in-law, so that outsiders found entry practically precluded. Aptitude and skill in the craft were no longer required. The masterpiece was examined perfunctorily or not even demanded of the "insiders," while others had their masterpieces examined so carefully that acceptance was impossible. This sort of thing became more and more exaggerated as the world moved on out of the Middle Ages and into modern times (and, as popular discontents seethed up to the eve of the French Revolution, guild officials did petition for change—they wanted to tighten controls still more!).

It has been emphasized that the guilds had religious, fraternal, and similar aspects. There were always organized connections between the guilds and the church and charities connected with church work. Just as the church had become involved with feudalism, with bishops becoming feudal princes and landed lords, so the church became involved with the guild system. This too was never planned, but grew by natural evolution; guildsmen were also good Roman Catholics and interested in the concerns of their church.

When we envision the way in which medieval cities were built up, we can see that the members of a guild normally lived as intimate neighbors, for the shops which sold a given service or commodity were almost always concentrated in one street or neighborhood or square. In those days a shopper who wanted silver went to the silversmiths' street, and all the silversmiths were there together; if he wanted shoes he went to the cobblers' alley; and so on. As a result, all the members of a given guild were parishioners of the same parish church, and that church might well have several different guilds, perhaps a half dozen or so, within its parish if it were located in a neighborhood where guilds were concentrated.

Of course this meant, in turn, that parish work could be financed by arrangements with the guilds in the parish; different guilds were sure to take over the responsibility for care of the church altar, of some special chapel, or of some other aspect of church work. There might be several different chapels in a given parish church, each dedicated to a saint who was the patron of the guild which supported the chapel. As a result, a given guild would organize its worship around that chapel, carrying provision for its maintenance in the guild budget and supporting a junior cleric or perhaps a full priest for their chapel. Some parish churches had several different clerics, all of them drawing their pay from the several different guilds which supported them in the parish church.

Guild members found it desirable to know how to read and write. They did not have to be able to read Aristotle in Latin or Greek, but they had to be able to keep accounts and to write the notes which were connected with their business. Commonly one or several of the guilds supported a schoolmaster (who could be the same cleric who took care of the guild's altar in the church) to teach their children, thereby furthering the connection between grammar-school teaching and the church.

The guilds were also expected to contribute to the building of the church, its repair, its beautification. A tremendous amount of church building went on in the towns where lively manufacture developed. Every town in northern France or Flanders, for example, which was notable for cloth production by twelve hundred, is the site for a great cathedral or of one or more fine churches—Rheims, Beauvais, Chartres, Ghent, Arras, and so on. The people who paid for the great cathedrals were the residents in a town and the area around, but chiefly the funds came from lay and clerical land owners and from the guild treasuries. At Chartres cathedral a fair part of the expenses were taken care of by the city guilds, and this is recorded in a number of the chapels in beautiful windows for which the guilds hired the decorators; a double sort of recognition is to be found in the scenes and symbols of many windows honoring both the Christian church and the guild.

The work of the guilds extended also into public spectacles and entertainments. This started above all with religious spectacles. What we might call charades, showing such things as Jonah in the mouth of the whale (which would be to the taste of the fishmongers), were put on by the members of that guild on holy days. These religious spectacles would be worked out so that the actors would do some particular thing and the spectators would then be supposed to know what it was. The spectacles were done on the porches of a church or on floats dragged through the town. There was as much desire to have fun and to parade around in front of the neighbors in a medieval community as there is in one of ours. But the point here is that the guilds tended to do much the greatest part of all this. As time went by they added more and more of what is called stage business. People on the floats or on the stage began to move around and do things, first in pantomime and then with spoken words. After a while authors began to write scripts and definitely work for laughs. Little dramas were produced which were often funny, and were sometimes even very lowbrow despite the religious auspices; the guilds in effect were pioneering in the development of the European stage.

The guilds also hired painters to paint pictures, just as they hired glass-workers to put glass in churches. Also, all along the line they were very active in charity work, within their own group primarily, but also in general. Some guilds invested gifts and surpluses and ended up owning enough in income-bearing city real estate or land in the country to become wealthy.

Many guilds lost their endowments in England at the time of the Protestant Reformation, and on the Continent a good part of their assets were lost at the time of the French Revolution, in both cases because of close connections with the Catholic Church.

Management of Production: The Merchant Capitalist

We have considered the organization of the masters and their employees inside the guilds, and now we must turn to the men who organized and managed production, marketing, financing, the finding of raw materials, and so on, for without these men there could have been no export industry.

First we must turn back to the small local buyer, if we are concerned with local business inside a small town, or with the neighborhood business in a big town. In such places people who wanted something made, a pair of shoes, a cloak, a kitchen knife, went to a shop and ordered it to be fashioned. Goods could be taken to a shop to be made up, or both the goods and their making could be purchased in the same place. Such would be the case in the cobbler or tailor shops, for instance.

But there were many guildsmen who sold articles such as butter or salt fish which they had themselves bought from still other persons. They were the retailers who did no processing, but whose skill consisted of knowing their business, knowing how to choose what they wished to sell and how to advise purchasers to buy.

From the point of view of the Middle Ages the man who handled retail goods, whether he worked on them in his shop or not, was a guildmaster at this level, selling over his counter. It was upon this guildmaster that both retailing and manufacturing patterns depended, whether the articles manufactured were for the customer across the counter or for a general export market.

However, in a large industry producing for the export market, in getting the work for workers it was not the guildmaster who purchased the raw materials at their very source. The master would be too busy weaving, let us say, to be able to make a trip from a Flemish manufacturing town over to England to buy a few sacks of wool. Instead, there had to be someone whose function in the whole industry was as a supplier and someone to function as merchandiser of the finished goods. Then the working craftsmen, whether masters or journeymen or apprentices, could keep working at their crafts.

This arrangement for handling procurement of materials and export of finished goods could be tied up with the division of labor in the processing of goods, a division of labor which was found in many other industries, but which was most striking in the case of textiles. This industry will be taken here as an example, although all the metal industries had step-by-step processing also, from the first digging in the mines to the final sale of helmet or pot or pan.

It was possible for a person to shear his own sheep, wash and card the wool, spin it into yarn, then weave it, and so on. He would finish up weeks or months later with a few yards of woolen cloth (as would an American frontiersman) very poorly made, although he would have had to have used relatively expensive machinery, such as a loom, at some points. His end product would have been a bit of poorly dyed, poorly woven, and poorly finished cloth, produced at tremendous relative cost in equipment and labor.

Division of labor, allowing each step to be carried on by men who were especially skilled in doing just that, and who had the expensive equipment but could afford it because they were using it all the time, came to be the principle in the textile industry, and in others, too, where there was an export market.

It was always possible for a person who had a specialty to go to market and buy the goods on which he needed to work. A weaver could go to the market and buy just the sort of yarn he wanted for his bobbins. It was also possible, once he had his cloth rough woven, for him to go to the market to sell it to a fuller who was acquiring materials for his own shop, and so on along.

But far more often it was the merchant capitalist who took care of such things, the man who had brought the wool to town in the first place and who was ultimately to take the finished cloth away. It was he who owned the materials as they moved between one extreme of their production and the other.

The merchant capitalists were well-to-do merchants dealing in spices, leather, and foreign exchange as well as in cloth, alum, dyestuffs, and other manufacturing supplies. They were the men who went to the fairs of Champagne with several dozen bolts of finished cloth and who carried on transactions at the wholesale level, as described earlier. But in their home towns their main interest lay in the production of the bolts of cloth which were to be taken from that town to those fairs; it was their function to run production by local artisans whose contributions were so well divided in the fabricating processes that they had almost no contact with one another. It was the merchant capitalist who saw to it that the materials moved from the spinsters to the weavers to the fullers.

First of all he saw to it that in England a given amount of wool was bought for him at some Cistercian monastery. Often he made payment in advance, sometimes as much as two or three years ahead of time. The monastery might be in need of cash because it was building a beautiful priory church for which it was running deeply into debt, or because King Richard the Lion Hearted had been captured in Germany and was being held for a king's ransom for which the king's chancellor was requiring money from all the monasteries, or because some feudal dues had to be paid. In any case, for some reason or another the monastery might need to sell its wool ahead of time. The merchant capitalist could be regarded either as the financer of the monastery's debt, taking its promise to repay in wool, or as a businessman making sure of his supplies in advance—and incidentally playing the futures in wool.

Once he had obtained the wool, the merchant capitalist had it carried to a port where he had to pay heavy taxes to the king of England for the privilege of exporting it. At the port he placed it on a ship which he and a group of other merchants might either own or have chartered, or on a ship in which another group of merchants had sold him so many of their own places for his wool sacks. The ship carried his shipment to Bruges, and from there the merchant had it transported to his home town.

Here he took the wool to a wool washer, or to several dozen wool washers, who had agreed to cleanse his wool at so much a pound or at so much for the lot. When the washing had been completed, the merchant inspected it, took it back again, and paid off the guildmaster who had done the washing or had had it done. The merchant then took the wool to the carders. From the carders the merchant took the wool home, where spinsters came to the door, each to take a few pounds of carded wool home where she would spin it. When it had been returned to him he would then take the yarn to his weavers—several weavers might be working in connection with him—and days or weeks later he got back his woven piece from each weaver. He paid the weaver off, the weaver having in turn been paying his own journeymen and apprentices inside his own shop. And so the processing went on, through the fulling or walking of the rough-woven goods, through shearing and dyeing.

In each case, in these export industries, the working guildmasters had had the work—the goods and the orders to work on the goods—put out to them by the merchant capitalist. This was the "putting-out system," as it is called, where the capitalist had put out work to the specialists at all the different stages in the manufacturing process.

Entirely finished, the bolt of cloth, still owned by the capitalist, started on a mule's back or in a wagon toward the fairs of Champagne or, after the later twelve hundreds, back to Bruges to be sold there. It reappeared in the channels of trade as a piece of merchandise.

All of this had called for a great deal of expenditure on the part of the capitalist. He had had to pay for the wool over in England, for the king's export license, for all transportation cost, for the carding, washing, spinning, for the weaving, dyeing, fulling, and shearing and then for transport down to Champagne. It was here that he got something back for the first time, after many months of steadily accumulating costs as each bolt of cloth was made. It had been a long way from his first expense to the liquidation of his cloth venture. Yet even here what he collected was not coined money; it was in turn merchandise—spices, for example. These he had to carry home and pass on to England and keep in trade. It is quite clear from this account that the merchant capitalist needed to have a very considerable reserve of resources in the form of credit, money, merchandisable goods.

In actual fact, a merchant capitalist at any moment had wool coming in, work going on, and goods for sale going out, with return merchandise coming in—all moving along simultaneously. He had to be very alert and knowledgeable, as thoroughly trained as any of his craftsmen specialists, and more so. He had to know the likelihoods of wool production in England and the political situation there so he could guess whether future prices were likely to be up or down. He had to know the general risk involved and the transport costs from England to Bruges. He had to have a good idea as to what men to give work to and to whom to give what, and so on. He had to know the markets at Champagne. He had to be a specialist in geography and politics, and markets and money rates, for the whole of western Europe.

It was possible that the merchant capitalist had no more connection with the workers who took care of processing his wool than that which came from making a deal each time he had a job to be done—an individual deal to have that work done and to make a payment for it. In the export industries, such deals were being made all the time. Some of the masters were well enough off so that they did jobs for merchant capitalists just as simple transactions. These masters owned their own small shops, or at least had long-term leases on them, they owned their own tools, they were in a position to make private individual deals, a number of them, in the course of a year. There were men like that at all times.

But a very large proportion of all the master fullers, master weavers, and master dyers were not financially and otherwise well enough off to play an independent role as equals with the merchant capitalists. In the big textile cities and in other towns where other industries went on, in considerable measure the merchant capitalist was the person who financed the people who did the work.

This financing went on in the following way. Let us say a merchant capitalist had some work to be done, and a given weaver had illness, a wife who was spending too much, or something like that, and he wanted to get some cash as well as some immediate work. In such a case quite commonly the capitalist paid in advance, or made a part payment anyway, for the work that was being done. So he figured in his interest charges. He might get a reasonable twenty to twenty-five percent per annum or an unreasonable sixty to one-hundred percent per annum for any advances he made, made deductible by one dodge or another when the work was done. Men fell into the hands of merchant capitalists who were quite as much lending usurers as givers of work.

The merchant capitalists in cities such as Douai, Ghent, Arras, or Ypres owned a very large part of the urban real estate on which stood the tenement buildings in which people such as the weavers and shearers had their rooms. In such a room the weaver and his wife, perhaps a journeyman and one or more apprentices, did their eating, sleeping, and cooking— one room without a glazed window, with no running water nearer than a pump or fountain down the street, and a walk-up of several stories above the street. Of course, not all the working masters lived in such tenements, but a good many of them did. The tenements were owned by rich real estate proprietors, and when one lifts the lid and looks in at such a rich real estate man, he is likely to find one of the merchant capitalists.

He was a giver of work to weavers who lived in his tenements and who might be behind on their rent. Worse than that, some of them, far back when they were young and ambitious at twenty-three or twenty-four, had gotten married without having any resources; such a man might have taken a stake from some merchant capitalist who set him up with a room and loom and materials—and debts. They would still be in debt twenty or thirty years later. The wife might have lost her teeth, but the debt remained, with the poor fellow and his family always one or more months behind on the rent. The merchant who had been keeping them as landlord was the same person from whom they had taken all the work they had ever done. They were not hired by him; they were just tied to him by a debt that never was finished. Furthermore, when he had given them that initial stake—a rented room—he would have given them some of his own weaving equipment, for he would have had quite a little in a courtyard or shed, since he was in the habit of setting young weavers up in business with their equipment in return for understandings which were quite indefinite but enduring, to do his weaving for him. As a result, such people lived in his place, worked on his machinery, were in debt to him for advances, and he was the only merchant capitalist from whom they were in a position to take work. If one of them ever took work from some other merchant capitalist, he lost his equipment, the place where he lived, and risked going to debtors' prison because of his debts. He could not bargain very well; his position was to say the least weak when it came to making deals on his work for the merchant.

The tying of the master weavers and their peers to the merchant capitalists created situations which, generally speaking, are no longer true in the United States.

It should be remembered that master guildsmen who were in this miserable position were still actually the employers of the journeymen who were another notch below them. The masters were not laborers in the sense of laborers in a labor union. The nearest equivalent to the modern craft-union man was the journeyman and the older apprentice. The master weaver or fuller (the boss, we might say) who oppressed the journeyman was the fellow just described as owing such heavy obligations to his landlord.

The merchant capitalist was not the manufacturer with a big factory whom we might know today. He had his resources partly tied up in material, machinery, and housing, but there was no big roof over his working staff, there was no factory; in most industries of the time there was not much in the way of a power system attached to a water wheel or any kind of engine. He could stop business any day, gather together all the things which had been put out, and remain inactive for an indefinite period, using up his assets only slowly.

This sort of development characterized the big industries in the course of the first great medieval boom period. It was town industry. The putting-out, the guilds, the merchant capitalists—all of these were town processes and town persons. In general, this kind of industry survived in European manufacture with astonishing vigor into the eighteen and nineteen hundreds. A good deal of eastern European manufacture was done this way in the early twentieth century. As a matter of fact, this type of industry in the towns, with the putting-out, the guild, with the master pretty definitely subordinate to the capitalist, and so forth, still operates in the case of some processes. A great many persons alive in the United States in the mid-twentieth century have known it at first hand.

On the other hand, the industry inside the towns began to run into rivalry from similarly organized putting-out industry in the country and the villages from the thirteen and fourteen hundreds on. The rise of village or cottage industry simply meant a shift of some, never all, industry. It was especially characteristic of textiles and metals, which migrated in considerable measure from the towns to the villages ten to thirty miles from the towns. Cottage industry, though, never had any guild organization.

Some of the shift of industry to the country came when manufacturing processes began to rely in some part on water power, and there was a movement of industry toward power centers. This was exactly what we think of as so characteristic of the industrial revolution or of modern industry, but it began as early as the later eleven hundreds.

The first of the operations in the textile field to use some mechanical power was the fulling process. Water wheels could keep fulling hammers rising and falling on soft cloth, and they had such machinery by the late eleven hundreds. After that the tendency was to move fulling operations out to places where water was to be found which could turn the wheels, and to have a considerable establishment wherever the wheel was set up. As a result, fulling was the first of any of the manufacturing operations to come to look like later factory processing. By the twelve hundreds, therefore, a kind of an early dawn of the industrial revolution was to be seen when a fairly large fulling shop, with a number of workers, was set in operation at a place where water power was to be found. But this does not mean that we should put the date of the industrial revolution back to the eleven and twelve hundreds.

Of course, once the fulling process began to be carried on in the country, there was a tendency for much of the rest of the cloth processing to move out to where the fulling mills were. So weavers, dyers, and finishers began to move into the country near the fulling mills. Since the mills themselves could be modified to grind grain or tanbark, villages and new towns tended to grow around mill sites. But this did not develop to the extent occurring during the industrial revolution.

Controlled by the merchant capitalists, this shift to the country was given impetus by the rivalry between guilds inside the big older cities, and by the rivalry between all of the craftsmen and the merchant capitalists.

The Upheavals of the Thirteen Hundreds

In the thirteen hundreds there were all sorts of troubles across western Europe. Great famines lasted two and three years, cutting the population down badly; the great Black Death hit in 1348–49, and then came again and again, about once a generation for a number of generations; there was a collapse of international and of local banks such as occurred in the United States in 1932. The population shrank, and the end of the long boom came.

As a result the merchant capitalists had to cut down on the amount of work they gave out, and they tried hard to tie their guildmasters and journeymen to them more tightly. As rich men, they also had the most important positions in city governments; they were the aldermen and the mayors. During this period most of the town constitutions in the north—Flanders, France, and England—and many in the south came to be closed so that only persons whose ancestors had been aldermen had any opportunity to stand for city office. Aldermen chose only the sons and brothers of other aldermen when elections took place; aldermen were the only people allowed to choose. General elections were eschewed.

During those harder times, there came to be great explosions of different parts of the populations against one another. However, a comment should be made: there was not a single one of these explosions or revolutions which was completely due to internal causes. Instead, every one of them was connected with foreign warfare, and was at least supported, if not thought up and organized, by an enemy. The great revolution of the

Flemish workers and masters against the Flemish merchant capitalists was bought and paid for by the king of England; we even know something of how much it cost him. The great explosion of the workers in Florence was partly bought and paid for by *condottieri* and rivals of Florence who were trying to weaken the city. Such revolutions are not likely to occur without something there besides a grievance; the person or force which is indispensable to such affairs is the outside subversive influence with money and a purpose.

Viewed institutionally, these revolutions were in part an attempt of the outs to get in. It did not matter who was out; a rebellious group was usually a coalition of nearly everybody who was out. In these affairs we find what seems a weird thing to us today—the most aristocratic nobles and the lowest gutter sweepers in alliance against the butter and eggs sellers, because both the gutter sweepers and the aristocrats happened at that moment to be out. There was not a nice neat pattern of the lesser against the greater; frequently it was the two extremes against the middle, and in fact that pattern was the most common of all.

It is impossible to miss the fact that these were not purely economic and political revolutions, but were also involved with religion. Inside the Christian faith are certain very strong streaks of feeling and sentiment which are, to say the least, critical of the rich. As a matter of fact one of the few direct quotations of Christ is to the effect that a rich man who dies rich cannot go to heaven. As a result, in those explosions or revolutions of the thirteen hundreds there was a strong element of the worker with a grievance—or a poor person with a grievance feeling he could justify rebellion against a rich man because that was Christ's will. There were strong religious organizations, above all the Franciscan begging friars, which preached public service, charity, and social reform from about the 1220's and 1230's on. They did this vigorously. There was leadership and a good deal of direction as well as prayers furnished by individuals from the most vigorous branches of the church, the friars.

This tie-up of religious, political, and economic elements of revolution was to be seen in a nickname which was to be found in northern Europe, of "blue nail." The word had originated rather the way some nicknames have today, for certain classes or professions in our population, such as flat foot, sand hog, and gandy dancer. In the world of workers, blue nail meant a weaver; the name may have come from the fact that their nails were blue either from dye or from the cold rooms in which they worked. But during this time, blue nail came to mean not only a weaver, but also a political revolutionist who was trying to throw the rich merchants of

Flemish cities out of office. Finally it was used for heretic. It meant all these at once, so that to call a person a blue nail came to be a serious charge.

Once in a while revolutionaries were successful, the capitalist merchant upper class was put out of power and the blue nails came in. In Ghent the guildmasters of the weavers, fullers, and others (not to be mistaken for a revolution of journeymen, for it was not) managed to gain control at different times in the thirteen hundreds. First of all they threw the merchant-capitalist-aldermen-landlords out of town, killing a number in the process and burning their houses. Then no more wool came into town because the merchant capitalists were not there to bring it in. The revolutionaries did not have to pay rent, but neither did they have any work. The work which had been finished was not carried to the international markets, for the merchant capitalists were not there to take it. Saturday nights no pay was made for the work which might have been done, for there was no work to do and no one to pay.

Furthermore, the craft masters showed themselves to be utterly unable to be any kinder to other people than the capitalists had been to them. As soon as they were in power they acquired many enemies in addition to the merchant capitalists they had ousted. Almost instantly they got into warfare with the peasant villagers all around the city. Since they knew the cottagers were also making cloth, they organized scouring parties to go through the villages; there they went into all the houses, burned the looms they found, and cut off the right hand of each peasant who had been weaving without their permission. Furthermore, they became very upset because the peasants raised the prices of butter and eggs and other produce brought to the city market. So they set prices themselves and enforced them harshly; after that there was no butter. They were also just as unreasonable to their own journeymen. They fixed wages low, and then did not have any work to give them. Finally, the fullers and weavers locked horns with one another. The weavers wanted to have the fullers, who came next in cloth processing, pay them as much for woven cloth as the traffic would bear, and a little more. The fullers wanted the weavers to cut the price of the woven cloth so they would have a wider margin of profit. The result was conflict in the streets of Ghent between the master weavers and the master fullers. At this point the landlords and merchant capitalists came back, supported by workers, peasants, and most guildmasters in other trades, under the banner of the county's government.

But it is easy for us to see that there was no call to cheer when the weavers of Ghent threw out the officers of the count of Flanders and the merchant capitalists. Other revolutions were not just like it, but they were similar. Money for this particular upheaval had been furnished by King Edward III of England, who did not care who lost, and perhaps hoped that all would. He did all he could to induce craftsmen to move to England, intending thus to build up a competing textile manufacture.

CHAPTER VI

Towns
and Townspeople

THE Romans, Greeks, and other people in the ancient Mediterranean area centered their lives on fortified urban centers which were religious, legal, and business centers. The Greeks called a center like this *polis*, which we have incorporated for the names of cities such as "Minneapolis." To the Greeks the *polis* was not only the fortified center, but also the country around, where the peasants and the landlords were all free men of the *polis* who could either live within the walled city or, residing outside, could walk to it for business, for religious ceremonies, or to participate in military and civil affairs. Athens was all of Attica, which had originally been made up of a number of smaller units that had all come to be fused into one city unit.

The Romans had the *civitas*. Rome proper had started in that way, as a fortified hilltop with a cluster of market and public buildings and cottages below, and a wall about the whole settlement. The open village was outside the walls, and the farm land where the Roman peasants and nobles plowed and tended their animals was also in the civitas. Rome lived in a world of such city-states; its early records are of the wars of Rome against those neighboring city-states, then of coalitions of its city-states against other coalitions of city-states, and so forth, until Rome had won all the wars and come out with a great cluster of hundreds of city-states all dependent on her, the only one to have control of foreign affairs and command of the army. All the rest had to follow Rome's orders.

From the evidence of archaeology we know that in the West at least the urban centers had come to be badly shrunken during the two hundreds A.D. For example, in the days of Rome's glory the urban center of Paris had covered an island (known today as La Cité) in the Seine River and considerable land on both banks to the north and south. Archaeologists have found the ruins of beautiful villas, baths, a circus, and so on in these places. By the year three hundred, after a period of desolation, Paris had become a fortified island in the river, with the fortification partly made up of stones and bricks from the ruined villas and other buildings in the old suburbs. During the four, five, and six hundreds the urban centers all across Gaul, in England, in the Danubian lands, along all the edges of the great Empire, had shrunk to tiny cities covering not much more than from eight to thirty to eighty acres, with walls around them constructed largely from the ruins of abandoned suburban buildings.

We find that the residents of those small towns were almost exclusively made up of, first, garrison soldiers with their women and children and the working craftsmen attached to the army, a great many of whom were quasi-military discharged veterans; second, the command forces of the government with a few persons such as judges and tax collectors who had jurisdiction over the neighborhood; and third, of the church officials —bishops, priests, and deacons—with their servants and households. There were also people who had small retail enterprises catering to such civil, military, and ecclesiastical personnel.

Generally, every walled town, if it had any sort of a population at all, had a bishop as well as an army commander. Had the bishop moved away with his curia and the pilgrims he attracted, still more of the town's residents would also have departed. The bishops came to be so important inside the walled center that the word *civitas* began to shift in meaning. Originally it had meant a whole area, the rustic as well as the walled urban part. During the five, six, and seven hundreds it came to mean the walled urban part only, and the word in French became *cité*, or "city" in English. In England today, a city is technically a town with a bishop, and a town without a bishop is called a borough. During the earliest Middle Ages, cities survived partly because the bishop was there; we can even say that in many cases they survived only because the bishop was there.

As a result of all this, the older, ancient idea that the city-state or *civitas* was a large area with an urban center was revised so that the *cité* or city was just the urban center and a new name had to be found for the open country around it. In the latest day of Roman and of Romano-barbarian government in the West a count was the official governmental, military, judicial, fiscal officer in any city, with the open country as well as the urban area under him. But when the bishop inside the city walls, or right near them, came to be identified with the government as well as with the church, the distinction between his "city" and the count's open country holdings began to be important. Linguistically this is a division which is still widely made. In some states in the United States we speak of the city police and of the county police, and have the jurisdiction of the city police going to the edge of an urban area while the county police do their work outside the urban area. "Count" meant the lord of the county, and in Italian the word for a rural villager is *contadino,* the "dweller in the county," while a city person is a "city dweller," a *cittadino.* We have a division in modern English and other languages reflecting a change in the political organization which had developed since about thirteen or fourteen hundred years ago.

The area in which a bishop held jurisdiction was small. Many of those cities were merely circles of wall inclosing only a few acres. Of course some were larger, but in the West there were few cities where there was anything like a sizable population filling up the space inside the walls. In some towns, like the city of Rome itself, the inhabitants were like dried peas rattling around in a shell. The massive Roman city walls which had been put up in the late two hundreds went around a great stretch of ruins and pasture; only a few thousand papal nobles, employees, and garrison troops resided where there had been gardens, tenement buildings, forums, and temples, most of which were coming to be covered with sod where goats were pasturing. This was the case with many of the cities, and inside most there was open land, small as the walls were in circuit.

The decay was most pronounced along the frontiers of the old Roman Empire. Except possibly for York and London, there was not much of an urban population left in Anglo-Saxon England, although there may have been a few other towns where a handful of merchants lived, or where a bishop had reinstated his episcopal government inside walls after the Anglo-Saxons had turned Christian in the six hundreds. In the northern part of Gaul, the northern half of modern France, the cities had faded until they were settlements of church officials with only a few persons other than that living inside the walls, and these were usually dependents of the bishop. This was also true in the lands between the Alps and the Danube, in what is now modern southern Germany, Austria, and Hungary —land which had been quite thoroughly Roman as late as the four hundreds, but which then turned Germanic in language.

Here is a rough picture, drawn from the work of archaeologists and the slight amount of documentation we have for the period. For about a hundred miles inside the old Roman frontier of Britain, the Rhine and the Danube, the people in the seven hundreds were German. The population had been Germanized—English is a Germanic language, and the Anglo-

Saxons had done a thorough job. In the lands along the Rhine the German language was always to be found, far inside the old Empire. By the later seven hundreds, in the time of Charlemagne, there were no urban centers in those areas save for a few stockaded, palisaded Frisian port forts in the lower Rhine and along the coast. We have the scarcest evidence of city activity or population.

Instead of living in capital cities and governing from those urban centers, the kings lived in rural areas and moved from villa to villa, eating up the surpluses accumulated, then moving on when the surplus in any villa or group of villas had been exhausted. We have no evidence that in the north of the Carolingian world important wars were settled by the taking of cities. Instead, there was maneuvering in the open country by fairly small armies. Battles were fought in the open, and defenders did not retire behind city walls to try to hold strategic centers or make recoveries after the enemy had wasted his strength. When cities exist, such fighting has centered on them. The Danubian and northern Gallic areas give all these evidences of decayed urban life and its nonexistence to all practical purposes.

This was not true in France in the lands along the Mediterranean, or in Italy. In Italy there were urban centers. The Lombards who ruled Italy retired behind the walls of their cities when there were raids by the Avars and Hungarians and Franks from over the Alps. They came out from behind city walls to make counter thrusts at enemies. We have evidence that their city walls were continually being repaired, that when they had been broken, measures were taken to put them together again. We also have evidence that the bishops lived permanently in their cities.

We also have evidence from the south of that thing which really makes a city—trade. There were people designated in passing by other documents as merchants, and some of these were Italians. There was a continuity between the city life of southern French and the Italian towns and the city life of antiquity. It had become poor, mostly by the decay of trade, but neither the cities nor the trade had disappeared altogether.

Another thing is that in southern Europe life centered in the cities. In Italy and Provence and Languedoc important officials seem to have lived in the cities. In Italy the king lived in Pavia a good deal of the time and in a palace. Local rulers seem to have had country estates, and fortified country castles, but for the most part their lives centered in the cities. While the cities in the south were not large, still they were definitely alive and functioning.

In both the south and those areas in the north where urban life had died more or less completely, we find (especially in the relative peace of the Carolingian period) that in the seven and early eight hundreds there was still another sort of center which was attracting population. The six and seven hundreds saw many monasteries founded by Roman, English, and Irish monks. By choice these monasteries were almost always set up far away from settled places, and yet many monasteries themselves rather rapidly attracted a non-monkish population.

Generally speaking, in Italy and central and northwestern Europe new monasteries were given large territories of back country waste land, and the monks, who in most cases (as that order became popular) were Benedictines, went to work to improve their properties. Working hard, they cleared the land, built bridges, built milldams, improved the property and attracted settlers.

Sometimes they imported settlers from other monastic properties further away to help work the land. But in any case, free volunteer settlers tended to come to their gates, and to settle down, attracted by the prosperity which stemmed from all the activity at the monastery. For one thing, craftsmen who knew how to work with metal and leather and textiles would find customers right at the gates of the monastery. Inside the monastery was a prosperous community able and willing to acquire fine goods, and itself able to make fine goods; many of the monks were skilled at gold and silver smithing, or steel and iron work, or with leather, and so on. In addition, by and large Christian fighting men left the properties of monks and monasteries untouched, or at least not violently touched. Neighboring lords would and did work out some legal theft of monastic properties, but not the kind of violent stealing they perpetrated upon one another. Consequently, on monastic lands there was a chance that even those who were not monks could live their lives out without having their throats cut and their property carted away by random raiders.

Then too monasteries afforded hospitality to all comers as far as their resources would allow. That tended to attract refugees from other parts not only for the protection just mentioned, but also for food. Once there, the able bodied were likely to be able to find work and to settle down in and around the monastery gates. This giving of hospitality was extended to wayfarers who were just wayfarers, but they also might be papal emissaries, imperial legates, and other such persons in governmental and ecclesiastical hierarchies, and they might also be merchants.

Merchants could find food and lodging simply by knocking at the monastery gates. This is, as a matter of fact, true of monasteries to this very day. This knocking at the monastery gate was in effect the way in which a man registered in the only hotels which then existed. Since merchants were on the road and needed hostel service, monasteries tended to be the places where merchants stopped as they went across country. More than that, merchants who had wives and children could leave them at some monastery which had advantages of location and security. Around the gates of monasteries, even when they had not yet become cities, there came to be a population of non-monks drawn there for protection, for food, because many monasteries were good centers for trade, and so on.

During the time of the greatness of Charles Martel, of Pippin the Short, of Charlemagne, and even for a while after the time of Charlemagne, there was a false feeling of security in most of western Europe. Men pulled down old city walls around the little episcopal cities to obtain materials for church or monastery or private dwelling construction. Some of the bricks and tombstones in those city walls have an interesting history. First they were Roman tombstones in the suburbs; then around 300 A.D. they were gathered and cemented together in a hurry to form city walls; in the seven and eight hundreds they were quarried out and put into the walls of churches, monasteries, and private dwellings; at the next stage, in the eight and nine hundreds, they were to be put back into city walls again. Finally, in modern times the walls were dumped as rubble into the moats, and where the bulwarks had stood the boulevards were laid.

Europe, once the Carolingian Imperial armies around the edge had been bypassed or passed through, was relatively wide open to the kind of hit-and-run raiders who came in the middle and later eight hundreds and well into the nine hundreds from east, west, north, and south. This was the period in which urban life as such hit bottom, at least in the north. It was only by development of defense in depth by the feudal fighting forces that these raids were finally stopped, and the possibility of counterattack began to be developed.

Those places which were attacked once and again in the late eight and nine hundreds were some of them abandoned, but more often they were made into forts, or castles. The Roman word for a fortified spot was *castellum,* whence comes the English word "castle." In the German language the word for such a fortified center is *burg.* In English other words for castle are "borough," which is found in all the names of towns which end in borough, as Peterborough, or "burgh" as in Edinburgh (pronounced Edinborough), or "bury" as in Salisbury or Canterbury. Burg, borough, or bury was the German term for what was called *château* in French, *castello* in Italian, or castle. To be sure, the people frequently had little work to do in building a fortification save simply to put the walls back up where they had been allowed to fall apart or been taken apart a generation or so before. In the nine hundreds most of the largest *cités* were strengthened all over again, and fortified in solid fashion. Walls were put around many monasteries, both where the monks dwelt and where merchants and other non-monks had come to dwell.

In the nine hundreds Europe began to be studded with castles that were purely garrison points, and with castles that had other population in them in addition to military men. It was at this time that development of burgs which were big enough to hold a considerable number of nonmilitary, nonchurch, nongovernmental population began to make itself evident. As the nine hundreds came toward an end and the ten hundreds began, we find the word burg beginning to take on a new meaning, which was tied up with the merchant and artisan population which had at first lived outside the military walls. This part outside the burg was in French called the *faubourg*, in modern English "suburb."

In one spot and then another, the population in the *faubourg* or suburb began to overshadow the population inside the wall; the population in the suburb began to be more numerous, wealthier, and even in a military way more powerful than the armed garrison inside the walled core of the burg. To be sure there were many castles which never attracted more than a handful of residents to their gates; there were monasteries which did not attract much population either; there were old Roman cities which had flourished under Rome, but for some reason were off center and did not now attract any population. Many of them still exist today, in the nineteen hundreds, with little walls around them, looking much as they did centuries ago.

But whenever a monastery or a feudal fighting castle or a walled city was well located for trade, a suburban population would grow up around one or several of the gates. This often came about when the nucleus was at or near crossroads left over from the old Roman road system. It is to be remembered that the Roman roads were still quite good over long stretches, although most of the bridges were out. Even the ruined stretches still served to mark the routes for most of the traffic. Another place where settlers would be likely to cluster would be around a castle which had been built to defend a river crossing, such as an "Ox ford," or a Paris bridge, or a London bridge; or at a point where roads led away from a port which may have been a good landing place for Vikings, but was also a good landing place for peaceful merchant ships. Roads leading off to the interior were equally good for Vikings or for merchants to travel. Or they would cluster at the mouths of important passes through the Alps, usually one at each end. In other words, castles, monasteries, and old Roman towns, so situated as to attract merchants, attracted population into the suburban settlements.

As any suburban settlement grew, the problem of walling it in soon made its appearance. The first step was usually to dig a ditch around the new settlement, throwing the dirt up on the inside, and so making an entrenchment an attacker would have to fall into before he could climb out. Then came putting up wooden palisades on top of the dirt pile, and then finally, in the ten hundreds and after, construction of fortifications made of stone or brick to make them stronger against attack by fire or battering ram, and more durable.

The walling in of the suburbs created a wall plan in which two or three or four series of walls might exist simultaneously. Inclosing only a few acres could be the original walled monastery or feudal castle, the burg proper (*burg, kremlin, château, kasbah, steen, stein*—one may take one's choice of the region and language!) still manned by its garrison which came in to it from feudal holdings in the neighborhood, to do garrison duty in the burg. But outside, along at least one and perhaps along several of the roads leading in to the main gate of the castle, would be a walled suburb. But of course, since it was walled it was no longer a suburb but part of the burg. It was at this point, in the ten hundreds, that a word which had been used everywhere for the fighters who garrisoned a burg began to take on the meaning of peaceful merchant citizen. The word was *burgher* in German, *burgess* in English, *bourgeois* in French, and in Italian *borghese*. Everywhere the word burgher and its variants, which had meant a feudal garrison man, came to mean a merchant or craftsman living inside his part of the walls.

The addition of new suburbs to the old core of a city by the building of additional walls was a process which in some places was repeated more than once, perhaps every twenty or fifty or hundred years, depending on the speed of growth of a given city. The rings of a tree somewhat parallel this development of further and further walls as a town grew. Of course the walls did not come in concentric rings, like those of a tree; given parts of a city's suburbs would grow more rapidly than others. Many times the old walls were left standing for a long while, partly for inner defense, partly from laziness—but also there was little incentive to tear the old ones down, for they did not matter.

In the case of many old towns successive additions to the walls are still traceable today. Of course, as soon as walls were put up in or around a town, all of the streets and buildings which came near them of necessity took their position into account, and when the walls were taken down the streets and buildings still stood, retaining their alignment. Maps can be made today showing in town after town just where it had expanded in the nine through the twelve hundreds. Documents often tell just when a new extension had been begun or when it was being carried on, so it is even possible to date most of the extensions pretty closely.

There came to be more and more walled towns; the largest were growing still larger, and little new ones were starting, all across the map of western Europe. It was only in the thirteen hundreds that the process stopped, rather suddenly. By the time the towns had begun to grow again the use of gunpowder had come in, and towns were in general defended by other means.

In the course of the development of European towns there were differences, to begin with, from one area to another, and, as development went on, there still continued to be differences.

Italy and the nearby parts of southern France had never seen the disappearance of towns. Individual towns had been ruined—Aquileia, a great town in northern Italy, was by Attila and has never grown again; there is a big pasture and forest area there now. But Aquileia was succeeded by the town created largely by its refugees, Venice. In the case of most towns even that sort of gap did not occur. Pavia and Milan and most of the rest survived. In Italy there were always towns, and the development of the medieval towns was simply a matter of growth, or rather of regrowth inside and new growth outside the walls left from Roman days. (The nearby coast of southern France should always be included when speaking of Italy through the Middle Ages, for it had almost exactly the same development.)

In addition to Italian nobles who continued to be city folk, there were the craftsmen whose prosperity and increase both in numbers and wealth had a great deal to do with the reinvigoration of every healthy urban center. Recruits came in from the villages, and it was because of the influx of these that most of the population growth and physical growth of the cities took place.

Some new towns appeared. One of the most famous of these, Venice, grew up out in the mud off the coast of the Venetian Plain. Another was Florence. It had been just a little river bridge center, while the main town was on a hill to the south where the Etruscans had had a fortress and the Romans a hill city, Fiesole. When in the eleven hundreds Florence in the valley by the bridge began to grow, it had a war with its mother city,

Fiesole, and destroyed it both demographically and politically. But most of the new cities in Italy were nearly everywhere exactly where they had always been, and with exactly the same old Roman names.

Along the Roman border with Germany, from Hungary out to the North Sea, in the upper Danube, the Rhine, and the Moselle regions, were the Imperial Roman bishops' fortified cities. These had been fortified Roman cities; when Rome disappeared, the walls at least remained. The most famous example of this was Cologne, where a great fortified Roman camp had become an important city and had then become Germanized when the Franks moved into that area in the three, four, and five hundreds. We are not sure today whether there was a population inside the walls all the time or not. But we do know that about when the Franks became baptized Christians in the late four hundreds, they reactivated the episcopal organization there, if it had in fact decayed. Thereafter the walls of the old Roman city Colonia Agrippina surrounded the Frankish bishop and his household. From then on there was never a moment when it lacked a bishop or, after his jurisdiction had expanded, an archbishop.

In the period we are turning to now, the nine and ten hundreds, a considerable *faubourg* developed between the bishop's walls and the river (the city core being a bit away from the river), and walls were strung between the city and the river to protect the new *faubourg*. We are not sure how early this was done, perhaps before ten hundred. From then on successive increases in the population of *faubourgs* resulted in formation of the medieval and early modern city. Around an old Roman episcopal center a new German town had grown.

In addition, the same sort of thing could happen around German monasteries; one of the most famous of the monasteries to develop into a modern city bears the name Munich, which means "monk town" or "monk center," and Munich in southern Germany is a monastery grown into a town.

There had been fortified defense centers pushed out onto the frontier against the Hungarians, and one of these became the capital of the eastern frontier; Ostmark or Austria had as its capital Vienna, which grew up around an advanced fort the German emperors established there in the nine hundreds on a still older Roman site, typifying another sort of medieval urban center. Cologne, around an old Roman city; Munich, around a monastery; Vienna, around an advanced frontier fort—these are the patterns followed by the various cities in the Rhine-Danube frontier areas.

Then, as Germany began to be Christianized and the Slav lands eastward were penetrated by Germans, new cities were founded outright.

Nearly all of these at the beginning had a fort as a core or center. Among the important ones was one which was placed in Saxon lands to guard the mouth of the Elbe River, named "The Fort of Ham" or "Hamburg." Hamburg came into existence as an advanced fort, with a bishop as its chieftain so that it was a bishop's city from the start as well as a defense center. Another frontier fort placed out in Slav land to guard the main east-west interriver route was Berlin, a German fort in the middle of alien Slavs, many of whom are still there in the marsh country nearby to this day. Then there were trading ports, established above all by the Hansa merchants, or by their grandfathers before there was a Hansa, at the mouths of the rivers east along the Baltic; such a place was Danzig, founded by Germans but in lands which were otherwise held by Prussians, for the purpose of trade with those people in the back country.

In the Low Countries, northern France, and in nearby England along the North Sea and English Channel, there were old walled Roman towns such as Canterbury, London, Arras, and Cambrai. We know that some of them were empty, or practically empty, during the four and five and six hundreds.

Just when these towns began to regain inhabitants, or when the population still there began to grow again, we cannot be sure, but we know they had begun to shelter a population which had trading and manufacturing interests during the Carolingian period, and then most emphatically sheltered merchants from the nine hundreds on. During the interval, most of these towns had been held by a permanent nucleus of episcopal officers and garrison troops. The town of Canterbury, as the Anglo-Saxons called it, is an example of this. It had Roman walls, and at almost all times in its history a bishop, even though there was a gap of over a hundred years when the Anglo-Saxons were not Christians. And the king of the Kentish men lived there. The town was an old Roman city in the original sense of the word; as a bishop's center, it became a city in the sense of the six and seven hundreds; and then it once again became a trading place in the eight and early nine hundreds. Other English towns had similar histories, such as York in the north, and Chester to the northwest.

But in England there was still another origin for many of the towns which had become famous and important by the ten and eleven hundreds. In the defensive fighting against the Danes in the later eight hundreds, King Alfred and his successors built large fortified camps, in part imitating the Danes who were doing the same thing. There was room for quite an army in some of those fortified camps, a few of them being as much as forty to eighty acres in extent, and once they were built a good many never lost their population. Instead, neighboring squires, thanes, and sheriff's men continued to garrison them, and fortified as they were, they gave protection to traders and craftsmen as well as to the king's officials. Since in most cases these towns had no bishops, they continued to be called forts, or boroughs.

In the area of Flanders, Brabant, and northern France some towns simply started and developed in a way that Americans are likely to consider the natural way for a town to begin and to grow. Without any forts or administrative centers, these towns rose in neighborhoods which for one reason or another were good for manufacture. This could only occur where there was a general government over the area, strong enough to give any town protection, as has been the case in most areas of the United States during its development.

The most famous of the towns which were industrial from the start was the Flemish town of Ypres, which grew to great size and then faded when its industry moved elsewhere. Ypres grew up as a place where men made cloth. Situated in Belgium near the French border, it was not walled nor fortified, had neither a bishop nor any administrative officers with much power in the neighborhood. Its beautiful Cloth Hall, built during the twelve hundreds, was looked upon as one of the greatest examples of Gothic architecture, but of Gothic architecture dedicated to a purely secular building instead of to church use. Unfortunately, this magnificent building was blown to nothing in the fighting in World War I.

Along the edges of the seas of which the Vikings had control during the eight and nine hundreds, we have seen how they established what were in origin beachheads on the lands they wished to plunder further. Such places as Dublin and Limerick in Ireland began as beachheads from which to raid and dominate the country round about. At all the places where they went regularly the Vikings built fortified centers which were sometimes fairly large, palisaded, and with a ditch. There was a resident population for part of the year, but with most of the men absent during a good part of each year for the purpose of raiding and of trading. Many of those towns faded back out of use and existence quite soon after they had been founded; they were put up, lasted only a few years, and then the army of Vikings who had established them went away again.

But many of them became quite permanent, and all across the coastal lands from Ireland into Russia we have seen that there are towns today which had their origins as Viking establishments of the eight and nine hundreds. As the lands in which these towns were situated turned Christian, and as the Vikings became Christian and subject to influences from older areas, most of these towns began to conform to the general pattern of western European towns. They almost at once lost their original characteristics of being pirate centers from which the countryside had been raided. The best of them, like Kiev and Dublin, became the capitals from which the country was governed and the church administered, with an active local manufacture and foreign trade.

The Middle Class or Burgesses in the Older Social Structure

As already noted, in Italy there were few bars to entry into the lesser nobility on the part of other townsmen who had started lower down in social rank. Entry was more or less on a basis of cash and the passage of time; a man who first succeeded in a craft and then became a well-to-do merchant could expect to obtain recognition for himself or at least for his sons by buying land in the country which gave feudal rights. These men took titles of nobility; in effect they called themselves "Sir" without going through formalities. They might or might not do homage to some greater noble, but they took the privileges of rank simply on becoming rich enough to exercise them. On the other hand the lesser nobles in Italy were quite commonly subject to degradation, not in title, but in economic condition as family estates were divided and subdivided. As a result there were rich merchants who were easing upward into the nobility, while at the same time there were very poor nobles whose ways of life were but little better than those of the poorest craftsmen inside the same town. This has been characteristic of the Italian scene ever since, rich men seeking titles and titled nobles with no money.

Of course, the nobles in Italian cities bore arms, and so did everyone else who had any pretensions at all; in Italy the bearing of arms was taken for granted, depending chiefly on the wish of the person who bore them; it was not regarded as something which in itself stamped the person as noble. Italian nobles had no compunctions about arming their poorest peasants in order to form them into bands for private warfare, and the countryside would be scoured by rich nobles leading *bravi*.

Even more important, from the very beginning intercity rivalry and warfare in Italy made it necessary that as many men as possible should be able to fight. Our historical sources show very clearly that as early as the ten hundreds the ranks of the city militia were made up of young men and boys, journeymen and older apprentices, who were part-time soldiers. From fighting from behind their city walls they soon graduated to fighting in the open fields in campaigns which lasted a few days or a few weeks in the best season of the year. (Medieval wars were normally fought when the weather was best for fighting, not in the winter time or when it was raining.) The cities in Italy being close together, it was possible to have a major war in June and have the soldiers back to business by the fourth of July, having marched five miles toward an enemy who had marched five miles toward them for a battle. The common fighting in Italy was in general quite as much a matter of the ranks of the city militia, made up of craftsmen and journeymen, as of nobles mounted on horses. Militarily each was important. With such a lack of distinction between the professional arms bearers and those who normally worked at trades, there could not be the sharp line between nobility and non-nobility in Italy which was to be found elsewhere.

In the Scandinavian areas and in England, which was so heavily Scandinavian in matters of this sort, there was, as in Italy, no feeling that it was ignoble to be a merchant. A book, *The King's Mirror*, shows very clearly that in the twelve hundreds it was considered a proper thing for a Norse noble to go into business or for his son to go into business. A man could be a king's courtier, or he could be a respectable merchant; the choice was up to him, and he lost no regard by choosing the merchant's career. Or he could be both a powerful Norwegian earl and a wealthy merchant. This was true up to the time of the Norman conquest of England in 1066, and to some degree thereafter, although the conquest brought a French upper class into England which had somewhat different ideas on the subject.

The key to this matter in England can be found in the legislation having to do with army and administrative affairs. Both the kings of England before 1066 and the kings thereafter, William the Conqueror, his son, and grandson, appraised men for fighting purposes according to their wealth. Our documents are poor but probably Anglo-Saxon law was followed by the similar provisions of later English law, which were that a man with an estate large enough had to bear a fighting man's burdens and the expense of heavy fighting equipment. In other words, if a man became well-to-do, he was supposed to be able to buy a good fighting horse and the equipment which went with it, and to stand up in war as a nobleman.

In the administrative law the same thing held true: the king of England always relied heavily in matters of government upon the local well-to-do. Such a subject owed service in the king's court as a juror, a member of the panel of citizens who told the king what was true in assessing taxes or appraising crime, and was expected to do a good deal of work each year for the king. No questions were asked as to how wealth had been accumulated. A man could have inherited his land or business; it could have been given to him by the king or some patron; or he could simply have gone into business and made a good profit. In England at all times it was possible for successful persons to rise into the nobility. It was also normal for the younger sons, even of earls, to slide down into the ranks of respectable common people.

A little later than the period under discussion here, in the twelve hundreds, the principle of primogeniture became more firmly established in England than in any other country in Europe. On this principle an inheritance always goes to the oldest of the sons in a family. There is a nice illustration of its working in the career of Sir Winston Churchill. His grandfather was a tremendously rich duke. His father was a younger son, called a lord out of courtesy, for legally he was no more a lord than was Tommy Atkins. Sir Winston Churchill, the grandson of a duke, his father a brother of a duke, he himself the cousin of a duke, was plain Mr. Churchill until the Queen knighted him. This principle of primogeniture threw all inheritance into one line and threw poverty, or relative poverty and insignificance, into all the other lines in each important family. However, a good deal of respectability followed into the second, third, and fourth generations of the great families. Descendants of the younger lines could still be part of the noble group socially, even though they were commoners. As a result there has been intermarriage and, in political matters, much coöperation in England between those who belonged to the younger or cadet branches of noble families and those who belonged to the wealthy branches of merchant families.

In the twelve hundreds lesser gentlemen in England, including persons who were brothers and cousins of earls, came to sit as shire or borough representatives not with the nobles in the House of Lords but with the burgesses in the House of Commons. As a result, in England leadership in political matters, while it was the leadership of the organized boroughs, was in part exercised by adults of the younger branches of the great noble families and by the leading well-to-do gentlemen of the country—the knights and squires. This was a development unique in England, as the developments in Italy and the Norselands were unique to them.

In northern France, in the nearby Low Countries, and in Germany, by and large the people who lived in the growing towns had no vestige of noble ancestry. Almost all of them were peasants, and many of them were former serfs, or serfs who were in the process of evolving into something different. There was no tradition that the nobles live in the towns; on the contrary, there was a strong tradition that noblemen live out of the towns, on their country estates. There was a strong prejudice against allowing a tradesperson who had become rich also to become noble. The king of France and some of the chief sovereigns in Germany did sometimes exercise the privilege of making individuals noble by formal ennoblement, but it was a very slow process. A French or German merchant might hope for it but in Germany and France ennoblement still did not give a man's family all the regard of the other nobles until several more generations had gone by; ennoblement came slowly and its sweets were seldom tasted in a family until the third or fourth generation. By the twelve hundreds ennoblement was becomiṅg a royal monopoly, and was given grudgingly, for service or for money payments to the king. In those areas the upper class on the whole held its ranks pretty tightly shut off against ambitious persons in the middle class, and it was far more difficult to break into the upper crust than in either Italy or England.

This French attitude had pretty well crystallized by the ten and eleven hundreds, at the time of the First Crusade and just after. It made itself felt in many other parts of Europe because in the course of the eleven and twelve hundreds French prestige in all sorts of things became tremendous, as it has remained to our present day in the attitudes of many western Europeans. French literature became dominant in literary circles as the French romances, epics, and other forms of literature developed to a very high point. From the middle eleven hundreds on, French architecture dominated the architectures of England, Germany, Italy, and northern Spain. The Gothic style of architecture is northern French in origin, and its excellence was so great that it was impossible that it should not have been adopted by other peoples all over Europe, once it had been created. In addition, French table manners, dress, and fighting style were imitated in England, Germany, Italy, and Spain, and even in the Byzantine Empire.

Furthermore, French architecture, institutions, attitudes, dress, and language were carried out of northern France into other areas by French conquerors. In the ten hundreds considerable fighting forces of Frenchmen were to move in all directions. In about 1020 to 1030 north Frenchmen were conquering southern Italy and Sicily; they took about fifty to seventy-five years to accomplish it, but they ended up by having founded the Norman Kingdom of southern Italy. Northern French armies conquered southern France just after 1200 in the so-called Albigensian Crusade. After 1066 French armies had conquered England, and in the eleven hundreds the grandsons of those conquerors in turn penetrated Wales, Ireland, and Scotland. Forces of Frenchmen conquered part of

Portugal and helped found that nation. Frenchmen dominated the great effort of the First Crusade and subsequent ones, for the core of the army and the leadership were northern French. The French upper class carried with it the attitude toward merchants and merchant life which had originally been restricted to northern France and the nearby parts of Germany.

When the Rhineland Germans came to rule, either directly or indirectly, the peoples of Poland, Hungary, and Bohemia, a very similar but German variety of aristocratic prejudice was carried over into eastern Europe. There the attitude of Germans toward the non-Germans was somewhat the same as the attitude elsewhere of Frenchmen toward non-Frenchmen. So attitudes toward merchants and the merchant classes which had originally come from that small area of northern France and the nearby Moselle and Rhine country were carried elsewhere, either in German or French packages.

As the towns grew up, it became necessary that the whole pattern of society be rearranged—the traditional Carolingian pattern of society, as men of the time described it, wherein three classes were recognized: the clergy, the nobles, and the peasants. They thought in terms of services rendered, not of position. A person was in the uppermost class, the clergy, whether he was a pope or a cardinal or a poor parish priest; he was in it because his function was to pray and keep the whole population in the proper relationship with God. A man was noble—in second rank—whether he was emperor of the Holy Roman Empire or a poor sergeant with one sorry nag to ride, if he served by offering his body, his honor, and his goods in war, and also served by ruling, however large or small a force he had to rule. The peasants, whether free villagers or lowest serfs, served by producing the food everyone, including themselves, needed, and so formed the third class.

There was no place in this pattern for a person who served by buying, selling, or making goods. In France and nearby Germany the general idea was that these men were still peasants, even when they began to make or sell cloth in a town like Ypres. In England, Italy, and Scandinavia the general attitude was that they were respectable, even noble when wealthy enough. But there was a problem, however the new class was rated. Should it outrank the clergy? Manifestly not. Should it outrank the nobles? In Italy opinion would not let the townsmen outrank the nobles, but was willing to allow the wealthier ones to become part of the nobility as already described. Yet then there were the lower-class townsmen who were not nobles, but who carried weapons and won wars with them. It was impossible to reckon these townsmen as peasants, for they themselves refused to be so considered. They had many reasons for their refusal, and eventually even in northern France and Germany succeeded in making their case in opposition to the upper classes. A townsman interested in foreign trade could not afford to be treated as a serf; it made it hard for him to stay in business.

There were privileges for which townsmen were willing to fight. Important among these were freedom for a man to come and go, at any distance, without fear that his lord might drag him back as a runaway serf; freedom from any of the physical labor required of a peasant, such as reaping the lord's corn or carting his lord's goods; freedom from a court system which enforced a village and agricultural law, but which made no sense as a business law. To put all this positively, the merchant townsman had to have a law system and jurisdiction that would cover his own kind of existence, which village and manorial law were totally incapable of achieving. In some countries, at least, the townsman thought he needed, or actually did need, power to control trade in his own neighborhood to his own advantage. He wanted to have power to bar rivals, to control raw materials, to control working hours and conditions, and so on, in the industry in his town. In Italy and Germany, where they actually accomplished this, the townsmen wanted to be able to negotiate with other townsmen for purposes of protection of business—they wanted some of the powers of sovereignty. In Italy they even wanted to be able to form armies and kill one another; the Italian townsmen wanted the privilege of fighting on their own terms and for their own causes. And negatively the merchants did not wish to be taxed at any time a lord decided he wanted money.

All of these and some other things were what the townsmen wanted to have, and which they managed to obtain by gradual steps. It was not always the same story everywhere. In Italy the townsmen got so much that by the twelve hundreds they were swallowing up the countryside and forcing the country nobles and villagers—there were true country nobles as well as those who had one foot in the city—under controls which were irksome to them. The towns began to be very high handed and harsh in the treatment of their own neighbors out in the country.

Even a curious sort of collective serfdom was later imposed by the so-called democratic government of Florence upon the countrymen all around the city. The peasants were unable to leave their villages without the permission of the city government, were unable to move to town unless the city government gave them license to do so, and were forced to buy, sell, and work under the control of the city government. A kind of collective serfdom was imposed by a kind of collective lord in the course of the thirteen hundreds which made the peasants in the country around Florence quite miserable, just at a time when it looked as though the town itself was enjoying something of a democratic government.

In Italy the town in general destroyed central government for all practical purposes. In the 1170's the northern Italian towns so thoroughly beat the Holy Roman Emperor, Frederick Barbarossa, that he could no longer really govern those towns. As a concession, the Emperor made an irrevocable legal grant to the towns in the 1180's of practically all of the royal or regalian rights. From that time on in Italy there was, in effect, a whole group of small powers. This was the outside limit to which town ambitions could carry the communities.

In England and in general in France the towns were closely held under the king and were never given that kind of privilege. But the towns in England began to have their representation in Parliament.

As we have indicated, in the Middle Ages men did not employ the word "class," but instead used the word "estate." While this is fundamentally like our word "state," it does not mean a territorial state, but a status. In France and England by thirteen hundred, and in most of the other countries, there were three privileged estates—the old top two, clergy and noblemen, and then the new one which had arisen, the estate of the burgesses (in England) or bourgeoisie (in France) or burghers (in Germany).

Peasants, whether free or unfree, were not regarded as belonging to one of the three privileged estates, though in Sweden they formed a fourth estate. Outside Germany and Italy, where they fought their way to practical independence, the townsmen found that their main lever was collective bargaining with their kings, especially collective bargaining for taxes. What the kings could take from the clergy and nobles was limited by old law and custom, and what they could get from people in the towns was not so restricted, so rulers could legally grab the assets of merchants.

But by about 1300 in England under Edward I the burgesses were accustomed to pay regular taxes after discussion between the king and the House of Commons. From this came the concept that any kind of tax touching the commoners had first to be asked for by the king from the Commons. After discussion by the Commons it could then be voted and submitted to the lords and clergy for final passage. This is approximately the pattern followed today in the United States in our budget and taxation procedures which start in what is our House of Commons, the House of Representatives.

Strata Within the Middle Class

A burgess, or burgher, referring to anyone living in a town, was a general term for a townsman. At first it did not mean privileged or un-privileged, rich or poor, but simply all the town dwellers. Only in later medieval and early modern times, increasingly especially in the sixteen and seventeen hundreds, did the term burgess or burgher make another shift in meaning until it came in most cases to refer to a very privileged stratum belonging to a narrow upper crust of wealthy townsmen who alone had the right to vote and to stand for town offices. The period in which this more confined meaning of the term bourgeoisie was most pronounced was roughly the time of Plymouth Rock and Jamestown and the French and Indian Wars; it was not during medieval times. The word burgher came to mean a very privileged upper-class aristocrat inside the town in Germany; the bourgeois was the same sort of person in France. There was a curious reflection of this in the development of English boroughs or towns. By 1800, speaking generally, the longer a town had held its original charter, the wider its franchise and the easier it was for the poor people to vote; the later the franchise—and this was espe-cially true of the franchises of about seventeen hundred—the tighter the charter was in restricting burgess privileges to "the best families" in the towns.

As cities became important, within the cities men had to determine to their own satisfaction the ranks and interrelationships of the urban groups.

Within the whole middle class or bourgeoisie, in the medieval and original sense of the term, working from the top down, there were those who stood as the topmost citizens. In modern scholarly textbook usage these persons are often called "the patricians." That is borrowing an old Roman term to use for the Middle Ages; it is not a term that, at least until very much later, was used by the men themselves to designate the topmost urban class. Or, borrowing an old Greek name which was not used in the Middle Ages, we can call them the aristocracy, but this can only be done while carefully keeping in mind their inferiority to the feudal aristocracy, the really topmost people; only in Italy and a few other places did the town aristocracy fit also into the general aristocracy, and even then not at the very top save as individual families like the Medici were outstandingly successful.

The merchant banker in Italy was always regarded as what we designate here a patrician. His ancestors were estate owners, or he had bought estates. The patrician inherited a rank which let him bear sword and spurs and live nobly, or in individual cases he might have taken these on by himself. Such persons also owned a good deal of the real estate inside the towns; they either owned it outright or held it on long or even perpetual rental terms, often enough from some church or monastery.

Like situations were particularly common in northern Europe. Where a town had grown up on a monastery's land, it was fairly normal for the leading townsmen to be reckoned as peasant tenants of the monastery, paying a few chickens and eggs a year for possession of what had once been garden lands near the monastery gates but had become downtown real estate bringing in hundreds of shillings or even hundreds of pounds' income per annum. The richest merchants of Arras were curiously subject to tiny peasant payments to the monastery of St. Vedastus for their real estate holdings in the city which had grown up around the old monastery gates. On the records of the monastery, it looks as though these rich merchants, as late as 1200 and 1250, were still serfs, for they paid old servile dues for perpetual possession of city building lots on which they had erected buildings bringing in great sums of rent money every year. The poor monks of the monastery got little more than a few eggs for the equivalent of owning the Rockefeller Center of Arras.

Patricians in the most prosperous towns were very rich. Even before 1200, a well-to-do merchant banker in an Italian city, in Arras, or in Provins, would make individual deals in sums which were as large as an English earl's annual income. It was the great wealth in the hands of men of this sort that helped the towns in Italy to throw off the rule of the Holy Roman Emperor. A person may well wonder how it was possible for the citizens of an area of the size of Milan to trounce so thoroughly the armies of Frederick Barbarossa, drawn from the spreading German lands. The wealth of a few Milanese patricians was as great as the wealth of great lords of Germany. As late as the fifteen and sixteen hundreds Venice, a city governed by patricians, put fleets on the seas which held the whole power of the Ottoman Turkish Empire at bay.

This stratum in the population also included at least the well-to-do doctors and lawyers, who in many cases were sons of patricians. But also individuals who came up through the schools and became, by their own talents, recognized leaders in law or medicine, or in the church, were socially a part of the same group. To be sure, some of the professional men did not become insiders. Apparently this was due to individual peculiarities or failures to make enough money as doctors or lawyers to be able to assume the status of patricians.

The next lower group of people, who understood perfectly that there was a difference in rank, were those who were prosperous retailers, or masters in the most lucrative crafts. These men did not have fortunes which put them in the ranks of the patricians, but nevertheless they had property and a position well up in town society. Nearly all of the retailers were organized in their different retail guilds, and so, of course, were the craftsmen—the goldsmiths being a good example. The master craftsmen, a few men or a few hundred in the largest cities, were never so extremely rich as the great banker nobles, but inside the towns they were a very solid group of citizens.

In the history of town politics it was often this class which gave leadership to what was known as the People's or the Popular party. This was the party of the *popolo* in Italy, or of the *popolo grasso*, or "fat people." The *popolo* or *popolo grasso* were solid and well-to-do citizens, frequently hostile both to patricians and to the classes next below themselves. During the nineteenth century, writers came to identify this party as the party of democracy, being misled by the label "People's party." They were just as tough about keeping the persons next lower down, and those next above, out of political power as were any of the other exclusive political groups of those centuries.

Underneath them, and divided into many still smaller groups, were those who were the small retailers, the masters in the less lucrative crafts and the journeymen of some of the other crafts, as well as the persons who came in from the countryside to do business in the city square but who, in the country, were important persons—the village rich.

In surviving documents we have evidence of the closeness that existed between the small retailers in the cities and the village rich; the patterns of their dowries and wedding contracts indicate this. There was a great deal of intermarriage between well-to-do villagers and this class of town retailers; they fitted easily together in the way their families lived, and many a village rich man moved into town and opened up a shop. This was one of the channels of migration toward the towns which has been noticeable at all times.

Next below came the great mass of the working poor in the industrial towns. These were the laborers who had no special guild organization or special skills. The small retailers and the "deserving poor" had a tendency to become mixed together, although they themselves were conscious of their difference. In turn the deserving poor were quite closely tied to the free peasantry in the country outside the town, and were often interchangeable where there was a seasonal migration between country work and city work. Those with strong backs and hands helped with the harvest; then they came into town to work at stevedoring, street construction, household service, and so forth; then once more returned to the country.

The deserving poor made up the largest part of the population. This group very seldom achieved a position of political leadership, and seldom held the position once it was obtained.

In discussions of societies earlier than our own, practically no one ever tells about the underworld; like juvenile delinquency, we seem to assume that it is something which has just appeared within the last few years, for which we or someone else is currently responsible, but which no society ever knew before. Socially the underworld is one of the most stable and unchanging and perpetual of all the strata of society.

The underworld is of curious composition. It is stable, but it is always made up of various elements, and this was so in medieval towns. Speaking generally, the underworld was made up of all the charlatans and true criminals which any population would have, some of them being hangers-on and parasites of the very well-to-do. Political and social life in most of the Italian cities and elsewhere demanded that the richest nobles have armed retainers (a fancy word for this service). For love and for money *bravi* ("bully boys," "goons") were kept in the houses of great families, and they were retained outside the city in the country castles and holdings of rich people. In England an organized force of this sort, in the fourteen hundreds, wore a common badge or "livery," and men like this carried on the feuds between great families during England's "Wars of the Roses" between the Lancaster and York branches of the royal dynasty. The rich maintained or hired for the job cloak-and-dagger and club men to do their dirty work for them. Because their connection with honest murder was intimate, they could be honest murderers or retainers depending on who was paying them that week, or highwaymen, gamblers, pimps, or mercenary soldiers. Mercenary companies were always full of such persons and were sometimes led by them.

Bravi, when employed, lived in the highest strata physically; that is, they slept in the castles and palaces of the nobles. At the same time, when out of a job, or when circulating through the streets or villages on their own, they were sure to be moving in the underworld. There were also those who were professionally outside the law—those who made a living by selling talents, goods, and services which were against the law. There were also the village bad persons. The connection between city, country, and village was not too remote. The worst of the lower class had cousins in small towns and villages, and vice versa. City slums were also the refuge of those who were outside the law somewhere. Populations like this went streaming off to do the most remarkable things; we do not generally think of the army of the First Crusade as containing a considerable contingent of underworld characters, but it did. They got honest Crusaders into all sorts of trouble, on the way across Europe and beyond into the Holy Land.

The Physical Aspects of the Towns

The physical aspect of the towns calls for some comment. In general, the nearer the center of the city, the further away from the city walls, the higher the real-estate values were. The nearer the walls, the more likely that a house might be hit by enemy fire. As a result, the buildings which housed the very rich were toward the center of things. And of course it was at the center of things that the main squares and buildings were located.

If a town had a bishop, the bishop's cathedral and palace, usually integrated together in one complex of buildings, stood near or on the main square. Very near by would be the chief building of the town government. In an independent town, this would be its capitol; in a town which was under some higher sovereign it would be the municipal court house or city hall.

Usually either the cathedral bell tower, or another tower built next to the city hall or as a part of it, served as the town bell for emergency calls. When the enemy was at the gates, the great bell would be set tolling. If there was a riot in the streets, the bell would be rung. If somebody wanted to start a riot in the streets he would try to get to the bell and toll it in order to set things humming. The bell was the symbol of freedom in the northern towns and, when a town had lost its freedom, the victor who had snatched that freedom away took the bells from the tower so that the town became silent. From the point of view of patriotic townsmen, that was the greatest of all tragedies. The belfry, or campanile, was like the bell towers we often find today on American university campuses; these are in many cases modeled after the Italian bell towers of the eleven hundreds, or the Flemish ones of slightly later vintage.

In prosperous northern towns, in addition to the church and city hall, the other buildings around the squares came to be the guild halls, club rooms, and administrative centers of the rich guilds. We often find, as in Brussels, that the town hall and the guild halls took up all the frontage around the principal square. In Brussels the cathedral happens to be a little way away from the square, and the guild halls are of relatively late construction, having been put up in the fifteen and sixteen hundreds. But Brussels was modeled on still older towns, so it can serve as an example.

Behind the guild halls, next to the cathedral, or behind the city hall and bunched in close thereabouts, were the residences of the wealthy merchant capitalists, the patricians. In the ten and eleven hundreds these houses were as solid a fortification as their owners could make. Not only did each have to serve as an inner defense in case an enemy broke through the city walls, but each had to serve as a final defense against next-door neighbors.

Family feuding was characteristic of towns everywhere, north as well as south. In Italy every family was enemy to some other family or group of families, or expected it might soon be. Shakespeare gave a very correct image when he pictured Romeo and Juliet and the hatred between the Montagues and Capulets. Such families did not like each other; they disliked each other so much that they killed one another on sight and by arrangement, year after year. It was taken for granted that a person who went over to the enemy or had any dealings with the enemy was the worst kind of traitor.

In the north the count of Flanders, the king of France, and the king of England held the feuding down, and fortified houses were not common. While the first few generations of patricians erected feuding houses, soon after their fangs were pulled by public authority, and great houses were likely to be smaller and less like castles than those in Italy, where feuding was worst of all.

In Italian cities where feuds and faction warfare ran rampant, the houses of a clan of patricians were built as instruments for killing neighbors who were unfriendly and for avoiding being killed. Some of the stoutest had walls which were ten or more feet thick, and without windows at the street level. There were arrow slots a little way up the wall, from which to shoot hostile neighbors as they came down the street. On the third floor there were windows out of which things could be thrown at those neighbors as they came in close.

The entrance was well fortified, with a great barred door wide enough for a coach or armed men on horseback to go through. When a visitor knocked and was admitted, he found he was not actually in the house. Instead he was in an alcove, and above it were gratings through which hot coals and hot oil could be dropped, while on both sides were arrow slits at throat level, constructed in such a way that a spear could not be easily poked through them from within the alcove. There was still another great door out of the alcove to the courtyard as strongly barred as the first one, while a portcullis was available to be dropped behind, over the first door. The visitor could be closed in with no way of getting out unless he had been invited to the house as a friend.

Once through the inner door, the visitor would find himself in a court-yard which had no doors or windows at the ground level. An open stair-way up one side of the courtyard invited the unwelcome visitor to fight his way to the door above, all the way subject to attack through slits in the wall on one side, while no railing protected him from missiles fired across the court.

Up from one corner of the house, or from the middle, would rise a stone tower some six to eight stories high. On the upper reaches of the tower would be machines which could shoot a cloud of arrows, and catapults which could hurl rocks or large bundles of pitch-soaked burning straw across city blocks at enemy towers. In the twelve hundreds such palace towers dominated the skyline seen on approaching Florence, Siena, Lucca, Milan, Genoa, and other Italian towns.

Eventually city fathers or tyrants had to require the tearing down of the fighting towers in order to achieve some sort of peace, but one little town in Italy, San Gimignano, which lies between Florence and Siena, still has a handful of its towers left. The picture given here has been that of the dream home of the very rich; mostly, even those with fighting tow-ers were less elaborate, as are those of San Gimignano.

In the north as well as in Italy, medieval city palaces had crowds of people living in them. We must not think that great wealth brought privacy in those days as it sometimes does now. In the household of a very well-to-do family would live the unmarried sisters and cousins and aunts to the third and fourth remove. Separate rooms or floors would be tenanted by households headed by married males—uncles, brothers, cousins. Then there were many men and women servants, with their spouses and chil-dren, for a respectable household required three or four or five body and food servants, sometimes a slave or two, and the family bastards. There were also hired bravi. The palaces of the very rich were crawling with people. What is more, they were cold-water walk-ups; there was no running water upstairs. Until the thirteenth or even the fourteenth centuries there were no glazed windows. Heat for cooking and warmth came from braziers, the fuel being carried up and the fumes mingling with all the other fumes.

Outside the neighborhood of the great houses were to be found what were called in one town the *sestieri,* in another the *quartieri,* and so on. In English we call them "wards." Such wards covered areas about the size of a few of our city blocks, and each ward had in a measure the character of a little town within a town. We have something like this in our American towns, but they are only by chance organized in wards. Our wards are artificial things, usually bounded by main streets or other surveyors' lines. Occasionally we do have little towns within our cities, a little Poland, Norway, Sweden, Italy, and so forth, and they usually also have a life of their own.

In the Middle Ages the boundaries and political organization of a ward coincided more closely with the character and interests of its inhabitants. In Florence there was a whole German ward for a long while, and in any town where there were students there was a segregated quarter for them. The Latin quarter in Paris is such a place, where the students could lead their own lives.

However, normally all the citizens of a town were of one speech and cultural background, and still the wards had a character of their own. To begin with, a ward usually had its local square, and its local church or churches. The ecclesiastical organization fitted fairly well the ward pattern. A ward (or part of a ward) would also be a parish; a parish (or part of a parish) would be a ward. One or two or three priests would be identified with the churches of a ward. Their church buildings served as centers for ward life. The local areas also had particular business interests. We have mentioned that there was segregation by craft, all the goldsmiths, all the cobblers, all the fish dealers, for example, being located along their respective streets or alleys or squares. With their shops and homes thus grouped together, there would be one or several guilds identified with a given ward and parish.

There was also ward responsibility, above all for taxes and police. (The word "ward" in English was originally the same word as "guard.") The militia which guarded the city walls was organized on a ward basis; a given ward unit was responsible for the guard or ward of a given unit of wall, and had a given position in the marching army of the city when it took the field. The ward unit was supported by money from taxes levied on the guilds and on the ward. The ward had charge of its own fire and police organization, the police and fire and militia units all being under the same direction. Sturdy apprentices and husky young journeymen formed the military, police, and fire-fighting force of a given ward. The adult men enjoying the franchise of the ward elected their representative to the central city government. The aldermen in the wards (at least in the north) in turn elected the chief magistrates of the city.

There was crowding, overcrowding, or supercrowding in the tenements. Unless a town had begun to shrink or decay, they were all crowded. But we cannot be sure their preferences in the matter of crowding were the same as those of persons who read books like this. Quite certainly they liked to live close together, with their shops downstairs, or with their working rooms (for example, those of the weavers) upstairs on the third or fourth or fifth floors.

If possible, the slums proper were kept outside the city gates. In modern America the country club is outside the city while the slums are down by the slaughter house, the tannery, and the gas works. In the Middle Ages it was the other way around (leaving out the gas works). The slums were outside the city walls for the best of all reasons: nobody cared if they got burned. As a matter of fact, if an enemy was approaching, city officers cleared out the slum people and drove them over the horizon if possible. In case of siege no one wanted to have those worthless mouths inside the walls. They also cleared the slum hovels away from the city gates so that the enemy could not creep up close under cover of the huts and get into a position to shoot or rush the defenders of the city gates.

The slums were likely to run along the main roads which approached a city. There was also housing outside for wayfarers who got caught after six o'clock or sunset or whenever it was that the city gates were closed. The inns on the outside of towns could either be dives, or they could be respectable enough and intended for such persons as Chaucer's pilgrims who were spending the night outside the city in hopes of getting an early start the next day.

Around the larger towns, the villages even quite a distance away were for all purposes reckoned as belonging to the towns. The administration of the town police, courts, and taxes usually included an area from two to six or even ten miles outside the town. That was a considerable area. The "league" or the "banlieu" was the name for this area under the town administration.

From our point of view, a large number counted as town dwellers were actually village peasants. The inhabitants of those villages came to concentrate upon the victualing of those living within the walls, stressing truck gardening, meat, milk and butter production, the catching of fresh fish, and so on. Villages around the towns also tended to house a considerable number of the deserving working poor. Those with jobs would walk into town and be near when the gates opened; then they would walk the three to five miles home after sunset.

It was the land outside the towns which was ravaged by any enemy. First warning of invasion was often given by smoke rising from distant villages, even before couriers could get in ahead of the straggle of refugees. When they had forewarning, a town's own forces often scorched the earth in advance of an enemy army, knowing it would be scorched anyway and wanting to leave as little loot as possible. Able-bodied young villagers were part of the fighting force of the city, and were lined up in its militia ranks.

In the first town development wood was largely used in building, as it has been in the United States, unless no timber was available in a neighborhood. In the Northern towns where wood was easily available there was a long, slow shift from wood toward fireproof materials, while in Italy the change came a little faster. But even in Italy, in the early ten hundreds, most of the city of Milan burned up in a single day. The city of Pavia was burned by the Magyars in the nine hundreds, and then burned again completely by the Germans a couple of generations later. Most of the towns were easily burned, and while no source tells us explicitly that they were built of wood, we feel sure that towns which burned up so easily must have been made of it. Local Italian town statutes or ordinances are to be found for the late eleven hundreds, and increasingly for the twelve hundreds, which require citizens to get rid of thatched or wooden shingle roofs, and to go over to stone and slate and lead—fireproof materials. To judge by the surviving buildings in many parts of Europe, it was in the eleven hundreds, first with church and defense buildings, then more and more with private dwellings, that they went over to stone where there was good stone in a neighborhood, or to brick, as in the Low Countries or Lombardy, where there was no good local stone to work with. Stone, brick, and such materials came in increasingly in the course of the eleven and twelve hundreds, although London burned up almost completely as late as the 1660's. London was a very slow and very backward town in the development of this sort of thing.

In addition to laws requiring changes in construction, there came to be regulations concerning such things as public hygiene, other fire hazards, and so on. One of the universal laws required fire to be covered in every household after a certain time of the evening. ("Cover fire" in French became "curfew" in English.) There were increasingly strict regulations about animal slaughter, household waste disposal, encroachment upon rights of way, and like matters, but even as late as 1800 A.D. most towns, especially in the north, would have smelled and felt filthy to those who live in them today. Italy was relatively sweet smelling and clean by the twelve and thirteen hundreds.

Public Works and Charities

In the development of prosperous towns, a very large amount of the activity and wealth of the citizens was devoted to public improvements. There was, all over western Europe, what we should think of today as a lively town spirit in any town which was doing well. A town could express its character, and show its interest in artistic matters and its love for the Christian religion and saints, by devoting a great deal of money to the erection of one great public church. In any city where there was a bishop in residence the erection of a fine cathedral was a primary interest of its citizens, from Sicily to the farthest north, and from Iceland to Kiev.

There had been much good building in the tenth century in some parts of Italy, southern France, and Rhineland Germany. When the population began to increase more and more rapidly around ten hundred and from then into the fourteenth century, it was actually necessary to keep building more and larger places of worship. It was also a matter of town pride to erect churches which would outdo those of neighbors. The rivalry between the towns and the resources which were available for this purpose promoted the prosperity of a very considerable number of great architects, and brought into existence large numbers of organized, skilled craftsmen who could supply the masonry work, the iron work, the glass work, and other things necessary.

Money for the work was obtained partly through the ordinary revenues of the church officials concerned, and partly through special subscriptions, bequests, and endowments from people in the area. The great work of building cathedrals led men with engineering genius to devise ever more efficient and effective construction principles. This takes us into the realm of artistic history, but it should be noted that the sort of genius which was making bigger and more efficient ships was also making greater and more efficient naves of cathedrals. Gothic architecture, viewed from this point, presents a triumph of invention.

The development of any city also called upon citizens to repair, extend, and adorn the fortifications of the city. Great city walls were erected partly by public subscription, partly by forced taxes, and frequently by the labor, much of it voluntary, of most of the able-bodied population. When a city was threatened, real miracles of rapid and expensive construction were achieved.

In addition, in towns which had any water frontage, there was need for docks, moles, warehouses, and the like. Even lighthouses were needed, and bridges and aqueducts were called for. City governments undertook these works, much as they would today, but the work was at all times furthered by very extensive endowment. Often volunteer work in cutting stone and moving materials into place was of great help. Wealthy men subscribed or donated to projects of this sort.

Several different monastic orders undertook to build badly needed bridges in areas where local resources could not handle the heavy expenditures, or local artisans were deficient in numbers or skill.

The ten, eleven, twelve, and thirteen hundreds saw Europe marvelously benefiting from public improvements of the sort mentioned. A very large number of the bridges, roadways, harbors, and moles still in use date back to improvements undertaken for the first time in the period we are covering.

The Christian religion taught men they should be generous to the poor, the sick, and those who were unable, because of misfortune, to make a way for themselves. Monasteries on the one hand, with episcopal and parish organizations on the other, did of course provide extensive facilities for what we should call today hospital and orphanage work. But it was in the cities of the period that a rapid extension of buildings for these purposes took place alongside those which were more clearly ecclesiastical in origin. Wealthy men, wealthy families, guilds, and other groups voluntarily set up hospitals, orphanages, and retreats for widows and spinsters and endowed them in perpetuity with "bonds" and with rents in city and country property.

The rapid growth of the towns and the flow into them of a great many persons whose economic position was precarious or downright poor called for expansion in what would be called, in modern society, social work programs. Relief of the poor and care of dependents had, of course, been sustained by parish organizations in the rural as well as in the urban communities. But the towns started to grow too fast, and the older machinery could not be expanded with sufficient rapidity to take care of the new problems.

First in Italy, at about 1200, organizations, ecclesiastical in every way but designed to take care of the more or less unchurched populations in the big cities, sprang to life. During the twelve and thirteen hundreds, and indeed ever since in Catholic countries, these organizations have played a large part in urban social work. From the point of view of the church, the organizations which were set up first by St. Francis of Assisi in a small town in central Italy, and by St. Dominic, who was of Spanish origin, were extensions of the monastic pattern. Brothers, as they were called, joined the founding saints to form monastic communities which were not, however, located in remote country districts but rather in the teeming cities. The brothers or friars in the Franciscan and Dominican orders ministered to the needs of the poor and preached to those who were not adequately reached by parish organizations. The Dominican and Franciscan orders became social-work orders on a very large scale, since they spread rapidly from their homes in Italy to all parts of the Roman Catholic community. Some other orders also grew up paralleling them, but did not become so prominent or so lasting.

The Dominican and Franciscan friars begged for their own livings, since they were under vows of personal poverty, but they also distributed what was given to the indigent, they cared for the poor and the sick in homes, and they provided shelters and little schools for underprivileged children in the bigger cities. They worked as well with villagers in the country-side, but it was in the cities that the need for them was most strongly felt and the effect of their work most noticeable.

Both Franciscans and Dominicans had an influence as well in the fields of lower and higher education, another need which the growing towns had made acute by twelve hundred. In this educational work the Franciscans and Dominicans built upon foundations already laid down both by the communities and by the church organizations of Europe. For a long time it had been felt to be the duty of the parish priest anywhere to give elementary instruction in Latin to such boys and girls as showed sufficient talent. This was partly with the thought that the recruiting of the next generation of church servants depended upon the education of the young, even in the Carolingian period and the tenth century.

With the rise of towns there was increasing demand for young men who could read and write, and there was reason, if only a social one, that well-to-do young girls should be taught their letters, although hardly ever in Latin but rather in the local speech of their communities.

School work might be carried on, of course, in any parish church. Some advanced work was normally associated with any cathedral where a master of the scholars carried on the instruction of young recruits for church service. But in addition, in the course of the eleven and twelve hundreds, there came an extensive development of private grammar-school teaching by schoolmasters who made their livings from the fees. These were largely centered in the cities, although larger villages also had free schools or fee schools, as the case might be.

Dominicans and Franciscans recruited for their own orders young men in the cities and villages who had a drive for social and missionary work which made them acceptable brothers. To train recruits, it was necessary for the orders to have schools too; and some Dominican and Franciscan brothers developed into the outstanding scholars at the rising universities. Leadership in the rise of the universities was not at all a Franciscan or Dominican affair, yet nevertheless some of the very greatest of the minds in the university communities at all times were those of leading brothers in one or the other of the two orders.

The universities themselves were in large measure the creation of the new towns and of the townsmen. Universities were unknown in Europe in the ten hundreds, although soon after they were being foreshadowed by gatherings of students and teachers in some centers. In the course of the eleven hundreds the first of Europe's really great universities—which still exist to this day—began to take shape. Paris in northern France and Bologna in northern Italy housed the first recognizable universities. However, other universities springing from them or founded in imitation of them were progressively established from Scotland to Sicily and from Spain to Poland.

University students lived in university towns and depended for their own sustenance upon remittances from their homes through the channels of trade. University communities rode upon the shoulders of the economies which had been developed by and for the townsmen in the first place. There are other reasons why great universities came to grow in the period mentioned, but it is quite inconceivable that they could have grown as they did, or lasted at all, had there not been the towns for them to grow in and the new trading channels by which they could be supplied.

The large cities had combinations of great luxury and great poverty at all times, despite what has been said so far about poor relief and other ameliorative measures undertaken by church communities and private charity.

Those who dwelt in the greatest houses lived in a combination of astonishing luxury and relative discomfort. There was sparse decoration in the private chambers of the well-to-do. The bed was frequently the only pretentious piece of furniture which a very wealthy family might possess. Sparse furniture and poor ventilation were often combined with a profusion of rich hangings, cushions, and covers in the rooms which were most frequented. There would be a most extraordinary sort of profusion for the meals in the well-to-do homes, and tremendous quantities were served. However, to judge by the recipe books which have survived to us, the food was crudely cooked and queerly flavored with bitter or sour juices, spices, flowers, and herbs.

Wherever possible in the yards or behind the buildings of the wealthy, there were gardens which served at one and the same time to provide some of the food, at least salads, and perhaps flowers for decoration of the interior of the house, and the little breathing space which the crowded cities made so desirable. Covered balconies or *loggie,* reached from upper stories or on the roofs of the wealthy, gave facilities for fresh-air eating and strolling. In the south bathing establishments were generally open to customers.

Work and Holidays

Crowding in the workers' tenements and the slums was ameliorated by the fact that fresh air and sunshine, in open fields, were only a few hundred yards down the road from every town gate, and even the largest towns covered far less area than cities do today. The walk from town center to city gates was never long.

Medieval townspeople, for all the crowding and squalor which seem so repugnant to us, had a great deal of fun and made an enormous amount of provision for the having of fun. Holy Days or holidays were days in which the routine of work was completely interrupted and everyone, from the richest down to the poorest apprentices and slum dwellers, turned out to take part in or to view processions and games, theatrical presentations, and mountebank shows in the principal square, along the streets, in the lesser squares, or even in open fields outside the town walls.

There were more holidays than we normally enjoy in our modern society. There were holidays for the principal seasons of the year, for the principal saints locally revered, and then the great general holidays for the highest feasts of the whole Christian calendar. Generally speaking processions were gorgeous. The wealthy burgesses were expected to parade themselves in the most elegant and colorful apparel, and in such processions to take their proper places by rank and social position. There were, of course, nobles and ecclesiastics garbed equally splendidly in all processions of any account. Foreign ambassadors and visitors from strange towns likewise had their place in such processions, and were also expected to show off startling, novel, and beautiful costumes for the pleasure of all.

The inns of the cities were, as they are today, of various levels of excellence. The very well-to-do usually counted on being put up by persons of equal rank in towns they visited. Well-to-do churchmen and noblemen usually maintained, in any town which they were likely to visit often, quite elaborate and relatively luxurious dwellings of their own. Most bishops and great abbots had permanent headquarters near the court of whichever sovereigns they were accustomed to attend. So did the very greatest of the nobles.

Cities with large interests in other great centers maintained similar hotel residences for their merchants and financiers who were away from home. The house of the Genoese in Bruges was rented from the Borsa or Bourse family. Trading in exchange and like matters centered where the Genoese lived, in the residence which has given its name to modern Continental stock exchanges. Venice had a combination big hotel and warehouse and isolation lock-up for German merchants. The German Hansa had great all-purpose establishments at Bruges, London, Bergen, and Novgorod, and lesser establishments elsewhere.

However, even the well-to-do merchants, unless they were put up as guests of equally well-to-do merchants in a town they were visiting, usually were thrown back on the accommodations of what we today call hotels. These were usually very crowded, with a minimum of privacy even for those with heavy purses, and, while the wine and food were lavish, the personal facilities, the bedding, and the other amenities might very well from our point of view be extremely distasteful. However, the well-to-do man who brought merchandise with him found that his inn and his innkeeper played a role very much more important than that played by a modern professional hotel and hotel keeper. The innkeeper took care of the guests' animals—he would normally have both pack animals and riding beasts—and also of his servants, who might be of considerable number. The innkeepers also provided storage rooms for the merchandise a merchant might bring with him. In many towns the innkeeper would go much further. He could act as interpreter and broker, bringing his guests in touch with local merchants for buying and selling. He might help to close deals, hold pledges for future payment, and even function as official sales-tax collector for the local government. The innkeeper might well be, in a town with a lively foreign trade, an extremely important cog in the machine of commerce.

Lesser inns, which were in most cases drinking places, existed in considerable numbers throughout the wards of a city. Many were respectable; some were not. Those which were not were oftenest located in the slum area outside the city walls. It was in them, in fact, that the lowest classes in the cities met and hobnobbed with the lowest classes from the country —where the country highwaymen and the city cutpurse were in brotherhood in the big drinking room provided by an innkeeper who served as tipster, fence, and stool pigeon.

Families who could afford it usually tried to have some small property, by purchase or by rent, in the open country. This was to serve many purposes. A small cottage with part of an acre or several acres of garden around it could well provide a fair part of the table food for the whole family in the course of the winter months. The cottage could also provide a pleasant spot for withdrawal when the city got too hot or when plague broke out within the walls. A small place in the country was desired by the middling well off inside the city walls, and a bigger place in the country was normally desired by those who had greater means—the great merchants and bankers.

Large places which could rival the establishments of great nobles were commonplace among the rich patricians in Italian towns, or in England or in France. While the purchase of such estates could be an end in itself, there was often enough still another thought in the mind of a wealthy merchant when he acquired property of this sort; if by chance some title of nobility or authority adhered to a given house and main property, it was possible by the purchase of such a place for a merchant to start his sons and grandsons on the way toward entrance into the nobility of the country at large. Purchase of estates which would enable them to live as squires was one of the common aims among Londoners, Bristolmen, and others in England. Similar ambitions moved well-to-do men in France, Germany, and Italy.

The work of the workingmen inside the cities was, except for the holidays, extremely arduous. To begin with, machinery, such as it was, was heavy and clumsy. The manipulation of tools left callouses on the hand and a crick in the back. Many of the trades were hard on the eyes or on the lungs, or resulted in malformation of the muscles of an arm or of a leg, and so on. It was commonplace in the Middle Ages for the passer-by to identify the trades of persons he saw on the street by the malformations or other manifestations of hard physical usage of their bodies.

As a normal pattern, the workday was from sunup to sundown. That meant that in the winter the day of actual work was rather short, and there was constant temptation to lengthen it with the use of artificial light. Artificial light was frowned upon by respectable crafts, partly because work done with its help might well be substandard, by accident or by intent, and also because it was possible to work more secretly away from the eyes of guild inspectors after curfew time, behind drawn blinds.

However, since most of Europe lies rather far to the north, the summer days were long. The workday, the day from sunrise to sunset, was divided into our normal number of hours, but the hours began at the start of the day and finished at the end with the high or noon point in the middle. This meant that the hour itself was longer in the summer and shorter in the winter through the working day. A six-hour day would have far more than six of our hours in June and many less than our six hours in December.

Daily life, among those who dwelt in the crowded craftsmen sections and in the slums, was rather nearer the starvation level than we like to think we would find today in our own metropolitan centers. Poverty was a barrier against marriage and was furthermore quite severe in its effect upon the lower classes in cities. We lack anything like good reliable statistics for town populations, either as to the over-all size of the city population or as to the percentages, within the city population, of various elements. But one thing which strikes anyone who gets involved in the records we do have is the high percentages of adult men and adult women who were unmarried at any one moment. Marriage for those in the lower classes came, all too often, late in life if at all. As a consequence there was a very serious problem of town morals, solved in different ways in different cities, but hardly ever solved by making marriage easy for the hardworking lower craftsmen or for the unskilled. It might be noted that one of the endowments popular among the wealthy charitable in any progressive city was a fund which could supply poor but honest maidens with dowries. These played a part in combating this over-all difficulty in getting the younger people to form into families. Lorenzo the Magnificent Medici embezzled the fund which Florence had built up for this charity.

It was hard on children to be brought up in the dark, disease-ridden city streets, and conditions were also very bad for women in childbirth or in the period of childbearing. As far as our poor evidence can show us, there was over-all failure generation by generation on the part of town populations to replace themselves. In general, town population was maintained and, if there was an increase, it was increased by a flow of migration from villages both near and far into the city. A town population did not supply enough new healthy young adults, born in the town, to take the places vacated by the death of the older persons in the same town. Even when many children had been born to a couple, wills show that the adolescent and adult offspring were few as a rule. Life expectancy, even for healthy young adults, was far shorter than it has now become in European urban societies.

CHAPTER VII

Republics,
Oligarchies, and Tyrannies

TOWN governments varied, of course, from place to place, and nearly all varied from time to time. Perhaps no political history contains so many incidents of reshuffling of constitutions as that of Italy in the period with which we are dealing. Instead of a dead-level stability, there was a boiling activity as men tried to devise constitutions for the government of towns in a period when they were growing and when there was little over-all historical experience upon which to draw.

In northern Italy, speaking generally, somewhat the following sequence of developments took place. From about ten hundred to eleven hundred towns were considered to be local centers under the government of the king of Italy who was also the king of Germany and the Holy Roman Emperor. The link between the town area and that sovereign was sometimes a local marquis or count whose title to govern came from Carolingian grant. More often the government was exercised locally by the bishop or archbishop who had, by Imperial grant, the powers to rule as count. While this appears to be a somewhat monarchical and autocratic form of government, we find some evidence—although not perfect evidence—to show that at least in his civil and military activities such a bishop was aided by what we might today call a committee of well-to-do citizens, many of them noblemen whose properties and interests lay inside the city walls and in the country as well, perhaps as far away as thirty or forty miles toward the horizon.

While the bishop had the authority, the government in fact was handled by these wealthy and noble gentlemen schooled in war, in the holding of courts, and in the exercise of power generally. These men formed the council around the bishop where important policies had to be discussed. They led the bishop's armies, they undertook the care of city walls. They were his feudal vassals, functioning as such.

Late in the ten hundreds or early in the eleven hundreds, this theoretical episcopal monarchy was in general developed into a limited constitutional monarchy—to use very modern terms which, however, somewhat describe the situation. In the bishop's name the councils of leading citizens undertook to do practically everything that independent governments do today. Backing the bishops, in an attempt sometimes to hold onto the powers which were slipping away from them, the German emperors conducted wars against city governments which were engaged in this rebellious development. On the whole, the Italian city governments had made good by 1190 or 1200 their claims to handle their own affairs themselves. This finally recognized and made legal a situation which had in fact been existent for many generations in the case of such cities as Milan, Genoa, Pisa, Bologna, to name only a few of the cities in which somewhat this development of a "college" of consuls took place.

Whether they were already recognized as legally exercising such powers, or whether they had not yet obtained such legal recognition, the free towns had a great many powers and functions which had to be performed. The town nobles and merchants managed taxes, trained and commanded the armies, built and manned the strong points in the town or the nearby country, ran the courts, and in general until about 1200 acted much as a board of aldermen would do in a northern city. Feuding, however, between such patricians as customarily occupied the high offices resulted in a general distrust of government by these boards of six or eight or twelve local magnates, who were normally elected as consuls for a year's term, but who passed office-holding from one member of their own class to another.

It became customary to hire what we today might call a city manager from the outside. Usually this official for whom they developed a name—*podestà*—was a professional at the trade of managing cities. The podesta was hired on a very tightly drawn contract to come to a city with his own staff of judges, military leaders, and palace guard, and to take over for a period of one year all, or almost all, aspects of city affairs. He might leave the old consular board under him, or he might simply wipe it out completely. At the end of his year's service, however, he was required to remain in the city, stripped of his powers, to be investigated by a special board set up for that purpose and provided for under the original contract. If, during his year in office, he had misused his power, he was subject during the period of post-official inquiry to make restitution or to suffer severely in his property or even in his person. Once he had been acquitted he was paid a very lavish salary for the year's services and sent home in high honor.

Podesta government was a device designed in part to win wars with neighboring cities, as well as to keep down feuding within the city itself. A city at any one moment was at war or likely to be at war with all its neighbors. Towns which were vigorously competitive for markets, for taxes over border areas, or for the loyalty of one another's citizens, were inclined at all times to break the peace, usually in the name of general political principles such as adherence to the Guelf or Ghibelline causes. The podesta was conceived of as bringer of unity for the purpose of winning wars with rival towns.

However, in the middle of the twelve hundreds the great rivalries of popes and emperors, combined with feuds of the factions in most cities, brought about still another general development in town government. In any one city, a clique or a single party would seize the government and put into office a podesta not designed to keep the Guelphs and Ghibellines from one another's throats or to provide stability in general within the town, but with the task of eliminating all opposition to the dominant party. (The Ghibellines upheld the authority of the German Emperor, the Guelphs opposed it; either one or the other faction was almost always in power.) One-party rule by faction or clique then came to be the general pattern. The party might be Guelph in one city, it might be Ghibelline in another, although it usually had some special local nickname.

Rivalry between the two great parties, expressing itself in local conflicts between the factions in the different cities, kept all Italy in an uproar through much of the twelve hundreds. Then one-party rule, the management of all affairs by a party boss, led rather rapidly in most towns to true despotism. The boss himself, put in office at first by either the Guelphs or the Ghibellines, might develop into the founder of a line of hereditary tyrants in the town which first had trusted him. Or the new despot might be the descendant of some old noble family of the town itself, which, holding onto rural castles and followers, had always exercised some influence and whose leader now moved in to protect the town from all enemies and the townsmen from one another. In exchange he took the right to exploit the town as if it were private property.

There had always been mercenary soldiers in the armies the towns marshaled against one another, but in the thirteen hundreds the hiring of mercenaries from foreign lands as well as from Italy itself became the general rule when towns set to war with one another. Mercenary leaders, or captains, or conductors (*condottieri*) of troops of soldiers sometimes seized the government in towns which had employed them, or in towns which they had conquered in the name of an employer.

By these various means despots came to dominate most towns which had not been swallowed up by others. It might be noted that the number of towns which had freedom went down rapidly once the imperial government relinquished its legal right to rule locally. The great majority of towns thereafter fought, quite literally, to the death, for the loser in a war between two towns had its lands annexed, its trade cut off, its taxes raised, and so on, by the victor. To be sure, sometimes a victor would show a certain sort of magnanimity by allowing the defeated town to become a quiet center for university studies, or a center for artistic activity, or a royal residence. For example, the Visconti of Milan utterly crushed the freedom of Pavia. But instead of killing Pavia as a town, they turned it into a fine center for studies and a center for their ducal court. In much the same way the Florentines, after exterminating the power and prosperity of rival Pisa, made Pisa into a center for university work. However, this did not always happen to the defeated towns, for there were far too many. Such towns vegetated, functioning economically as local market towns, governed by state officials sent from above.

The despots, as they got into power, were of course always afraid of being overthrown. This might come from the victory of a rival city, or from revolution within the walls, or from a palace assassination and replacement (and this last was the greatest danger).

Once in office, the despot was able to give efficient government and, if he was enlightened, to provide a beneficent rule in which the lower classes especially were given a great many quite tangible benefits at the expense of the upper classes, which might well be stripped of a good part of their wealth. Enlightened despots were great patrons of art, architecture, literature, scholarship, partly to bedazzle their own subjects, partly to give themselves prestige in their world of fellow despots and outside monarchs. There were also many unenlightened despots.

However, it was necessary for these men to maintain a complete system of secret espionage, a whole system of secret arrests and imprisonment, without trial or even notice to kinsmen. Torture, execution and other violence characterized the activities of secret policemen under the control of such despots. Especially the tyrants' own fathers and brothers-in-law, sons, wives, and mistresses and boon companions had to be regarded as dangerous. In the family of a despot, family squabbles were more serious than those of ordinary people. A hard word and a frown might well result in somebody's death, the despot's own or one of his relative's, within a very short time. Danger of poison or of the dagger, from a wife or from a husband, was something that actually did exist in the households of these men.

It can be noted that the city of Venice was quite an exception to this chain of development, partly because in Venice it was impossible to have a riot or a revolution in which the rebels could ride through the streets and take possession of the principal centers of power. In Florence, for quite other reasons, despotism came much later than in most cities, and so on. There are, it should go without saying, exceptions to all these general statements which have just been made.

North of the Alps—and this covers most of the Rhineland and Danubian Germany, the lands colonized eastward by the Germans in the period we are talking of, and northern France and England—the movement toward city independence never did work itself out completely. While in the ten hundreds citizens of many of the northern cities had ambitions quite like those of Italian town dwellers, by the eleven and twelve hundreds the central state had in all cases proved itself too strong for the cities to get the independence which such cities as Milan acquired at the same time in Italy.

The king of England, the count of Flanders, the king of France, and other rulers in Germany maintained sufficient authority, even inside town walls, to make it impossible for the burgesses to become wholly independent. However, maintenance of royal power in most of these countries was furthered by a political alliance between townsmen and rulers. Instead of fighting the towns, the rulers in the north almost everywhere made common cause with the merchants and craftsmen against the local feudal lords and bishops.

The vehicle for the conferring of powers on the townsmen themselves was normally a royal charter granting local government, but in which the local government was subordinated to the ruler. The king of England allowed the citizens of London wide authority over their own taxes, over their police, their walls, and their fighting forces, but he maintained his authority well above that of the sheriffs and other officials of London itself. The king of France was sometimes generous to his subjects in Paris, but at the same time managed their affairs directly from his own court.

In the chartered northern towns there was commonly an alderman for every ward, serving for one year. The aldermen together usually elected their own chief official or mayor. As mentioned earlier, the mayor served as head of the whole city, but each alderman (or pair of aldermen) served in a way as a little mayor over his own ward.

In most of the cities there was a tendency for economic and social discontent to make itself manifest in the course of the later twelve and the thirteen hundreds, and this economic and social discontent took on political and religious color as it spread and became strong. An epoch of urban turbulence was manifest through the thirteen hundreds. These hard times have been mentioned in another context; it is now needful to notice their effects on town populations and affairs.

There were some serious general famines, and we know there was the Black Death in the middle of the century, with later waves of the Plague following at twenty-year to twenty-five-year intervals for nearly a century after. We know that population in many towns was dwindling and that probably over-all population was dwindling. We know too that there were shifts not only in trade routes which worked hardship on older centers, but also in the pattern of manufacture which moved many of the processes in the textile and metalworking trades to new centers or even into rural areas which had not earlier been important in that kind of work. This left older towns with shrinking populations, shrinking tax roles, and other distressing local problems. We also know that great wars between the kings of England and France, paralleled by wars between other potentates in other parts of Europe, drained countries of men and money, and in many cases caused outright physical destruction of the countryside and of important cities.

It was in this period that we find more rebellions and civic disturbances within the cities than had been characteristic of the earlier period—not that that earlier period had been altogether tranquil anywhere. As the thirteen hundreds went along, we find that rebellious groups in old industrial and trading centers, in both the north and the south, fought against the entrenched governments of aldermen, or consuls, or podestas, or despots. The rebellions nearly always combined programs of religious, social, economic, and political reform.

From the point of view of religion we find that the rebels generally demanded church reform, especially reform of the tax and other financial patterns which supported the church. There was a distrust of and dislike for rich prelates and wealthy clerks who lived by church endowments or by the gifts of the poor, and even distrust of the friars. In many cases individuals or groups expressed their dislike of the upper clergy in such ways as to bring upon the rebels quite well-founded charges of heresy.

The heretics of the thirteen and fourteen hundreds in some ways fore-shadowed the heretics of the Protestant Reformation period, and in other ways had teachings and beliefs which were quite their own.

By and large opposition to at least part of the clergy and part of the beliefs of the church was paralleled by what would be called ultra-democratic or leveler sentiments in the political and social world. Opposition to rich men as rich men, and to constituted authorities as such, was characteristic of many of the rebel groups. Anti-rich reform and anti-dictator reform was demanded by rebels in the streets of northern towns as well as in Italy.

Whether the hard times helped cause all of this, or whether these helped cause the hard times, is a matter for debate. But on the whole, these turbulences in the towns of the period did not result in any very serious or great remodeling of social, religious, or economic patterns. In some cases a little success was followed by disruption into warring sub-factions of the winning group; in other cases the whole of the revolution-ary movement was put down by the rallied forces of king, prince, or despot, as the case might be.

When the revolts failed, there was in general a period of stagnation which in the case of many towns has lasted on through the rest of history. There are towns which were prominent up to 1300 or 1350, went through distressing developments such as those mentioned, and have been left since as museum pieces. However, that generalization should not be made too broad a one, because Paris and London, to mention only two great cities of today, themselves had very violent developments of this sort in the thirteen hundreds.

Section III

SOCIETIES OUTSIDE EUROPE

WE NOW turn to the peoples outside Europe who were to be tremendously changed by the pressure of Europeans upon them. This pressure commenced in some instances in the thirteen hundreds, broadened to affect more and more peoples in the fourteen hundreds, and has been general from then until the present day. The history of European contact with those peoples is being currently written in our newspapers; it has been a governing force in all human lives for the last four to five hundred years.

Since we are especially interested in giving an account of the economic and social structure of Europe, it is from this European point of view that we shall approach the outlying peoples: we are not going to study any of them from an over-all point of view, bringing together an integrated picture of their theologies, arts, literatures, and learnings along with their economies and social organizations. We are going to go even farther in specialization of interest, and especially look for such weaknesses in their economic and social structures as were to facilitate European penetration. There may have been very admirable traits in most of the societies that were broken down and ruined by contact with Europeans. But from the point of view of our interest, those very things have sometimes been "weaknesses" which made those people vulnerable either to European military and political penetration, to outright conquest, to displacement and outright elimination by Europeans, or to very deeply shocking influences from the Europeans which broke those societies, their religions and their governments.

Some of them were strong enough to resist and strong enough, occasionally in the least admirable aspects of their original cultures, to stand up to European penetration. In some cases where this happened it was due to an ability to take over the worst weapons of the Europeans, and to use them in self-defense.

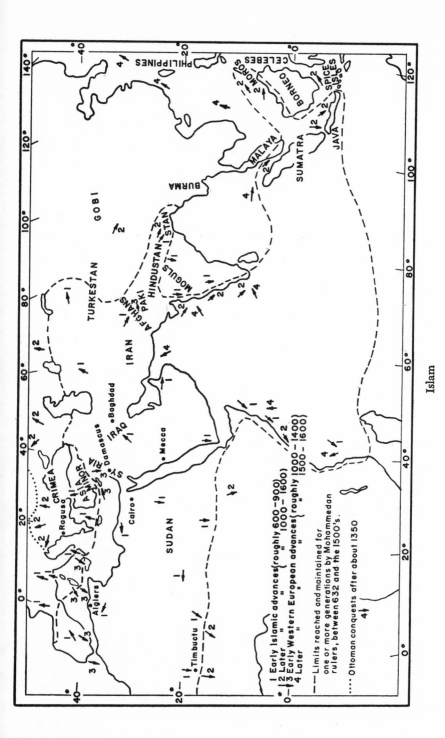

Islam

CHAPTER I

Islam by the
Fourteenth Century

MOHAMMED died in 632, and ever since the six hundreds, the Islamic peoples have been next-door neighbors to western Europe.

Mohammed was a city Arab from Mecca, born an aristocrat but a poor relation of the richest aristocrats. He was an Arab to the very heart, and his holy book, the Koran, according to dogma the words of God transmitted through his mouth, was of course in Arabic. As a result, ever since 632 any learned man anxious to succeed as a teacher, religious leader, or judge in the Islamic world has had to use the Arabic language. Mohammed established Arabic, up to that time not considered a very aristocratic language, as the language of learning and of government for the Islamic world of learning, law, and higher studies. This did not happen all at once, nor exclusively, but it was very general. It gave, and has given ever since, one sort of unity to the world of the Mohammedans: it became easy to find Arabic-speaking persons in any community from the Atlantic Ocean in Morocco to the farthest reaches of Indonesia. Learned men spoke it, and speak it, everywhere. This unity has been important in the economy, for merchants can go anywhere, and traders from one end of the Islamic world to the other can keep in touch with one another quite easily, because of their common tongue.

While there are different sorts of law inside the Islamic world, they are all basically Koranic law. The resultant common pattern of law has been important in the world of commerce. Private customs, public law, and morality are all of one general character through Islam.

The Arabic core of the Islamic world is itself diverse. The Arabs of Mohammed's day were not uniform in their culture and interests. In

Arabia there were and still are some almost uninhabitable deserts which have only become useful now, since oil has been found under them.

But it was not all desert. A good part of the total area was more properly dry steppe country, with periods lasting for months when animals could not graze and water holes were not full enough to care for men and beasts. In these same areas there were also months when across the ranges there was grazing, which was carried on by tribes or clans with grazing rights, either recognized by the other tribes or fought for. The changes in conditions in their ranges made it necessary for clans to keep moving about.

Dispersed through these areas were places where underground water or pools collected from run-off kept the ground quite moist, and given the fact that the climate was hot enough, there was a very heavy production in such spots of barley, wheat, dates, garden truck, and citrous fruits, with two or three crops a year possible where things were handled efficiently. Such small areas had a very dense population per acre right in the midst of great steppe or desert areas in which for a good deal of the time there was no population.

But the Arabic core was not the only part of the Mohammedan world. First Arabs, and then Arabs plus converts and conquered followers, pushed out in every direction after 632, building up a great empire. Until about 800 or 850, this was to be the most powerful single state in the European-African-Asian world.

Managed by the successors of Mohammed, Arabs of his immediate clan, this state was known as the Caliphate. (The word "Caliph" means "successor" in Arabic, the substitute on this earth for Mohammed who has gone to heaven.) The Caliphate extended its boundaries to the Atlantic, north into Central France, across the whole south and over both the east and west ends of the Mediterranean, up to the Gobi desert, and out to northern India. All of this was one area of government. The Caliph lived either at Damascus in Syria or, after 750, at Baghdad in Mesopotamia (Iraq).

Very considerable parts of the Caliphate consisted of lands which had been in the old Roman Empire and in its successor, the Byzantine Empire. Syria, Palestine, Egypt, the lands of modern Tunis, Algeria, and Morocco, had all been Byzantine, while the land of Spain was Roman-Visigoth when the Mohammedans overran the country.

The peoples were still Christian for a long time after the Mohammedans came in. The idea that the latter came with the Koran in one hand and a sword in the other is completely wrong. That they came with the Koran in one hand is true, but the tax collector's money bag was in the other. A person who was a Jew or a Christian had to pay more money in taxes; Mohammedans were not required to pay an important head tax. Perhaps this moved more people to turn Mohammedan than did any threat of the sword. Conversion took a long while, however, and as a matter of fact it has never been fully completed, for the Christian Arabs of Palestine, the Coptic Christians of Egypt, and Jews everywhere have remained uncoverted after over thirteen hundred years of Mohammedan domination.

As the Mohammedans extended their control over so many peoples and lands, a great civilization was created through the blending of elements from the civilizations of the highly advanced peoples who had been conquered. There were elements from Persian and Indian sources, from Turkish and even, through them, from Chinese sources; there were strong elements from the ancient Roman and Greek civilizations, and strong elements in Spain from the preceding Roman and Visigothic-German cultures. There came to be a civilization which was not provincially Arabic. It was so much more than Arabic that the simple term does not fit it; our best word for that civilization is Saracen or Saracenic.

Saracenic civilization developed rapidly. It took shape in the seven, eight, and nine hundreds, to become one of the great historical civilizations, with tremendous influence upon learning and science in western Europe. All across the world over which the caliph ruled there came to be a common art, a common literature and theology—so much so that even when political break-up came, Saracenic culture remained intact.

It is easy to conclude that the world of Islam was falling backward economically and militarily in the ten, eleven, and twelve hundreds. It actually did in the West. The Saracens in Africa and Spain began to suffer during those centuries from attacks by the Europeans from one side and by Africans from the Sudan on the other.

But from the twelve and thirteen hundreds on, Mohammedans in the farther East were rapidly expanding their territory. In the fourteen hundreds this movement had become very rapid in the farther Southeast. As a result, it was precisely just before the Europeans came along that the advanced populations in Malaya, Sumatra, Java, the southern Philippines, and the shores of Borneo and Celebes were going over to Mohammedanism. Its growth was suddenly stopped by the political and military competition of western Europeans, starting in the early fifteen hundreds.

Resources, Peoples

The European part of the Mohammedan world lay within the Mediterranean climate belt. However, much of Islam was not near enough the sea to be influenced much by ocean-collected moisture; the high plateaus and salt deserts of Iran or the deserts of Turkestan either lacked the rainy season or had only scattered, very torrential rains at wide intervals of several years, and sometimes at intervals of ten or fifteen years.

The Mediterranean zone, we have noticed, is one where transhumance is rather normal, from the lowland to the highland or from the south to the north—from the green pastures of one season to the green pastures of the next, and back again. Seasonal rains dominated the lives of all of the people except seafarers, settled oasis dwellers, and those living in areas irrigated by man-made canals. Where water permitted, there was a very intensive gardening culture. These people give the same attention to the raising of date palms, wheat, and barley that other persons in other countries might give to roses—and they give it to roses too.

Over Islam there was a much greater dependence on animal products than in western Europe; so much of the land would grow grass but nothing else that reliance upon flocks and herds was very profound. For the most part the sheep and horses, camels and goats, lived on seasonal ranges. Around the wheat fields, where there was enough water, there was herding of the animals in one place all the year around, but a good part of the land was cropped by moving the animals across it, the people in turn living almost entirely, so far as their own production went, on animal products—milk, which the Turks liked fermented, or sour milk, cheese and curds of different sorts, the meat of animals, and the main fiber for clothing was wool or camel's hair from the flocks.

Peoples of the desert and steppe lands had certain needs or appetites which they could not satisfy. Any food—grain food especially—other than animal products, had to be bought, stolen, or exacted as tribute. As a result these people were great plunderers. In addition they were short of metal. They had their own smiths living in the steppes with them; however, the iron itself had to come from outside. But the production of iron and steel was handicapped not only by the paucity of good, easily-worked ores but by the scarcity and high price of charcoal. Weapons of finest quality were made, but there never was cheap, abundant iron for the farmer or craftsman to use.

All across the Mohammedan world both the steppe and settled peoples were in need of timber, which was always in short supply. Areas such as the Lebanon forest which produced famous cedars have for millenniums been drawn upon for a great distance around for timber with which to build such things as temples. But timber on the whole, because it was in very short supply, became one of the items of trade between Europeans and Mohammedans, being exported from Europe to Syria, Palestine, Egypt, and North Africa. Although the popes in the eleven, twelve, and thirteen hundreds opposed the trade and tried to prevent its sale—because of its ultimate use—timber, sometimes fashioned into boats, was a standard article of export to the Mohammedans.

In addition to the products of Islam's own lands—the aromatic perfumes and gums—there were some things wanted in Europe which the Islamic people could supply. From the dawn of civilization and history the sailor and desert-caravan Arabs had been great middlemen, going formidable distances between the terminals of long trade routes. Throughout the whole of the Middle Ages and down until the eighteenth century they carried the products of the Spice Isles by land and by sea to where they could be forwarded to western Europe. (The idea that the Europeans stopped the spice trade of the Arabs by sailing around Africa does not fit the facts.)

Over-all, the world of Islam has always been poor in the really useful metals. There had been some rich silver and gold finds; in fact, in the seven, eight, and nine hundreds there were mines in Afghanistan which produced so much silver that Yukon types of wide-open, roaring camps grew up around them. So much silver came out of those mines and went into distant currencies that scholars think it had an effect on money supplies in both China and France simultaneously. But Islam was short in iron, copper, and the other useful metals, placing the Mohammedans in a position of dependence upon Europeans, Asian mountaineers, or other neighbors for those things.

There have been wonderful jewels from mines either under Mohammedan control or on the edge of the Mohammedan world, such as the rubies of Burma, the diamonds of Africa, or the lapis lazuli of Persia, but no great economy can rest on gold and precious stones.

Westerners are often vague as to the significances of terms which must be used in describing Mohammedans and the various peoples who make up their religious and cultural commonwealth. Since a survey of important terms can also serve to bring out economic and social factors in that society, an analysis of names can be useful.

A Mohammedan is anyone who has accepted the teachings of Mohammed as true. Such a person can also be called a Moslem or Muslim, meaning a person who has surrendered or made obeisance. Salaam is a cognate word in the Semitic pattern of languages; a man who has made his bow (his salaam) in surrender and obeisance to Islam (or to Mohammedanism) is a Moslem. Kin also to the same word is Islam, meaning the world of Mohammedans, with two subsenses which are not necessarily identical. The first is that any land in which Mohammedans are dominant politically, numerically, or culturally can be spoken of as an Islamic country, or can be thought of as included in Islam. The second, that Islam, in a more completely abstract sense, is the world of the thirteen or fourteen hundred years of Islamic history; the world of the Mohammedans in the cultural, intellectual, religious sense; and the world of all Mohammedans everywhere, which would include those who go to the mosque every Friday wherever they may be. Even though the United States is hardly an Islamic land, we can think of Islam as existing here and wherever else there are Mohammedans.

In the narrowest sense of the word, an Arab is an Arab in the way a Norwegian is a Norwegian. He is a person from Arabia, with Arabic ancestry, speaking Arabic. But this does not cover the full use of the word. Many of those in Arabia, of Arabian ancestry and speaking Arabic, are black slaves from Africa, whence slaves have been imported time out of mind and within the last few years. Arabs can also be found in the Philippines, on the coasts of India, or in Morocco. These can be descended from emigrants who left Arabia twelve, eleven, or ten hundred years ago. Or they can be descended from persons who never came from Arabia, but who adopted Arabic as their language. The Arabs of Morocco today are many of them native Moroccans who turned Arab. In this connection it should be noticed that the modern Christians of Egypt, Syria, and Palestine, who are descended not from Arabs but from the old Syrian or Coptic Greek Christian populations, speak Arabic and hence are non-Muslim Arabs.

Moor is an old western European term for any dark person, or for any Mohammedan. Europeans have always been vague in their use of the word. They speak of white, brown, and black Moors. But Moor, while it is an old loose term for any Mohammedan or North African, even more specifically refers to a person from Algeria-Morocco. Such a person does not have to be an Arab, and as a matter of fact the typical Moor is a Berber.

We find the word Berber coming over into English in several uses.

For example, we have the Berbery or Barbary Coast of San Francisco—which meant that once it was full of rough men acting like pirates, the Barbary coast having been originally the coast of North Africa along which the Berber pirates lurked. The Berber is not an Arab any more than a Russian or a Scot is an Arab. He is a Mohammedan, and often a heretic Mohammedan who does not speak Arabic. In ancestry a fairly high percentage of all the Berbers are light blonds, and even the blue-veiled Tuaregs of the Sahara Desert are likely to turn out to be blond with "Nordic" heads and hair once their sunburn has faded.

The Turk is any person who has Turkish as a language, and may be short and dark or tall and blond, a desert warrior, an oasis dweller, or a city craftsman. Asian Turks were predominantly Nestorian Christians during the five and six hundreds at home in Turkestan where they originated. They had become Mohammedan by about ten or eleven hundred, in part by mission activity and in part by conquest. During the ten hundreds they began important migrations into the Mohammedan world of Persia, Iraq, Syria, and Asia Minor.

One group of them came to dominate Asia Minor, and as a result we now call that part of the world Turkey. Others settled in South Russia and the Crimea, while still others went into India. Nearly always they became strict Mohammedans by the time they were very far from home. But they are not Arabs, and do not speak anything like Arabic, although their learned men, like the learned Berbers, of course use Arabic as the holy language.

The Persians or Iranians are linguistically close to Europeans. From them Mohammedan civilization picked up a considerable part of its art and literature. They are dominant in Persia (Iran) and Afghanistan today. Once again, the Persian, especially the Persian on the frontier toward India, is likely to be physically a "Nordic"; blond and blue-eyed individuals make up a fair part of the population, showing some blood kinship from remote times with many of the peoples of the Baltic area.

The term Malay is a loose one. There are a great many kinds of peoples speaking languages which are like the Malay and related to it, but not identical to it. The true Malays have long dominated the shores and part of the interior of Southeast Asia's mainland and islands. They have become Mohammedan since the eleven and twelve hundreds, as have similar peoples along the shores all through Java and in many other parts of Indonesia. In the Philippines a Malay, or any other Filipino Mohammedan, is known as a Moor, called so first by the Spaniards who knew all Mohammedans as *Moros* back home.

Beside these mentioned, there are many other Mohammedans (including millions of Chinese), but these are the main groups.

Strengths and Weaknesses

At very early times, even before the death of Mohammed, the Mohammedans tended to break up at the top as different subclans related to Mohammed fought for leadership. Dynastic and clan rivalry beginning at the top and going on down through society has always existed in the Mohammedan world, especially among the Arabs. It is said that there are feuds in the Mohammedan world which are thirteen hundred years old. Dynastic rivalry began to crack up the Caliphate as different clans gained control of different sections and went to war with each other.

Furthermore, religious sects have been rife in the Mohammedan world almost since the beginning. These sects correspond for some practical purposes to the Christian sects. There are sects among the Mohammedans which are rivals to one another just as Lutherans, Presbyterians, Mennonites, Catholics, and many others are rivals for allegiance in our Christian society. Most of the Mohammedan sects have had organizations. What is more, many of the sects have been militant, going out to make converts or to attack unbelievers and other sects. One of the most important today is the sect which dominates Arabia, the Wahabi, the sect of the family of Ibn Saud and his successors. Another is the sect which is run by the Aga Khan, which has its followers chiefly in Persia, East Africa, and Pakistan.

Division into these sects was caused by such things as religious debate, debate over morals, and debate over constitution and law. Strongly organized sects, in turn, often formed a core around which independent governments were built. At the same time some of the sects became influential as secret societies, whose members might be found everywhere but were often enough centered in some part of Islam actually governed by the supreme leader of the sect.

In the Middle Ages, during the eleven hundreds, there was an extraordinary sect called the hashishans, or the Assassins. Its members smoked hashish (the hemp cannabis, or marijuana) and became so skilled at killing political enemies that they gave their name to the words "assassin" and "to assassinate" in all the western European languages. In the beginning they were a religious sect. When their head, the Old Man of the Mountain, wanted to have someone killed—a count of Montferrat or a high Egyptian or an Arab—he would stimulate the assassins he had designated and send them off to do the job.

As we would expect, in the Mohammedan world there were layers in society. Some of the main lines of division were the deep ones between town and country. The towns were located where there was a high-level agriculture and plenty of water, while the country was usually the land of steppe peoples who were organized socially, economically, politically, and militarily very differently from the town peoples. So there were antagonisms: town versus country, or settled people versus mountain or steppe people. Although living right next door to each other, their lives were so different that the joining of country and village and town people under one government was extremely difficult.

In the settled areas there was a strong division between landlord and tenant. Notice should be taken here of an important aspect of land-lordism in the Mohammedan world. A very important part of Moham-med's teaching was the one which enjoined charity; it was one fifth, or twenty percent, of the gross of his income that a good Mohammedan was supposed to give to charity, double what Christian teachers have often enjoined upon Christians. A great many Mohammedans have always taken this injunction as a teaching which ought to be followed. Over the Mohammedan world the result has been the building up of thousands of foundations for charitable work, in turn bringing a very considerable part of the ownership of productive land into the hands of charitable corporations. These are run by local boards of trustees, the incomes being devoted to maintenance of teachers and students, or of mosques and worshipers, or of plain bread-and-butter charity for the poor. While rich landlords are found everywhere too, still, quite widely in the Mo-hammedan world, the landlord has been a corporation organized for religious purposes, and the dispossession of the landlord has usually meant the termination of academic work, of support for the local sewers and drains and aqueducts, and of almost all charity and poor relief work.

In 750 governmental fragmentation first set in. After only about a hun-dred years the great Caliphate began to break up. Initially some of the people followed one branch of Mohammed's family, the Ommiads, who had conquered Spain; most followed another branch of Mohammed's clan, the Abbassids, who made their headquarters at Baghdad. Thereafter both of these Caliphates began to break down further, chiefly because it was the normal pattern of Mohammedan government to delegate any great area remote from the capital to a trusted lieutenant, who was often a kinsman, and to give him, as a sort of viceroy, control over religious activities, judicial, military, taxation, and financial matters. These men, as they became established in Morocco, in Northern India, and in other regions, began to develop practically independent states, even when they still nominally recognized their Caliphs. Finally, such lieutenants or the families they founded became completely independent of headquarters, or recognized their caliphs only in the prayers on Friday.

Another weakness in Mohammedan government was the likelihood of too many sons being generated in a harem. It was very difficult for the sons of one father, born to different mothers, to be agreeable to one another. That was partly because the sons would take up their mothers' hatreds of the other mothers. Harems were difficult things to run; the occupants squabbled too much, they killed too much, and the sons were likely to grow up not just as candidates for the throne the father was to leave, but also set and determined to kill all the other sons, having had that idea implanted by their mothers. A striking demonstration of what happened in an Oriental household, when the sons by different mothers were watching an old father get ready to die, is to be found in the account of the doings of the children of David—Absalom and Solomon and the rest.

Another weakness in the Mohammedan states was the way in which a son, when he had obtained the position left by his father, would be likely to let actual control of affairs be taken over by a prime minister. Such things happened in western European history also, as when the kings of the Franks allowed their mayors of the palace to take over an increasingly important amount of power, which eventually led to a mayor's setting himself up as king in fact and establishing his own line. Somewhat the same thing happened in Japan when the shogun took over the mikado's power. In the Mohammedan states powerful prime ministers sometimes made their positions hereditary. Then a line of hereditary prime ministers might hold the real power while a line of hereditary sultans or caliphs or emirs held only the title. It should also be added that a fair share of prime ministerships fell into the hands of slaves.

By the eight hundreds, and for a long while thereafter, Mohammedan rulers were suspicious of their own relatives and tribesmen. As a result, they preferred to hire or to buy foreigners as their bodyguards. The only people who really saw the sultan or caliph, except for his harem eunuchs and women, was often the palace guard of young slave boys he had purchased. The commander of the guard, usually a slave soldier (mameluke) who had worked up from corporal to lieutenant to brigadier general, became the wielder of power. This went so far in Egypt that from the twelve to the eighteen hundreds the throne of that country was in the hands of a series of mameluke captains, most of whom had been slaves when they came to Egypt—Nubian, Russian, Mongol, Turk, European—and had worked up through the guard, eliminating rivals and predecessors, and reigning until they in turn were eliminated. This pattern also obtained in Spain where the captain of the mameluke guard under the later Mohammedan rulers was often the real power. It was also true in India and elsewhere. The weakness in politics resulting from slave rule was very important. Many Mohammedan states were ruled by adventurers, desperate men who had reached power by the dangerous path of killing their predecessors, and who feared to lose power the same way.

In many ways the strongly integrated tribe, clan, or village was more important in the Mohammedan world than the central governments. The weakness of the central government did not penetrate down to this level.

The Arab tribe, or tribes among many of the other peoples, the Berbers in Africa, or the Iranians on the Persian plateau, was often a very strong unit. There were many tribes with hundreds of years of history behind them and a strong consciousness of their unity, whose members were likely to obey very strictly any orders which came down from their chieftains, even when such a chieftain was a long distance away. Often the individuals were scattered but had a home range or homeland and would be very loyal to the tribe residing there.

They were often even more loyal to a subdivision of the tribe, a clan, which usually owed allegiance to the descendant of some one of the original heads of a tribe. A tribe might have several clans. The tribes and clans were much harder to destroy or control than most of the other units in the Mohammedan world.

In the world of the village cultivators, the strength of village organization was very considerable. People in a village were accustomed to working their fields and handling their public and group problems according to patterns which were very old and well adapted to their needs. These were fitted to the local climate, geography, and agriculture, and it was the stability of their villages which was most important to the people in that world. Dynasties could come and empires go, Babylon and Assyria, Alexander and Rome, the Sassanids or Abbasids, it did not matter so long as the village stayed together. For all the upper level instability described above, the people of a village had a stable society so long as they kept the village pattern.

The social pattern could only be seriously dislocated by the breaking up of villages, which was extremely difficult. But strong as the village unit was, it was not everywhere strong enough to prevent the dislocation which came with European penetration, although the villagers were to continue to regard as their property that which their ancestors might have lost or relinquished three or four hundred years before. They were never to give up title, nor to forget their obligation to reconstitute the village as their ancestors had known it.

The general economic position of Islam requires some notice. During the Middle Ages, even until the thirteen and fourteen hundreds, Islamic technology had been relatively high and relatively fruitful. In the world of books and science Europeans learned a great deal from Islam; they also learned a great deal in horticulture and the crafts. Many European commodities were imitations of what had first been invented or manufactured in Islamic lands. (Examples are morocco or cordovan leather, mentioned in another connection.) When it came to the tools, to the products, to the skill of the men, Islam was long superior to the Western world in the following fields—fine intensive garden culture; in handicraft work of all sorts, iron, glass, fine textiles, and so on; in matters of warfare, having better siege machinery, fortifications, superior armor and weapons, better strategy and generalship, until the early eleven hundreds; in seafaring, the building and operating of ships, the daring of the ship men, a superiority which lasted until the ten and eleven hundreds; in the arts of commerce, the ability to organize partnerships, to handle coinage and finance, and so on. In the course of the ten and eleven hundreds the Europeans had begun to catch up fast in all of these fields, and in general had outstripped Islam by the thirteen and fourteen hundreds. Of course, there were exceptions; there were parts of Europe which were backward and parts of Islam which were especially advanced.

This was not altogether a matter of the world of Islam sliding backward; largely it was a matter of the Europeans surpassing them in development of techniques and the exploitation of skills, until the relative superiority had been lost by Islam.

But part of the European advance to superiority was due to barbarization and the breaking up of society and the channels of commerce in Islam, resulting from invasions from the outside.

These invasions came from several directions. There was a series of destructive invasions from south of the Sahara Desert into northern Africa and Spain in the eleven and twelve hundreds when, for example, backward south-Sahara Berber heretics smashed and burned Islam's libraries in Spain. A country which had been noted for its books and scholars no longer had many. In the East there was invasion of wandering Turkish tribes, which became civilized later, but not until they had done considerable damage. And last of all there was the invasion of the relatively uncivilized Europeans which, in the form of the Crusades, wrecked prosperity and trade in the rich lands of Syria and Palestine. The western European must be reckoned as one of the three great groups of barbarians bedeviling the civilized Mohammedans in the ten, eleven, and twelve hundreds.

But just to keep the record straight, one invading group, the Turks from around the Caspian Sea, who gained control first of Persia and Mesopotamia, then of Asia Minor, and finally of much of the Balkans, were not lacking in ability to rule and organize empires. Western Europeans began the Crusades by a great attack on Islam around eleven hundred; the high tide of Western penetration came when they took Jerusalem. By about sixteen hundred the Holy Land had long been lost to the Europeans, and so had the Byzantine Empire; but the Ottoman Turks were attacking Vienna in the heart of Europe. The counter punch of the Moslem Ottoman Turks was far harder to withstand than the initial blow of the Western Christians.

The Ottoman Turks, when established on the edge of Europe, in intimate contact with the Venetians, Genoese, Germans, and Greeks, not only took over the culture of the older Saracens but also devised ways to set to their own use the technology of the Europeans. The Ottoman Turk troops were better organized and led than European troops, although they were partly organized on European models, and the elite foot soldiers were Albanian, Serbian, Greek, Bulgar, Armenian and Roumanian boys taken from their parents by a kind of baby tax and brought up to be Turkish infantrymen. Often enough they were officered by renegades. The Ottoman Sultan had fine artillery, often designed and cast as well as operated by Dutchmen or Englishmen, Germans or Italians, who had taken service with him. By the fifteen hundreds the Ottoman Turk also had fine fighting fleets and the best leadership, under such people as converted Greeks, Italians, and even Dutch and Englishmen.

Roughly between 1350 and 1500, the Ottoman Sultan spread his control over the whole of the Balkan peoples. The Greeks, Albanians, and Vlachs (of Roumanian speech) had for long centuries been Christians of the Orthodox faith. Spread widely over the interior, from the five hundreds on, were south-Slavic immigrants. Ruling the Slavs in general, first steppe-nomad Avars and then the similar Turko-Finnish Bulgars had held sway and threatened the Byzantine Empire from its back door. The Bulgars had completely Slavicized, turned Orthodox Christian, and taken on Byzantine culture. But by 1500 all these peoples had been brought under Ottoman lordship and largely isolated thereby from the rest of the Europeans. They were to re-emerge as "Europeans proper" only in the nineteen hundreds. Important as they are now, they lived through the centuries discussed here as subjugated fringe peoples within the horizons of Islam.

The pirate commonwealths of Tripoli, Tunis, and Algeria were an important force in war and politics as well as in commerce in the fifteen to sixteen hundreds, and well into the nineteenth century. (Morocco was similar but more "inland" and it had a legitimate dynasty.) Their pirates raided ships and seacoast communities not only around the Mediterranean, but as far away as Ireland. In a rather informal fashion they lived under the wing of the Ottoman Sultan, attacking his enemies and friendly to his friends (oftenest the French, but also the Dutch and the English for considerable periods). The city of Algiers had its own commercial prosperity, partly in plunder and partly in trade goods, especially in slaves brought across the Sahara. The United States, in the nineteenth century, was the first European power to counterattack them, after the Spanish Hapsburgs had failed to restrict them in the sixteen hundreds.

At all times there has been a continuous activity in the field of commerce. The Arab peoples had been great traders by desert and sea, and they have continued to be until this very day. They are still excellent merchants, but usually limited in the scope of their activities by their lack of finance and connections. The middleman position of the Arab merchant was not destroyed immediately by the discovery of the route around the Cape of Good Hope. It was hurt for a while, but soon revived, for by the fifteen and sixteen hundreds there was still a considerable flow of commerce going from and to the East and West, with an increase in the amount going from West to East. Venice and other Italian cities continued to prosper down to the sixteen and even to the seventeen hundreds, as did the Mohammedan towns with which they did business in Syria, Asia Minor, and Egypt. The great changes which hurt Moslem commerce came with the development of the clipper ship and the steamboat. Until then the Islamic merchant continued to be important, even after he had lost his relative position of importance in the world of trade.

CHAPTER II

Africa
South of the Sahara

EVER since Neolithic times, the Mediterranean has been a boulevard, uniting the peoples of Italy and Tunis, Spain and Morocco, Greece and Egypt. What has been difficult to cross has been the great Sahara Desert to the south of Algiers, Tunis, Tripoli, and Egypt. This difficulty was profound when men had to cross it on foot, and the result has been the cutting off from each other of the lands to the south and north of the desert ever since the last great glacial epoch.

In relative isolation people in the lands to the south developed physical, cultural, and other traits making them very different from those in lands to the north of the desert. The Tunisians, Algerians, and Egyptians are connected in every way with west Asians and southern Europeans in their physiques and historical background, while the peoples to the south of the desert have been cut off from Mediterranean peoples. Africa proper is a kind of island, the northern shore of which is not the Mediterranean, but the Sahara Desert.

Resources and Liabilities

The isolation of Africa is pronounced even when the land is approached by sea. South of the Sahara, practically the whole of the continent is relatively high tableland, a great mesa of continental size. There are few places where the land slopes down on an easy grade to the sea. The tablelands come out to great cliffs or sharp drop-offs fairly near the ocean's edge. As a result, all African rivers of any size form up on the tableland and flow to some point toward its edge, then drop over in a series of great falls or successive rapids such as the cataracts of the Nile, the rapids of the Niger, the falls below Stanley Pool in the Congo, or the

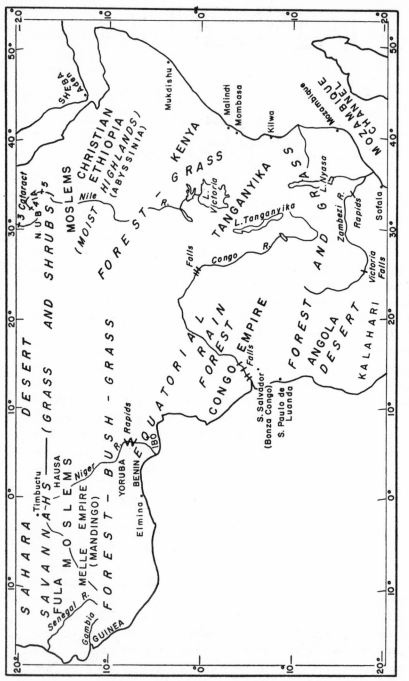

Africa south of the Sahara

Victoria falls of the Zambezi. As a result it was impossible to take a sailing ship from salt water up any African river to the interior. In ascending it is necessary to cross a coastal swamp land, then overcome shallows, rapids, cataracts, or falls, until the higher level is reached, where the river allows navigation again to a great distance inland.

Another barrier is the low country along the coast; it is nearly everywhere fever-stricken. Africa is not so overrun with disease inside as it is along its margins. This made the effort to get around the falls or cataracts especially risky. What is more, a good part of the diseases prevalent in that flat country are particularly lethal to Europeans. Later we shall notice the effects of European diseases on other peoples; it also happens that African diseases are particularly bad for Europeans. Diseases are both a protection and a weapon when it comes to contact with others. Africa's diseases were one of the great shields against penetration from the outside, especially against the Europeans.

On the whole Africa's coast has poor harbors, especially poor for European boats. The fact that harbors are poor is complicated by the fact that in both the Indian and Atlantic Oceans there are tremendous swells. Out at sea these are not very noticeable, but close to shore breakers sweep in so that landing in a small boat is hazardous. The first combers are sometimes met miles off shore. Moreover, there are bars at the river mouths which can trap a large boat if it is driven on the sand.

Inside Africa the general pattern of climates follows the lines of latitudes, stretching in bands across the continent.

Southward from the Mediterranean the land becomes progressively drier, until the belt is reached where it is necessary to carry all food and water needed for man and beast. Southward again comes grassland where the desert begins to turn into what is more properly steppe country, or savannah, or the Sudan. From sparse grassland this turns into land where there is tall grass, after which the bush begins.

The bush land, depending on the elevation, starts at about ten degrees north of the equator, turning into increasingly dense tropical forest as the equator is approached. It is in this land of heavy equatorial rains that pygmies and Congo Bantu peoples are to be found. In Kenya and Tanganyika to the east there is open country even under the equator, for the land is high. Going further south the pattern is reversed, with grassland fading into a belt of desert, but by that latitude the continent has narrowed so much that the Kalahari Desert in South Africa is not nearly so big and important as its sister desert in the north. Then the very tip of Africa is once more a land with the Mediterranean climate, even verging toward the temperate.

The bands of climates described here, however, are greatly turned from an east-west pattern by the influence on rainfall and temperatures exercised by altitude all along the eastern half of the continent. A glance at a map shows that no important river drains into the Indian ocean north of Madagascar; while the mighty Congo's tributaries collect most of the rainfall of the equatorial surface, with help from the Nile. The eastern highlands have great savannahs which provide pasture to immense herds of wild and domesticated beasts, and high forests on the flanks of mountains. On that side of Africa cattle-herding peoples (growing maize, too, since that crop was introduced from America) have flourished.

Pushing southward from the northern savannahs along this natural cattle range, successive waves of migrants had for centuries before 1500 been carrying northern speech and ways ever nearer the southern tip of Africa, restricting the range of the Bushman hunters.

The inaccessibility of the land has had added to it the inaccessibility of its resources. Through history the Africans have had resources of great value which their technology did not allow them to exploit and to which their interest was not drawn. The industrial use of the iron and copper of Africa has depended entirely on the application of the most advanced techniques. Most of the ores did not appear in forms which could make them very useful to primitive peoples. (Still, a high proficiency in hand-working of iron was early reached in some regions.) On the whole the minerals of Africa have not been of any historical importance until the last seventy-five to a hundred years. In the Middle Ages the industry of Africa went very little beyond the gathering industry, either for local use or commerce.

While on the whole all people south of the Sahara are much darker skinned than the peoples to its north, this does not mean they are uniformly pigmented or in other ways especially like one another. The variations of peoples of darker skin south of the Sudan are even greater than the variations of people in the European-Asian land mass. There are tremendous differences, such as those between the west African and the Bushman. What is more, both prehistorically and historically Berbers and Egyptians and Arabs have contributed to the development of subvarieties by crossbreeding to the south. As a result people are found whose features and head shapes are like those of Europeans and whose skins are black, or, vice versa, fairly light-skinned peoples whose features are more properly those of the native Africans. In Africa there is every shade of dark skin from sallow to brown to practically yellow to blue-black. Africa also has the shortest and the tallest varieties of peoples, living near one another. In addition it has the most tremendous variety of languages that we know of, perhaps equaled only by the great varieties of languages spoken by the American Indian groups before Columbus.

There is no African language as such. West Africa, for instance, has a very complex pattern of languages, only remotely or not in the least related to one another, some of which are spoken only by small groups, others by groups numbering many millions. But from the eastern highlands, largely through the Congo tropical forest region and down nearly to the tip of Africa, there is one great language family, that of the Bantu. The Bantu language family is one of the world's great families of speech along with the Semitic languages or the family of Indo-European languages.

In some areas social patterns are extraordinarily complex and highly developed. Many African peoples show a high aptitude for the invention and maintenance of a complex social structure; highly developed, intricate patterns of organization are to be found among African tribes. Some of these were very ancient.

There had been superstates in Africa, evidences of which are to be found in some of the earliest references to African peoples. Several of them were functioning when Europeans first came in touch with Africa south of the Sahara, in the middle and late fourteen hundreds. Some states in Africa long before the Europeans appeared were large both geographically and in population. Similar states continued to be built up by African statesmen and conquerors on down to the early eighteen hundreds.

Some of them were on the savannah grassland edge, toward the Sahara, and were deeply under the influence of Mohammedan teaching and education. The Mohammedan faith jumped the Sahara in the ten to twelve hundreds. Important Mohammedan empires flourished in the region of Timbuctu and further east in the Upper Nile region. In addition there was the very ancient Christian empire in the Abyssinian lands, which descended directly from the Ethiopian empires which were as old as Egypt, both politically and as cultural entities. The Abyssinian empire is one of the ancient civilized empires of the world, and has been Christian since the five and six hundreds.

The last of the great African empire builders in the south were the Zulus, who came close to creating a great Bantu-Zulu empire in the late seventeen and early eighteen hundreds. Under white influence they built up a most effective army. Its equipment consisted of bull-skin hide shields and broad-bladed stabbing spears or swords. In fighting discipline and morale no force has ever surpassed the Zulus, though the fighting morale in the Zulu empire was matched by that of some of the military forces of the west African empires, including regiments made up of women who fought like tigresses and who gave a very impressive account of themselves.

These empires were ordinarily built up by what we would call a dominant tribe. Some tribe would gain control over its neighbors and create a superstate resting on military and financial support of conquered tribes, just as Europeans have done. The rivalries of these empires would have filled the historical record of Africa had there been such records. Yet we know practically nothing about them save what was learned along their fringes by Moslems or by chance European visitors to their interiors, until it was too late to take down good records of their pasts. All our surviving accounts and descriptions are fragmentary.

It was in part from the wars these empires waged that the slave trade was nourished. Loot to go onto the market at the end of a war consisted of long chains of slaves sent out for sale somewhere else. Also, the empires maintained themselves in part by a tribute of slaves. Since Europeans were doing much the same thing as late as the ten hundreds A.D. this can hardly be considered as evidence of cultural lag.

Native and Foreign Traders

Native exploitive techniques were poor, but trade organization and aptitude for trade were at a fairly high level. As far back as we have any record, there were well-recognized trade routes crisscrossing Africa, with controls and arrangements made by traders with different potentates along the routes. In many of the tribes there were no such traders. Instead, there were tribes or clans who were trading specialists as a sort of ethnic or clan craft. The same kind of man, with his same home and dialect, was to be found trading in different parts of Africa.

The trade was carried on to a marked degree by persons, too, who were only visiting Africa. Across the east and central part these were either freshly arrived Arabs, or part-breeds, or black Arabs descended from Arab traders. Or they might be coastal peoples under Arab influence. In this respect Africa was not so different from the Europe which knew a widespread but thin trade, especially in slaves, during the five, six, and seven hundreds, also in the care of merchants who were not natives of the places they frequented—the Frisians, Syrians, and Jews.

That they did not carry a great volume of goods was partly due to the weakness in transport; most of the routes were paths, and the transport animal was usually two-legged, since horses and camels had trouble living in a good part of Africa. On the inland waters dugouts or reed-bundle rafts were the only vehicles.

Some commodities were always in demand, salt being an important item. A good part of Africa is short of salt. A hot climate creates an appetite for it, not only for preserving food but for keeping people healthy. Salt was at a premium and was used for money. As a matter of fact, salt is today still a kind of auxiliary money, but once it was the only form of money in many parts of equatorial Africa, the value set on it being very high per pound.

A very large part of the African top soil is not very rich. Tropical rain forests which look so lush have to be counted among the areas of low productivity, for not only in Africa but in the Amazon River rain valley opposite in South America, men get a rather low yield per acre in food stuffs. This is partly because the heavy downpour of rain leaches out the minerals in the soil, so that the soil is not very fertile in a state of nature. Forests grow, but they are not nearly so thick as they would be if growing in the soil of France, for instance.

Outside the rainiest areas, in other parts of Africa, there are some good lands, but here diseases have been a serious problem for a long time, especially diseases which kill animals primarily and men secondarily. The worst of these comes from the bite of the tsetse fly, the African sleeping sickness. In great sections of Africa this has been an obstacle to development down to the last few years; and there are other diseases of almost equal importance.

For many generations now some of the very best food crops raised in Africa have been of Western Hemisphere origin, notably Indian corn or maize, which has become the staff of life for peoples from Egypt to the Cape. Europeans introduced other foods from the Amazon rain forests and the Caribbean coasts. When Europeans first came in contact with Africa, the population was scantier almost everywhere than it is today; at least all the evidence we have points to the population level having been much lower. The Africans were in a low stage of agricultural technology (quite unlike the Western Hemisphere Indians who were very advanced) and good foods were scarce.

Not only was their productivity low because of their lack of skills and crops, but also the climate made it almost impossible to rely on successful storage of their crops. This left the people open to sudden famines which might come as the result of war, invasion, social and other upsets, bad weather, or disease. When a shortage occurred, a local population could die off within a month or six weeks; it would take a long time for that area to become repopulated.

The resources of Africa were in general much like those of earlier medieval Europe. The Africans produced raw crops which were scarcely processed at all. They had no furs, for tropical animals do not produce good furs, but they had the elephant, which produced a tremendously valuable commodity. Ivory from Africa was carried, far back in antiquity, across the Sahara at great cost in human lives. It was one of the most precious of all things, the sort of material the Greeks had used in building statues to put in the Parthenon.

By the eleven hundreds African gold was being brought north from the Timbuctu region in quantities, and before twelve hundred it was helping the western Europeans balance their accounts with other parts of the world. Ostrich feathers always had a good market. Through the later Middle Ages fancy dress helmets for the knights and hats for the ladies called for them and, along with peacock feathers, that of the ostrich was used as a symbol of magnificence. Except for ivory and feathers, the animal products of Africa were not important. Until modern times the vegetable products were of no importance at all; while Africa was rich in palm oil and some other basic foods, there was no demand for them and they were of little value in trade until the late eighteen and early nineteen hundreds.

Most important of all the products were the slaves. They were shipped into Islam, where slave guards, harem slaves, and slave Sultans were important in such countries as Egypt. In Arabia, Persia, and Morocco-Tunis, African slaves were always in high demand. They were also shipped on to Europe, where the use of black slaves was high fashion in Renaissance Italy. Such a family as the Medici in Florence showed off its wealth and magnificence by having them in the household. The last prince of the main line of the Medici (his half-sister was queen of France) was the illegitimate son of one of its black waitresses. Cross-breeding with the master's family was not at all an uncommon pattern where such slavery existed.

However, Europeans developed cane sugar and cotton culture in their colonial possessions during the thirteen hundreds. The first were in Syria,

Cyprus, and Crete, and later ones out on the Atlantic islands. As sugar cane and other plantation crops grew important, black slavery for field work also developed. Portugal's exploration enterprise around Africa was tied up with the demand for black slaves; they brought profits which largely paid for further exploration. This pattern goes back to the thirteen hundreds—the opening of plantations by European managers and financiers, with black slaves. It continued through the fourteen hundreds and was then transplanted ready-made to Brazil and the Caribbean islands, and in the case of the English-speaking colonies, to the Carolinas in the sixteen hundreds.

The Arabs Around the Indian Ocean

Arab interest in Africa's trade goes back at least to the days of the Queen of Sheba and to Solomon, about a thousand years B.C., and it may have been old even then. Sheba came from the region of Aden, at the mouth of the Red Sea, where there was once a much greater population than there has been in modern times, with fields watered by reservoirs held by tremendous dams. Sheba was rich not only because her land was rich, but also because her traders bought and sold northward in Palestine as well as far south along the African coast. She had gold, slaves, ivory, and ostrich feathers to sell. Furthermore, the trade which centered on Sheba's land also tapped India and the farther coasts of the Indian Ocean.

Sheba's area, south and southeast Arabia, has been too little noticed by Europeans at any time, either in the Middle Ages or since. Southeast Arabia has not been a land notable for sheiks on beautiful steeds. Instead it has been a land either of gardeners or of daring overseas navigators and traders. The southeast Arab has been one of the world's great exploring seafarers and sea fighters. Facing out on the Indian Ocean, his land was not at all the kind of Arabia the Crusaders found a good many hundreds of miles away to the north.

From that region, since at least the days of the Queen of Sheba (for at least three thousand years), skilled seamen, merchants, and conquerors have been sailing in all directions to which the coasts would lead them. By the eight hundreds apparently they had reached down to Madagascar; and long before they had gotten to Ceylon, and then to Formosa, around and through the Straits of Singapore.

As they went along distant shores, these Arab sailor-traders usually tried to gain control of harbors which they could use as bases both for

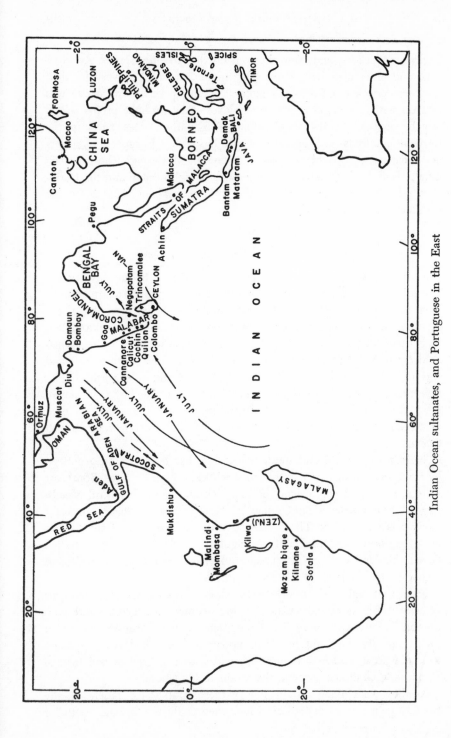

Indian Ocean sultanates, and Portuguese in the East

their naval operations and for trade with natives. In this they were much like the ancient Greeks or like those other seafaring Semites, the Phoenicians, who had founded colonies all around the Mediterranean.

A sheik or sultan would lord it over such a harbor, with a few subjugated tribes in the near neighborhood, while a few dozen Arab traders and fighters and slaves made up his town's population. The sheik himself was usually its chief merchant, and in fact often he was the only merchant, all the others working for him. The small holding he possessed could be passed from father to son for hundreds of years. It would not get any larger, and at the same time it would not decay; it flourished from trade which passed through it.

By the thirteen hundreds there were Arab or Arab-controlled coastal ports all the way from Madagascar around to Java, along the east coast of Africa, around Arabia proper, along the coast of India, the coasts of the Malay Straits, and out to the Philippines and Java on the far side. These sultanates lived by supporting one another in trade, for essentially it did not pay them to fight one another. Trade went through them all to everybody's profit.

They did not need to control any of the interior. By making individual arrangements all the way back to the middle of Africa, it was possible for the Arabs around Zanzibar to get the trade of that whole part of Africa to flow out to Zanzibar where it would go into the channels of the Arab Indian Ocean trade. The Indian Ocean Arabs were interested in naval hegemony and trade, not in a land empire.

As we shall see, it was this Arabic network of coastal stations that the Portuguese took over beginning in the early fifteen hundreds. The pattern of the Portuguese empire in the Indian Ocean and farther east had been set long before the Portuguese by the Arabs. When attacked by the Portuguese, the Arabs were unable to defend their empire because of the inferiority of their ships, their guns, and their organization. The Portuguese took over what the Arabs had built up, a fully constructed, ready-made naval empire, with commercial connections into the hearts of both Africa and Asia.

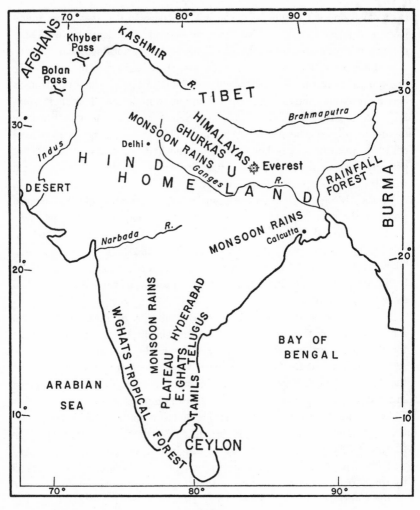

India

CHAPTER III

India and Hindu or Buddhist Asia

THE Indian climate is dominated by the overwhelming presence of the great Asian land mass. Monsoon winds develop when this great land mass gets warm in the northern hemisphere's summer, the air over it begins to rise, and surface air all around begins to blow in from the sea. These wet winds drop much of their water as they come. Then, in winter, as the land mass gets colder than the ocean's surface, the winds reverse; the winter monsoon is dry, for the wind blows off the land toward the sea. As a result of the monsoons, India is essentially a two-climate area; when the rains come, much of the peninsula is as wet as a tropical rain forest, while it is nearly as dry as a desert otherwise.

Locally, however, there are crisscross mountains which trip the winds, creating too much or too little dryness. The thick wedge shape of India is due to the way lower mountain ranges run toward one another at the south end. On either side of these low mountain ranges even wetter jungles and drier desert lands than those of the rest of the continent are to be found in close juxtaposition to one another because of their interference with both the wet and dry monsoons.

India has always had areas of very rich soil and has most of the useful minerals. While distribution of its riches was spotty, gold, silver, and jewels of every sort have always been associated with India. India did not produce them all, but it produced more than its share of precious articles, giving it riches to export, from before the days of the Roman Empire, both to China and Europe.

In some places India was well endowed with iron and fuel. Local working of iron has been a very old and well-developed art. Indians made art objects out of iron so pure that it will rust hardly any more than would gold.

From as far back as the times of Babylon and Pharaonic Egypt, there has been a high development of nearly all the crafts in India. In Hindustan and the neighborhoods nearby and in some of the coastal areas, there were crafts highly developed by 1000 B.C. and perhaps even three or four thousand years earlier; the dates of some of the oldest sites where artifacts have been found are not known. But very near the neighborhoods where crafts had been so developed there were—and today there still are—aboriginal tribes living in the Stone Age or even in an older culture than that, using wooden spears and arrows. Over thousands of years the jungles have been guarding some of the world's least advanced peoples while simultaneously the coasts and the plains of the Indus and Ganges have produced some of the most advanced.

India has always had an uneven distribution of population and soil resources. In the wide alluvial valleys in the north, and in some other places, the soil has always been rich to a depth of hundreds of feet. In other districts the soil is extremely thin and not very fertile. Where rains are too heavy, they have the usual effect of leaching the soil, which diminishes the fertility of tropical rain forests. In other areas dryness has resulted in wind erosion and the loss of the soil. And of course the ground is rough in the mountain districts, which cover much of the surface.

The Many Layers of Peoples

There is a population in India which seems to have been aboriginal and which spread at first everywhere in the country. Dark, even blackskinned, this population seems to have been in various ways somewhere between the Australian Bushman and the western European—if it be akin to any other particular breed—and not much like either the Chinese or Africans. This basic aboriginal population seems to have been there in Neolithic times, and it still survives, remaining practically pure so far as we can tell, in some of the most backward areas.

Living in small tribes or clans, many of these groups have a pattern of life much like that of the most backward of the American Indian tribes or the most backward of the Africans. They are hunters and gatherers, with no particular skills and no tools of an advanced sort. What appear to be kindred stocks are also found throughout the peninsula, mixed in varying proportions with still other sorts of people who have come in from the outside.

In general the population which has entered India in successive waves from the northwest has been physically like the population in western Europe. There is similarity in physiques between the Afghan stocks and such stocks as are to be found in Germany and Ireland. We can only surmise that the invaders who went into India fifteen hundred or twenty-five hundred years ago became more thoroughly mixed into that earlier population than did those who arrived only three hundred or four hundred years ago.

There has also been some intrusion of peoples from the Tibetan-Burmese side to the northeast, creating such populations as those in the Ghurka country, from which come the men who have climbed Mt. Everest. They are generally closer to the Tibetans in blood than to the Indians. Still, much the greater part of the new populations have come in from Persia, Afghanistan, and Central Asia through the Khyber and other passes.

The successive peoples penetrating from the northwest have come as invading conquerors, and on the whole, in theory, have been against mixing with the peoples who were there before them. But the theory that they are of unmixed blood falls apart when their complexions are studied; they obviously must be of mixed blood to have become the color they are.

The most influential of all the layers of invaders were those who brought with them the basic pattern of the Brahman or Brahmanistic faith, and who have developed in India not only the religion but also the governmental and cultural pattern of Hinduism.

Until the eight to nine hundreds, all of the invaders from the north fitted themselves into the Indian religion and society without too much trouble. They tended to give themselves a different social position, with this as the general rule: The later in arriving, the higher, and the movement down does not come until someone moves in above and forces a downward step. This layering, as it can be called, is very deep, and in general the last layer is nearest the top. In modern times the English were the topmost but, as the English have left, those who were on top before the English came have again become the upper layer.

When the newest invaders were Mohammedans, layering became difficult. Beginning in the eight and nine hundreds, more importantly in the eleven and twelve hundreds and again in the fifteen hundreds, the successive invaders from the north had already embraced the Mohammedan faith, and these people did not wish to intermarry with the earlier Indians. Religion dominated so much else that the process of integration with native stock began to be troublesome. To this day an integration has never yet been worked out, and is now a cause for political and military problems.

From the north came the language which, in turn, is the ancestral speech of the dominant Indian peoples. The wave of Indo–European-speaking peoples which went into India fifteen hundred to two thousand years B.C. brought with it a language related to Persian or Greek, or English and German. The language, Sanskrit, is one of the earliest of the recorded Indo-European languages. But long since, its dialects have split apart so far that different peoples of Indo-European speech cannot talk with one another. Some of the aboriginal groups took over the advanced Hindu civilization, and in taking it over adopted the Indo-European language. This was especially true in the great plain and the valleys of northern India, but it did not occur everywhere; other powerful peoples—Tamils and Telugus, for examples—took up Hindu civilization but kept their ancient languages.

Mohammedans were dominant by the time the Europeans originated their contact with India, with Arabs on the coasts and Afghan-Persian Mohammedans in the Indus and Ganges valley areas. During the fifteen hundreds, these latter peoples began to develop a great Mohammedan empire; creation of a single Indian state goes back, not to the English invasion, but to the last of the invasions from the northwest, that of Turkic-Persian Mohammedans who called themselves Moguls or Mongols.

These men claimed to be descended from Genghis Khan's Mongols, and their founding monarch claimed descent from a courtier of Genghis Khan's court of some three hundred years earlier. It was under this control that the Indian Empire was created during the fifteen hundreds. In the seventeen hundreds a business company of Englishmen began the piecemeal annexation of the already-created Indian Empire.

In the fifteen and sixteen hundreds India did not have political and military weaknesses. If anything, the empire of the Moguls in that period was one of the world's great states, well organized and powerfully supported by armies. In the seventeen hundreds, however, weakness at the top—the court harems beginning to pull court policies apart, local submerged units beginning to rebel, and like troubles—were to make the empire crack. The English were to move aggressively into India in the late seventeen hundreds, approximately during the lifetime of George Washington. Political weakness appeared late in the history of European contact with India; it was not something which had been there all the while, and the means by which the English were to take over were supplied mostly by the Indians themselves.

Various Indian potentates asked the British East India Company to support them; the troops were chiefly Sepoys (Indians trained in European fighting methods) and the money was furnished by Indian taxes. The conquest was not achieved by large armies sent from England. In sum, the first real empire in India was created by the Moguls just after Europeans came into close contact with that country, and the English were the successors of the Moguls at a time when others in India itself were also trying to wrest that Empire from the Moguls.

We are accustomed to thinking of India as a densely populated land, where there are several hundred million people. When Europeans first got there, it was nowhere nearly so densely settled. Even in antiquity there had been areas in the Ganges and Indus river valleys where intensive agriculture had maintained a dense population, but even there it was nowhere nearly so great as it has become in modern times. There is no misinterpreting of the fact that their contact with Europeans induced growth of the great populations now found in China, Japan, Java, India, and many other places in the world. The Europeans have imposed peace, brought the means to cut the death rates from famine and disease, and stimulated over-all production and consumption. But in the meanwhile, we must think of India during the fourteen and fifteen hundreds as containing wide, sparsely-inhabited spaces featuring stretches of wild jungle or semi-desert brush or mountain country, or even good fertile plains, with hardly anybody living in them.

In advanced areas the Indian population was overwhelmingly village-pastoral and agricultural. There were districts where hunting and the gathering of honey were dominant occupations. There was no single uniform economy. In some districts the general pattern of life was a good deal like that of Europe in those times, while in others men were far more primitive.

There was a general tendency for diverse language groups to coincide with diverse economies. The bush people and people of the southeast coast did not speak Indo-European languages, and still do not today. On the whole they were living both socially and economically in a way very different from that of the people who lived in districts where Indo-European languages were used. In general, the Indo–European-speaking peoples in the northern plains valleys tend to have the economy and social organization which we think of as "Indian." This includes the caste system ("caste" from the Portuguese word *casta*, which means the layer system of society) which predominates overwhelmingly in the Indo-European districts. Other groups and districts have been influenced by the caste system, but hardly anywhere to the same extent as the Indo–European-speaking peoples.

The system of castes is usually taken by Americans and Europeans to be a frozen and rigid thing, but the idea that castes stay petrified, like so many layers of limestone, is incorrect. Instead, there is constant restless movement within the caste system, with units moving up, moving down, pushing and hurting each other as they try for little advantages within the system. We are also struck by the more modern tendency for the caste system to stratify according to crafts or occupation, so that street sweepers will be at the bottom while priests will be at the top (noting, though, that some Brahmin priests are among the poorest of people).

Historically the castes do not seem to have been associated with jobs. Instead, it is more than likely that the castes started as racial subdivisions, where the lower represented the greater amount of crossbreeding with the aborigines, while the higher were connected, at least in theory, with purity of Brahmanistic blood. This is possible, although we are not too sure of it. At any rate the caste system, when the Portuguese first went to India, was not quite so ramified as it is today. It has continued to add ramifications and has been a factor giving stability in the social pattern, but it is also a source of weakness, especially in economic matters.

It has been very hard to change the economy in India, and it has been the noncaste people who have most profited in trade and industry and done most to strengthen it. Among the Hindus proper there has been a tendency for persons of the best education, with the most capital and the best general knowledge of the world, to remain aloof from craft work of any sort. On the other hand, also among the Hindus, the persons who were able to use tools have been in caste levels and groups which were devoid of general education and without capital. As a result there has not been any drive on the part of weavers to put in weaving machines, or of rich Hindus to set up textile mills.

The economy of India was to be changed by contact with Europeans, especially the contact with Europeans by groups which were not primarily in the caste system. Important among these were the very small population of Parsees or Persians who were descendants of refugees from the Mohammedans back in the six hundreds. When the Mohammedans pushed into the Persian or Iranian plateau, most of the Persians gave in, but a few thousand who were mainly members of the aristocracy and city merchants fled into India. Their descendants have been there some thirteen hundred years now, and still use their old speech for religious purposes. In modern times Parsees have become big capitalists, founders of modern banks, insurance companies, iron mills, and many other businesses. Their leadership in such affairs seems to have been generated by the caste system itself, which so largely left the field open to them.

On the whole the Mohammedans have been fairly exempt from the whole pattern, although many converts from the Hindu faith have failed to be converted away from the caste system. Over the years the caste system is to be reckoned as one of the things which made conquest or penetration by the Portuguese, Dutch, French, and English fairly easy.

In India a conqueror at any one moment has been at the top of the social system, if not the caste system. The result has been that in large parts of India the man at the top of the social heap was a foreigner in language, traditions, and religion—above all in religion. An example of this was the Nizam of Hyderabad in the middle-south, ruler of a wide territory until it was taken away from him by the Indian government. The Nizam had always been a Mohammedan ruling a state which included millions of non-Mohammedans. There were just a few Mohammedans, who were close to the throne, and always a bodyguard of south Arabians specially imported to care for his family business and to act as the palace guard. The fabulously wealthy Nizam was in no way connected with the people he ruled, having nothing in common with them in the way of language—he spoke a different kind of language as his household tongue—or religion, or in attachment to the country. After four hundred years of ruling Hyderabad, the Nizams were to all intents and purposes still foreigners.

The pattern of Indian society was predisposed to accept a handful of outsiders as heads of the states, and it was into that position that the Portuguese, Dutch, French, and English were to step during the fifteen, sixteen, and seventeen hundreds. The English needed relatively few of them to handle the reins of government which had previously been controlled by the Moguls.

Indian Culture and Religion Outside India

While India was subject to outside conquest, it was itself the center of some extraordinarily dynamic and expansive religious and cultural movements. The greatest of these movements was that originated by the north Indian preacher-prophet, the Buddha, whose followers have spread his teaching outside India to a tremendous extent in the course of the

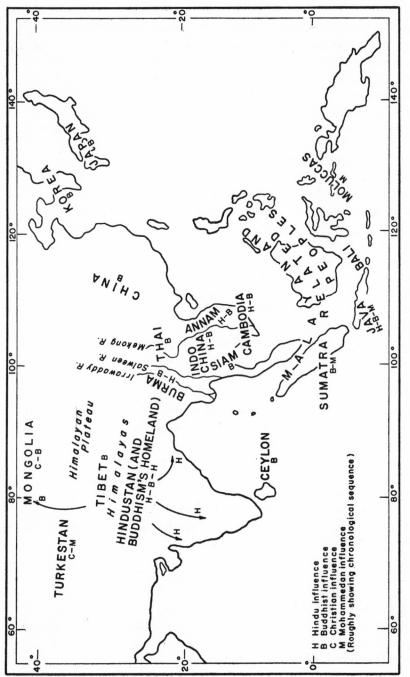

Hindu and Buddhistic Asia

last two thousand years. In the case of Mongolia it has been spread only in the last five or six hundred years.

Buddhism started out as an Indo-European religion, and its holy books were written down at the start in the main languages of north India. In fact, Buddhism grew out of the Brahmanistic religion. It flourished in India a while after its start there over two thousand years ago, but tended eventually to die out in its homeland under the pressure of a revived Brahmanism.

But it did not die as a movement; quite the contrary. It maintained a peaceful missionary movement which penetrated the central Asian highlands, China, Japan, and eastward toward Indo-China. Later on Buddhism spread into Ceylon. The missionaries took with them different sectarian interpretations of the teachings of Buddha; it is not uniform, with exactly the same teaching everywhere, any more than Mohammedanism or Christianity are completely uniform. Sects among the Buddhists came to exist early and have been very important since.

Wherever they went, Buddhist missionaries carried with them the holy books of the religion; that meant that they carried with them the need for their converts to study Indian languages and literature. Just so missionaries of the Roman Catholic Church have taken with them wherever they have gone their holy books written in the Latin tongue, thereby spreading the culture of ancient and medieval Rome along with their religious teaching. So also have the Mohammedans carried Arabic, their holy language, all around Islam. Buddhist missionaries carried their holy books, language, and outlook on life from India to hosts of people quite different in language and ancestry from the peoples of India.

Along with the content in thought, the framework for thinking and philosophy, went trade and arts and crafts. Buddhism and Hinduism proper were vehicles by which Indian art styles and concepts were spread into central Asia and even to Japan, to Indo-China and the East Indies. Temples in Java or Japan were built by architects who followed Indian patterns although the workmen were native. The same Indian influence appeared in architecture elsewhere through the Buddhist world as well as in painting, sculpture, and dance, and costumes. A whole world outside India was partly Hinduized, even though this was mostly done by a religion which no longer had much influence in any part of India itself.

Trade went along. The first tie for trading purposes of any durability between India and the Spice Isles was created by navigators who took missionaries in their ships, two thousand years ago, in the days of the Roman Empire. At that time Indian traders who were Buddhists, or who

carried Buddhists in their ships, were important in the region of Singapore
and Java. They traded, and they carried missionaries and pilgrims from
Java and the East Indies to the holy places of India. For Buddhism's
spread was associated not only with missionaries going away from India,
but also with pilgrims who went to India from even great distances. At
all times over the past two thousand years the holy places of India have
been known by Chinese, Japanese, Burmese, and others, who visited
Buddhist holy places and relics. The ties of trade and education, culture,
literature, and art, between India and the outside world have been
kept strong by this means.

Buddhism is strikingly like Christianity in its generation of vigorous
monasticism. Monks have been a very considerable part of the population
in any Buddhist country, and until very recently were politically dominant
in Tibet. Many of these monks were wanderers of the highways, like the
European Franciscan friars in the Middle Ages and today, but most of
them have lived in monasteries where they have been the special guardians of Buddhism in Mongolia, Tibet, Burma, and Siam.

Monasticism in the Buddhist world has resembled that in Europe
in another respect: the monks introduced superior agricultural and craft
methods in regions which had been lacking them. When monks moved
into Tibet they represented a vigorous force in the economy and society.
The monastic movement also provided the great libraries which have
been guarded in monasteries of the Buddhist world just as those in
western Europe were guarded for centuries in the Catholic monasteries.

There are some special features in the climate and topography of
Southeast Asia—which we might call Indo-Asia. Most of the land to the
south and east of the Bay of Bengal is wet tropical. There are, however,
spots where there is a shortage of water, usually on the down-wind side
of a mountain range which may have an annual rainfall of two or more
hundred inches on its other side. So while there may be very dry spots
locally, generally the summer monsoon soaks the land. Only a few places
in the world are in a class with the lands of upper India-Burma when
it comes to getting drenched, and during the rainy season it is not an
easy climate in which to live. But when the monsoon wind is blowing
off the land it becomes fairly dry, and the inhabitants can grow their
crops.

In general it is very mountainous. The great folded ridges of the
Himalayan plateau continue down into this extension of Asia, forming
its backbone. As they bend southward, they become lower, with wider

valleys between them, and the high-mountain character of the land is gradually lost. These are fairly new mountains with quite steep slopes, although their lower slopes can be terraced. On the rolling ridge-tops there is another place where crops can often be grown. The deep valleys as they approach the sea hold increasingly more alluvial soil, until the deltas are reached. The population of the area is concentrated on the deltas, either the big ones such as those of the Red, Mekong, or Irrawaddy rivers, or on the little deltas of small streams which come down from the hills and flow into the ocean only a few miles from where they start.

The alluvial coastal strips and deltas are capable of supporting an extraordinary population per square mile by rice culture. These people have good swamp rice as well as highland rice from the upper levels, which they grow in tremendous quantities in good years; and most years are good.

There is also very rich soil on the main islands such as Java and Sumatra, where terracing on the mountains makes possible use of a volcanic soil which is just as rich as that of the alluvial deltas.

In all Indo-Asia there is not a very large population in the back-country hills and jungles. Just through the fringe of jungle bush at the edge of village land there will be miles and miles of land in which no one lives except outlaws and hunters, who go through occasionally, or small bands of Stone Age aborigines.

Vegetable products have always dominated the diet and economies of the area. Rice is the staple, although the introduction of American maize several hundred years ago, for growth on the ridges, has made a big change in use of highland fields. People who eat Indian corn in some neighborhoods do not even remember that it was brought in; just as the Negroes do in South Africa, they think that it is native.

The inhabitants are overwhelmingly a rice and fish eating population, the fish coming out of the sea just off shore, or out of canals, ponds, and rivers. From shrubs and trees have chiefly come the export commodities, above all such spices as pepper, cloves, and nutmeg. Mineral resources are excellent in many cases, but were not to be exploited at all until very modern times, except for precious jewels. For instance, Burma has been famous for its rubies for a long while, but otherwise its mineral resources have not been particularly important until within the past two generations, when western Europeans began finding oil in Borneo and Sumatra, tin in Malaya and Siam, and other minerals.

The mountain folds circle southward into this part of the world and one continues to form the Malay peninsula. The valley lines of rivers have been the lines of migration of successive layers of people, from the Tibetan area and from what is now called South China. In that whole region peoples of great variety have been generated by the sharpness of the valleys and difficulties of local communication. People who lived even three hundred miles apart, but in the same valley, were closer to one another than to other people who lived twenty miles away over a mountain ridge in the next valley. As a result, there have been a great many different tribal languages and cultural groups, generated one after another or existing side by side at any one time. It is an area of wide diversity in linguistic groups.

The hillier parts are in general backward areas, being least accessible from the sea or the river valleys, and are sparsely inhabited. The linguistic and cultural relatives of some peoples are gone so that they seem to live by themselves. An example of these are the little Negrito peoples, or Negrito-like peoples, who are often to be found in the hill country. They either live or are known to have lived in the Malay States, the Philippine Islands, Sumatra, and elsewhere. These people are few in number and are different physically in every way from the peoples who live about them. Their culture is in most cases that of the Stone Age, and they have hardly any resources or ability to exploit resources except what they can do by hunting. There are peoples within hunting distance of Singapore at this moment who are culturally in closer touch with Neanderthal man than with that city.

The important peoples in these parts, both numerically as well as culturally, politically, and militarily, are immigrants from the north or from the sea. (The Malays apparently did not spread from the mainland out to the islands but instead came from the islands into Malaya.) The most famous of all the peoples to come down the valleys from the north are the people known as Thai or Siamese. They are a very numerous part of the whole population in the peninsula. Siam, or Thailand, covers only part of the area they occupy; there are also many of them in Burma, and many more in Indo-China. The Thai are immigrants from south China who were driven out by the Chinese. They have been on the run from the Chinese for a thousand years; they have settled successively in parts of what is today China, then in parts of what is now Burma and Indo-China, and have then been pushed still further south. The peninsular Thai are refugees from China, and back in China there are still other Thai who are pretty well Chinified now.

A large number of Tibetans moved long ago into the Irrawaddy River valley, where they became known as the Burmans or Burmese. They created their modern empire at about the time of the Americans' revolution. Burmese conquered all the other different peoples around them in the late seventeen hundreds, and then were themselves taken over by the British in the late eighteen hundreds.

In addition to the Burmese and Thai there were other important immigrants, such as the Annamese who went into Indo-China, and the Cambodians.

Four major factors or elements playing a part, but playing their parts in different degrees of importance, have created the cultures, societies, and economies of Indo-Asia.

First of all, there were native indigenous civilizations with variations from Cambodian, Annamese, and Malaysian to Siamese and Burmese. Then there were the Indian-oriented Buddhist influences which were especially important up to a few hundred years ago. On top of this was the Chinese influence from the north which has been steadily exercised for over a thousand years. Since the twelve hundreds, especially along the coastal fringes, there has been a Mohammedan influence which came in by sea, especially strong upon those who were properly Malayan in their language and background.

Central governments in Indo-Asia have not been stable; thrones have been overthrown many times. But while central governments are rather fragile things, coming and going in history, there are other elements in government which are not so fragile.

The central governments, at least the imperial governments, have been nearly all erected somewhat on the theory that the emperor or king was the father of the whole population. This idea is basically Chinese. In China the father of a family is a personage of great importance at all levels of society, and the father of all the families, as will be noticed, was thought of as the greatest of all fathers—the Emperor.

Examination of the biological family tree of any king or emperor in those parts, however, is likely to lead back to a successful village rebel-bandit. Such a man would have started his family toward a throne when some preceding central government had begun to grow weak and ineffective. He himself would have been a village bandit or headman who had begun to lead rebellion, carrying on guerrilla warfare and bush-whacking until he had put himself in control of a large section of the country. After that, with a regularly organized army he would have swept on to victory, wiped out the preceding royal family, built a brand new capital somewhere while allowing the old capital to revert to its original wilderness, and founded a new dynasty. Each dynastic family had a very limited attachment to much of the population under it.

For one thing the royal family was usually of one language group in a kingdom where there were many others. The interest of the ruler centered in his own particular clan and group which had risen with the royal family. Cut off from most of the population, the head of the state did not have much hold on his people save as it rose from his success. As soon as he was no longer successful he was no longer obeyed. Often enough, though, bandits trying to gain control of the government were unsuccessful, and the previous dynasty would re-establish itself.

Save where there was some copying of Chinese patterns, the governments in that part of the world had no organized bureaucracy or established tax rolls. Although advanced in some ways, they were not advanced in those which make for bureaucratic stability. The shift as one government began to fail and another to rise was simply a matter of the villagers' no longer paying attention to orders which came from the fading dynasty and giving taxes and obedience to the new bush bandit or to the foreign invader who was taking over at the top.

The brothers, cousins, and second cousins of the king constituted about the only nobility there was. This was a world in which there was not much in the way of an hereditary nobility resting its power upon long-time ownership of lands. Instead, portions of the winnings of the ascending dynasty went to government officials who were relatives of the monarch. These officials did not own either the land or the people; there was no serfdom or slavery in that sense. Instead, the official was given a territory in which he collected rents and taxes; that was the nearest they had to a nobility. Such a man was often supposed to maintain a military contingent available to the ruler when needed, which was about the closest they came to feudalism.

In Imperial days the Chinese had a regular gradation from the emperor down; these people were likely to follow the Chinese pattern by which in general the dignity of positions granted went down one notch with each generation as branch families became more distant from the throne. Persons whose father had been emperor were one step down; those whose grandfather had been emperor were another step down; at nine or eleven steps members of the family had no claim for official position. As a result, it took about nine generations for a branch of a family to lose its nobility. But nobility was always dependent on the reigning dynasty and could be lost at once should that dynasty lose its power.

Monks were of great importance in the civilized communities of Indo-

Asia. In Burma, Siam, and Annam they have constituted a far larger proportion of the total population than anything ever known in Europe. They have been most important in learning of every sort and in charity work. While there have been perversions of the original intent of some of their orders, by and large they have kept their faith well. Usually they have lived on endowed charities, and begged each day from door to door in the streets. In general these monks have been of different orders and groups of Buddhists. In some of the countries, especially where there was an alphabet akin to ours, they have managed to maintain a fairly high level of literacy among the people by running small schools at the grammar-school level where a basic education is provided. As a result literacy has always been more general in many parts of Southeast Asia than outsiders have assumed.

The village has been the stable organization everywhere. Its council has been the real government, with its elders and headmen and women. (Women have been important citizens in that part of the world, with large share in the decisions and management of all communities.) The villages have been stable, and strongly integrated, with considerable practical equality in affairs enjoyed by all adults of good character.

By and large there have not been lords over village communities; instead there has been a particular tax-rent roll by which payments had to be made to a delegate of the king. In times of chaos villagers often benefited, for then they had no one to whom they had to pay taxes, although they suffered raids and blackmail.

Among the more advanced peoples, the village has been the focus of personal loyalties. A man did not so much live in Annam, Siam, or Burma as in his own village. It was partly due to this concentration of life within the villages that so many different languages and peoples could live in near proximity and still maintain their individualities. The occupants of one village cared little about what happened to those in the next. There have been no theories attached to this, only a working principle which is neither Chinese nor Hindu, but native, and goes back to different roots from either China or India.

The basic food of the whole of Southeast Asia was rice, grown in the marshy valleys and on terraces on the hills. On the seacoast, fish was likewise important; in local trade rice went to the seacoast and fish to the interior. This was an ancient commerce and necessary to both the coastal and hill communities. Except for this, the communities could be very nearly self-supporting.

Thus people in that part of the world were able to get along with almost no contact with the outside. To them embargoes meant nothing. Their products for export were chiefly crops which were gathered, or were grown at a very low level of agriculture, such as mother of pearl, cocoanut, birds' nests for soup, various kinds of dried fish from the island or coastal areas, the surplus rice, and above all spices. To the people in the villages it did not matter vitally whether these things were sold or not.

However, their spices have always been a commodity of the most tremendous interest to certain outsiders, who have been anxious to obtain as much pepper, clove, and other spices as possible. Away from that part of the world, from very early times the spices began to be worth their weight in gold. Spices brought multimillions to outsiders who were able to control the export, and getting control of the spice trade has historically been a matter of displacing those who were previously in control. There were two reasons why the influence of India spread so actively through Burma, down Siam, and out to Java. One was that missionaries were spreading their faiths. The other was that traders, especially from Ceylon, were pushing the spice trade. Buddhism (and Hinduism in Bali and Java) and the spice trade had been developed for a long while when, during the eleven, twelve, and thirteen hundreds, Moslems began to intrude.

Arabs from South Arabia, trading as far as southern India, established contact with the Malays, who might almost be called the Arabs of the farther East, for the Malay communities east of the Bay of Bengal adopted much the same religious and trading pattern as that of the Arabs. The Arabian-Malay faith and trade radiated to Java and the Spice Isles in competition with the fading Buddhist-Hindu influence. Moslem sultans began to overthrow Hindu rajahs in Java and Sumatra. In the fourteen hundreds the trade in spices had become dominated by the Malay-Arab combination; then the Portuguese took it away from the Malay-Arab group; a hundred years later the Dutch took it away from the Portuguese, and it remained in the hands of the Dutch until 1940.

Foreign trade in the islands has been managed historically by foreign traders who have taken control of strategic points along the coasts or rivers, and have then subjected local rulers to some kind of tribute. The tribute has been arranged in different ways, with outright buying of the spices fairly rare. As a result, the villagers did not often make much of a profit from exported spices; they were not an export, they were a tribute. The collection of spices was a required labor tax and the produce was carried to the ports to be picked up by the sultan's or rajah's coastal vessels which carried the merchandise to concentration points for shipment toward China or India and the Mediterranean. The villagers did not obtain the wherewithal to buy corresponding imports; their rajahs and sultans did. The villagers were not particularly upset when trade was cut off, nor were they particularly benefited when it was flourishing.

It was to outsiders that the export-import business was important. It was particularly important to one group of outsiders who lived inside the different countries, the Chinese. For hundreds of years Chinese, especially southern Chinese from Foochow (now Minhow) or the Canton area, have been migrating into Southeast Asia. This migration in recent centuries has been especially heavy where European governments have established stability, such as in the Philippines after the Spanish had arrived, or in Malaya after the British had calmed that region down.

The Chinese have made themselves an extremely important part of the economy wherever they have gone. While individuals have concerned themselves with foreign export trade, the majority have concentrated on local business. They have managed the concentration of goods from the coastal village and its small hinterland, then dealt with the wholesalers or collectors who have come along the coast. They have run the gambling, loan-shark, and vice businesses in the towns and villages where they have resided, as well as the local shops, and dealt with the outside world, making themselves the middle men between the Malay, Filipino, or Siamese and the outsiders. They have never become natives, although mixed bloods have become natives. The Chinese has considered himself to be a member of some specific village community and family back in China; his relatives would make a real effort to send his body home for burial, even generations after his ancestors had left for Siam or Java. All through that part of the world Chinese have been completely at home, and yet, contradictorily, they have remained Chinese in every way. Although they controlled a very large part of the local affairs in a village in the economic sphere, they did not take a part in local politics. As operators of the opium and gambling establishments, and especially as loansharks, they have been targets for the antagonism of the local population.

There were no castes, as in India; Mohammedan influences made the setting up of castes even more difficult than it would otherwise have been. But the differences from tribe to tribe made up for this in part; there was some tendency, not to have castes, but to have specialization in economic activity which was based on ancestry, with certain activities considered Chinese business, others Siamese, others Malay, and so on.

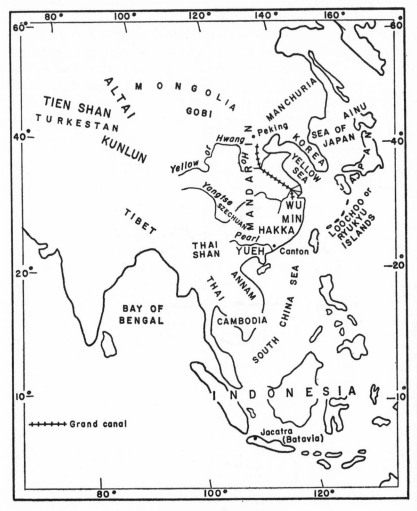

China and Chinese Asia

China

and Chinese Asia

C HINA, and the large neighboring areas of Asia which have, to varying degrees, been "Chinified" over the last two thousand years, lies on the map across the top of India and Burma, and the Indo-Asia just discussed. The central Asian Moslem lands, a combination of desert, steppe, and oasis, lie to the west. East is the Pacific and the Ryukyu and Japanese archipelagoes. On the north, from Central Asia to the Pacific Ocean, its frontiers run through the lands of steppe, forest, and mountain, of warm summers and bitter winters.

Within these modern political boundaries, many peoples, speaking other tongues and devoted to other religions, with their own inherited economies, societies, institutions, arts, and literatures, do in fact, taken all together, cover more territory than China proper, but the Chinese for countless years have dominated all of them in numbers, in art and crafts, in wealth, in war and government.

The cradle of the Chinese people, of their language, civilization, and polity, clearly lay in the great valley of the Yellow River and on the nearby rolling country and wide deltas, roughly south of modern Peking.

The true Chinese in earliest history occupied a land which had a continental climate, at about the same latitude as that of Chicago. Behind them to the west were the high, dusty plains of Asia, while the Yellow Sea and Pacific Ocean lay downstream and out to the east. In this region the land is a great deal like the Middle West of the United States. The homeland of the Chinese is highly productive in crops suited to temperate climate.

The Chinese there had begun to develop its civilization at about the same time that similar developments were taking place in the Indus

Valley, in Mesopotamia, and in the Nile regions. Its civilization is very ancient, but just how ancient we cannot be certain. From that region Chinese political influence and settlement have spread so far that what was the core of China is far outweighed by China today—a much more variegated and wider land.

Modern China is a territory containing some of the highest mountains in the world, some of the coldest plateaus, some of the driest dusty deserts, some of the wettest semitropical swamps, and almost all the different kinds of lands between those extremes. It is like the United States in that it is continental; and it is not possible to speak of a typical Chinese climate.

China's varieties of climate account for great unevenness in the spread of population. There is practically no place in the world which is drier and less hospitable than central sections of the Gobi Desert. On the other hand, on the Canton Delta and in some other places there has been such a concentration of population that the people have even spilled over into the rivers, living in boats moored along the banks.

The varieties of climates and resources have been responsible for a tremendous diversity in the ways in which the soil has been exploited, ranging from tropical or semitropical rice culture in the southeast to the yak's milk and cheese economy in the mountainous west.

Historically, of course, the resources of oil, coal, and uranium which rumor tells us are being found in Mongolia, Turkestan, and other regions fringing China proper were of no value for they were not exploited. China's usable resources were, earlier, rather slim. Its people had iron and knew how to use it, but some areas had too little. Neither did they have abundant supplies of copper, although there were districts which produced copper long ago and which still do. There were decided shortages of some of the metals, making necessary considerable importation of them. One of the metals which China has consistently imported has been silver, for which there has been a great demand for use in jewelry and other ornaments. Yet silver was not used for money until western Europeans began to bring milled dollars, the so-called "Shanghai" or "Mexican" dollars into the port cities.

The Chinese proper call themselves the Children of Han—the name of the ancient, semi-legendary dynasties which seems to have held sway for some six or eight hundred years, if the legends are correct. Historically the Children of Han have been the proprietors of their unique kind of culture—their art, their script or writing which they developed along lines very different from the alphabetical system of southern Asia and Europe, and their governmental pattern.

Over the past twenty-five hundred years they have expanded quite extraordinarily in a geographical as well as a cultural way. They have done it both by what ethnologists would call acculturation and by colonizing. The culture of the Chinese proper has been infectious, and peoples living near have been caught up in it. Other people, admiring the Chinese way of life, have invited Chinese missionaries and settlers to join them; leaders have gone to China themselves, studied all things Chinese, and returned to try to put those things into their lives at home. Peoples all around the Chinese proper have been, to one degree or another, Chinified; the Japanese and Koreans, the Mongols, the peoples in Indo-China who have been under Chinese influence, and the Tibetans have all taken a great deal from China in different degrees and times. For instance, about a thousand years ago the Japanese adopted a great deal that then was Chinese. Today, many things which we consider properly Japanese are really from the Chinese of long ago, such as some features of Japanese art and costumes.

There has been extermination or expulsion of peoples whom the Chinese wished to absorb but who resisted. The most notable of these movements has been that which brought about expulsion of Thai people from great stretches of what we today call South China. Many of the Thai, or "free people," moved down into Indo-China, Siam (Thailand), and Burma to get away from the Chinese. These have maintained their identity, as have some of the Thai who remained behind, while others simply became Chinese and make up an indistinguishable part of the wholly Chinese population in the region of Szechwan.

All peoples who were very near the Chinese proper were likely to become completely identified with them, so that the line between the Chinese proper and non-Chinese is almost impossible to draw. As a result of this, from north of Peking to south of Canton, originally non-Chinese have become themselves Children of Han by imitation of their neighbors, by taking in immigrants from areas to the north, and by generally assimilating themselves with the proper Chinese. A process which can be seen as partial in Japan has been carried to a conclusion in the region of Canton, where the people are now really Chinese. It is not only hard to draw a line between the Chinese proper and the non-Chinese, it is also hard to draw it along any political frontier, for historically the frontiers in that part of the world have been very flexible.

Economies and Societies in China: Their Strengths and Weaknesses

The Chinese have had a marvelous degree of cultural unity, with a single kind of writing, a single kind of family organization, and usually allegiance to a single state. But within their own group they have had also a tremendous diversity, which has been partially due to diversities in climates and in the economies the climates could support. In the north the Chinese have relied considerably upon millet and wheat, while in the south they have relied on rice. There has been a great difference in the planting, custody, and division of the crops from one area to another. In some districts some crafts were highly developed while in others the same crafts were practically nonexistent. Regional peculiarities were very pronounced all through China.

This has always been true even of the dialects, which could differ so sharply one from another as to be mutually unintelligible. Some southern Chinese cannot understand a northern Chinese, and vice versa, any more than a Norwegian and an Englishman and a German, all speaking Germanic tongues, can converse face to face. But the Chinese have always surmounted this difficulty with their picture writing, wherein the pictures meant the same things in any dialect (and even in Japanese). This complete unity in written language has been a bond holding all the Chinese together despite diversity in spoken languages. There has also been the main dialect, Mandarin (Pekingese is the standard form), which was spoken by all educated men. Mandarin also meant a public official of the professional learned class of the empire, and a mandarin spoke the same language on the Russian frontier as on the Hindu.

Like governments in the Indo-Chinese area, the government of China has been, in principle, the government by the chosen head of a dynasty within a clan, a single great all-father ruling the families of families. Historically such a dynasty came up from a given village, or descended from a given foreign conqueror; foreign conquerors have provided a large number of all the dynasties in China.

In its three to four thousand years of governmental history, China has had for periods a single ruler of the Chinese people (not of the territorial China we know today, but of whatever was at the time the territory). There have also been long periods in which as many as four, five, or a dozen Chinese states existed simultaneously so that the country was broken up as feudal Europe was in the nine, ten, and eleven hundreds.

In some centuries local war leaders (but they were not feudal lords), princelings, dukes, and counts (to use Western terminology) had their own followers and fought with one another, paying little or no attention to any emperor. Dismemberment of that sort has been historically very common in China. Such conditions obtained during a good part of this very century, when different war lords took over provinces or sections or groups of provinces to rule them with only a nominal recognition of the head of the state. After 1912–1913 the war lords went quite a way toward making another fragmented China, with subdivisions which might number several dozen one week, and only a few another week, as overturns took place with great rapidity.

For long stretches of time in Chinese history the rulers were foreigners. Above all, these foreigners were nomads from the steppe lands to the north and northwest. Not just once, but repeatedly, peoples from those outside areas formed large armies under warlords or tribal chieftains and struck down toward the great plains and deltas of China proper, with their eyes on conquest if possible, and booty in any case. The Great Wall of China was built to hold away such people and, though it helped to some extent, it was not infallibly successful. Yet the Great Wall was not the only defense on which the Chinese relied; they also used ambassadors, money, bribes, titles, and the conferring of royal brides to cause barbarians to fight one another or at least to be quiet. When the Chinese were vigorous and active, their influence was known in Central Asia and even as far as the Caspian Sea area. But on the whole the policy has been defensive, symbolized by the Wall behind which the Chinese have stood, ready to beat off intruders.

Nomads much like the Huns, Avars, and Magyars who invaded Europe also pressed into China. Among them were the Khitai, from whom the name "Cathay" seeped over to Europe as the name for China. The Khitai and other Tartars or Mongols or Manchus have ruled in China.

Since Europeans really became acquainted with China in the middle of the 1200's, it has been under the control of first the Mongols into the 1300's and then of a native dynasty, the Ming, for about three hundred years, and then of another nomad dynasty, the Manchu, which ruled until 1912.

The Ming dynasty was native to begin with, but the Mongols were steppe nomads from the north and west who took over China in the twelve hundreds. They struck China just when they also struck in Europe. They even tried to take Japan, but their great fleet was completely knocked apart by a typhoon which the Japanese called a "kamikaze," a "holy wind," which blew the Mongols to destruction (the word has come to have a different meaning in modern times).

Both the Mongols and the Manchus did the same thing quite quickly after obtaining control of China; they Chinified so completely that only a few generations after they had come in as alien conquerors they were living in Chinese style as individuals and ruling China according to China's traditional pattern. To be sure, among themselves the Mongols kept their clan organization, law, and speech, becoming bilingual; and the Manchus did the same thing. But for all practical purposes, in their tastes, in their cultural activities—many Manchus especially becoming highly educated in Chinese art and literature—they had been absorbed.

By the time European contact with China became really important, the Manchus were the rulers, though in the fifteen hundreds, when the Portuguese first touched China, the decaying Ming dynasty was still ruling. But before the Portuguese foreigners were in any position to think of taking over China, the Manchus, themselves foreigners from the north, had seized it. Also, by the time the Muscovites began to nurse ambitions of conquest, in the sixteen hundreds, the Manchu-Chinese Empire was far too strong to be a victim.

During the time of the American French and Indian Wars, the Manchu state was extremely strong. The Manchu ruling clans were very tough, very military, with considerable auxiliary forces of organized native Chinese, a people who have always fought well when well led, and not fought at all when poorly led. For the first time in all history a strong Chinese control was created over Chinese Asia. Mongolia, Turkestan, and Tibet were added to the Chinese Empire a considerable time after Massachusetts was added to the British Empire or Quebec to the French. Among the vigorously growing empires of the world in the sixteen and seventeen hundreds was the Chinese (led by the Manchus), which did the most complete job of all in conquering foreigners, then absorbing them governmentally and militarily. It was at this epoch that the territorial China of the modern maps was created.

Such strength meant that China was not to be overrun or annexed by Europeans. Any attempts on the part of the Europeans to disrupt Manchu control collided with a strong state until about the 1830's. By then the Manchu grip was beginning to be relaxed, especially in South China, and western Europeans, together with Americans from the side toward the sea and Russians from the other side, have since been able to extend influence into China.

In the fifteen hundreds, China's fringe areas were basically non-Chinese. Over much of these areas Buddhist monks had a very strong influence, even to having control of the government. As a rule, where the Chinese could not grow crops as they were accustomed to doing, there would be incomplete Chinification. The Chinese agricultural pattern was deeply imbedded in the whole of Chinese culture. In an area where transhumance was necessary, where great herds had to be driven between northern and southern pastures each year, a completely Chinese culture could not take hold. Likewise, in areas where the climate was too tropical, Chinese culture as such could not make itself completely at home.

Fringe peoples could borrow tremendously from China in their thought; their script and literature could be deeply influenced; they might even put on Chinese clothes, although Chinese clothes were not very good for horseback riding nomads; but until they could also borrow the intensive small-plot agriculture at which the Chinese were so skilled, they could not become truly Chinese. Such agriculture did not fit in well with the Mongols or the southern mountaineers, for example. As a result, fringe peoples, by their economies which in turn were determined by geography and climate, were measurably protected from Chinification.

On the other hand the Chinese pattern of life was at home where basic family support came from small plots of intensively cultivated soil. This sort of economy could be established in river bottoms or in great deltas where the people lived in settled villages, frequently fortified with mud walls. These were villages made up of a few dozen or some score families, the heads of the families being the important persons in the economy and the politics of the town. The very largest part of the population in these villages was on the whole self-supporting and self-sufficient.

The economy of the villages was supplemented by cottage industry (in a few parts of China, people lived in isolated establishments, but in most parts they lived in villages), which is very ancient in China, as it has also been in the agricultural parts of India. This type of manufacture by which a family, both parents and children, specializes in making something for sale has been used to supplement the raising of crops in garden style. It has usually required a high level of skill but simple craft methods and tools; the villager contributed hardly any capital for tools, and none for materials, relying on a putting-out system. As in medieval Europe, a city merchant or specialist furnished materials and often the tools, traveling about to start the manufacture, then paying money as pieces were done and depositing more materials for the next round of work.

Manufacturing has been regionally specialized, some areas concentrating on metal work, others on porcelain, others on straw work, woodwork, or boats, and so on. As a result there has been a very considerable interregional trade since the beginning of Chinese history, with one area making straw hats for almost everyone else, another weaving widely appreciated textiles, and so on. The greater part of all commercial activity has been involved in getting the articles made, collecting them, shipping them to other parts of China, and distributing them. Over-all, trade inside China has always been of paramount importance.

Since China was so very large, its internal trade was rather like the international trade of medieval Europe in general character. The sort of movement of goods which we have above called international trade between Flanders and Italy was like the trade between Peking and Canton. Internal trade has been the great interest of the Chinese merchant class, and the great support to the Chinese cottagers who have done the actual manufacturing.

On the other hand, Chinese goods have enjoyed a tremendous reputation outside China for their excellence, novelty, and beauty, and have been in the highest demand. For instance, for a long while no one outside China knew how to make a vitrified porcelain which was called "china," and which was greatly appreciated anywhere that it was taken. It was only in quite modern times that the British and French learned how to make it, and until then there was a great demand for such things as Chinese teacups and saucers. Until the very most recent generations Chinese cloths were superior to competing cloths from Europe, and so on.

To the Chinese, the outside trade has been simply a little extra on the side, and something of importance only to the merchants of Canton and a few other sea ports. As far as China as a whole was concerned, it was insignificant, since it affected the prosperity of literally only a few hundred merchants out of a population of millions. It was the home trade which made the wheels of Chinese commerce and manufacture go around.

But outsiders, first the Portuguese, then the Russians and Dutch, then the English and Americans, found that what seemed very slightly important to the Chinese was tremendously important to them. There has been a great deal of warring among Europeans for the opportunity to trade with China, with the Portuguese and the Dutch fighting it out, then the Dutch and English fighting it out, as they have tried to eliminate one another.

The Chinese economy was above all agricultural, with intensive cultivation of flat plains or rolling country. This economy was both vulnerable and strong at the same time. There was not much storage of food, and not much carry-over of crops. Most farmers did not have either the facilities or the capital to keep a large supply of grain in granaries.

Also, the very small size of individual holdings was a constant source of difficulty for the farmers. So a local crop failure or a regional crop failure produced catastrophe to those affected. One or two years of general crop failure could cause millions of deaths. This has been true in modern times as well.

For another thing, since so many lived in the valleys of great mountain-fed rivers, the Chinese plains were subject to catastrophic flooding whenever the dikes were broken. One of the chief activities of any good government has always been to keep the dikes in repair.

On the balance, however, although crop failure or floods resulted in death for great parts of the population, there was a great resiliency, and a few years after such a catastrophe the people could be back to a prosperity equal to that before the disaster. There was no permanent disruption such as would occur in the United States should our transport and manufacturing machinery be badly broken up.

Social and economic disruptions in China have always been connected with land ownership. In China most holdings historically were small, a single piece of property which covered two or three acres being considered large. Only temples and persons of great wealth owned more than ten or fifteen acres. There could be as many as three families making their livings from a single four or five acre unit—a hired man and his family, the tenant and his family, and the owner and his family. This was not so bad in the south, where two or even more crops of different kinds could be raised on the same land in a given twelve months. Everywhere the land has always been made amazingly productive by our standards.

There was not great uniformity from region to region in China in local land laws, money lending customs, and so on. From Peking to Canton several different types of land ownership patterns existed in different regions, and with many variations in between.

There were no hereditary family nobilities in China, but the head of the clan of Confucius had been recognized as ducal through the centuries. Other families which have gained power have done the same step-down described in connection with the Indo-Chinese, Siamese, and Annamese nobilities, whereby after a dozen generations away from direct relationship with some king or emperor, the ex-noble family became of common rank.

However, while there were no hereditary nobilities in the western European sense, for thousands of years in China, especially beginning several hundred years before 1500, there was a scholarly civil service system by which high position was open to anyone who could qualify.

This lasted until the fall of the Manchu dynasty in 1912 but was especially strong in its functioning at the time Europeans first began a regular contact with China. By this system endowments and scholarships made it possible each year for a good number of poor boys to start an ascent in the educational world which led to the highest positions in the state. Examinations were the only means by which to enter the civil service, and further examinations were the only means for advancement. An able boy who managed to enter the civil service through examination, and then to pass further examinations, could end up as one of the highly revered scholars of China, entrusted with the most important of governmental positions, with all the privileges of a nobility attendant on such a position. Wealth or nobility in his own family had nothing to do with his achievements in this line. Such men, working with the "best families" of a given area, were the actual rulers of the different sections of China, having been appointed by the emperor who delegated authority to them and only checked on their activities from time to time.

Classes in China were not much like our status classes. The most important of all groupings was that of the scholars. This is still true in China, although the scholarship is not focused on the Chinese classical writings as it once was. In 1500 the Chinese recognition of classes followed a more or less set pattern. Scholars were in the topmost place. Next came farmers, no matter how poor, although within the group of agricultural people of course there could be the landlord, the tenant, and the ordinary hired man. Below the farmer came the merchant, no matter how wealthy. At the very bottom came the soldier, the lowest of all.

This class pattern did not fit at all with anything known in Europe, nor did it resemble the pattern obtaining in India. It took for granted that any persons from any family might become scholars and move into the highest class. It placed the responsibility of whether he was to move up or down directly on the individual. Merchants, as such, had no high standing in society unless by chance they were also learned. This class system of China resembled nothing in western Europe, nor did the Chinese recognize the European class system in return. All of this was to be of some importance when western European merchants began trying to trade in China with a people which did not want, need, or highly regard them.

Japanese, Korean, and Loochoo (Ryukyu) Fringe Cultures

The Japanese, Loochoo, and Koreans who lived on the peninsula of Korea and on the off-shore island chain, which stretches from the far north southward nearly to Formosa, were alike in a number of ways. The Japanese, Loochoo, and Korean languages were related and there was a historical connection between them. They had all been deeply influenced by Chinese civilization, especially in the form that civilization had had in the nine hundreds, when they had adopted much that was Chinese.

Another thing they had in common was their mixed genealogies, there being an admixture of southern islander blood, especially strong in Loochoo, less in Japan, and even less in Korea. This had derived long before from a Malayan-Polynesian(?) migration by sea from the south. There had also been influences from the north. In the northern side of Asia and, in the Japanese islands nearby, there still are people whose physical characteristics are astonishingly like those of Europeans. The Japanese have called them "the hairy people" or Ainu. Ainu men have long beards and hair on their chests; the women and men are likely to have the fairer skin of the western European; gray or green eyes are common among them, and their hair is often light brown and wavy instead of black and straight. In other words they look like remote cousins of Germans and Englishmen. Also, they do not have the secondary fold of the eyelid which gives a slant effect to the eyes. Prehistoric crossing of the Ainu with South Sea Islanders and with people from the Chinese mainland seem to have produced the Japanese, Koreans, and Loochoo peoples.

In many matters basic to the culture, especially in Japan, the southern islander influence is strong. It was the southern group which bequeathed to Japan the shape and make of houses, and the shape and make of governments—an essentially South Sea governmental pattern rather than a Chinese one.

The people were, broadly speaking, organized under chieftains who, along with their followers, lorded it over different local areas. In the fifteen hundreds territorial holdings, in the hands of chieftains and their followers, were the key units. Power did not rest in the Japanese mikado but in a chieftain of all the chieftains who was known as the "shogun."

Members of the warrior class were tied to one another by clan loyalties which were very strong. The head of a territory was usually a head clansman, and his swordsmen were of his own clan or members of clans which had hereditary connections with his own. He and his followers lorded it over his district, but there was no system of grants and subgrants of landed holdings as in the feudal system of Europe in the nine and ten hundreds; collections of rice and use of services from the peasants were taxes, rather than feudal or manorial dues.

There was anarchy among the shogun's followers for decades in the fifteen hundreds, even though there was nominally a holy mikado and also in theory an all-powerful shogun. This anarchy invited the Portuguese and Spaniards to think of invasion and conquest. There were projects for it parallel to those of Cortes in Mexico, Pizarro in Peru, and de Soto in Alabama.

But the would-be invaders ran up against too tough a fighting people in the Japanese. For all their insubordination the Japanese were stubborn fighters, hard to break in any kind of battle. Furthermore, the Japanese were very quick to learn, especially about fighting. The warriors lived to fight and were extremely eager to learn about anything in armor, weapons, tactics, or strategy. The Japanese only had to face Portuguese naval cannon once before they began to make every effort to obtain such weapons. They only had to watch Dutch ships navigate and maneuver in the wind and against the wind in order to covet Dutch ships. And so on. The Japanese learned with astonishing speed how to cast European cannon. They soon learned to make European-type maneuverable ships. By the late fifteen and early sixteen hundreds they were practically as well off in matters of war technology as the Dutch, Portuguese, and others who might attack them.

The Japanese were likewise extremely perceptive and active in the matter of Intelligence. They used it endlessly in their own wars, and were very touchy about other people coming in to look at Japan. So in the early sixteen hundreds they finally barred everyone from coming in, and that bar held until the 1850's, and it still held more or less until 1945.

Partly because the threat from Europe helped draw the Japanese together, and partly because they could make their home-country campaigns bigger and more effective with the use of European-type weapons, certain Japanese lords fought their way to control of Japan and possession of the shogunate. In the late fifteen and early sixteen hundreds a succession of three warlords unified Japan. They got rid of the rebels and made themselves supreme over all the other fighting men. The Tokugawa dynasty of shoguns, once in control, held it until the 1870's, a few years after our American Civil War. It was they who closed Japan to the outside world, ruled with strong military controls inside, and saw to it that the mikado had nothing to do except write poetry, appreciate flowers, and other such civilized activities. Life around the mikado was very highly polished, with no blood letting or crude manners, while around the shogun life could be very rough indeed.

In the process of Japanese unification a great many fighters were driven from the country. Most of these exiles took to the sea as pirates or became mercenary soldiers. Thereafter something which seems like a curious anticipation of the twentieth century was to be seen—Japanese mercenaries taking part in Siamese, Philippine, and Javanese wars. They worked as mercenaries and pirates, usually in the pay of the Dutch, in European conquests in South and Southeast Asia.

Although they owed much to the Chinese, the Japanese social pattern was very unlike the Chinese. In Japan the fighting men were at the top. (The Koreans had been more deeply influenced by Chinese thought in this.) There were ranks within Japanese fighting classes, the lords being at the top and swordsmen at the bottom. Next under the swordsmen came rice-growing peasants who were, at the time Europeans first touched Japan, nearly without legal or any other rights. (For example, a European wrote that he saw a group of Japanese swordsmen marching down a street in time of peace come up to a small group of ordinary civilians and, swords in each hand, cut their way through the civilians.) Japanese noble tyranny was not so much a matter of enslaving the peasants as it was of reducing them, through dues payments, taxes, and social and legal repression, to a miserable state.

Low socially, but actually very important, were craftsmen and merchants. The craftsmen organized themselves into something resembling guilds, forming corporations under the patronage of temples and temple bodies, or sometimes of nobles. Those who could do this increased their prestige.

Merchants were very important in the economy, first those who dealt with China, and then (before the bars went up) with the Portuguese and Dutch. They usually had men of the nobility in debt to them, but nevertheless were socially of a low status. It is only in modern times that the great Japanese merchant families have come to the top in importance. This came about when the fighters found that they needed wealthy merchants.

Japanese products were in great demand among foreigners. Japanese porcelains and fabricated or crude iron, copper, or brass, carvings in ivory and wood, and silks were extremely valuable to outsiders. But they were not at all important to the population as a whole, which was mostly fed with handfuls of rice and raw fish, pickled radishes, seaweed, and the like. Rice cultivation and the work of Japanese fishermen were all-important. With the exception of a few merchants the population was not greatly touched by foreign trade and commerce, one way or the other.

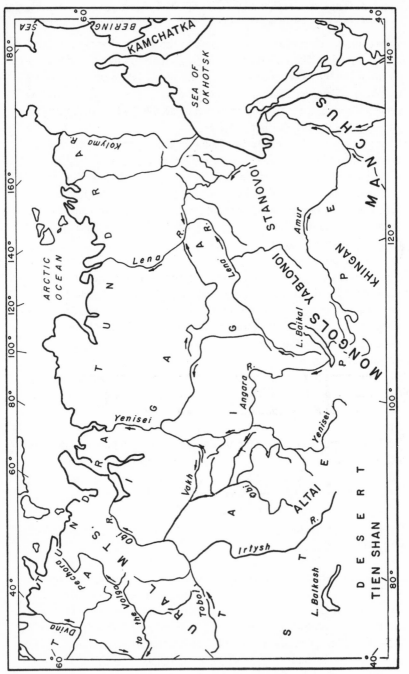

Continental Asia: vegetation zones, rivers

CHAPTER V

Continental Asia

ARCHAEOLOGICAL and historical records of the peoples living in central Asia show how they have been dominated by the continental climates of that tremendous expanse of land. It is the greatest of the land masses, cut away almost entirely from any sea influences, and in climate arranged in great belts which run roughly east and west. According to their latitudes, different regions are correspondingly hot or cold, and these great belts of climate have determined not only the kind of animals or plants which will grow, but also the patterns of economic life for human beings who have lived there and learned to use the resources offered.

On the whole we have the same climate zones on the North American continent as those which obtain in Asia. They are not arranged quite the same way, however, primarily because our mountain chains run north and south, while those in northern and central Asia run east and west, giving the climate belts in Asia a much better alignment east and west than we know here.

No people on earth has paid so much attention to the scientific study of climate and soil as have the Russians; it is modern Russian scholars who have given names to their home country's belts of land and climate. Scientists in other areas have picked up the terms, so we call the three main belts of climate the tundra, the taiga, and the steppe.

The tundra extends from the Arctic seacoast southward for a varying distance into the continent, hundreds of miles in most parts. Perpetual frost is found in it only a few inches or feet below the surface. In the warmest weather the surface melts and there is a quick growth of scrubby vegetation and mosquitoes.

But down below is the everlasting frost. In general, the surface is low, with rock outcrops which are bare of vegetation save for a few lichen, and the land is overwhelmingly marshy. This is not due to heavy rainfall but to the fact that whatever moisture falls, either in the shape of snow or of rain, evaporates only very slowly, and the land is so flat that drainage into rivers and northward toward the sea is at a minimum; runoff from higher inland areas brings still more water.

In the tundra there are hardly any trees which grow much above bush or shoulder height. These are mostly scrub willow and birch. There is a great deal of moss, regular bog moss and other forms, which supplies much of the food for animals such as reindeer and rodents; these, in turn, along with fish in the rivers, supply a good part of the food for the carnivorous animals, the great bear, the seal and walrus in the ocean, and various kinds of foxes, minks, and weasels.

As a matter of course, human population in that part of the world has always been extremely scanty, and there is great reliance on fish, seals, and other animals for food and, at least during the past thousand years or so, on the reindeer, the one domesticated animal to be found in the North. The Lapp and Samoyed and other peoples all the way from Norway to the Bering Sea domesticated the reindeer, which they used for riding or for pulling sleighs, and for its milk, which they used in the same ways we use cows' milk. They used the hide for harnesses and clothes, the bones and antlers for tools, and the carcass for meat.

This thinly settled land in the north has for centuries been dependent on imports for some important items, notably metals and salt, but also for anything which might be called a luxury.

Going south in Asia, the tundra begins to turn into forest land, just as the tundra in northern Canada begins to turn into Canadian forest areas toward the south. The land becomes a little higher, better watered in parts, and without so much standing water (though still a great deal) south of the belt of eternal subsoil frost. At this point trees begin to grow, at first in isolated patches and then more and more until the taiga or coniferous forest area is reached. This happens as one comes south from the White Sea and from Finland into Russia, or south from the Arctic Ocean itself into any part of northern Asia where the slope of the land is fairly gradual.

On its northern edge the forest belt is full of coniferous trees which gradually change over into deciduous, oaks and beeches and so on, to the southward. A person traveling southward from the tundra through the taiga will find he is also constantly, but not steeply, climbing higher into land, of which some has been glaciated and is rolling and covered with a usable top soil. When the trees are cleared, the land will bear grain crops and provide pasturage for sheep, goats, cows, horses, and swine.

The taiga is interlaced with rivers which flow north across the tundra out into the Arctic Ocean, but which in the forest belt have interlocking lateral headwater streams. It is easy to travel from the far west of the continent to the east by going down one tributary and up another branch, and so on, making only short portages between the river basins. The forested lands of the northern European plain are westward extensions of the taiga of Asia.

In earlier times the population was not dense in the forest lands. Real settlement in the old forest belt has been chiefly done by the Great Russian Muscovites, rather slowly over the last three hundred years, and has been a settlement largely of and by Muscovites from Europe. Before the sixteen and seventeen hundreds, the peoples who lived in the forest were under the political overlordship of the much more prosperous and numerous peoples of the steppes, still farther south. The Muscovites themselves, taiga dwellers, were in the same subordination to steppe overlords, until around the time of Christopher Columbus.

The steppes do not extend in an unbroken band from the Pacific over to France, although they do form quite a continuous belt. The steppes begin to appear as one goes south from the forest belt. At first there are open grass prairies with trees here and there in clumps, and finally there are no trees save in the hills and along the streams. Continuing from north to south the rainfall in general lessens, so that steppes with deep grass in summer begin to fade into steppe lands which are more and more like desert, with stunted grass which is good for pasture in only certain seasons.

The steppes extend roughly east and west across the whole continent, between the forests and the mountains, in belts a few hundred to many hundred miles wide, and on westward across the great European plain north of the Black Sea. Regarded this way, the open prairies of Hungary and even of France are a continuation of the Asiatic steppes.

There were few obstacles to the movement of men and animals in the steppe lands and, ever since they domesticated the horse, most of the peoples there had been nomadic or semi-nomadic. They moved great distances north and south on their ranges, and in case of war or the beginning of a great drought could go long distances east or west without disrupting their own economies and societies. Their whole society was designed to make movement easy, and in the course of only ten or fifteen years of marching cross-country and of fighting those across whose ranges they wished to go, some groups were able to move from the region of the Gobi Desert into Hungary.

With their equipment and mode of life they were able to move intact with astonishing speed. Generally speaking, the rivers were not much of an obstacle, for they could go across most of them taking their wagons, their animals, and their wives and children, either east or west, with fair facility.

The steppe lands merge southward into desert, mountain, and plateau lands. In the mountains proper there is ice on the peaks, rich green valleys below, and desert plateaus at the lowest levels. Many of the parts of central Asia such as Turkestan and Mongolia are a great deal like the region of the Great Basin and central plateau of Utah, Nevada, Arizona, and Colorado. There is rich pasture in the hills, the middle valleys, and on the foothills; then, only a few miles away from the foothills, there is desert. Where there is sufficient water, dense settlements of grain and fruit growers and towns of craftsmen and merchants have flourished.

In the north of central Asia, through the tundra, taiga, and steppes, rivers generally flow pretty much toward the Arctic Ocean and are gentle most of the way, but in desert areas there are great landlocked basins like the basin of our own Great Salt Lake. Rivers flow into the basins, but may not even flow as far as the local salt lake because the land is so parched. In central Asia there are several huge landlocked lakes which are either fresh or slowly turning salt, or which are already very salty, such as the Aral Sea which is fed by two beautiful broad rivers which flow down from the Hindu Kush Range, or Lake Balkhash and other seas from which there is no outlet at all. Landlocked river and lake systems are common enough, more or less surrounded by mountain ranges difficult for humans to go through.

The great rivers which flow northward across the plain to the Arctic are not obstacles. Until the building of the Trans-Siberian Railroad under the Czars, they had been avenues of travel, and most of the landlocked peoples in central Asia have been good river boatmen. These people have been almost amphibious. Although the typical Cossack has usually been depicted as a swashbuckling man on horseback, it would have been equally correct to picture him as a river-boat man, good at an oar or sweep or poling up and down a river with a keel boat, or floating along as a raftsman, just like river men in the Middle West of the United States when the great forests were being cut down.

The mountain, steppe, and tundra areas were all rich in gold and silver, although in earlier centuries these were not exploited to any great extent.

Still, there were rich barbarian iron mines in Mongolia and Turkestan, the iron from which was used for trade. And ever since the days of Herodotus the flow of gold dust and nugget gold from river washings in that area has been important to Europe. During different periods in the seven and eight hundreds there were also big silver mines in the high plateaus. Rich as it was in minerals, the ores were in general beyond the ability of the people to exploit, and historically speaking this whole area has not been a mineral-producing part of the world until modern times. The minerals were nevertheless among the lures which drew the Muscovites eastward.

What the land produced chiefly were vegetable and animal products, mostly for the sustenance of the residents of those different belts of territory, but with some products which had a very high trade value.

The tundra has been at all times famous for the production of elegant furs. It is the home country of the sable and other of the finest fur-bearing animals in the world. The catching of fur-bearing animals always has been a big activity among the tundra peoples, partly for use for their own clothing and partly because furs were the export commodity they had for exchange for needed things.

There is almost no vegetable production of any importance in the tundra, but the taiga was to become a timber-producing country in modern times, while historically it has also been fur producing. As soon as the timber was cut off, it became quite adequate for rye and vegetable growing, first with enough for the residents, and later with enough for export once the development of transportation made export possible.

On the steppes the great products were those of the herds and flocks. Either the camel or the horse provided transportation and milk, while sheep, goats, and cattle produced nearly everything else that was needed. Many of the steppe peoples in Asia have preferred to use the horse alone rather than to have cows also. They have gotten their milk and meat from horses as well as their transportation.

There are well-watered areas in both the steppe and desert countries. In the desert, by the true oases or along those rivers which flow down from the mountains and then disappear in the desert sand, there were communities dedicated to intensive agriculture. Here grain especially was grown, but also fruits, which made a coveted supplement and balance for the diets of the steppe nomads.

Primarily, the trade of continental Asia has been between its different climate belts. From the forests the tundra people have drawn iron, some vegetable food, and a good deal of the timber they needed; in return they have sent back, either as tribute (the tundra people were always tribute-paying to the people south of them) or as trade goods, the precious furs of the northern lands. The peoples of the forest belt passed on furs from the north as well as furs of their own, and when avenues for trade were open these furs were sent to China, always one of the great fur-using areas of the world, and to Europe, which has been the other great fur-using area. (In both China and Europe furs early became associated with rank.) The taiga area was well placed to export furs to either Europe or China, and it was that trade which above all attracted Europeans into the country. It was to exploit the Asian fur trade that the Muscovites began their imperialist expansion around sixteen hundred, just as it was the fur trade which drew Frenchmen and Englishmen into the interior of North America, then on to the Rockies, and finally to the Pacific coast, in the same generations.

Peoples and Economies, Governments and Cultures

The tribute paid by the tundra peoples to the forest peoples was paralleled by the tribute the forest peoples paid to the steppe peoples. Until the rise of the Muscovite Russians the steppe peoples had always been dominant in continental Asia. In the six hundreds, in the time of Justinian and thereafter, several successive Turkish empires were created by steppe conquerors in the lands between the Caspian Sea and China, and from time to time steppe peoples either threatened or actually conquered China. As we have seen, people of the same sort also conquered parts of Europe, the Huns in the three and four hundreds, the Avars in the six and seven hundreds, and the Magyars in the nine hundreds.

Genghis Khan's empire was not the first of its sort, but it happened to be the last and most far-reaching of the great central Asian empires, resting upon the military skill, bravery, and excellent equipment of the steppe nomads. These peoples were far more numerous and far better organized than the peoples north of them in the forest and tundra belts. They could put thousands of men into military formations, instead of the scores or perhaps hundreds that the forest peoples could or the mere handfuls that the tundra peoples could muster.

As well as superiority in numbers, the Mongol-Turkish armies also had great mobility, which made them dangerous even to the civilized armies in China, Persia, or the Roman Empire. They cultivated physical bravery, and since the time they had become known historically, they had devoted themselves to fighting. Their weakness lay in their incessant war of clan against clan. But when they were all under one control, pushing in one direction under one leader, they were a terrific threat to all the peoples around.

The settled peoples of the forest usually had to pay tribute to the steppe nomads, and so did the settled peoples of the river valleys and oases. Tribute was often more important than trade, steppe lords demanding iron, grain, fruit, slaves, gold, and luxuries. This greediness for the products of neighbors, the desire to make different settled peoples work to produce tribute, was a big factor in the creation of nomad empires. The nomads who were descended from the followers of Genghis Khan exploited the Russians on the western fringe of Asia in just this way, making the Russians of the forests and Ukrainian steppes produce grain and other tribute to be consumed by the Tartar Mongol hordes farther out on the steppes. They exploited the peoples they had under them as simply as they exploited their own mares and sheep and goats: they milked or worked them.

The peoples and government groups of central Asia were quite diverse. Between the Great Wall of China and the Volga River were three main biological varieties of people, distinguishable in height, complexion, shape of head, and so on. In general, the nearer to northern Europe, the closer to "European" in physical type were the people, the greater the percentage of light-complected persons. These people's eyes were blue, green, or gray—but also brown and dark. In height they were neither predominantly big nor particularly short; they were either tall or rather broad and squatty, and everything in between. While that variety of human was most common near Europe, it was also to be found everywhere, even as far as northern China or in Persia and India, but less frequently in parts farthest from Europe.

In the desert and steppe regions there was a predominance of people with darker, swarthy, or olive or brown complexions. They were likely to be tall and slim rather than short and squat, their hair could range from straight to curly, and would be dark, but not always black. They were black-eyed or brown-eyed, and frequently had deep-set eyes and eagle-beak noses. Among groups speaking Turkish they have always been especially numerous. They were to be found over toward Europe (and, of course, everywhere in Europe itself) and as far away as the Great Wall in the other direction, but they were predominant in the desert and steppe areas. Chinese painters of fifteen hundred years ago often pictured nomads as looking like this, emphasizing the eagle-beak nose which was a disagreeable feature to any Chinese, and especially so to artists. From this we can be quite sure that there was a strong manifestation of that type, even alongside the Great Wall of China.

Near China the tendency was for what we might call Mongoloid (Mongol-like) features to be important. The term, invented by anthropologists a couple of generations ago, is probably wrong, for the earliest "Mongols" seem to have been of the beak-nosed sort. Development on that side of Asia of the so-called Mongoloid features was probably the consequence of an emanation from China, whence that strain had long been breeding itself into the blood lines all across Mongolia and Turkestan. Incidentally, Genghis Khan himself may well have been gray-green eyed; if so he was not "Mongoloid" in physical type although he was the greatest Mongol of them all.

With three main physical varieties, but with an endless amount of interbreeding through all centuries, the population of Central Asia has been uneven in physical characteristics. While whole peoples have been overwhelmingly "Mongoloid" in features, others overwhelmingly "European," others overwhelmingly "Turkish," still, among the various groups there have always been individuals who showed recent or earlier crossbreeding.

In part the mixture was produced ever since the beginning of time by stealing women. Wives and concubines were acquired by slave raid and slave trade and warfare. The family of Genghis Khan was of the most mixed breed, for he added various females from all around to his collection, and his sons and grandsons did the same. His great-great-grandsons had in them the blood of most of the people the Mongol Empire ever touched, thanks to such crossbreeding with women from different stocks. To a tremendous degree the whole of Asia has had mixed breeds, and the three main types are only that.

Among the great families of languages in central Asia was the Indo-European speech, found also in Europe on one side, in India on the other, and in islands of people all across from Russia through Armenia and Persia to Pakistan. We know that until not long ago the inhabitants of still more areas spoke Indo-European tongues, but have since changed to other languages. In that part of the world the speaking of Indo-European languages has been more or less associated with light complexions, yet "Mongoloid" people whose native speech was something akin to ancient Sarmatian or to Persian (both Indo-European languages) were to be found.

The south part of the steppes and many cultivated districts were occupied in general by people who spoke varieties of Turkish. The kind of Turkish spoken in the Ottoman Empire or in modern Turkey was an offshoot, as we have seen, brought there from Turkestan when migrants moved into Asia Minor in the ten and eleven hundreds. The original and chief home of the Turks was back in the steppe country, in foothill valleys, and in the interior oases of desert basins of Russian and Chinese Turkestan.

As in Europe, in central Asia culture groups were more important than either language or physical type. It has been a part of the world where religious affiliation has been even more important as a criterion. It did not matter so much what a person looked like, nor did the language he spoke matter much more than his appearance. What was really important was how he worshiped.

The following religious groups were dominant about 1580 and 1590, at the time when the Muscovites began expanding there. The whole of the desert and steppe area was dominated by Islam. So true was this that the peoples speaking Turkic and Indo-European were almost everywhere normally assumed to be Mohammedan. From the nine and ten hundreds until about 1900 in central Asia, in the lands known as Khiva and Bokhara (the Asiatic Mesopotamia into which Alexander the Great led his troops), were the leading intellectuals and cultural advisers of all the Mohammedan peoples east of the Ottoman Empire. The Bolshevik government after the 1917–1918 period liquidated the great Mohammedan libraries, universities, and congregations of scholars there, which had been rivaled only by the libraries and universities and congregations of scholars in Cairo, Egypt. This Islamic center was not far out on the fringes of the Mohammedan world; it was one of Islam's two great hubs.

Muscovite conquest of that great eastern center of Mohammedan culture and religion took place between the period of the American Civil War and the end of World War I. It is one of the newest colonial areas in the world.

There has been an extremely active Buddhist expansion from Tibet into Mongolia, mostly in rather recent times. Tibet-Mongolia is now dominantly Buddhist, but earlier it was either Shamanistic or Nestorian Christian. The Tibetan form of Buddhism has been dominant since 1580 and 1590 across the regions of the steppe and forest plateau peoples nearest China. Beginning in the late seven hundreds and through the eight and nine hundreds, the Nestorians had had a marked success in converting peoples in Turkic-Mongolic areas to their form of Christianity. Nestorians are not completely gone even now, but there are very few of them, for they have lost their followers to Islam or Buddhism; but in the days of Genghis or Kublai Khan, it was possible to travel from Jerusalem to Peking, along the Mongol military routes, and to find at all stopping points communities of Nestorian Christians.

The trip of Marco Polo from Venice to China and back has been of great interest for hundreds of years. But at the same time there were Mongol ambassadors, chosen because they were Nestorian Christians and so could get along with other Christians, who went all the way from Peking to Bordeaux. From the other side of the fence, so to speak, we have an account of what Europe looked like to such a Nestorian Christian Mongol ambassador. A part of Genghis Khan's own immediate household was Nestorian Christian.

Most of the people in the taiga and tundra areas were devoted to nature gods, known by different names, and propitiated mostly by such rites as dances and incantations performed by witch doctors. In one of their dialects the people of the region called such a person a shaman. The witch doctors cured people, took care at least of entry into the next life, and got rid of droughts and ghosts by rattling, hollering, and performing sleight-of-hand tricks. Apparently they did good.

Great empires rose among the nomads when one clan won dominion over the other clans and peoples, and at such times the steppe nomads also ruled the oasis peoples to the south, and the forest lands to the north, even penetrating sometimes as far as the tundra. However, there was a tendency for such empires to rise rather rapidly, and then to fall apart in two or three or four generations in a sort of cyclical fashion.

Either by conquering neighbors or absorbing them in friendly fashion, a single clan would create a military power which, in turn, would spread its influence all across the steppe lands until its chieftain had made himself Khan of Khans, ruler of all the other lesser Khans, drawing tribute from them and requiring their aid in warfare. With that instrument of conquest, conquerors would go on to attack the states of more sedentary and advanced peoples. China was nearly always a target; so also were the lands of modern Iran, Afghanistan, northern India, the lands around the Black Sea, and Eastern Europe.

The steppe empires had a deep-seated weakness. Inheritance of power was passed along according to the rules of a simple clan which had only cattle and range land and dependent families to divide when the dominant clan's chieftain died. The great empire of Genghis Khan was divided up into ranges just as would have been done with the few hundred square miles of the home pastures which his father had had in Mongolia. By this division the Khan of Khans or Great Khan took as his share the eastern range, including the Chinese part, leaving great ranges to his brothers and cousins. One such range was central Asia, another Persia, another the west toward Russia. Those subfamilies tended in two or three generations to identify themselves with their subjects. Kublai Khan, the great ruler dwelling in the Peking capital, identified himself to a great extent with Chinese culture, as did the Mongols immediately under him.

Meanwhile, the descendants of his brother, the cousins in Persia, turned Mohammedan and identified themselves with the literature, religion, and life of Islam. The cousins on the European side also identified themselves with Islam in south Russia. When the Buddhists won over the Mongols of the central ranges in Mongolia proper a little later on, the unity of the old inheritance of Genghis Khan was finally broken up, for the branches of the family no longer spoke the same language and were at swords' points on matters of religion. So far as our scanty records can tell us, much the same sort of thing had happened to the earlier empires of steppe nomads. We chance to have much better records in the case of Genghis Khan's Empire, especially records which were created and preserved by the peoples on the fringes of the Empire, in China, Persia, and Europe.

The process of dissolution by division at the top went on in turn within the various great units which had first splintered off from the big central empire. This was particularly true along the edges of the Russian world. The group which held its authority from the northern shores of the Black Sea and the Caspian, up through the valleys of the Don and Volga rivers to the tundra, and lorded it over the Russian princes in the region of what is today Moscow-Kiev-Novgorod, was called the "Golden Horde."

The Golden Horde began, in the fourteen hundreds, to split in turn into three lesser subhordes or khanates. These khanates, whose rulers were of the royal Mongol family but had become Mohammedan for the most part, quarreled with one another. There were dynastic troubles on the inside of each khanate and other troubles with the subjected Russians. All this combined to weaken the fighting strength and to lessen the political efficiency and power of these khanates of the Crimea, of Astrakhan, and of Kazan. In the northern part of the old Empire of Genghis Khan, across the center of what is today Siberia, a weak little khanate of Siber or Sivir was ruled by another branch of the old royal horde of the Mongols, but had hardly any really effective fighting or governing strength even over those who were nominally its subjects.

The Mongols made a tremendous impression upon Russia. The Russian princes were the subjects of the Mongols, either brutally or very generously treated, entirely at the whim of the nearest Mongol khan. Then the Russians became one of the many successor peoples, absorbing a small element of Mongol population within their own, and then striking for independence. In the course of the fourteen and fifteen hundreds they began to reunite the Mongol empire from the west end, whereas it had first been built up from its center. As a result the Mongol empire had an heir, both geographically and politically, in one of its subject states, something which had often happened in the world of the steppe and central Asian empires. The Russian empire was also in part set up and managed according to patterns which had been deeply influenced by Mongol example during the centuries when the Mongols had the overlordship of the Russians of Moscow.

CHAPTER VI

The

Western Hemisphere

THE linked land masses of the Western Hemisphere lie nearer to the North than to the South Pole. They stretch across all of the latitudes from the Arctic through the north temperate and the north semitropical to the equatorial, then back up the scale in the Southern Hemisphere to the subarctic at the very tip of South America.

The mountain ranges generally go north and south in such a way that their effect upon the climate, in the temperate zones where they lie along the western shores, is tremendous. The ocean-tempered, ocean-moistened westerly winds come in from the Pacific (as they come in from the Atlantic over Europe) and are seriously affected by the fact that they quite quickly, coming inland, strike mountain ranges. This results in the creation of rainfall belts running north and south instead of east and west.

There is very heavy precipitation close to the coasts where the mountain walls trip the winds. Then, just inland, there are dry belts where, if the passage of air had not been interrupted by the mountains, there should be something corresponding to the moist lands of central Germany. But instead of the broad oceanic temperate zone of well-moistened lands running east and west, as it does in Europe, the Western Hemisphere has a narrow temperate oceanic climate zone running north and south, twisted in that direction by the great mountain ranges on the western coast.

The deserts and grassy steppes of Asia and Africa run generally east and west. Similarly, in both North and South America there is a belt of Mediterranean climate next toward the equator from the zone of westerly winds, and of Saharan desert next farther toward the equator. Southern California and the peninsula of Lower California, respectively, represent

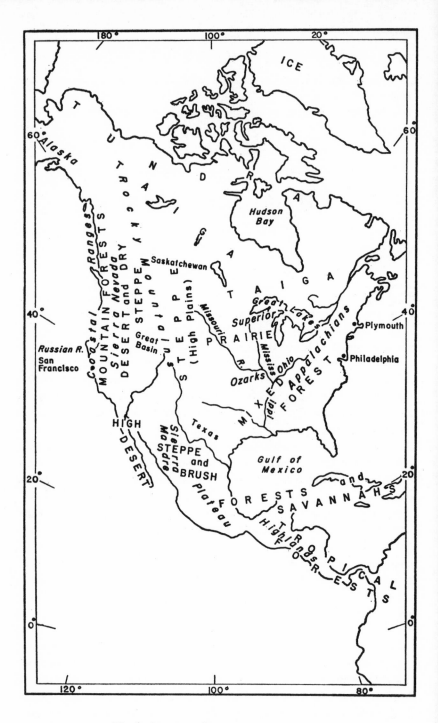

North America: climate, vegetation zones

these belts. But in North America, those two belts are not extensive east and west for mountains running north and south break them off too; and the land masses are not so wide, east to west, as they are in the Eastern Hemisphere.

Much more importantly (returning to the temperate zones), the arid belts are twisted, east of the mountain ranges, from east-west into north-south orientations. The steppes and prairies run in broad belts from Texas to Saskatchewan, not from San Francisco to Philadelphia.

Finally, the forests, too, lie north and south in North America, not as in Europe and Asia. They exist at all only because the great cyclonic air movements across the United States and Canada, in working eastward, also pick up heavy loads of moisture from the Gulf of Mexico and to a lesser extent from the Arctic and Hudson Bay. The tapering off of southern South America eliminates this type of temperate-zone climate from that continent.

The great backbone of mountains in general runs along the Pacific edges of the continents. The slopes are usually gentler toward the east, but on the west coast they are very precipitate as they come down toward the beaches of the Pacific Ocean. In some latitudes the slopes from the great backbone out to salt water to the east are several thousand miles across. That is the case in Canada and the United States, and to a lesser degree in the belt of equatorial South America. In a few places the slope toward the Atlantic is only a few score or a few hundred miles wide, as is the case in the isthmus lands of Central America.

There are stubby older mountains and plateaus and some smaller ranges rising from the eastern plains of the continents, such as the Ozarks, the worn-down mountains of northern Wisconsin, the Appalachians, and in South America the Guiana plateau and the plateaus of eastern Brazil. These ranges are like the lesser mountain ranges in Europe north of the Alps. They are not new, rough, rocky, glacier-draped mountains, but instead are generally covered with vegetation to their tops and the passages through them and around them are not very difficult. They slow down but do not actually bar penetration from the Atlantic coast to the wide inland areas.

There is easy access to both the North and South American continents almost everywhere on the Atlantic side. The mouths of the best river systems, such as the Saint Lawrence, Hudson, Mississippi, Amazon, and Plata, are easily reached by boat from Europe. Furthermore, the larger of those systems are so extensive and their flow so gentle that tremendous parts of the interior can be reached without going over difficult falls and rapids. It is possible for good-sized European ships to go high up into the continental interiors, and then for good-sized river vessels to go on even farther into nearly the best lands of either North or South America.

What is more, again on the Atlantic side, the Western Hemisphere is penetrated deeply by two great salt-water gulfs. The more important is the combined Caribbean Sea–Gulf of Mexico. This salt-water avenue goes deep into the heart of the two continents, almost dividing them, and leaving them open to penetration by European sea-going vessels practically to the backbone ridge itself between the Isthmus of Panama and Mexico.

The other great gulf, important in its own region, is the gulf or bay named for Henry Hudson, the navigator—Hudson Bay. There is a third system, almost as useful in penetrating to the center of the North American continent—the Great Lakes chain by which both primitive boats and the most modern ships have been able to move cargo and passengers far into the interior.

The isthmus between the two continents is narrow and at that same point the backbone mountain chain is lowest. It was very quickly discovered (and was put to use within a generation after Columbus' finding of the western islands) to give access to the Pacific Ocean in general.

The land masses of the Western Hemisphere do not straddle the equator at dead center, with equal amounts of the two continents north and south. Instead, there is a great deal of the northern mass which has subarctic and high-temperate zones, while there is very little of the land mass in the corresponding subarctic and temperate zones to the south; the greatest part of the land mass in South America lies in the tropical and subtropical zones, while only a little fringe of the northern land mass comes that near to the Equator.

All through and along the great backbone, on plateaus and in valleys between the ridges, were developed the civilized Indian societies found there when the Spanish first entered by way of the Caribbean–Gulf of Mexico gap in the early fifteen hundreds. The civilized Indians did not extend their culture very far into the temperate climate zones to their north and south. Yet, while they were in tropical latitudes, the Indian civilizations flourished best in districts so elevated above the sea as to have agreeable climates fitted also to the growing of maize (Indian corn) and other vegetable crops.

Of importance for the initiation and expansion of European colonization is the fact that the North American forests come to the water's edge nearest northwestern Europe on a front of nearly two thousand miles. This fact invited northwest Europeans to move in with their whole culture—crops, livestock, tools, costumes, and social and political patterns.

The Spanish, for their part, were already habituated to the Mediterranean climate and to high plateaus and valleys, semiarid steppes and mountains, and to irrigation agriculture. Their horse and saddle, mule and burro, long-horned range cattle, sheep and goats, tools, housing, costumes and customs, were prefashioned for life in the highlands they invaded. They were also experienced in conquering, controlling, and exploiting civilized Moors, which helped in handling Aztecs and Mayas. The Portuguese had worked out sugar-plantation culture, using African Negro slaves, before invading Brazil.

Offshore, on the Atlantic side of North and South America, but above all in the region of the Caribbean and the Gulf of Mexico, there were island chains and archipelagoes on which Europeans could make lodgment considerably before they had to tackle the land masses themselves for the purposes of conquest and settlement. Strategically it was to be a lucky thing for the Europeans who came boat-borne from Europe that they could initially establish themselves for a generation on the islands, where mistakes would not be so costly, and where they would not be set upon by hostile natives in numbers sufficient to dislodge them. On the offshore islands the bases were established for the penetration of the mainland itself.

Europeans have always been ready to move into inhospitable mountain country for the purpose of getting out minerals. The great desert and dry steppe regions never have attracted them, although favored spots could be made fertile by irrigation.

The tropical rainfall jungles which are predominant in the lower lands in South America were of little use in a state of nature, except for furnishing vegetable products which could be picked up by gatherers. This was a world little known to Europeans until twentieth-century technology and medicine began to make it possible for them to flourish there.

All across the top of North America lies the tundra belt, not so extensive as that which runs along the northern side of Asia, but nevertheless a very large stretch of territory. Save that its natives never have had domesticated reindeer, conditions were like those of the Asian tundra.

We know now that the Western Hemisphere was tremendously rich in minerals, yet they were of little significance to the Indians. Indians

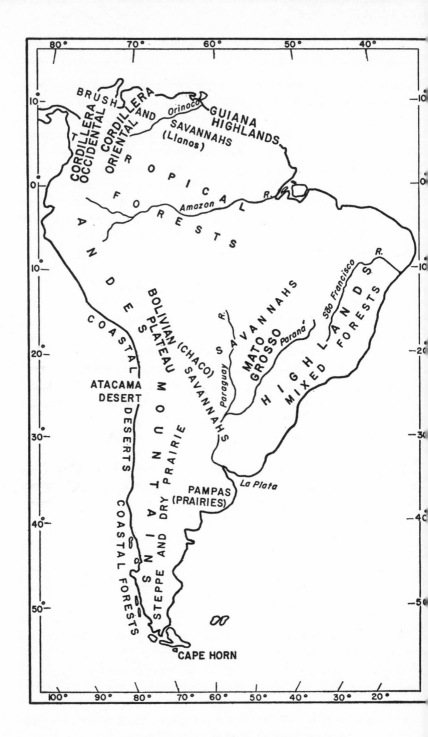

South America: climate, vegetation zones

used metals to a modest degree. For jewelry they used precious stones, gold and silver, and to some extent the copper which was to be found around Lake Superior, in northern Canada, and also in places in Central and South America. It also was made into tools, albeit the sharpness and hardness of copper tools were not very great.

When Europeans arrived, the people from the northernmost to the southernmost ends of the two great continents, even the most civilized, were in the Stone Age. For tools and weapons they used easily chipped sharp stones such as flint and obsidian, supplementing and combining stone with wood, bone, horn, and shell.

The Peoples: Languages and Cultures, Products and Economies

A long time back, in the Eurasian and African world, the domestication of a number of grass-eating animals of the families of the horse, the cow, the goat, the pig, the reindeer, the sheep, the camel, and the elephant had been successfully achieved. Strangely enough, many of those animals, or species somewhat like them, had ranged in the North and South American land mass until a geologically very late time. Animals which were nearly horses, nearly camels, and nearly elephants had lived in Kansas and Nebraska with human beings.

However, by the time a few cultures in the Western Hemisphere had first developed away from primitive savagery, animals of those sorts had largely disappeared. A few animals of the cow, goat, camel, and reindeer families existed, but the varieties found in the Western Hemisphere were not amenable to training. About the only animal which had been widely domesticated was the dog, and it probably was an import from the Eurasian areas.

In one small corner of the Andean highlands there was one other domesticated animal, a cousin of the camel called the llama, a mountain-climbing beast of burden and a producer of wool, hides, and meat of considerable use to the Inca Indians in Peru.

Because of the lack of domesticated beasts, human affairs had to be organized very differently from the ways they could be organized in the Eastern land mass. In the Western Hemisphere there were no animal-raising nomads; there never could be a Genghis Khan with his Mongol horsemen descending on civilized peoples, say in Mexico or Peru. In the Western Hemisphere there could never be an integration of crop growing and animal raising such as had been so very highly developed in medieval Europe through the manorial pattern.

Transport overland had to be by pack loads carried by humans, making it impossible to move great masses of goods in trade or in war while also making it difficult to concentrate great amounts of supplies in imperial capitals or populous trading centers, as was possible in the Eastern Hemisphere.

For still another thing, all the work had to be done by human beings. When we consider that these men were laboring with tools of wood, stone, and shell, we can see that the amount of work which could be accomplished per annum would be lower out of all proportion to the amount a similar number of men, supplied with iron tools and with their animals, could get done in the Eastern Hemisphere. The lack of domesticated animals was a handicap in transport, in war, in the maintenance of agriculture, and in making goods everywhere in the Western Hemisphere.

In addition to these deficiencies was the technological lag, characterized above all by ignorance of the wheel, but also by ignorance of how to harness or transmit the power in wind or running water, and how to construct sizable boats.

Quite different in every way from the picture in respect to animals, tools, and machinery was the picture in respect to useful vegetation. In the Western Hemisphere a great many plants had been domesticated at an early stage in human development. Not only had these plants been domesticated, but strains had also been carefully and intelligently selected and propagated for special qualities until some of them had been remarkably transformed from their primitive ancestors before Europeans encountered them.

The most famous of all the plants of the Western Hemisphere in this respect is maize or Indian corn. This grass plant had first been cultivated in the central belt of mountains, probably in Central America, or in the northern part of South America, and had been so changed by selective development that it had become unable to survive without mankind's constant care through every single successive crop generation. Not only that; some varieties had had their cobs increased in size from a tiny ear only about the size of a small thumb to a great tremendous ear. There were varieties that had kernels which were red, brown, black, white, or yellow. Some varieties would grow far up in the highlands while others would grow far to the north; some would pop and some were soft; some could be eaten raw, green and soft, some flinty-hard dried seeds had to be ground into meal. The varieties of corn developed by the Indians—or by the Indians' wives, for they did the work—was almost beyond belief.

The Indians had also done well with tobacco, and with many other plants which had received their attention. The list of plants which they could raise, and which in turn were to have a tremendous effect on all the other peoples of the world after about sixteen hundred, is long. Potatoes, tomatoes, maize, a wide range of gourds, squash, pumpkin, very useful varieties of beans, a great many kinds of peppers, some very useful tropical root plants, cocoa, and tobacco must be numbered among their contributions. The diets and agriculture of other peoples all around the earth, of Europeans at home and in colonies overseas, of Africans, and of Asians, were to be deeply modified as these products of Indian agriculture came into use. In medicine, quinine and cocaine were also Indian discoveries.

At the time of Columbus the Indians in general were far less numerous than the populations which now reside in the same areas. That was especially true in the temperate lands where Indian methods of cultivation and their general economies simply could not support anything like the dense populations of modern Canada and the United States. Moreover, their numbers soon dwindled further after the arrival of the Europeans because they were so susceptible to a great many European and African diseases which had apparently never before reached the hemisphere.

Nearly all the humans in the Western Hemisphere, the so-called American Indians, were members of one human family; the Eskimo and Aleutians in the far north were local exceptions. Within that family there was a tremendous range in particularities. For example, some Indians were longheaded and some were roundheaded. Some had flat noses and some had beaked noses. Some were slim, some were pudgy. Some were tall, some were short and stocky. But they all had about the same complexion, the same sort of hair, and most of the other basic traits of a single family of people. It was not uncommon for secondary differences to be seen in a single clan.

Quite in contrast to the over-all uniformity of the physical stock was a great variety of languages. There were some large families of languages. We have referred to the families of Turkic speeches, the families of Bantu and of Indo-European speeches, and so on, in the Eastern Hemisphere. In the Western Hemisphere, for example in the region which is now the United States, were some great families of languages such as the Iroquoian, the Muskhogean, the Siouan, the Algonquin, and the Uto-Aztecan. Those five speech-families in turn numbered several dozen good

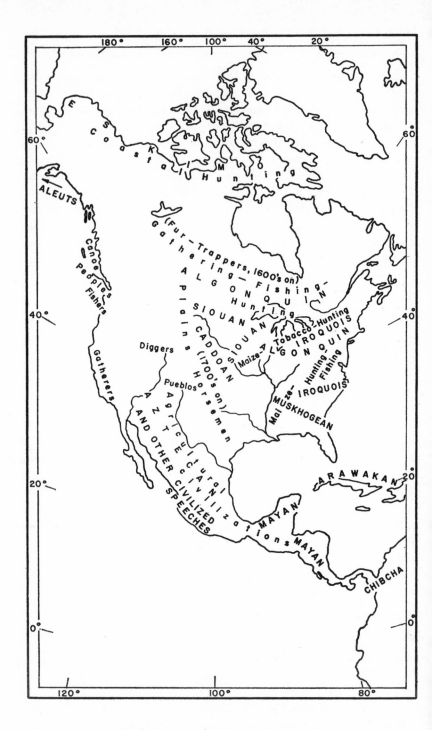

North America: language, culture groups

languages, and most of those languages had several or even many dialects. In the other extreme, there were whole language families in the Western Hemisphere represented by only a few hundred isolated individuals, usually in the mountain regions in western North America or in pockets in tropical or mountainous South America. Along with all these great varieties of languages there were extremely varied culture patterns, which are the most important for our purposes.

The cultural groups were of course in considerable measure conditioned by climate and basic resources. In addition, there were differences in the culture patterns which can be traced to the migration of peoples from one area of culture to another, or to the borrowing by Indians living in one culture area from Indians of another. For example, as we can tell by archaeological evidence, some of the highest civilizations of the mountain and plateau regions were carried by migration into new districts in the course of pre-Spanish history. We can also note that the Indians of the present-day United States were all influenced by their borrowing of the maize and bean culture of the Mexicans, and might go on to say that the Indians of the southern parts of the United States, especially those in the southeast, seem to have owed a considerable debt to the civilized Indians of Yucatán and Mexico in matters of government and religion.

In the New World there were several main culture groups. One such group was the tundra dwellers who were fishermen and trappers, lacking the domesticated reindeer of the corresponding tundra dwellers in the Eurasian land mass. They were few and of little power politically and militarily. They had one great asset, the furs of the country about them, and were disposed, once contact with the people of Europe had been established, to go over to a fur-traffic economy almost instantly.

A second group in both North and South America, but chiefly in North America, was the forest and grassland peoples of the temperate zones. Almost everywhere they lived in villages located close to water courses; at least for those in North America, travel by boat was easier than going across country, and they made great use of the fish and shell fish found in the water courses. They were hoe croppers, relying chiefly on maize and squashes, and fishermen and hunters, with hunting perhaps the least important of the three major sorts of food-producing activities.

In the tropical rainfall forests was a third group, some of whom supplemented hunting and fishing with digging stick and hoe agriculture. On the other hand the poverty of the soil of much of the low country in the tropics accounts for their rather low reliance on plant resources.

South America: language, culture groups

A fourth sort of culture was imposed on those who lived in the deserts, or rather around their edges. These people were almost entirely simple gatherers of a scanty supply of food, and were at a very low stage of culture. There were never more than a few thousand of them; and they were, for example, the sorts of people to be found in the Great Salt Lake basin and other like areas in both continents.

A fifth group was to be found on the Pacific coast, both in the north and to the south in the temperate zone, relying heavily on fish and animals to be caught by the shore. Fishermen—sea-going canoe people—lived in Chile on the south end and in the area of Alaska, British Columbia, Washington, and Oregon on the other end of the mountain chains.

The Plateau Civilizations

To return to the civilized Indians, we find that they lived in settlements nearly everywhere that agriculture could be carried on, in the plateau and valley folds between the main mountain ridges, from the Chile deserts north to Chihuahua and New Mexico. They relied on potatoes in the Andes, and corn and beans everywhere, for their food.

On the Mexican plateau, where the mountain ranges spread apart to form eastern and western ranges enclosing a mile-high plateau between, during several thousand years (exactly how long is still not clear) successive peoples had developed settled governments, art, literature, science, and systematized religions with organized priesthoods. Some of the peoples had contributed a great deal, others had contributed a little, while still others had merely picked up their patterns from neighbors.

Speaking generally, there had not been any great empire in the earlier history of the Mexican plateau, although we suspect that several bigger-than-usual states had been developed. Instead, whatever their language, and whatever variety of the common civilization they had cultivated, most of the civilized Indians had always been politically organized into something very like the city-states of ancient Italy, Greece, Asia Minor, Syria, and Palestine.

In each city-state a fortified capital contained the palaces of the highest governmental officials and military leaders and also the temples of the religion with the dwellings of the priests. There would be sections in those capitals for merchants, craftsmen, and common laborers. Outside the city proper, for quite a distance in every direction, would be villages, and around the villages, in turn, tilled fields with the tillage going a considerable distance up the hillsides. Such a city-state would have a

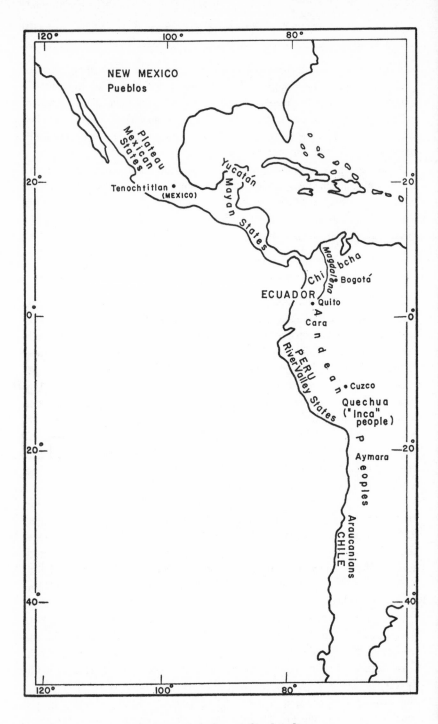

Mexico and Andes, civilized Indians

distinctive religious organization, its own pattern of gods and sacrifices, calendar, and so forth, but they all conformed to a general pattern.

Mexican city-states were almost endlessly at war with one another. The reason was partly religious. Warfare provided the captives who in turn provided the victims for the human sacrifices, which were extremely important in many of the different religious cults found all through the Mexican world. But warfare was also generated by hate and rivalry, by desire to get riches and tribute, and by simply wanting to be the dominant people in their world.

When a city was more than normally fortunate in warfare, it could begin extending its power wider and wider over other city-states. In most cases there would be no attempt to exterminate, drive out, or replace the subjugated neighbors. Instead they would be left with somewhat their old organization, but subject, because of conquest, to sending tribute—cocoa, foodstuffs, cotton goods, salt, and above all captives for temple sacrifice.

There were city-states in Mexico which had languages different from other languages in the same neighborhood. Many of the states had local varieties of the common culture which were quite distinctive. On the other hand, in general the dominant language was Nahuatl (Aztec), related to Ute in the United States, and the dominant population was that of one single city-state at the time the Spaniards got there.

In the thirteen and fourteen hundreds this city-state, on an island in some extensive lakes and marshes at the center of the Mexican plateau, had begun to extend in all directions at the expense of its neighbors. Then called Tenochtitlan and today called Mexico City, it made alliances and won wars, so that when the Spaniards arrived its outmost frontiers were those of an empire. They reached the Pacific to the south and west, touched the Gulf of Mexico to the east, stretched northward almost to the Rio Grande region and southward almost to Yucatán.

When the Spaniards came it was still expanding. But the number of subjugated city-states which had been rather newly brought under control was at that time considerable, and none of them supported the Aztec yoke very happily. Their pride had been injured, and they hated the Aztecs for having beaten them. But they also hated furnishing the unending procession of young men and women who had to be sent from the subjugated cities, the young people marching off to have their hearts torn out on the bloody altars in Tenochtitlan's temples. Of course, in addition there was irksome tribute in warriors, in food stuffs, and in craft products which had to be sent up to Mexico on the backs of porters who were drawn from the villages of the subjugated. The hate for the Aztec overlordship was tremendous, and was to be a great help to the Spanish when they came in to take over the Aztec Empire.

There was a special character to warfare in Mexico, one of the weaknesses which the people there suffered from when opposing Europeans. To a great degree the object of war in Mexico was to acquire human sacrifices for the altars. The best and most divine of all sacrifices was the enemy warrior taken alive in battle. Consequently, Mexican armies were quite prone to turn any body-to-body engagement into a series of wrestling and roping matches by which those in the front ranks sought to make captives for sacrifice of those who opposed them, and to avoid capture themselves. When they fought one another, this was not too great a disadvantage; or rather, both sides suffered from the same disadvantage. But when the Mexicans fought Spaniards it was quite another thing, because the Spaniards simply wanted to win the battle and would kill, while the Indians were trying to take live captives. Needless to say, once the Spaniards and Mexicans came to grips with one another, the attitude of the soldiers in the front ranks was important.

There is another curious fact. The Mexicans initially thought the Spaniards were gods, and of course their horses and the few guns they had heightened that impression. Although not for long, for a few critical weeks, on their arrival, the Mexicans persisted in considering the Spaniards as superior beings from another world, allowing them a chance to get in touch with rebel and seditious elements throughout the Empire before the Mexicans developed an attitude which was clearly and completely hostile. Even then, subject to worry over the matter, the Aztec ruler shilly-shallied between decisions to kill the invaders and decisions to treat them as superior beings.

The Mexicans had a cultivated and learned priestly class. Despite their bloodthirstiness, many of the priests were the products of a long and rigorous education, with ability to read and write the Aztec hieroglyphics, with considerable astronomical and mathematical skill, with engineering talents of a high order, and so on.

There was also a warrior and command organization, and persons of originally modest position could move up the ranks by manifestation of bravery and of skill in taking captives or by leadership talent.

There were merchants and craftsmen; the merchants traveled not only throughout the empire of the Aztecs itself, but far around and beyond its frontiers, usually in trade with foreign civilized Indians, and the craftsmen were highly skilled in the working of stone, gold, and silver, in the making and embellishment of buildings, and in making textiles. The great mass of the population was a village peasantry depressed, rather harshly ruled, and heavily burdened. They lived on beans, pepper, and ground corn and provided labor for the fields and for construction work and bodies for the sacrifices in the temples. They were burdened with taxes, labor, and rent. There was little in the pattern as the Spanish found it which would make the Indian villager, even in the dominant city-state itself, a dangerous subject for the Spanish provided they only slightly improved the general working conditions. As a matter of fact, the Spanish bettered conditions in one important point, for they abolished the blood sacrifice. Otherwise they enjoyed the products of the work of the villagers much as had the Mexican overlord class.

There were other civilized Indians, the ancestors of many of the Mexicans, Guatemalans, and so on, who were not necessarily either Mexican or Mayan. They lived to the east and south, as far as the narrow part of Mexico, and all were heirs of the same ancient culture based on corn.

There was a great deal of communication between the Mexican plateau and Yucatán, Guatemala, and Honduras. There were wars, which provided their own form of communication, and their merchants and priests went back and forth. Some of these other peoples may have been the earliest civilized Indians.

The Mayan Indians had been established mostly in Guatemala and Honduras. Many of them were still there when the Spaniards came, but by migration large Maya colonies had been founded northward and eastward in Yucatán, the peninsula which points out toward Cuba, and for some hundreds of years Yucatán had contained most of the Mayas—and the Mayas with the highest civilization.

The Maya stock was vigorous, its civilization was high, but, as in Mexico, the political structure was not particularly strong and stable. Once again, city-state nobles and the priestly caste ruled over a peasantry which had very little culture and rather little patriotism. More important, for several generations before the Spaniards came, the Maya city-states had been subjected to a type of long-drawn-out depression. Because they did not have domestic animals to manure the land, the fertility of their fields was running out. They mostly slashed and burned and planted crops, and had worked farther and farther into the jungles around their cities. The soil close to the cities had played out and food was getting hard to come by.

While their agriculture suffered from poor tools and fertilizers, there is no question but that many of the New World's most marvelous gardeners were Mayan. Among other things they were the first people to use rubber, especially for the making of rubber balls in order to play a game which was lacrosse, hockey, football, basketball, and murder all mixed into one; they played in great walled courts and the losers were sacrificed.

The Mayans were also among the earliest to cultivate the cocoa bean, which was a very important product to them as well as to the Aztecs. They had also domesticated turkeys. But they were in real economic difficulties at the time the Spaniards came and not anything like the strong people they had been somewhat earlier.

All the way down to Panama there were civilized isolated groups, many of them Mayan in language and connection. It was at Panama that a zone of civilization emanating from the Andean Mountains south of the Isthmus was met.

In the upland region of northern Colombia and Venezuela, with headquarters at Bogotá in modern Colombia, were the Chibcha. They were the leading people in the upper Andean highlands, although there were other civilized Indians or near-civilized Indians in the same parts.

The Chibcha were not a particularly fierce and pugnacious people. They lived in big open villages, in a semi-tropical climate, raised corn and vegetables, had a king and a series of chieftains up to the king; and so on. They do not seem to have had anything like the inclination toward organized warfare, human sacrifice, and cannibalism which characterized the Aztecs. They were friendly when the Spanish came there, and, although they were reasonably brave and well organized, the first Spaniards, about one hundred and twenty-five of them, conquered the Chibcha empire with only one scuffle in which one Spaniard was killed— and apparently he was killed by mistake by another Spaniard. The Chibcha intermarried with the Spanish. Their land was isolated, difficult to get into, and equally difficult to leave once in; it turned out to be one of the easiest to conquer and most pleasant to rule of any that the Spanish took over.

All the way from the northern Andes down to the region of Chile, the valleys and high plateaus were occupied by civilized Indians. The little valleys of the rivers which ran down from the Andes into the Pacific were likewise held by civilized Indians. These valleys, only a few miles long between the foothills and the sea, supported rich irrigation cultures. Other Indians back up in the mountains were equally civilized, with their own particular different ways of making pottery, textiles, working metals, and worshiping.

In the high valleys running through the modern countries of Ecuador, Peru, and Bolivia, such civilized Indians had lived for a long time. For some generations before the Spaniards arrived there had been one particular sort, originally a small tribe, of civilized Indians who had been extending a military political empire over that whole land.

These Indians should not properly be called the Inca Indians, for "Inca" was the title of their king of kings (they spoke Quechua), but we have fallen into the habit of calling them "Incas" for short. The area as a whole had different languages and other differences with which we need not bother. The Inca center was in the highlands of Peru, and their imperial capital city was at Cuzco. From that center they had sent ambassadors and armies north and south along the great valleys, down the short rivers to the Pacific, and over the ridges into the next valleys, progressively drawing all the other civilized Indians under their sway. Fifteen or twenty years earlier, just before the Spaniards came, they had completed the conquest of Equador, whereby they had annexed the last of the great civilized peoples of the highlands.

As the Spaniards found it, the Inca empire was an extraordinary structure, unlike political and social entities found other places, either in the Western Hemisphere or anywhere. The head of the state was always the Inca, who had the purest descent possible from the founding Inca great-great-great-great-grandfather and grandmother. Under the Inca constitution and law the Inca's only legitimate wife was his own full sister. Each Inca was therefore a son of a sister and a brother in the full blood. This inbreeding had gone on in the royal family for some six to eight generations—it is a little uncertain how long. This custom has appeared among other peoples around the world; for example, the Ptolemies did the same thing in Egypt, and the Hapsburgs of Austria and Spain were nearly as closely inbred in the fifteen to sixteen hundreds.

The original Inca stock must have been good, for the Inca ruler and other princes of the blood found by the Spaniards were all quite outstanding people—strapping handsome men with real physical and mental vitality. Unlike the Aztecs, they were humane and entirely paternalistic in their organization of their state.

The Inca armies were brave, well trained, supplied, and led. They won wars, but the Inca government preferred to conquer by peaceful means if possible. Most of the conquering had been done through negotiations by the Inca himself with neighboring kings and princes, which brought them into his family if everything worked out well. The Inca would take several of the princesses of the other royal family as additions to his harem, which was an official harem, part of the government. In the same way in which he had officials, he had wives who were all of them representative of different political interests throughout his empire. To the subordinate royal family he gave individuals from his intimate kin. Cross-marriages were the way in which the chieftains of the other peoples were tied to the royal family. The women everywhere had a pattern of loyalty to their husbands; it was normal for a young woman of princely rank to acquire a husband from some other tribe and thereafter to give her loyalty to him.

The Inca state cannot be defined by any term known in the American-European political, social, or economic language.

Everything was fixed in advance by the planning of the Inca. The Inca government maintained storehouses from which all subjects drew the food allotted them; into the storehouses went all they grew. They built paved roads (which were for men to run on, not for carriages) all through the high mountains, tying their whole empire together just as the Romans or Persians had tied theirs. The subjects built roads, temples, city walls, and terraced the mountainsides according to the directions of the various highest, middle, and lowest ranks in the chain of command. At every level there was demand from below for orders, the passage from above to below of those orders, and complete obedience when the public-spirited orders came.

For such a detail as making sure there would be a sufficient number of marriages, proper requests went up the line; down the line came the commands that certain villages had to send their young marriageable women to a given festival, and the young marriageable men were sent from the same group of villages. The young people were lined up, the males in one line, the females opposite. The officer gave the command and each young person paired up with the person opposite. After that the couples went to the cabins assigned by the state and, as far as we know, a series of happy marriages followed.

The Incas were the first to use cocaine, found in the leaves of coca, a wild plant. Chewing the coca leaves, they could put a heavy pack on their backs and trot up a mountain; they did this to the astonishment of Spaniards who watched them while they themselves could scarcely walk on the level in the rarefied atmosphere. According to observers, there is nothing quite like watching a very fast soccer game played by the descendants of those same Indians, at an elevation of about 15,000 feet; American spectators, sitting still, are panting from shortage of breath.

But the Inca system had two weaknesses which were to be fatal when the Spaniards arrived. First of all was the loyalty of the women to their husbands. Pizarro and his Spaniards learned of this in the first few weeks they were there; they took some Indian princesses for brides for themselves (whether they had wives back in Spain did not matter) and thus acquired the loyalty of Inca princesses—who knew politics inside the Inca empire and so were able to guide the Spaniards in all their important political moves.

The other weakness lay in the Inca who was in charge of everything at the very moment the Spaniards arrived. He was an unconstitutional rebel usurper; love had wrecked the constitution. The reigning Inca's father had first lived in the old capital, Cuzco, and by his sister had had a legitimate family. But in conquering Ecuador he had, of course, married a daughter of the king of Ecuador and then (something he should not have done) had fallen in love with that lady, and never gone home to his wife. Instead he had lived in Ecuador in its king's palace, and there raised his son by the Ecuadorean. He came to wish for this son's succession to the highest throne. When he died, his constitutionally ineligible son and his legitimate son had fallen into a tremendous civil war which had wracked the empire. From the point of view of the constitution the worst had happened and the son without the birthright to the throne had won just a few months before the Spaniards came in. Though there were legitimate Incas in the back country still on the warpath, Atahualpa, the winner, was a usurper in the eyes of a great part of the people. Meanwhile, the army had been badly wasted.

Given the paternalistic pattern by which the whole empire operated, there was danger for the first time that orders from on top would not be obeyed, which would ruin things; or worse, that the Spaniards would get control of the chain of command, which is actually what they did. The Spaniards got themselves established at the top very quickly, and the Indians went along, doing everything in routine, with only a little fighting, until it was too late to rebel against the Spaniards successfully. The Spaniards seized Atahualpa, defeated his cousins and brothers who were lurking in the hills, then installed themselves at the top of the governmental pyramid, sending their orders down a chain of command which still operated, using royal puppets.

The Inca highlanders had not succeeded in penetrating the wet Amazonian jungles immediately to the east; they were afraid of them and had reason to be. The jungle natives there were as primitively backward as the Incas were advanced. Today, on the edge of the Chibcha lands, live the Motelone and other like Indians. Within just the last few years the Motelone have attacked American jeeps and helicopters with poisoned arrows; a man dies quickly from a little scratch of one. In spite of every effort, these Indians have never made friends; they did not make friends with the civilized Indians, they refused to make friends with the Spaniards, neither will they make friends with Standard Oil of New Jersey. That was characteristic of many bush Indians all along the Amazon Valley, along the wetter coasts of South and Central America, and everywhere in the jungle.

What the Spaniards were to occupy were the lands of the civilized Indians. The very northernmost edge of the Mexican civilized area lies in the modern United States. In a sense the Pueblo Indian culture and the Pueblo people are on the outermost fringe of Mexico. It was only that far that the Spaniards extended their dominion, for the Indians had to be at a certain rather advanced stage in order to be susceptible of Spanish-European conquest and occupation. On the other hand, the civilized Indians were advanced enough so that it paid the Spaniards to exploit them rather than to get rid of them. The Spanish nobles and priests aimed to enjoy what the Aztec or Maya, the Chibcha and Inca nobles and priests had enjoyed—the livings produced by peasants. They did want them to be supplemented by goods from Europe or the wide world, purchased with precious metal dug by forced labor.

EUROPE ON THE EVE OF ITS GREAT EXPANSION

WHEN we were last discussing western Europe, we noticed that for various reasons there was a great leveling off and then a drop in the prosperity in most areas during the course of the thirteen hundreds.

But after a pause in the later thirteen and early fourteen hundreds, there began to be a marked upswing once again in such matters as trade, industry, and agricultural production, and a resumption of population increase.

The greater part of the most recent writing on the subject has been quite insistent on the point that it is not right to think of the Middle Ages, economically and socially at least, as one single period continuously developing along the same lines all the way from the eight and nine hundreds through the fifteen and sixteen hundreds. The judgment is that there was the very vigorous and lively development of the economy along several lines through the nine, ten, eleven, and twelve hundreds, as already described, and that new developments became significant after the very marked break in the thirteen hundreds.

Economic historians are reluctant to break off the history of the Middle Ages at the traditional date of 1500, for that is midway in the history of Europe's second wave of prosperity. Rather, the economic historians think the new developments which began in the late thirteen and the fourteen hundreds had a continuity which went unbroken into the Industrial Revolution, to the time of the French Revolution, and in many ways to our present generation.

CHAPTER I

General Social and
Economic Changes after the
Mid-fourteenth Century

GRICULTURE in the old pattern continued. Most of farming was done simply for the sake of keeping one's neighborhood supplied. Manors continued to be commonplace. Where it did the job best, or where there was no drive or action in a neighborhood to change it, the big open-field system continued.

Where the manorial system had never come to be important, there was less change, or at least less manifestation of important change, in economies and societies than in the more populous and productive areas where the system had been most influential. On through all of the generations to which we are now turning there was less modification of basic patterns in the fringe areas, or in the mountain and transhumance areas surveyed some chapters back, than came about in the areas where the manor had been earlier or later implanted. Life and production largely followed pre-existing patterns in Ireland, the Scotch Highlands, Scandinavia, the plateaus and garden lands of the Iberian peninsula, Switzerland, and the Balkans, to name the most important.

But right at the heart of the old manorial area, in northern France, Belgium, and southeastern England, there were developments which broke up the old pattern. Increasingly, as time went by, the manors were decaying from within or being legislated out of existence because important persons and groups wanted something different. For one thing, by the fourteen hundreds men were doing much more plowing with the horse, and the ox team was no longer needed in many of the districts where it had earlier been indispensable.

For another thing, growers in areas where it was possible were increasingly tempted to shift from sustenance agriculture to agriculture for profit. This did not mean that earlier no one had wanted a profit. In Italy agriculture for profit had always persisted near the towns and there had also been agriculture for profit back in the eleven and twelve hundreds around Ghent and Ypres and other manufacturing towns in Belgium, as we have seen. In these places garden truck such as cabbages had been raised near the towns; pigs, fattened for the sale of their bacon and ham, were tended, as well as cows for the sake of their milk, cheese, and butter, to be sold in the town market. Truck gardens had long been, in essence, very much like those around modern American cities—small plots intensively cultivated with nothing much about the way they were set up and run which would suggest a manorial pattern of agriculture.

What was important in the fourteen and fifteen hundreds, as towns once again began to flourish, was the increase in this type of truck gardening around an increasingly large number of places. Agriculture on the old big scale for local village consumption gave way more and more to truck gardening, with large areas being divided into small plots as they changed over from grain and pasture agriculture to truck farming.

Even more significant was the further development of cash-crop agriculture in whole areas. In part that too had been known earlier. There had been a tendency in southwest France, which raised fine wine grapes and had Bordeaux as an excellent port for shipment, to specialize in wine growing in the twelve and thirteen hundreds. But in the thirteen, fourteen, and fifteen hundreds, southwest France tended to become a single-crop country, importing a very considerable part of everything the country people needed to eat from such places as England. In turn, the people produced fine wine and sent it to England and Flanders and to the north where the Hansa merchants carried it on to Sweden and Russia.

There were other cash-crop areas. Certain districts in the Po Valley went over to rice culture. In that part of the country today the Italian diet is based on rice, not on spaghetti. Other districts went in for the production of hemp or dye stuffs; woad, for example, was a dye stuff that was raised in every district where the crop would grow. The wide new lands which had been opened east of the Elbe and in Prussia by the German settlement became specialized in the growing of rye, and to a lesser degree in the production of salt beef, salt pork, and the like for shipment to the west in Europe. Great sections of the Norwegian timber land developed as logging country, where logs were rolled down hill to the fjords, and put on small boats or rafted for shipment to Bergen for sawing and export.

The addition of the western Hemisphere as a sugar cane country to the other countries already supplying the European market meant simply the transfer overseas of one specialized-crop agriculture which had long been developed by Europeans. Reliance upon overseas suppliers was in a pattern already well developed in Europe, before 1492. A big factor in the shifting of agriculture in this way was the growth of investment in land by city people, or by persons who had been city people and were trying to turn into country squires.

Almost everywhere the main current of migration continued to be from the country to the city. Cities were not self-sustaining in the matter of population, and it was the steady flow from villages everywhere into the cities that kept their populations stable. But there was one kind of city man who, after establishing himself in the city, began to be interested in edging back out, either for himself or for his son or grandson. This was the man who had succeeded financially, come to be wealthy, and wanted to invest in land.

From some points of view, and especially in northern Europe, investment in land was rather difficult in the earlier days. As long as feudal law rested upon military needs, a man could not procure rural land at the noble level unless he had been invested as vassal by some overlord. Vassals could not sell their land freely, for the overlord might object. On the other hand, a city person who took over land at the servile level might find himself considered a serf, or at least called upon to provide servile dues. Either way, from the point of view of the city investor, was undesirable. But as early as the eleven and twelve hundreds there was a rapid development of a new kind of law affecting real estate all across feudal Europe, and especially in England and the Low Countries. City real estate had been freely buyable and salable for a long while, and a parallel freedom came to be allowed for rural property through rather rapid change in the law concerning real estate.

The investor in business affairs wanted a profit. When he bought a hundred yards of cloth, he wanted to sell it at some mark-up; similarly, when he bought rural property, he proposed, in the same way, to have it bring in a profit. As a result, there was a strong tendency for the city investor, when he had acquired either a large or a small piece of land, to treat it as a money-making proposition, and to be perfectly open-minded on making any rearrangements which would bring in a greater profit for his investment. This might be possible through selling away any rights which he might have purchased as the new lord of an estate —the rights this lordship gave him over boon work, week work, carrying, and all the other servile dues—for cash; he could sell them out (that is, take a lump payment from any serf and thereafter have no claim) and have the same work done by hired labor at less cost to him.

Another thing he could easily do would be to have his investment in a piece of land take the form of long-term leases rather than ownership. That was a common way of investing in rural property. Even more than the owner, a lease-holder would be willing to cash out a long-term right for a present advantage. If he had been paid for allowing peasants no longer to do week or boon work on an estate, he no longer cared what the situation was once his twenty-nine or ninety-nine year lease had expired. With money-making as the paramount interest, the leasing as well as the ownership of land became increasingly characteristic of a new sort of land investment.

Then, too, many rural persons who had accumulated money and the knowledge of how to manage property began to acquire control of land. In this group it was not so much noblemen, or would-be noblemen, as reeves, stewards, or bailiffs who had put money aside and began to suggest to their lords that instead of giving an account each year, they be allowed to give a flat sum every Christmas from then on for a perpetual lease.

Such an arrangement was known as a "farm," whereby the profit of the land was "farmed out." There came to be more and more farmers, who paid the lord, duke, or bishop an annual "farm." First the payment was known as the "farm," and then more and more these persons who were running their estates which were the property of someone else, but on a long term or perpetual "farm," came to be known as "farmers." Farming came in during the twelve hundreds and spread during the thirteen, fourteen, and fifteen hundreds. Since most of these farmers were not the least bit high and mighty and had no feeling they should keep their hands off the plow handle, many a farmer of a small farm, paying a fixed annual rent, was working the land himself.

The farmer came to be interested in consolidating his holdings. Going all over the great open manorial field, from one acre to another, did not appeal to him. More and more this whole arrangement came to be associated with commutation, which had started earlier in the eleven and twelve hundreds, but which progressed very rapidly in this particular period of history.

Commutation was the final settlement, on a perpetual basis, of one of the old binding contracts or customary rules requiring boon work, week work, carrying work, and the like. It meant changing over (to commute, to change over) from a payment in work to a payment in cash. Commutation of work was one of the most important factors leading toward freeing of the serfs.

It also developed that a person who had made an early agreement was able, in generations of rising prices, to enjoy unearned increment—an increase in his wealth for which he had done no work, and which came with an increase in prices. For example, with the rise in prices which in fact took place throughout most of the Middle Ages, the sum in cash which had at first represented a bushel came to represent three quarters of a bushel, then half a bushel, and so forth, until at last it was not a large enough sum for the lord to bother to collect from the descendants of the peasant who had first made the agreement; eventually it could cost the lord more to collect than to ignore the payment. So, as prices rose, lords let their payments from their serfs slide. When the serfs did not have payments to make, they were, in fact, free.

This change in status was also associated with the development of cash savings by the peasants. Earlier the peasant could not save goods because of course they would spoil. But a silver penny or a gold florin lasts. Once the saving of money became a possibility, it came to be feasible for a peasant to buy an acre here or there from the farmers, who were the persons next above him. Eventually he might acquire a small piece of consolidated acreage and become a farmer himself.

As soon as he had obtained enough acreage to count as quite a substantial person in his neighborhood, he was called a "yeoman" in England. In the fourteen hundreds reeves and carpenters and prosperous plowmen were turning into yeomen in large enough numbers so that they were essentially a new class in society. They were not pretentious about being gentry and squires, let alone knights and lords, but they were not serf villagers either. A yeoman farmer was likely to live in his own isolated farmstead, with his acres about him, and with his own small house and barn. That is the class from which the agricultural population chiefly sprang in the United States. Ours has been essentially a yeoman country, although our farms have been a good deal larger than were those in late medieval Europe.

Decay of serfdom in the West came also from sources other than commutation of work.

After successive waves of the Black Death had temporarily reduced the number of agricultural workers, many landlords became desperate and were forced to make very favorable arrangements with peasants who were willing to move onto their land. Farther east, Slavic peasants were able to run away and become part of the population on the eastern frontier toward the Mongol-Tartar-Islamic world. The same sort of men left the land in Hungary and went off to the frontier there. It was much this same impulse for betterment which was to take men, when they found out about North and South America, across the Atlantic to new frontiers.

Other reasons for the development of legal freedom in some districts were the putting-out system and enclosures. These may not have brought an improvement in the lot of the peasant. However, both provided alternatives to serfdom; they gave an alternative means for the support of a man and his family.

In some ways the decay of serfdom began with the rise of the cities. The nearness of cities induced persons who wanted to do so to go off to town. This was often considered running away, which is why there were rules in many of the cities that a year and a day spent there freed a man. The Germans had a legal phrase which said "the city air makes [a man] free."

But much of the migration of serfs toward the towns was with agreement, or at least with an understanding, whereby serfs for whom there was no land were allowed to move. However, frequently the serfs who went to town continued to pay, in cash, for the various things they owed as serfs back in their old villages. Although away from the village, their serfdom continued, and sometimes a person such as a lord mayor of an English town might legally be a serf of some manor where his grandfather had been the reeve or some other type of serf.

The steady military pressure of the Mongol-Tartar-Turkish enemies near them generally forced the Lithuanian, Polish, and Muscovite landlords to try to tie their workers to the villages. Earlier the villagers in Poland, Lithuania and Russia had had a good deal of freedom to move about, but we have seen that in the fourteen and then the fifteen hundreds the controls were tightened, and the peasant was prohibited from leaving his village. Only the runaways who had managed to get to the Cossack frontier could be reckoned as the free lower class in Lithuania, Poland, and Hungary, while the great mass of the villagers had become depressed into serfdom—one which was not historically the same as that of western Europe, and which grew as that of western Europe faded.

There was another paradoxical factor which caused serfdom to become increasingly acute in the lower-grade lands in France. After the Black Death the lords who were strong enough made serfdom more burdensome and reinstituted at new levels old work which their fathers had stopped requiring. In some parts of Europe the peasants were worse off in the fifteen and sixteen hundreds than their ancestors had been earlier. That was true in the Central Massif area in France, and in some other districts. But around Paris and in the citified north nearly all the peasants were free in the fifteen and sixteen hundreds.

It has been noticed that in some instances (for example, Florence) a big city might come to dominate the countryside as if it were a single lord in itself, and thereafter impose harsh regulations on rural villagers. The villagers were not allowed to come into the city unless they had passes; and they were required to go back. They were not permitted to leave their jobs in the country; they were required to sell and to produce at a low rate, and to pay the city market prices at a high rate. They were liable to road service, bridge service, trucking, and even fighting in the army. These were mostly burdens on serfs under manor lords, but were now the burdens of villagers under the lordship of a great city. Here was a rural servitude produced by "democratic" city governments which cared nothing for the welfare of the villagers outside. There were still true slaves in Sicily.

The putting-out system, in its first development under the merchant capitalists, had concerned town-dwelling craftsmen. As early as the twelve hundreds small "factories" had developed, above all fullers' mills which needed water power. As we have indicated, some manufacture had then shifted from the cities, which had no waterfalls or rapids, to the country, where water power could be found. As an example, the great textile industry in Florence was concentrated within the city walls and suburbs, but fulling work was done in valleys from two to ten miles away, and any spot with water power was likely to acquire a fulling mill. Some of these were fair-sized establishments, with several dozen employees. The cloth was carried to them to be fulled, then carried back to Florence. Also, because dyeing and tanning (which also needed mills for grinding tanbark) were rather unpleasant processes (as fulling also is), there was considerable effort made to have them operated in the country. All this was true even when most of the manufacturing was still done by putting-out within the cities.

However, there was an increasing trend toward doing more of the other textile work in the country near the fulling and dyeing establishments, and this brought even the weaving and spinning industries out to the country too. There was, also, a great dislike, even on the part of the merchant-capitalists who lived in big cities, of the city and guild laws which restricted freedom of manufacture. This was felt especially by those merchants who wanted to make cheaper, narrower, or flimsier cloth than the city laws allowed. It finally developed in Europe that city-made cloth was of a quality and price which appealed chiefly to the well-to-do. Other manufacturers wished to make great shiploads of inexpensive cloth to be sent to the Russians through Novgorod, or to the inhabitants of the eastern Mediterranean who rather liked the lighter cloths. Once trade was set up overseas after 1500, with the American Indians and others who wanted to buy very cheap goods, there was unceasing pressure to produce textiles fitted to such demands.

When the industrial capitalists, yearning to have a cheap cloth to vend, tried to have such cloth produced in their towns, they found they were not allowed to do so. So they put out their work more and more to rural workmen. If that was forbidden by their city guilds and governments, they even moved their industries to other countries.

The "countries" on the Continent were not so very large. When, in Flanders, the great Flemish weaving capitalists found they could not get the permissions they wanted in Ghent and Ypres, they tried having their goods made up in the villages. Then the city weavers raided the villages and harassed the villagers, breaking their looms, cutting off their hands and fingers, in an effort to stop that sort of competition. But the capitalists won after all, for they moved over the frontier into Brabant, another feudal "country" only ten or fifteen miles away from Ghent. In Brabant they were welcomed and encouraged. Development of a very prosperous Brabant industry was tied up with this flight from restrictions which the older centers had made too rigid, and the Brabant towns, such as Antwerp and Brussels, took the heart and life out of the older Flemish weaving industry. (We in America have had something very like this happen to our textile mills, in their move from New England to the South.)

The flight to England was indicative of something of the same sort for, when Flemish capitalists could not have things made as they wished in Flanders, they began having them made in England. The capitalist lived in town, had his stocks there, and was a city merchant, but his work was done on the putting-out system in villagers' cottages. In England that was called cottage industry.

Village workers tended to treat their spinning and weaving more and more as a full-time job, and to become therefore industrial workers who worked at home at a very low rate on piece work. Usually cottage industrial workers did no work on the land except perhaps as seasonal extra hands at plowing or harvest, when their labor supplemented the private farmer's own work. As a result, industrial workers quitted the loom or spinning wheel only for short-term high-pay seasonal farm work, just as American workers have done in the past few years in such seasonal jobs as the canning industry has to offer. So agricultural work came to be the supplement to their industrial work instead of the other way around.

Historically the word "enclosure" has two meanings. They are closely connected, but different. It was common enough in the eleven, twelve, and into the thirteen hundreds to allow an energetic individual, usually a peasant with extra drive or a person with no holding, to go out into the forest near an established village and to make a clearing. He was allowed to hold that clearing, which was usually a single unit with a thorn hedge around it. Such a holding was therefore an enclosure, but was found in the forest or in the waste land of brush and pasture around a village, not in the fields proper. Such enclosures were common in western Europe and well over into eastern Europe during the first great expansion of population. Not enough land was commonly involved to throw an estate's rotation of plantings out of gear.

But the new type of enclosure which spread progressively through manorial areas in the fifteen, sixteen, and seventeen hundreds was of a different sort, and when it developed fully it threw the manorial pattern completely out of working order.

The lord of a manor had frequently had demesne acreage right around his house, with a stout thorn fence around it. It had always been separate from the great open fields. But during this period the lords began to try to have their share of acres in the open fields also, either consolidated into one unit and then enclosed, or individually enclosing every one of their individual acre strips across the open fields. Men such as the reeves who worked directly under the lords then began to enclose their holdings also.

When individual farmers began to hold their lands by commutation, there was real trouble. The whole of manor operation depended on common holdings and team work on the part of the villagers. It was bad when one man enclosed two to five acres of meadow land which had always been openly mown; and it was bad when an individual tried to cut off sections of the village stubble and waste and to have his beasts kept away from the manor herd, in an enclosure.

From our point of view this development toward enclosure was progress, and we would consider that each individual was making much better use of his land when he enclosed it. However, it was very hard on the person who did not wish to change, or who did not have the resources to obtain an enclosure of his own. Such would be the case with the majority of the villagers; they did not have much money saved, and they had to watch the land their cattle could pasture become smaller and smaller, their rights in the forest dwindle as it was cut and other men's enclosed acres replaced the old timber. Because of enclosures, a great many people were forced to go over into industry for their livelihoods, as their village land rights slowly diminished. They grew free of serfdom, because nobody wanted that kind of work from them any more.

The period of the fourteen and fifteen hundreds saw the double process going on—a rapid extension of putting-out, with a large part of the rural population supporting itself chiefly on the income from piece work, not only on textiles but also on stockings, hats, wooden ware, metal goods; the list was very long on the one hand. On the other, in the same period a certain other part of the rural population, getting its hands on acreage more or less in its own right, began to develop into the farmer-yeoman class.

Another important change was taking place both in military tactics and in weapons which gave increasing importance to the foot soldier. For example, the yeomen of England became highly important in England's wars, especially in the Hundred Years' War which was a series of fights and truces which lasted from the early thirteen hundreds until 1453. In that war the English yeomen proved themselves able to cut feudal cavalry to pieces on the battlefield with showers of well-aimed long-bow arrows. That the long-bow arrow was a very formidable weapon was proved at Crécy and Agincourt. The English yeoman foot soldier became the winner of battles, as did other sorts of foot soldiers in other countries at the same time. This gave relatively less importance to the feudal mailed cavalrymen, and even started or helped them change their status from feudal lords into landlords. This rise of the foot soldier was closely connected with the rise to freedom of the forest villagers in the Swiss Alps when the core of the Swiss Federation was formed. Similar free peasant armies won wars in other places, in Italy, Bohemia, and in Germany. The deepest reason for sustaining the original sort of feudalism was gone once peasant soldiers could win battles.

Yet peasants who had become soldiers needed leadership, and noblemen found an outlet for their talents in the new warfare. Many happily dropped into the ranks, a step not at all distasteful when the rankers in elite formations were all of them born to noble families. Many another formed his own private regiment, not in the fashion of the old feudal lord, to control a barony, but to lead into the campaigns of states, on a contract arrangement, such profitable mercenaries. No fiefs were usually granted to such company captains, or *condottieri*, but they swore fealty, albeit strictly according to the stipulations of their lawyer-drawn contracts as to wages, supplies, and length of service. They did no homage, although that remained a feature of inherited landlord feudalism for centuries more in most lands.

Still another factor which contributed to the change was the rise, again especially in England (though even in the twelve hundreds it appeared in Italy), of sheep farming in areas which had been growing grain. Sheep ranching on a tremendous scale had been introduced into northern England in the eleven hundreds, in the earlier rise of commerce, especially by the Cistercian monks. But that had been done in empty country, without displacing villagers. Then, in the thirteen hundreds and increasingly in the fourteen and fifteen hundreds, landlords and yeomen who had enclosed their holdings were likely to put sheep into the enclosures. Where there had been teams of villagers who plowed their strips in the open fields, there came to be only a handful of shepherds to watch sheep in enclosed pastures or, as they called them, the "sheep walks." Desertion of whole villages began to be noticeable.

This became more and more acute in England as the fifteen hundreds went by. The men, women, and children who were lowest in the English social scale were those displaced villagers who had not become yeomen, and could not or did not become cottage workers. "Sturdy beggars," as they were called, were a new class which began to frighten the countryside and cause kings and parliaments great worry—the sturdy beggars of England who gave rise to such nursery rhymes as "Hark, hark, the dogs do bark, The beggars are coming to town." Such beggars moved across the countryside in gangs and were not whining little persons; they were often discharged mercenary soldiers who knew how to fight and were very tough. They cut throats, slit purses, burned houses, terrorized isolated communities; and what to do with them was a major problem. The good people of the time usually blamed such beggarliness upon imprudence and wickedness and thought it was sinful. We can look back and say many were persons who had been uprooted, but some of them were also undoubtedly sinners.

CHAPTER II

Industry,
Commerce, and Government

O N THE eve of European outward expansion, and as it progressed, the fields of the manor were steadily being put into enclosure and the villages were becoming little industrial centers.
The fastest development along this line, incidentally, was not in England,
where much of the attention of modern research work has been focused,
but in the Netherlands and near the big industrial towns of south Germany such as Augsburg and Nuremberg.

There were some governmental attempts to slow up or to redirect these
developments. Most governments tried hard to hold wages down, and to
control the prices and quality of staples immediately after the Black
Death. The plague had struck universally and so made national legislation necessary in many countries in place of merely local regulation.
Maximum-minimum wage laws were set in operation. The Parliamentary
Statute of Laborers and Apprentices in England was passed by Parliament in 1350, its object being to prevent rural laborers from going elsewhere to bargain for higher wages. This was modified occasionally from
time to time, but remained on the books for two hundred years or more.
At the same time laws were made which regulated the quality and prices
of ale, beer, and bread, the basic staples of the countryside, in order to
keep them from going too high in price. While these laws did not operate
perfectly, still they were national statutes with an economic-social impact. There were similar legislative developments in other countries.

We have seen that during the eleven, twelve, and into the thirteen
hundreds business units using larger amounts of merchant and industrial
capital than a single individual could amass were being created. Especially in Italy the company houses had then become prominent and their

activities had spread all over western Europe. The Florentine banks carried on operations in Scotland and England, Flanders and Naples, the Holy Land, and the Black Sea area. The same house would have connections all the way from the Holy Land to Dublin.

But in the course of the fourteen hundreds, the older amounts of manageable capital which previous industrial and mercantile enterprisers had assembled in turn began to look small themselves, compared to the massive assets assembled by such families as the Medici of Florence, the Fugger in Augsburg, and some of the Genoese houses. Sheer increase in volume called for even better managerial arrangements. So there was rapid comparative perfecting of the law and operation of share holding in corporations and of the law of partnership. There was increasing perfecting of bookkeeping methods, and a rapid improvement in messenger-courier-news services between towns and between branches of the same company.

In the late fourteen hundreds and into the fifteen hundreds the Fuggers had their own news service, and some of their news letters have survived. In a way the Fugger news letters, and those of other business houses, were forerunners of modern metropolitan newspapers. Traders passed news about, then newsmen began to publish the news in the Bourse or Stock Exchange offices, and more and more the exchange and gathering of news developed in the fifteen hundreds toward the merchants' news service or newspaper.

The rise of premium commercial insurance greatly stimulated trade in general, while it also allowed successful insurers to add such income to the general capital they could use in mercantile and exchange operations.

At the same time, widespread development of the device of sending goods on consignment to reliable factors in distant commercial centers gave greater flexibility and speed to business. Both senders and receivers could take greater advantage of differentials in supplies and demands across the whole world of the markets which were integrated into the international mercantile machine.

It is needful here to return to and expand our earlier discussion of business and colonizing companies—chartered and joint-stock.

All of these developments had a great deal to do with further development, in turn, of the laws which allowed trading companies increasingly greater freedom of action and broader scale operations. The trading company was more ancient than the period dealt with here. Companies had existed in Florence, Siena, Milan, Genoa, and other cities in the eleven and twelve hundreds. These organizations had been called "companies," and the name itself was an Italian word, *compagnia*. But in the fourteen and fifteen hundreds the company of the Medici, or of the Fugger or the Welser or the Hochstetter, the various English companies too, were very much larger than their predecessors, operated on a far greater scale, and with greater freedom because of new laws.

For example, the chartering of a company, giving it some fraction of the king's own sovereignty, was known in most European countries. In England the king could grant a charter to a company and delegate to it really considerable power to negotiate treaties, and even to make wars—both of them powers of sovereignty.

On the other hand, the Hanseatic League, which came from the bottom up, not from a sovereign down, made wars, defeated kings, and built a trading empire in the Baltic and North Seas; in the thirteen and fourteen hundreds it was one of the great powers although it did not have a government.

Regulation of the companies through their charters became increasingly extensive. In England, the trading companies had a logical development, while something parallel to it took place in other countries.

In the thirteen and fourteen hundreds the English exporters of raw wool had all been required by the government to send their bales and fleeces through a single outlet, The Staple, which was most often the English port of Calais on the French side of the Channel until its loss in the fifteen hundreds. Whatever city was designated as the town in which the king's officials would officiate was The Staple; sometimes there were several so designated at one time. This was to the king's advantage, for it allowed his officers to appraise and tax the wool. The export tax was one of his greatest sources of income.

Above, in another connection, mention was made of merchants who sold through The Staple, called the Staplers; no merchant could export wool from England who was not a member of the Staplers, who were organized into a corporation into which a man had to be admitted as into a club or guild, to which he had to pay an initiation or entrance fee, and which had an internal government. The whole organization operated under a royal charter, and the leading Staplers could meet and pass bylaws. Such an organization was not very new, for guilds and towns both did this; they operated under charters, passed their own bylaws, had their boards of aldermen or masters, and the like.

The difference here is that this was an export organization, which regulated the amount of raw wool to be exported from England in a given year, to what parts of the world it could be sent, by what means, etc. Beyond this no one in the Staplers was under the management of the organization any more than a shoemaker was under the management, in the buying and selling of his shoes, of the head of his town guild. The individual merchant traded on his own; he lost or earned, depending entirely on his luck and judgment in the market. In other words, there was no joint stock of merchandise nor joint management.

In the fourteen hundreds there was a very rapid increase of manufacture in England itself, mostly as the cottage industry was developing, above all in the manufacture of cheap cloths. With this development the export of raw wool began to fall off, and for a while most of the important export merchants had a double membership, for they worked inside the Staplers when they had wool to export, and inside a new group called the Merchant Adventurers, who were exporters of either rough or finished cloth.

As time went by the Merchant Adventurers rather carried the field, and the Staplers died out as an organization. The Merchant Adventurers, dedicated to the sale of cloth either more or less well finished, became the great exporters of England through the fifteen, sixteen, and into the seventeen hundreds. The organization did not die until into the eighteen hundreds, but it was pretty much moribund by a good century earlier and no longer then an important factor in England's trade.

The Merchant Adventurers also let each member venture his own capital. Yet often, especially in war or in times when war threatened, the central board took certain managerial control over all the members' goods. They required venturers to travel in convoy, directed what ships they could use, and so on, so that, especially during the fifteen hundreds, there was increased centralization of management, although the bookkeeping continued to assign the gain and the loss on each venture to its own participant.

At the time of the great wars between England and Spain in the fifteen and early sixteen hundreds some of the men involved in the Adventurers and like companies began to spread their risks by what we might call a type of pro-rata sharing of losses. In risky times the idea of joint stock of money and goods, by which the risk and responsibilities were shared, was increasingly attractive.

Joint stock was a new instrument in England, but not really new if we remember earlier Italian practices. Joint stock means, essentially, one single management handling all the capital put in by all the members of a company. In the language of the fifteen and sixteen hundreds that collection of capital was known as the company's stock—the company's purse and warehouse stock. Individuals bought shares in the stock, or stock shares, which were usually transferable, although untransferable shares were known then, and still are, in such joint stock companies. Instead of a man with a hundred pounds' worth of merchandise being admitted to the Merchant Adventurers and then venturing his own hundred pounds, he bought a hundred pounds' worth of stock in, say, the Muscovy Company, or the East Indies Company, and let the elected managers of the company buy and sell goods, run ships to the Indies or to the White Sea, for all stockholders. The joint stock company made its appearance in England, France, and the Netherlands in the fifteen hundreds. The big companies of the fifteen and sixteen hundreds, the East Indies Companies of England and the Netherlands, were, in their very size and scope of operation, something new.

There had been corporations in a wider sense earlier. The University of Paris was a corporation of the masters and students of Paris, when the University or guild or body of the masters and students itself came to be considered as a unit. About 1200, when the University of Paris was allowed to have a seal and was allowed to sue or be sued, it had become a guild. Today such a university as Harvard is the Corporation of Harvard. But a corporation which has business affairs is the kind of corporation we usually mean today when we apply the term.

Buying a share in a corporation could be made much less risky than owning a share of a partnership, for a partnership was a union of two or three private persons or a few more, each of whom was liable for all his goods in case the partnership went bankrupt. This amounted to unlimited liability. But with transferability of shares, it was possible to move into and out of positions of responsibility by buying and selling fortunately. This helped to make business investment attractive, drawing funds from noblemen, rural squires, and churchmen, who could put a little extra money into shares of joint stock with at least some lessening of risk. Final development of limited liability was to come very much later, and in the United States has been a matter of only the last few generations. But the whole idea of joint stock worked increasingly toward it. Joint stock allowed larger quantities of goods to be bought and sold and profits to be correspondingly increased and risks spread.

Increase in volume of trade was one of the reasons for development of new ways in which to handle volume, and in itself it had a considerable amount to do with what came next—shifts in the centers of operation. The new kind of trade in volume, calling for large sums of capital and large fleets of large ships, was beyond the handling powers of the old, small Italian states, to mention one area which began to lose as volume increased.

The Genoese and Venetians made noble efforts to increase the sizes of their ships and operations, yet they began to be outdistanced by merchants whose underpinnings were national kingdoms rather than city-states. England, France, Spain, and Portugal gave a foundation upon which very rich companies could rest, whereas the small states of Venice and Genoa, built up in a world when volume was not so great, could not support the necessary fleets. Well before the opening of the Western Hemisphere and the routes toward India, Dutch, English, French, and Portuguese ships had begun to edge into the Mediterranean itself and into business competition with Venetians and Genoese.

There was one city which had a great mercantile development during the fourteen and fifteen hundreds, with its foundations in the Ottoman Turkish Empire. The city of Ragusa on the Adriatic has been quite generally overlooked. It drew its trade from the whole of the European parts of the Ottoman Empire, and had great argosies of ships sailing as far as England. (Shakespeare and other writers in English, as well as in other languages, confused the city of Ragusa, which existed and was so rich at that time, with the ancient Argonauts and their search for the Golden Fleece, and spoke of an "Argosy." What they really meant was a "Ragusa.")

In the fourteen hundreds, the coastal seafarers of Portugal and Castile were coming up toward leadership. The great voyages of Columbus and da Gama were not the enterprises of foolhardy amateurs. Instead, they were the most spectacular of the wide-flung adventures which skilled Castilian and Portuguese seamen had been projecting for fifty to a hundred years. These men had gone far down the coast of Africa, a third of the way to Cuba, having already acquired the Azores before Columbus sailed. A shift was taking place, and the Castilians and Portuguese were rivaling or pulling ahead of the older shipping people in the Mediterranean.

The English and Dutch and French—especially the Brétons and the Normans in the north of France—were likewise, but more slowly, developing their own merchant marines—the size of their ships, the skill of their navigators, the competence of their mariners, the size of their corporations, and the size of their guns. Before 1492 they were all becoming more and more formidable in naval warfare.

This leads in turn to our next topic, the place of the new governments, with their concept of the divine right of kings, which were rising in

Europe. Some of the things which were happening in the world of politics had a great effect upon economic and social development; and, vice versa, developments in rural, industrial, and trading operations had a great share in giving shape and character to the new governments.

The important governments of the fourteen and fifteen hundreds were, increasingly, strongly organized monarchies in which the king and his chief ministers decided the law, the taxes, the questions of war and peace, without having to worry that great dukes and earls might be offended and start a feudal war. A shift in power and resources had taken place, some of the aspects of which have been described earlier, and the feudal lords were no longer in a position to rebel successfully. The king's yeomen, armed with rapid firing bows and with cannon, could defeat such armies as the feudal lords could put together, as could trained companies of foot-spearmen or pikemen. In England and France and elsewhere feudal castles had begun to evolve rapidly into landlords' pleasant rural homes; they may have been not too pleasant from our point of view, for there was no central heating, no running water, and far too many servants were under foot, but they were becoming palaces and rural estates instead of being the walled-in fighting keeps of earlier times.

The new governments were ruling over territories which were far larger than the old duchies and counties. France was a political unit from the Pyrenees to the English Channel, from Brittany to the Alps. It was not exactly the France we know today, but after 1453 it was much bigger than anything in Italy, for instance, and it was far stronger in diplomacy and war. Only England could balance France.

England had perhaps only a quarter or a third of the population of France, but with a good navy and high skill in war the English monarchy was the makeweight or counterweight to the French. Through the thirteen and fourteen hundreds, Spain had been taking on its modern territorial character as its various subunits underwent amalgamation. León and Castile, Andalusia and Aragon, Valencia and Barcelona, were fusing into bigger units, and then all the units except Portugal were finally fused into one by the marriage of Ferdinand and Isabella on whose credit and power Columbus's voyage was projected. Both Portugal and Spain were coming to match in influence the slightly older monarchies of England and France.

These new states were being built up by the new revenues which more efficient government and bigger business operations could generously provide. At the same time the new states enlarged the opportunities of the businessman. Here is one example of how that could happen: the Duke of Burgundy, who ruled practically as a monarch in what are now the Netherlands and Belgium, could allow cottage industry to compete with city industry simply by encouraging its promoters and preventing the cities from doing anything about it. Mention has been made of the way in which the weavers and fullers of Ghent in the thirteen hundreds disciplined the people in the country round about when they tried to engage in cottage industry. When the duke of Burgundy had become ruler of all of the duchies and counties of the Low Countries, he disciplined Ghent, and the Ghenters were no longer able to act as lords of their part of Flanders. The duke of Burgundy managed a state, an army, and a taxing and judging system which overrode the cities of Ghent and Bruges and others which had earlier been so stiff-necked. A national economy was beginning to appear, made possible by this new state, which was in turn supported by the national economy.

Such things as monopolies to trade here or there were in the gift of kings. A king could back up the power of trading companies by his fleets and armies, which could win wars to obtain monopolies or privileges for the trading companies, who in turn paid the king, with their profits, what it cost to build such fleets and armies.

The merchant class helped the new governments in another way; it supplied the kind of managerial talent to the royal governments which feudal and clerical counsellors were not in a position to give. Italians often had been hired to run royal mints, royal bookkeeping systems, and so on. But native talent could be trained quite rapidly in such fields, and the new governments were managed in affairs touching the economy and law by native merchants or the lawyer sons of merchants. At this time, for example, the judges in England were many of them the trained lawyer sons and grandsons of London and Bristol aldermen and other wealthy merchants. By the time the great explorations opened, the new governments had the use of the talents of this new class, as well as the armies of that other new class, the yeomen. Still, it is worth noticing that the "indispensable" secretaries of statesmen and monarchs—Cardinal Woolsey, Mary Queen of Scots, and France's Louis XIII—continued to be Italians.

CHAPTER III

Assets for Expansion:
Exploration and Trade

B Y THE thirteen hundreds and since, up to our present day, Europeans have always had superiority over any other peoples in everything which had to do with navigation. Even in the twelve hundreds, European ships had begun to be made large and stable, with increasingly effective rudder and sail controls. Large and small ships under sail could go against the wind by tacking, and could risk going into narrow channels and cramped harbors. No other ships built by other peoples could equal them in this.

The increasing size of seaworthy ships was important as well. The constantly improved rigging which they used, with blocks and tackle, winches, adjustability of the sails—sails which could ever more rapidly be hoisted and dropped, reefed, set at various angles—enabled ships to carry increasing amounts of cargo at greater profit. In every generation since at least the early twelve hundreds, ships have been improved by the shipmen themselves. They continuously worked out various changes in the design of their ships, modifying such things as the shape of a hull, the hang of a rudder, always with the intention of making a given ship or type of ship faster, easier to handle, and more capacious; and their shipwrights and financers forwarded such changes.

European sailors also improved their craftsmanship. From Norway to Greece, in all the coves and harbors where there were fishermen, a race of mariners who were almost internationalized was developing. The language of ships is (more or less) Mediterranean, with Italian and Arabic in its vocabulary, and it is nearly international. Irishmen and Norwegians, Spaniards and Italians, could all be on the same ship and with little trouble understand commands, names of parts and gear of the ship, and what to do with them on command. In those days as well as today there were

411

almost always strangers on board any ship, strangers of the most diverse sorts, in the forecastle.

The men who ran the ships were also somewhat internationalized. They were a breed who could professionally serve any ruler or any company of merchants and manage any sort of crew. As a result, there were Scandinavians sailing for the king of Portugal, Genoese sailing for the kings of France and England, and so on. It was not unusual in that period of great exploration that Genoese Cristoforo Colombo sailed for Isabella of Castile, that a Florentine named Verrazano sailed for the king of France, and that a Genoese-Venetian named Sebastiano Caboto or Cabot sailed for the king of England and also for Castile. Such arrangements had been ordinary earlier, and still are today.

Navigators also had increasingly good tools at their command. Europeans did not invent the compass, but they put it to work. They did not invent the sailor's chart, but better and better charts appeared; some very fine charts we have from the thirteen hundreds might serve as sailing guides today. Their charts were not perfect, but in basic construction they were much like the good sailing charts used by present-day sea captains. In the universities of the time students used standardized theoretical maps for some purposes, but in the command cabins of the ships maps could be found which really looked like the land and sea, showing islands, ports, and the rest; they were not only made to look right but were properly placed as to angles and distances.

In the late twelve hundreds there was also development of navigation tables by the mathematicians, at first especially by the learned men of King Alfonso the Wise of Castile. By this time mathematical tables and practical instruments had been worked out by which at least latitude north and south of the Equator could be calculated quite accurately. To be sure, until good chronometers were invented there was trouble in fixing longitude, but they nevertheless had ways of calculating it roughly.

Mathematical tables done by scholars in the courts of kings, or by university professors, made the raw material for navigators' manuals, put out after 1459–1460 by the printers, and available to any sea captain who could buy them. These provided sky maps and charts, showing the various elevations of the stars at different seasons and times of day. Arabic scholars had initially helped work up these things, and in 1490 some of the Arabs had, if not the improved European sky maps, the old basic ones of the eleven hundreds from which the Europeans had made their advances.

In these matters Europeans were remarkably quick to adopt good gadgets evolved by other peoples. They soon took them over once they had seen them in operation, and then improved on them. They did the same thing with anything else they found and thought useful or desirable. This attitude, which we take for granted, does not exist in many peoples or cultures. It will be noticed below as one of the great assets of the Europeans in spreading their culture and in dominating other peoples.

Firepower and Supplies

In the thirteen hundreds the Europeans began to work with heavy ordnance. Earlier they had used various sorts of catapults and *balliste* which threw clouds of arrows, sharp pointed beams, or stones. In the thirteen hundreds they began more and more to use brass or iron tubes that projected shot which gained its impulse from exploding gunpowder. In this field they used the help of bell-casters and others who had already been working with large masses of molten metal. When, in modern times, they learned to cast iron, Europeans could make iron cannon which no other people could make or use. The Europeans used first brass and bronze, then iron, and thereafter have always made better cannon at any moment in history than anyone else.

"Native" armies all around the globe have since been using obsolete European cannon, or imitations of European cannon made from European models of a generation or so before. Only the Turks, and later the Japanese, kept abreast of the Europeans, and they did so by engaging Dutchmen, Englishmen, Germans, and others to do technical work for them.

In handling cannon on ships the Europeans were again noticeably superior, especially after the Dutch and English of the fifteen hundreds developed the idea that the main objective in naval warfare should be to shoot an enemy's ship out from under him, rather than to board his ship and fight his army on deck.

European superiority in ordnance as to quality was matched by the relative cheapness of European guns, gunpowder, and shot. They benefited from the advances steadily made in mining, refining, working, casting, and machining metals. They not only had better cannon, but always kept improving their small arms. By the fourteen hundreds these were far better than those of anyone else, and by the fifteen hundreds they were strikingly better than that which they themselves had used a hundred years earlier. As they improved the effectiveness of their small arms with every decade, so they also lowered the price and raised the rate of output. Partly the increase in the quantities of munitions and the concomitant reduction in prices stemmed from European conquests themselves.

Incidentally, it was in the realm of gun making that the first significant application was made of the standard interchangeable part. At first crafts-men made the barrels exactly alike, then the various cogs and wheels, so that if a cog was broken through accident or enemy action, a new cog would be put in where the other had been, or a new flint when they began using flintlocks, and so on. European guns were always superior in quantity and quality to those of any of their enemies, and that superiority in fighting tools still obtains; the gap in technology between European and non-European is wider now than it has ever been in history.

Communication

The rapid communications which Europeans developed, and their monopoly of communications, gave them an ability to know where to go, what to do, and how to do it, in a way no non-European people could match. European rapidity of communication was the astonishment of all the world when other peoples first met them. To this day it has been a specialty. European packet boats and clippers, then European tele-communications of every sort, up to high-speed airplanes, have given them a monopoly of communications most of the time, and almost a complete monopoly in the technology for improving communications.

European pre-eminence in this respect was greatly furthered by the invention of the movable-type printing prss, which from just about 1450 on began to make it possible for one European to go somewhere, see something and describe it, and have any European who could read Latin (then the universal language) know all about it within a few weeks, thanks to the speedy circulation of printed materials.

News letters, then newspapers; scholarly letters, then scholarly journals; institutions organized and maintained permanently where trained men could gather and weigh and find meaning in reports and experiences touching geography, geology, climatology, zoology, botany and so on— all these and many more things were factors in the rapid and exclusively European exploration of the earth.

Growing Global Monopoly in Trade

Europeans were excellent traders, far better than most others, although in no way more skilled than, say, the Arabs or Chinese in this respect.

In many parts of Europe, notably in Tuscany and Lombardy, Catalonia and France, in England, in the Low Countries, and in the developed southern and Rhineland parts of Germany, there were a great many men accustomed to working for their livings by using tools and raw materials. As we have seen, some of these made finished goods while others performed a single process in the step-by-step manufacture of a finished article, in working metals or textiles, as well as others. The skills of Europeans were matched by certain non-European specialists in different special fields, but in many given fields the former were generally better than the majority of the craftsmen of the rest of the world. While the Incas were better than Europeans in their work with some sorts of textiles, the Europeans were better cloth-makers than most other American Indians and many other peoples; while the Indians of India or the Chinese were better than Europeans in some sorts of brass work, still the Europeans were better in this field than everyone else except the Indians and Chinese, to cite instances.

European traders themselves capitalized on the special skills of foreign peoples in two ways. In the East the people of India and China had no means of their own for selling their products to people any distance away, so soon after 1500 the Europeans built up a most profitable carrying trade, distributing the products of one place in the East to markets in other places. European ships and traders carried goods from Canton to Manila, to Calcutta, to Bombay, to Persia, to the islands of the South Seas. In return they carried all sorts of products from the places named (and literally hundreds of others) back to Canton. Through this carrying trade, the special skills and appetites of far-Eastern peoples furnished a most lucrative business to European traders, who were the only ones possessing both the ships and the knowledge of markets far away. As they came to monopolize the delivering of goods from one place to another, European ships and merchants could, if they wished, either handle those goods or not, as their interests led them.

Because of this monopoly, Europeans could capitalize on the special skills of special peoples in a second way: they could carry foreign articles with a tested profitable market home to Europe where skilled European workmen could learn to imitate them; once Europeans had begun manufacturing those articles, it was the European-produced goods which could be delivered to other parts of the world. They were in a fine position to push their materials and products in the world market, for they were the only ones who could carry materials and products.

For example, Europeans long prized the shawls which were made in the north of India in the Kashmir region; much later Scotchmen were making imitations of those shawls by the dozens per day; called "Paisley" shawls, they swept the Kashmir shawls off the general market. Europeans admired the very hard vitrified china of the Chinese, and for a long while bought it to sell to other peoples, taking it from China and distributing it. But then the Europeans began to make it in France and elsewhere, and shortly true Chinese china had become a rare article on the world market while Europe was making and selling enormous amounts of its own "china." For a good while Europeans bought cottons of a very fine quality from India for markets in Africa, Europe, and America, but before too long they had imitated them in England and were shipping cheaper machine-made cottons back to India where they ruined the Indian cotton-weaving industry in its own home.

European labor was relatively cheap, and became progressively cheaper as the first great wave of exploration and discovery swept on. It became progressively cheaper because of inflation, which raised prices faster than it raised wages. In the fifteen and sixteen hundreds the laborers in the textile industries, for example, were getting poorer in terms of real wages, which made the European cloths put out on the market of the world steadily lower in price as against prices for other things.

Furthermore, Europeans were endlessly experimenting with machinery. The great epoch for the application of water power and steam to the moving of heavy machinery was to come in the seventeen hundreds, but prior to that time Europeans constantly worked on improving mechanisms. Use of machinery further reduced the cost of labor in the making of a given item, and European goods tended to become less and less expensive.

The line of European goods was long, for they made all sorts of things on their own account. While in such places as India some kinds of iron and brass work might have been better, generally nobody could make such good copper or brass kettles, such good iron or steel tools, or such good implements for the hunter, housewife, or craftsman. Consequently, metal goods sold all about the globe tended to be of European manufacture. As Europeans came to any new area, their better metal goods came to dominate its economy, which became dependent upon further imports. The American Indians not only went over to use of French and Spanish iron and brass for their tools, they also forgot how to make stone tools. Only a generation after a tribe began to get a good supply, they had to have European tools or none. That brought dependence in many other respects.

Europeans were also very clever and seemingly had fun inventing all kinds of gewgaws which would amuse, interest, and please men and women in other parts of the world. Incidentally, Europeans liked these things too, and did not invent them just for foreigners. European dandies and ladies wore little tinkly bells on their clothes, little brass ornaments, and so on. They also invented good mirrors, and there is nothing which will sweep a virgin market so fast as a good mirror. Men love them. Anywhere the Europeans went, their mirrors with "silvering" on the back of good clear glass were a solid trade line. Cheap knives, spoons, bells, mirrors, were known as "trade goods."

Other excellent items were blankets and textiles of every sort. They came to have a good line of tobacco goods, not because tobacco was raised in Europe to any extent, but because they controlled the other parts of the world where it could be raised. They took the tobacco of Virginia, or Sumatra, or wherever it began to be grown (usually the Europeans began seeing that it was grown commercially) and sold it everywhere.

At a crucial moment the Europeans developed commercial distilling, so that they had distilled alcoholic beverages to sell. It was at or near the top of the European list. Most other peoples did not know how to make liquor, and it was always salable, and usually greatly facilitated sale of the rest of a line of goods. In business the first step normally was to give the customer a couple of good drinks, then to start talking.

European knowledge of how to gather large sums of capital and to manage such things as the great joint stock of the East India Company of England was tremendously important. Control of bookkeeping and of financial operations of all kinds, by a single man in one room, for an organization whose finances and books and affairs were spread over half the globe, was a European invention, something never before tried. Europeans were also very skilled in handling the financing of purchasing and selling all around the world. They were perspicacious when it came to sizing up those who could be trusted and those who could not, and clever at determining the amounts of discounts or charges which should be made. European knowledge of how to sell goods was never better than that of their nearest rivals, the Arabs and Chinese, but they went everywhere, while the Chinese went only to the Philippines, Indonesia, and Indo-China.' The Arabs lost leadership even in their home waters, and thereafter their ventures were never extended very far.

Return shipments from lands overseas were of the greatest importance also. For a European merchant it was those profits on the goods he brought home for sale that were his final ones. At home there was a great hunger for goods from abroad. China from the Chinese was in great demand until it could be duplicated and even improved on at home; embroideries and elegant articles for the luxury market were always in demand; desire for furs continued unabated, a demand which could be met with furs from either Siberia or the North American continent; and so on.

It was in the realm of food that one of the greatest changes in European habits was to come; a demand for foreign food products steadily increased. There was always the old demand for the spices of the Spice Isles, and added to this there came to be a demand for some of the new spices from the Western Hemisphere. Some of the chili spices the Indians used became an important part of the diet in Spain, while importation of cayenne and other hot peppers became important for the general European market.

There was already a home market hungry for sugar. Development of sugar plantations, first in the Mediterranean, then in the Atlantic islands and finally the Western Hemisphere, afforded sugar supplies on a large scale. In addition, cocoa, coffee, and tea, products never before known in Europe, came to be liked very much. In general, these were tropical or semitropical products which could be carried to Europe not for cultivation but only for consumption.

The ever-widening diet possibilities which came with the introduction of foreign foods and beverages to the European market brought about a considerable change in eating and living habits. During the late fifteen hundreds and thereafter, the European diet became much more varied than it had ever been before. Artistic cookery began to be important in both Italy and France. In England the famous coffee houses became popular centers where gentlemen of fashion, politics, and wit gathered (as well as some of the racier and more disreputable types), while their ladies entertained their friends at China tea parties—both phenomena made possible by the importation of tea and coffee from abroad.

Integration of Government and Business

It was a great asset to the Europeans in commerce that European governments put their whole strength behind mercantile enterprise, and considered the devising of ways and means for making their merchants richer and stronger a valid activity. The most powerful foreign states with which European merchants came in contact may have been equal to the Europeans in warfare, but none of them was so helpful in the promotion of trade and of the merchant class. In fact, as has been noted, Chinese, Japanese, Indians of India, and many others looked down upon their merchant classes. In general these peoples, who could match the Europeans in other ways, were indifferent to mercantile activity. Modern governments which foster trade are following a pattern established by the strong states of Europe some six or seven hundred years ago. Those European governments had a theory that if their merchants were strong and rich, the governments themselves would carry greater weight in war and diplomacy.

During the fourteen hundreds the European world had developed a curious shortage of gold as compared with other metals and resources, and there was a hunger for it. This was not to last in that acute form forever, but when we read of the almost hysterical greed with which Spaniards and Portuguese approached a pile of gold, we must remember that it was far more valuable per ounce in terms of purchasing power than it had been before or than it has been in modern times. The gold fever of such men as Cortes and Pizarro was something which drove men to exploration, stimulated their trading activities, and also stimulated them to conquest. Just at the time of Christopher Columbus's trip to the New World, the European money and price structure had gone somewhat out of equilibrium because of an imbalance between gold and silver, and of gold and silver against commodities. (It was one of the factors which pushed the Medici bank, as a bank, to the wall in the later fourteen-nineties.)

Assets for Expansion:
Conquest and Settlement

RAPIDITY of communication, superiority of ordnance, along with all those things which made for superiority in navigation and commerce, also were assets for conquest. Added to these was the fact that many people let themselves be conquered, or were conquered without hearing a gun go off, simply because they were overwhelmed by the European goods which came in through trade and had become dependent on such supplies.

Military Morale, Skill, and Efficiency

Europeans were not the only people who set a great store in hard fighting and who raised the fighting man to the position of a hero in society. The Japanese did the same thing, as did the South African and West African Negroes, the Iroquois and Aztecs, the Moguls in India, and many others. But the Europeans were as tough and as willing to give lavishly to successful warriors as any race ever known. In all their literature of adventure of the twelve, thirteen, and fourteen hundreds in which the success story was portrayed, there was an emphasis on the brave knight who won the girl; romances were partly love stories, but were also fighting adventure stories. Europeans could not hear enough tales of brave deeds. And of course that had its effect upon small girls and boys. This fostered men who were willing to die bravely just for glory. We should not overlook the willingness of a large part of a population to die for glory; such a population, if it has any other qualities which make it equal to its opponents, can be very difficult to defeat.

In addition to their idealization of the life of a warrior, Europeans had produced by the fourteen hundreds, and have continued thereafter to produce, a large number of poverty-stricken gentlemen. The English inheritance system whereby an entire estate went to the eldest brother, leaving the younger brothers estateless, produced many young men each year who were willing to go out, or thought they had to go out, to make their fortunes. In Spain the same sort of penniless aristocrat had been produced by the wars against the Moors; such men had first fought in the Crusades, but in 1493 and 1494, when the Crusades were over and the last of the Moors had surrendered, there still existed a large number of impoverished gentlemen. These penniless swordsmen had to solve the problem of how to live without an income and still maintain their positions in society.

In Spain, France, and Germany, in Poland and in Hungary, the attitude toward life, at least the attitude of the upper classes, was that a nobleman or true gentleman must not do manual work or engage in buying, selling, or money-dealing. He might go into the church or he might be a scholar, but the truly worth-while career for such a man was a fighting career, and it was the only one which he really expected could bring him honor, wealth, and glory. European swordsmen were plentiful; they were willing to die; they were greedy and cruel; they were willing to take what they wanted from anybody. Pizarro and Cortes and all their followers were this sort of men; the Balboas and the de Sotos and the rest of them were swordsmen, as were the gentlemen who made such a failure of Jamestown Colony in the first stage. So were the Cossacks.

Incidentally, the historians have done a great deal of injustice to that Jamestown colonizing effort, saying it was foolish to send a lot of gentlemen who did not know how to put in their own crops to such a place. But we should remember that when that colony was planned its promoters expected there would be much fighting, and sent the kind of men who could have won the fights. Had they sent a group of European peasants to Jamestown, the Indians might have wiped them out at the end of the first week, and second-guessers today would be asking why they didn't send some fighting men.

Generally, European swordsmen were well trained; they had an understanding of centralized command and operation unequaled by any save the Ottoman Turk, the Mongol, and the Zulu, who were also excellent.

The fighting man was more than a front-line hacker and thruster. As a squire or a young penniless knight, a good man became reasonably proficient in a number of skills. At his best he was a rough and ready field surgeon, blacksmith, horse doctor, cartwright, sapper, artilleryman, cook, court-martial lawyer, harness maker, and society dandy. The ability to read and write his own language was fairly typical, although "letters," meaning Latin, were only rarely possessed.

There was another reason why the Europeans were especially skilled. They were used to fighting the toughest people in the world, other Europeans. The Spaniards and Portuguese learned how to fight against the Moors together, and against each other. The Spanish, French, and English reached a high level in the understanding of how to run armies by fighting each other.

Comparative efficiency is important. In efficiency the European was always ahead of even the Chinese and Japanese and other comparatively efficient outsiders, while the military-social setup of many of the other non-European peoples was a parody of efficiency. Europeans came up against an Aztec army which was efficient down to the point where the Aztecs tried to make prisoners for their altars, as we have noted. Other fighting men could not be kept under control when loot was in sight. Still others had no means to keep forces supplied. On all these points European armies were far from perfection; they were simply nearer to it.

Then there was European bigotry. Down to the last generation or so, the European has never had the slightest qualm of conscience about imposing his will on other people. There may have been a few people who had qualms, but not the people who were actively conquering. The conquerors have known that their will was God's way, and that their faith was the only true faith; they knew that God was on their side; they knew that their culture was superior. They all—admirals, generals, seamen, clerks—looked down upon the Chinese and Japanese, the Indians and Incas. The conquerors could destroy anything of others without compunction—their institutions, their religions, their governments, their arts and literatures. European bigotry in all matters touching culture and religion was iron clad.

European command of the sea was a great advantage. In the later part of the last century the great American theorist, Captain Mahan, worked out the general principles of naval power (though back in the days of the Peloponnesian War Thucydides had done much the same thing). Both men came to the conclusion that with command of the sea it is possible to strike where you want; you need not strike until you are ready, for the opponent cannot touch you and must surrender choice of time and place for any attack. Also, unless you are very poor with the details, you have plenty of time to strike, to see whether or not the effort is a good idea, and, if trouble develops dangerously, to leave before you have lost your men and equipment. If we look at the globe of 1492 from such a point of view, and remember the European superiority in ships and ordnance, we can see that it would be reasonable for the Europeans to attack the soft North American Indians, not because they were soft as human beings but because they did not have the fighting equipment or the numbers, while it would be equally reasonable for the Europeans to leave the Chinese alone, because there were too many Chinese who were a match for the Europeans. Of course, Europeans actually did approach the Chinese, but they did not attack them until the nineteenth century, while they approached the North American Indians and began moving in as soon as they reached the beaches.

Furthermore, European command of the sea was a vital factor which, coupled with control of communications, made it impossible for enemies to join together against the Europeans. The enemies of the Portuguese in Brazil, Guinea, Mozambique, Malaya, could not join forces; they did not know where the fighting was going on, or even whether or not any fighting was going on away from their home localities. Thus the French, English, and Dutch were able to attack isolated peoples, who had potential allies elsewhere in the world but did not know it.

Political and Military Doctrine, and Christianity

Europeans have been remarkably careful to preserve the collective historical memory and strategic theory. The Europeans were not the only people who had books and a memory of their own and of other peoples' past. The Chinese had even better books and memory of the past; the Japanese and other peoples had memories and legends in books or oral tradition. But altogether the Europeans had about as good a collection of historical documentation as any, while in the case of most peoples there was practically no historical memory. The statesman or the general of a people without memory has to improvise as he goes along; he has only the memory of his own lifetime and what he has learned from his father to guide him in the choice of strategic points for defenses, for the movement of his troops, or, in the case of the statesman, for the development of his diplomatic negotiations. He has only the training in the reading of human character which comes from living with human beings.

Europeans had in considerable measure studied the historical records of the Greeks and Romans. In the Renaissance, in the period of the fourteen and fifteen hundreds, there was a very special revival of interest in and rediscovery of the literature of the classical Greeks and Romans. There was study of Thucydides on sea power, of the campaigns of Julius Caesar, of Macedonian and Roman army organization, and so on. And of course the western Europeans of the later Middle Ages had their own accumulation of historical records, of strategic and philosophical works. There was little impulsiveness in their choice of sites for conquest or attack. Instead, they were likely to study the situation.

The English maneuvered and touched in and out along the Virginia and New England coasts for seventy-five years before they chose to lodge in the Massachusetts Bay area and the region of Chesapeake Bay. These were not impulsive landings, for they had been trying to make a choice well before the age of Pocahontas, Captain John Smith, and the Pilgrim Fathers.

They also had a pattern or system for negotiations with foreign peoples. For example, when the sage and experienced Italian, Sebastian Cabot, drew up the sailing and general orders for the first English expedition into the White Sea, he gave the captains very precise instructions on how to negotiate, what to do, how to draw the papers, and so on. These were actually of great use once the English had gotten around the north end of Norway and began to negotiate with the Czar of the Muscovites. On the whole it was a very sage sort of exploration and conquest that the Europeans carried out. They did some silly things, but by and large their culture's historical memory gave them advantages. Within limits it is still a very great asset.

Another asset of the Europeans was the attractiveness of the Christian religion in all its forms to peoples who were not already possessed of an organized monotheistic or philosophical religion. From 1450 until now very few have been attracted away from the other great religions into Christianity; during the past five hundred years Christians have made almost no converts from Buddhism, or Mohammedanism, or several smaller groups. But those who had less well-established or inspiring religions were particularly susceptible to the attractions of the Christian religion. This was true in considerable areas in Africa and northern Asia, in the Pacific and Indonesian areas, and in the Western Hemisphere. European penetration was in very considerable measure by peaceful missionaries whose teachings struck the hearts and minds of others, turning those who became Christian into pro-European friends. In consequence, by this means European political domination and settlement was made easier. (Buddhism, Mohammedanism, and Communism operate in identical fashion.)

Expansion of Christianity into a great many parts of the world has had as a result the cultural, political, and religious annexation of peoples whose ancestries were not western European at all. For example, the mission work of, above all, the Franciscan friars in the Philippines whereby an offshore Asiatic people was made into a western European people in its religious, political, and ideological orientation in the late fifteen and sixteen hundreds. The Filipinos became predominantly Western without ever leaving their islands. And to this day we can still see the very large effect of that in the orientation of Philippine politics; they react and behave like Roman Catholic Europeans in all sorts of situations, instead of reacting and behaving like the Buddhists or Mohammedans in the same part of the world.

European Diseases; Alcohol

In addition to penetration in this way, of which we may approve, there was also penetration by the aid of disease and alcohol.

The distribution pattern of diseases over the world has had a great deal to do with contacts between peoples, allowing or cutting off contact. The African pattern of diseases made it almost impossible until the nineteenth century for Europeans to go far inside Africa. The malarial and yellow-fever areas and the like along the coasts killed the Europeans before they could climb the hills into the central plateau. Europeans were, in some measure, held at their distance by the diseases in the tropics, but they had their own package of deadly diseases.

We know that animals and human beings can become accustomed to specific diseases, but these same diseases are capable of harming non-immunized beings most decidedly. Long before the fourteen hundreds the Europeans had acquired some lethal diseases: chicken pox, whooping cough, measles, mumps. To us they are our "children's diseases" from which we expect most children to recover. Other children's diseases which were not so easy to recover from were smallpox, scarlet fever, and diphtheria. It was rare for a grown person to contract one of those, for many a person in a community of Europeans had had those diseases when young, suffered a mild case, and had acquired a life-long immunity.

On the other hand, the Western Hemisphere, although it apparently had some pretty dangerous diseases of its own, had not experienced those European children's diseases. In the communities of American Indians the descent of smallpox or measles on a population was brutal, and could turn a great tribe into a mere shadow of one. When the French became friendly with the Winnebago in Wisconsin, coming as missionaries and fur traders, their diseases killed the Indians off more efficiently than bombs. The Mexican plateau Indians did not really suffer very many deaths from the swords of Cortes and the Conquistadores, but the population of the Mexican plateau had shrunk to a fraction of its former size by the late fifteen and early sixteen hundreds, because of deaths which came chiefly from smallpox, yellow fever, mumps, measles, chicken pox, and other diseases imported by Europeans from home and from Africa. Many parts of the world, notably China, had the same immunities as Europeans, and in fact had immunity to diseases which laid the Europeans themselves low. Such diseases as cholera were present at all times in the Chinese and Indian populations without normally killing very many people, but were lethal to Europeans.

European diseases could be fatal to whole communities and peoples. When the Pilgrims sailed into Plymouth harbor, they found that the Indians there had made a good crop of corn, put it into storage pits, and then been overwhelmed by an epidemic of smallpox, probably contracted from some of the English fishermen who sailed along those coasts all the time. The whole Indian village, men, women, and children, had died, with the exception of one or two who had taken to the woods. One of these had visited Europe, had caught smallpox there, recovered, and of course become immune. He was able to tell the Pilgrims what to do with the corn, where the buried supplies were, and so on. For all practical purposes the Indians in the Cape Cod area had been exterminated just before the Pilgrims came. The Pilgrims did not have to ask if they could settle there, or fight to settle there; it was empty land.

Alcohol was just about as wicked as disease. Europeans had a social pattern governing the consumption of alcohol. A broad description of the European attitude toward wine and ale was that they consumed it on any occasion and in as large quantities as available. Furthermore, we saw above that early in the period of explorations they learned how to make, cheaply, large quantities of distilled beverages. They invented gin and other distilled beverages and took to drinking them. In each generation Europeans had a great many individuals who were ruined by the amount they drank, but the general run of European was able to drink a great deal and then manage a day's work without showing the effects too greatly. Their society demanded such behavior of them.

Many other peoples were not so inured to alcohol. Its effect on individual American Indians, Africans, Siberians, and South Pacific Islanders was so pronounced that not only did individuals go to pieces, but often whole societies dissolved in alcohol. The victims lost contact with their traditions, with their past, with their way of doing things, and came to the point where they were selling off their children, their mothers, or their fathers to slave drivers for a few ounces of gin. The European could easily buy traitors by drinks—and did. Alcohol, especially distilled alcohol, played an important role in the expansion of Europeans out over the rest of the world.

Increase in Population; Displaced Persons

There were drives and assets the Europeans had which made them able and willing to settle at points overseas or overland.

At the time expansion began we find that, among other things, the Europeans were just on the verge of having a great increase in the birth rate or, rather, probably, in the survival rate. During the next four or five hundred years there was to be a great increase in the numbers of Europeans, beginning first in Europe itself and then in its colonies as well.

The expanding population was to overcrowd some parts of Europe, temporarily reducing local opportunities for making a living. One of the solutions of this problem was migration away from such a district to another where opportunity was greater. This might be to another part of Europe, but it was also likely to be away from Europe, especially toward temperate lands in North America and Siberia, or regions resembling Italy and the Iberian peninsula in natural features and climate.

From the fifteen hundreds on, in addition to an expanding population, Europe also had a considerable number of persons who for one reason or another were dislodged at home. This dislodgment might be produced by a local depression. When there was a depression in the textile industry in England in the sixteen hundreds, cottages were left empty, and out of Plymouth and Bristol came the colonists for North America.

In addition, Europe began to have a considerable number of refugees from the religious persecution of various countries. This was especially true during the fifteen and sixteen hundreds. The splitting of Europe into two great camps, Protestant and Catholic, began about 1520. Then the Protestants split into subsects—Calvinists, Lutherans, Episcopalians, and still others—with the result that in all countries a religious minority was created, and there was very little tolerance of them. Protestants in Italy and France, Catholics in England and north Germany, all refugees, could move to friendly parts of Europe or to new homes in the New World. The experience of the Pilgrims who moved first from England, where they were persecuted, to friendly Holland, and then to New England was typical of what a good many of the religious refugees did.

The first settlements of Swedes along the Delaware River was a project of the King of Sweden for poor people who wanted to move to the colonies. For a person born into an authentic First Family of Virginia, the chances are mathematically large that the immigrant ancestor came over as an indentured servant, not as a planting gentleman. The kind of people Europe produces now as would-be emigrants is still very much the same as those who migrated in the sixteen and seventeen hundreds.

In England, France, Italy, and Germany, the younger son or the impoverished cousin provided the person in the family who would be sent abroad. Sometimes a family would make up a money purse for him to help him to leave the country, perhaps hoping he would have no occasion to come back or often counting on him to prepare the way for the others to follow.

During the fifteen and into the sixteen hundreds, the employed elements in the population of Europe were suffering from a rapid upward change in the price levels, which grew out of the overseas expansion. In the second and third generations after Cortes and Pizarro the importation back into Europe of great quantities of gold, but above all of silver, was stimulating to a great shift in European prices. Additionally came a rich flow of silver from new mines in the Tyrol, Bohemia, and Hungary; even by themselves alone these supplies of new European metal money would have markedly changed prices. The prices of things to eat and wear went up quickly as the quantity of money in circulation was augmented in these ways during the 1540's, 1560's, and 1580's, and as is usual in such situations, the wages of labor moved up very much more slowly. So the laboring force in western Europe was steadily earning less in real wages at a time when it was also increasing in numbers, which served to emphasize the effect.

Governments found they could drain poor individuals off into new colonies, especially if they could convict them of such crimes as poor persons are likely to commit, for example, stealing bread or poaching game. As a result, colonists who were to be sent out of the home country because they were poor, or because they were poor and had turned criminal, or because they were truly criminal, were available any time a government wanted to man a colony. They could also be used to man a ship, as Queen Isabella manned Columbus' ship with convicts, or they could be sent to the wilderness to build roads and work mines, as was Muscovite policy.

Europe also had a large number of honest poor people who were getting poorer, who disliked the process, and who were willing to break away and voluntarily go to a new country where things might be better, even at the risk of tomahawks or the Siberian winters.

Adaptability of Europeans and Africans

One of the assets of the Europeans, earlier mentioned in other connections, was their willingness to adopt and adapt when undertaking colonization. They had a quick appreciation of different ways to raise crops. The Pilgrims had to be told by only one Indian in the Plymouth Colony how to plant corn. Then, in one season they made a shift to a totally new grain culture—showing very extraordinary adaptability.

Europeans were on the lookout for new and better crops and animals, and were quick to move a good thing from the part of the world where they found it to still another (not at all necessarily to Europe). They picked up the seed package the American Indian squaws had prepared and began to raise potatoes, Indian corn, tobacco, tomatoes, and beans anywhere in the world that those things would grow well. In the other direction they carried European grains to the New World, as well as animals and fruits.

Another asset possessed by the Europeans when it came to settlement in new places was that they were willing and able to change their diet patterns quickly. In North America they rapidly learned to eat Indian corn, hasty pudding or cornmeal mush, and succotash. A present-day individual of European stock is habitually eating a hodgepodge of Arabic, American Indian, and African foods which is little like the diet of the medieval European.

The European was normally willing to force other people to migrate with him so as to be on hand—as slaves. Where the settler needed work hands in the sugar cane and coffee plantations of the tropics, and learned that white men died too fast, he imposed migration on a part of the population of Africa. The great migration from the Eastern to the Western Hemisphere was in fact a migration of Europeans and Africans; if we watch only the European migration, we see only part of the picture.

To be sure, no African built a boat and sailed across. In fact, the migrant usually went down to the coast in chains and ropes, brought there by brother Africans who were selling him for weapons, cloth, gewgaws, and gin. He was a victim of warfare, slave raiding, or court sentences. The shiploads of slaves filled up the empty lands of the

Carribean during the 1540's to the 1560's. Subsequently they filled up the tropical areas on the coast of Brazil, and to a degree the coastal plantations of Florida, Georgia, Alabama, and further on.

The migration did not bring with it African culture patterns to any marked degree. These people were mixed lots of victims from dozens of tribes and from all the shores of Africa, although most of them came from the coast around the Senegal and Niger River mouths, and on down to the Congo and Angola. Neither did they bring African governmental or social patterns. Where such social patterns did manage to cross the ocean, they were broken by the whites; but they hardly came at all, for broken populations of slaves, as we shall consider again later, do not carry such things with them.

The slave patterns were deeply imbedded in the society which the Europeans built. The African slave was another of the European's assets for his own migration and colonization. The very first of the white men to go through Texas managed the feat because one of the three persons in the party was an African "conjur man." He did "conjur tricks" and the Indians of the Texas plains were enough astonished to allow the little party to go through to Mexico. They sold their services and made new acquisitions as they moved toward Mexico from the Mississippi River area. The same "conjur man" was an asset to the expeditions which went north into New Mexico later on. The very first penetration of Europeans into almost any part of America was an African-European penetration, for from the beginning there were slaves who went along as part of almost any party of men. This was particularly true of most of the exploration into the southern states in our own South, as well as in the Mississippi region and all through Spanish and Portuguese America.

To a certain degree the Europeans who went overseas had medical and sanitary knowledge and practices which gave them an advantage over many other peoples in making permanent settlements. Today we are used to a world of medical research and practice which is making very rapid strides. As a consequence, we are likely to regard the medical practice and knowledge of even our own grandparents as barbarically primitive or medieval. It is quite unfair to the Europeans of the fourteen, fifteen, and sixteen hundreds who went overseas for settlement to hold that they were without medical knowledge, or that they were particularly "medieval" in the sense of backward.

There was a fairly usable amount of knowledge of the science of surgery, and in general Europeans were able to salvage many individuals who had been harmed in battle, or by working accidents, who might otherwise have been lost. European medicine had likewise come to use a considerable number of quite effective nostrums and pills to alleviate or to cure many of the ordinary diseases. There was an understanding of the effectiveness of mercurial and arsenical salts, and of the effectiveness of a great many vegetable compounds which could be made up from herbs and plants in Europe itself.

Of course, only some of the Europeans who went abroad were educated to understand and use such medicines. But in any European group there were persons, often enough noblemen or clerics, or schoolteachers or professional medicos, who had an eye out for the drugs and plants in any neighborhood penetrated. It was thanks to the quick eye and quick comprehension of its significance that Europeans caught on to the fact that quinine, gathered and used by only a few Indians in South America, could quite usefully counteract the effects of malaria. Other disease-arresting or disease-destroying drugs and herbs were noticed and added to the European pharmaceutical store.

European communications made it possible to put into use, far from the land of their origin, such drugs as turned out to be effective. Of course, they did not then understand the importance of vitamins in the diet, but they did know quite early, and long before laboratory science showed why, that certain fruit juices and vegetables, under certain conditions, retarded or cured such a disease as scurvy which we now recognize to stem from nutritional deficiency. The use of lemon and lime juice as a preventive or cure for scurvy was several centuries old before the cause of the ailment itself had been determined.

In many ways the European settlements faced difficulties that grew out of bad sanitation—which, in fact, destroyed or greatly weakened many. But along with a biologically inherited resistance to the effects of bad sanitation which came with them from districts in Europe which had long had poor sanitation, there was a certain amount of understanding that city disposals and home disposals should be adequate, and that it was foolish to drink most water, the danger from typhoid and what we would call dysentery being too great. Their habit of mixing wine with water or of using ale made Europeans to a degree free of water-carried disease.

By and large the Europeans started with certain advantages in the fields of health and sanitation, but much more important in the long run was the attitude of Europeans toward science and medical practice, which led ever-increasing experimentation to be carried out by surgeons and doctors. In the course of the sixteen and seventeen hundreds

European measures in these fields had become so superior that they helped still further to make European settlements dominant in regions where the natives still suffered from inadequate accommodations. The European advantage over many native peoples, in many parts of the globe, stemmed from the fact that Europeans could survive intelligently whereas the natives were blindly subject to diseases which wrecked them individually and as societies.

Tested Governmental Procedures

American history is so largely taught as having begun with Christopher Columbus that it is quite common for us to overlook the fact that Christopher Columbus not only was an experienced navigator but also was experienced in colonial activities before he petitioned rulers for their support.

The experience of Europeans in developing colonies for Europeans was indeed quite long. In a very real sense the expeditions of the Crusaders to the Holy Land, beginning just before the year 1100, were colonial enterprises; Europeans went for conquest, but they stayed for settlement; they erected governments on the western European model and imported settlers and instituted the social ranks of the Western world. They brought with them western European crafts and western European knowledge of navigation and commerce.

Following the Great Crusades were other colonial enterprises of western Europeans, above all of Genoese, Pisans, and Venetians, in the eastern Mediterranean and the Black Sea. European penetration of that area was successful partly because of the superior naval power which the cities mentioned could employ and partly, too, because of the large amount of economic control those same Italians were in a position to exercise.

But the holding of those colonies was, in a considerable measure, made possible by use of governmental institutions which the western Europeans established. Broadly speaking, they had worked out two general systems for tying colonies to a mother country.

One of them was to establish over any conquered area a duke or count drawn from the aristocracy of the conquering city, and given the sort of authority which feudal dukes or counts were accustomed to have in western Europe at that time. The mother city relied on such a feudal vassal to distribute in turn lesser fiefs to fighting men who would defend his fief against reconquest. He was also relied on to establish immigrant traders and craftsmen, or to control native traders and craftsmen in much the same way as lords controlled such people in their own territories. What we were to call in later American history "proprietary colonies" were early established and proved to be, on the whole, effective enough in maintaining relations between the mother country and the colonial area, and in holding the colonial area under control for the benefit of the proprietor and his country.

The other pattern which came to be developed, above all by the Genoese, was one in which a company of natives of Genoa would be given a charter by which they would monopolize the trade, products, and government of a considerable colony abroad. A trading company with its principal object profits for the stockholders could nevertheless exercise truly governmental powers to make war, coin money, and maintain navies and fighting forces in the colonial area. Company colonies were well developed in Genoese experience by the early thirteen hundreds, and at least one of them continued to flourish down to the time of the French Revolution.

In other words, experience in establishing and holding colonies across salt water had already been acquired before Christopher Columbus, himself thoroughly familiar with both proprietary and company colonies, came to the court of the Queen of Castile with an offer to establish still another on the traditional model.

As a matter of fact, those colonies of the Italians and other Europeans in the eastern Mediterranean had already been paralleled by the development of colonies in the Atlantic off the coasts of Europe and Africa. In the fourteen hundreds the Canary Islands, Azores Islands, Cape Verde, and Madeira Islands had all been explored and granted to proprietors or company developers by the rulers of Castile and Portugal.

In those colonies there had been established settlements of Europeans who came out either as subgrantees of the big proprietors or as the employees of companies which had in their plans the establishment of big timber and sugar and wine-producing plantations. Plantation economy in the sugar islands was well experimented with and developed before Columbus' day. Some of the largest and most successful of these plantation enterprises were developed by Genoese and other Italians who had been granted holdings by the Portuguese or Spanish authorities. Columbus had traveled and worked not only in the eastern Mediterranean colonies, but also in the colonies in the Atlantic before he conceived of going still further west on the expedition which ultimately took him to the Caribbean.

To a lesser degree the English obtained, in the course of the fifteen hundreds, experience with their own colony, Ireland, across the Irish Sea. Here again both proprietary and company experiments were carried out before the English very seriously engaged in planting settlements west of the Atlantic Ocean itself.

Finally, Great Russians had for centuries before the fifteen hundreds been establishing and bringing into connection with home authorities remote exploitive settlements in the northern taiga and even the tundra up to the shores of the White Sea.

EXPANSION BEFORE 1750

CHAPTER I

Government Policies
Through the
Period of Expansion

D URING the fourteen hundreds, leading governments of Europe had been modifying their machineries in the direction of centralization. In the language of the time and of political thought, "The Prince's" authority was being enhanced in theory, in constitution and law, and in all sorts of practical usages. At home and abroad the wealth and influence of a "prince" (he could be a king, a sovereign duke or bishop, or a republic, in fact) were expected to be the deciding factor in settling policies, regardless of moral considerations. These governments were designed for holding or gaining advantages over brother princes, not for exploration, conquest, or colonization. But they effectively served those ends.

Then, once these states began to expand, or their subjects began to push overseas, the power of the prince became increasingly the object of projects for expansion. Expansion proposals of different sorts were weighed and appraised from the point of view of "benefit to the prince." Given the outlay, would it be worth the gamble? Would the success of the enterprise meet the hopes which inspired it? Queen Elizabeth of England weighed everything proposed by Raleigh, Drake, and the later adventurers from the point of view of the prince's welfare.

The Age of Spain: Gold and Silver—Bullionism

In the successful cases of Spain and Portugal, England and France, and the Netherlands, the expansion which was carried on in many cases did result in a great increase in the prince's power at home, and this, after all, was where he wanted it to increase. (The English king always wanted to become stronger in comparison to the French king, and so on all around the circle.) As successful development of overseas enterprises resulted in an increase in princely power, so the princely power had to be there before the first overseas expansion could take place. Each built upon the other. By the late seventeen hundreds the European governments were stronger than they had ever been before, or than any governments had ever been in all history.

People who were concerned with the power of princes tended to develop theories as to how a prince's power could be increased, and always with such thoughts went the undercurrent of how to decrease the power of enemy or rival princes. Theories about this had been developing all through the Middle Ages. Venetians and Genoese had theorized on how best to cut one another's throats—by trade embargoes, by benefits to importers or to exporters, or by cutlasses. But the political-economic units involved then were small.

By the fourteen and fifteen hundreds the units had become the large monarchical economies. Kings were being told how to conduct their affairs by statesmen, professors, merchants, and churchmen, and almost all of the propositions which were incessantly being put to them had to do with the increase of power.

Princes also had special theories and interests. For example, the English kings, when they had found how effective their small armies of yeomen were in winning battles, began to do a great many things simply in order to increase the number of sturdy yeomen in English society. They tended to back away from suggestions which were otherwise attractive, but which seemed to threaten the welfare and numbers of yeomen. It might almost be said that the kings came to think in terms of flights of arrows, and a policy which diminished the number of arrows and the skill with which they were aimed was deemed a bad policy. In the thirteen and fourteen hundreds, and to a degree in the fifteen hundreds, there was an orientation of many other policies in England—the land policy, poor law policy, policies for encouraging or discouraging manufactures, policies with regard to migration—which were fashioned to help and not to harm the yeomen.

Other rulers were to be interested, not in yeomen, for they had none, but in such things as what policy might help the fisheries, et cetera.

Meanwhile, the theorists, practical politicians, and advisors studied contemporary or earlier princes and, having decided what had made them successful, advised their own princes to do the same things. Once the age of exploration and discovery had gotten well under way, it was easy to find a modern lesson in the ways of the Portuguese and Spanish.

From about 1450 on, the Portuguese and Spanish, in spite of rather modest population bases and rather poor manufacturing foundations, were thriving. First they built up overseas colonies in the Atlantic in the Canary Islands and Azores; then the Portuguese went into the East and the Spanish into the Caribbean. The rulers of Portugal and Spain came to be powerful out of all proportion to their wealth at home. During the fifteen hundreds they became the most powerful political and military powers, with the king of Spain also assuming the crown of Portugal after 1580.

Theorists and other rulers decided the secret of this power lay in the great flood of gold and silver which came from the Spanish colonies. Since the king of Spain could not make all the weapons he needed for his wars, he bought them from the Dutch—upon whom he intended to use them. And the Dutch sold them to him, too, for they needed his silver to buy the food and materials they had to have if they were to resist him. He maintained large armies in the Low Countries, Italy, North Africa, and overseas, and his armies won wars all through the fifteen hundreds. Then the king of Spain built a great fleet, the Armada, which threatened all the northern countries of Europe in the late 1580's. Spain could not have built the great Armada with its home resources, but it was able to buy timber from Norway and the Baltic countries, hire shipwrights from Italy and elsewhere, and pay them all with Mexican and Potosí silver.

The lesson drawn from all this by the theorists, the practical politicians, and the princes themselves, was that if a prince wanted to be great he should acquire rich silver and gold mines. Spain should not have been so powerful, but it was, and the secret was its gold and silver. As a result there was great emphasis upon the precious metals in the theories of the period. When reading back through the literature of the time, we of today are likely to think they were blind to other important factors in the economy; acquisition of gold and silver mines seemed to be considered of paramount importance.

This was the reason why princes hoped their explorers, conquerors, and colonists—sent abroad at great expense and risk, and in most cases at great loss—would find new mines. The first English settlers in Virginia, New England, and elsewhere were told to concentrate on mining. They thought of getting precious metal out of the ground, or from the Indians.

Then, in the late fifteen hundreds began the rather spectacular decline of the power of the king of Spain-Portugal. Into the so-called Spanish

Armada he had put a dozen princely fortunes, and he lost the whole gamble. Although there were still great resources in the Spanish mines—everything did not go to pieces all at once—it became clear that princes had to look for another and better policy than one which overly emphasized exploitation of mines of precious metals.

The Rivalries of the Northern States: Merchandise—Mercantilism

All through the later fifteen hundreds the gold and silver which poured into Spain had been coming through the front door at Cadiz and Seville and going out the back door to the merchants of the Netherlands or of Italy, the Genoese and others, who sold grain, leather goods, metal work, and all the products of industry and of forests and fields to Spain. With their new commerce, based upon a well-built, easily operated merchant fleet, with business connections established all over the north of Europe, the Dutch had the resources to beat the Spanish. They even became richer than the Spanish, and did so without a single mine that was worth noticing.

By and large the English pulled along fast behind the Dutch in the early sixteen hundreds, and in the late sixteen hundreds surpassed the latter in the volume and importance of their mercantile operations. The might of the English navy and army began to be felt even in central Germany when an ancestor of Sir Winston Churchill, the great Duke of Marlborough, won victories right on the edge of Austria, using armies which had been bought and paid for with the profits from business.

So the new lesson for the theorists, the practical cabinet ministers, and the kings was that princes could get rich and powerful through business. Stimulate the mercantile element in the community; give privileges and aids to merchants, and they will bring in the money.

Generally speaking this is what has come to be called "mercantilism" by modern economic historians. It is a general pattern, the aim and design of which is to make the prince powerful, to make the state strong against its enemies, and to hurt all other states even in time of peace. It has always been regarded as a way of making war; mercantilism is a means whereby a prince can weaken enemies as well as strengthen himself.

However, the theorists had no one policy for all cases. It was perfectly clear that in order to have an advantage the Dutch had to have something very like free trade. They were especially interested in making money from the carrying of goods. In the Netherlands there was hardly enough land, beautifully cultivated as it was becoming, to support all of the Dutch. They had no mineral resources; they had low hills and mud flats, with grass, cows, vegetables, and tulips on them. The Dutch had to develop local industries and a carrying trade to get on.

They began to carry goods not only from the Netherlands to other parts of the world, and from other parts of the world back to the Netherlands, but from one foreign country to another foreign country—for example, between India and China, between India and the North American continent once that had opened up, between South America and Africa. The Dutch sent their freighters anywhere that freight income could be obtained. They also enjoyed the income which came from insurance on the freight, from the sailors' wages, and the like. Since the Netherlanders also had to rely on a large navy and a force of sailors in order to remain independent, they did everything possible to improve ship construction and mercantile seamanship, using bonuses and other sorts of inducements. Thus, the Dutch emphasized what was most useful to them, establishing mercantile policies which would bring in an income despite their shortage of food and basic raw materials at home.

To feed their surplus population the Dutch needed fairly free access to grain and other supplies. As far as they could, they also developed local manufactures in order to earn income from the processing of goods. The mercantilism of the Dutch government was a policy which tried to obtain foreign and other trade concessions, or to retain those already established, in order to assure the import of raw material and food supplies which in turn could assure the Dutch of good markets for their processed goods.

The Dutch were also interested in fishing. In the fourteen hundreds the herring stopped going into the Baltic to spawn by the billions, and instead began to spawn in the North Sea near the Netherlands. Cod and other fish also became much more easily available to the Dutch. Protestants as they were by the later fifteen hundreds, the Dutch were very anxious to have a market for their fish in southern Catholic Europe, which was one of the reasons why they were willing to trade with the enemy, Spain and Portugal.

In basic principle, English mercantilism was a good deal the same as the Dutch. In both cases the idea was to sell more than had to be spent. It was in those days that the mercantile theorists coined a phrase—a favorable balance of trade—which might also be interpreted as meaning that you work harder than the other fellow; you make the goods and he uses them up.

Yet, in practice, maintaining a favorable balance of trade meant quite a different thing to the English. The English had many kinds of metals, and they had great flocks of sheep. As a result they emphasized the manufacture of metal goods, and did everything possible to increase English prosperity in the iron and related industries. They tried to keep wool at home where it could be worked on by English processors, to be exported only when it had become a product which would bring in the highest possible price per pound of original wool, meantime having kept many Englishmen well occupied. As a result the English were to be in favor of protective tariffs, export rebates, and the like—things which were an abomination to the Dutch.

Both countries were busily developing mercantilism, but in order to obtain what they wished, the English had to use methods different from the Dutch. They were to try to prevent the Dutch from carrying goods from, let us say, Boston to Charleston, which the Dutch wanted to do, and to insist that all the goods which were to go from Boston to Charleston should go by way of Bristol, Plymouth, or London, in ships manned by English sailors—with the result that Dutch shipping would decay while English ships would grow numerous and English sailors multiply. The Dutch were in favor of the widest possible open trade everywhere; the English preferred a tightly restricted trade, especially between England and its colonies, but also between outside countries and England.

As a result, while the two nations were trying to achieve the same thing, their statesmen clashed in practical policy. Thus mercantilism had various aspects all across Europe. Each country wanted the same results —a trade favorable to itself—but each had rules and regulations according to its own local conditions and resources. The theory of mercantilism is basically the great "ism" which all governments follow today.

Governments saw that in colonies there were markets, sources of raw materials, and places where the bothersome poor or noble could be sent. As a result, one of the aims of mercantilism, at least for those countries which had access to Asia or to the Atlantic Ocean, was to establish colonies, and even though the government might itself lose money on "plantations," it did so in anticipation of gaining greater strength for the Prince's estate—or the State—in the largest sense.

There was a race for colonies. A country which did not enter the race found itself left behind; the countries which successfully established colonies did in fact pull ahead in European politics. In the fifteen hundreds the first wars occurred in which colonial rivalry had begun to play a part, though a minor part at first. But in the sixteen, seventeen, and eighteen hundreds, colonial rivalry almost always played a great part in warfare; and it was sometimes rivalry for colonies which actually started wars.

Viewing their over-all experiences, it is safe to say that governments themselves always lost money on colonies. But this is somewhat like saying that government always loses money when it builds roads or runs the post office. For when colonies were taken from the point of view of the ultimate total strength of the prince, he could afford to spend money on ships, on garrison troops, on the cost of building roads and the rest, for from these things the country as a whole benefited. So governments fostered colonization directly and indirectly. They did this indirectly by giving bonuses to would-be colonizers who were willing to risk their bodies and their goods. There were gifts of feudal grants and titles; there were also special trade privileges and exemption from taxes. The governments of the time even encouraged piracy and privateering on the part of their subjects when it was directed against enemies, often enough even in time of formal peace.

In their internal managements the governments established all sorts of special tariff regulations designed to encourage the export of various commodities, always with an eye to the advantage of the prince at home and the disadvantage of somebody else, somewhere else. According to their idea, the best tariff of all would have been the one which by a single stroke would have driven all the other countries bankrupt. They never found one, but they kept trying. They even had two price systems, paying one price for what a farmer grew at home and asking another price, much lower, on the world market, with the government standing the loss and encouraging the farmer. That was true of grain farming in some countries. Such plans are old.

There were also programs by which new industry would be set up and encouraged if possible. Each country tried to draw skilled craftsmen away from rival countries. For example, the French, who used a great deal of ribbon and lace, buttons and cloths, in their ordinary costumes, had to buy those things from the Italians—from the Milanese who ran "millinery" shops, selling goods from Lucca and Venice and Milan which were extremely attractive for women's hats and men's coats and shoes and trousers and garters. Purchase of those things drew money out of France. So the French king began to attract workers out of Italy by offering skilled Italians rich compensations for moving to Lyons or Paris to establish the same kinds of businesses as they were operating in Italy. It worked. Fifty years later English kings offered bonuses to French workers to leave France and bring those same skills to England. The Genoese offered rich bonuses to bring Catholic refugee stocking makers from England to Genoa to set up stocking factories, a line in which the English were at that time pulling ahead. All across Europe countries tried to steal individual workers or whole processes; the Bohemians stole glass workers out of Venice, then the French stole them from both Venice and Bohemia, and so on.

These men were given government-built factories, exemptions from taxation for ten years or in perpetuity, monopolies of the market, letters patent which gave monopolies to inventors. "Letters patent" were "open letters" from the king, and inventors were encouraged by "patents" forbidding all others from selling an invented product. Men were induced to try to build expensive factory machinery—we may call it that, although it is a bit anachronistic—the government paying the cost of pilot operations in the hope that a profit would eventually be made. These were the various ways—and it is by no means a complete list—by which governments sought to build up their own strength.

Colonies were the largest and most attractive of all such investments governments could make. It was colonies which they pushed on the largest scale and with the greatest investment. With the aid of their governments, the Europeans began to take over the world. First by the Portuguese and Spanish in the fifteen hundreds, then by the English, Russians, French, and Dutch in the late fifteen and sixteen hundreds, European colonies were established wholesale. And in each case the home government was primarily interested in doing this in order to become strong enough to dominate the other governments at home in Europe.

CHAPTER II

The
Muscovite Empire

B Y THE time Ivan III died in 1505 the princes or grand dukes of Moscow had come to be paramount over all the other Great Russian cities in the forest region north of the steppes, in the headwaters of the Volga River which runs eastward for a good distance before it turns south into the Caspian Sea. Ivan and his predecessors had created one dominant political unit, and made it just strong enough to be able to stop paying taxes to the Mongol Tartars who had been collecting such tribute ever since the days of the Mongol conquest. Moscow was developing into a totalitarian state, held by a prince who was in truth omnipotent. He had boyars and other noblemen, monks and bishops, who were parts of his council, and local governments, but his word was law, on the model of both a Mongol or a Byzantine state, the two political bodies from which the Muscovites had chiefly drawn their ideas.

Novgorod and Moscow

Moscow had had one Great Russian rival, Novgorod. The rival state was a republic of rich merchants who held a tight grip on their city government, very similar to the republic of rich noble merchants which ruled Venice. The place was like Venice, too, in that it was in the middle of tremendous marshes, though they were sweet-water marshes instead of the brackish lagoons of Venice. Like the Venetians, these people of Novgorod had to trade or die. They could not raise meat and they could not raise wheat where they lived, so they had to import food either from property they might themselves own on dryer land, or from food-raisers in return for goods.

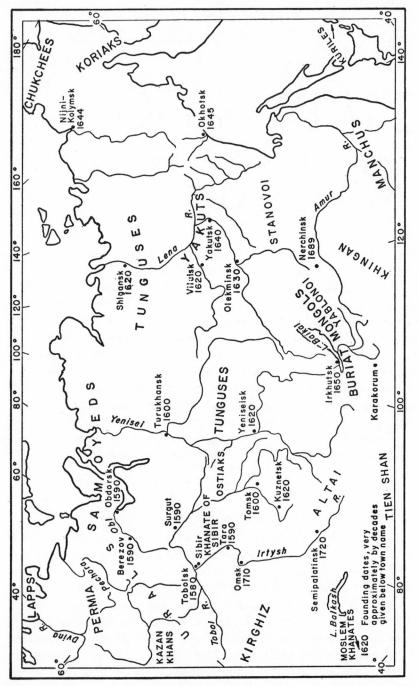

Muscovite expansion

They permitted the Hanseatic merchants to come up from the Baltic and even to have a walled quarter in their city. In the thirteen and especially in the fourteen hundreds, the Hansa merchants brought western European manufactured goods to Novgorod for use there and to be distributed farther. Merchants from the East came in with Chinese goods brought across the Asiatic caravan routes, depending on the chances of politics and wars along these routes. Grain and meat came from the East, especially from Moscow, for Moscow straddled the main food supply routes of Novgorod.

To pay for the things they needed, the Novgorodians had their fur trappers and traders bring in the wonderful furs of the taiga and tundra, all the way from the Arctic to the north and all the way from the Ural Mountain margins northeastward. Over that wide area Novgorod had a kind of empire. The land was occupied by various bands of Finns (not the Finns of Finland, but various related people who by and large were backward, not very numerous, and constituted no threat). The Novgorodians made these Finns trade and pay tribute. The Novgorodians had cloths and metal goods from Germany and England to sell, they had grain and meat from the Muscovite area (although that was not quite so important), and they had other goods which the Finns needed badly.

The Novgorodians obtained from them sable, mink, ermine, fox, and other skins. Only a few score fur traders actually did the work. But even these men did not do much trapping or catching on their own accounts. Instead they traded with the natives, as did the French, English, and Americans when they developed the American fur trade contemporaneously with the great development of Muscovite power. Novgorod's traders brought in great wealth, the city was proud and powerful, with strong armies and defenses.

But Ivan broke its power by starving out the city, chiefly by turning off the flow of grain and other food. When the "empire" of Novgorod was absorbed by the Muscovite prince, he personally took control of the fur trade, turning it into what we might call a state monopoly for himself. Then he used and greatly enriched some loyal merchant capitalists, who were given concessions within his monopoly.

The greatest fur trading family in all history, greater than John Jacob Astor's or any others, was the Strogonovs, enterprisers who made imperial fortunes for themselves and for the Czar by developing his empire northward and eastward. They opened iron and copper mines, developed salt-producing and gunpowder-producing establishments, foundries for guns, and founded trading stations. They endowed monasteries, and brought in colonists wherever that would pay. The Strogonovs were one of the great factors in the development of Muscovite power. Their hired men were the first who went into Siberia.

Mongol-Tartars and the Muscovite Revival

During the thirteen hundreds, the breakup of the great empire of Genghis Khan and his successors had been going on quite fast as different branches of the Mongol-Tartar royal family went to war with one another. In the course of the thirteen hundreds small parts broke into even smaller parts. The fourteen hundreds saw those Khanates which were nearest Moscow break off from the others, then break into three fragments, two having been ravaged just before 1400 by other Mongol conquerors, Tokhtamish and Tamerlane.

The Khanates of Kazan on the upper Volga, of Astrakhan southward near the mouth of the Volga, and of Crimea were weak, fighting with each other and also having internal civil wars. The Muscovite Czar at first refused to pay tribute any more to his overlord the Khan, for he could argue about which Khan he was to pay, and end up by paying no one. When, as anticipated, the Tartar Mongols tried war, their forces were too weak and they were beaten in seesaw warfare.

Then the Muscovites began to absorb them. They ended up by taking over the two Khanates to the east of them while the Crimean Khan saved himself, not by his own strength, but by becoming a vassal of the great Sultan of the Ottoman Turks across the Black Sea.

In addition to this opening up of opportunity to the east in the fourteen and early fifteen hundreds, there was a combination of difficulties in contacts with the West. During the fourteen hundreds the Hansa began to grow weak, the volume of its trade began to diminish, and in the late fourteen hundreds, after there had been quarrels between the Hansards (men of the Hansa) and the prince, the prince simply threw the Hansards out. After this the window to the West was partly boarded up. At the same time two powerful political states appeared on Russia's western frontier.

One was the combined political state of Poland-Lithuania. This was not truly a single state, being composed of two different states which had the same king, and usually had unified politics and war policies. The Polish-Lithuanian combination was hostile to the Muscovites most of the time, and blocked their direct access to Germany and central Europe.

Next to them was a very strong Swedish state, which also included what we now call Finland and a good part of the southeastern coast of the Baltic.

These two powers combined to bar the way to the West. They would not let English, German, Dutch, or their own traders into Moscow, for they wanted to blockade Moscow to keep it from getting strong. Neither would they let the Muscovites out. In Muscovite lands the price of German, English, and Dutch goods rose. A sort of chronic pressure of Russians toward the West and a counter-pressure of Swedes and Poles against them caused a series of great wars in that area, in which the Russians were generally beaten, for they were still fighting with antique weapons while their enemies used "modern" cannon.

There was something of a penetration of Italian influence into Russia in the fourteen and early fifteen hundreds, largely through Hungary and the Black Sea where Italians were importantly established. The architects who built a number of the most beautiful Russian buildings in the Kremlin came from Italy. Such architects and engineers could go to another country, observe its architecture and then build typical Russian (or whatever country it might be) buildings, better than those which native architects could build.

Italian Renaissance influence was important in Russia not only in building and engineering, but also in the introduction of the printing press and of Western philosophical and other literature. Also, since the Russians could not obtain guns and metal from western Europe, the Italians set up arms factories, metal refining plants, and helped develop mines as paid servants of the Czar. Although they were important, their over-all effect was not very tremendous.

To the south and east of Moscow were Cossack communities. The Cossack was a masterless man—a runaway serf, an out-of-luck nobleman, a captured enemy who had been adopted and brought up in the Cossack way, or an outlaw. They raised grain, herded cattle, and did some trading. But most of all they were pirates, on land and river and sea. They were an irregular army always at war with the khans to their south and east. Even when the Czar made peace, they kept on with war. Sometimes they made war on the Czar too. If he tried to rule them, they proved extremely unruly; so he tried to persuade them and to coddle them, to attract them with honey rather than to repel them with vinegar. During the fourteen and into the fifteen hundreds, the Cossack frontiers-

men were multiplying, becoming ever better organized in their quasi-
military republics which they ran in an alliance with the Czar, but not
under his control.

Finally, the high development of the Greek Orthodox or Russian
Orthodox monks in the fourteen and fifteen hundreds, and the sort of
monastic pioneering which those monks did, was a feature of Russian
colonization and frontier development. This was parallel to the pioneering which had been done in western Europe during the seven, eight, and
nine hundreds and thereafter by monks, especially Benedictines and
Cistercians. Another parallel was the Jesuit mission development in
Paraguay; another the Franciscan and Jesuit mission developments in
Mexico and California.

Characteristic of the Russian monastic frontier stations was the isolation which those monkish frontiersmen sought. Benedictines, Jesuits, and
Franciscans too sought to make converts and turn waste country around
into prosperous land. Many monks in Russia were really trying to get
away from the world and buried themselves in the ice and snow and
black forest five hundred miles from anything else. But they could not
avoid needing supplies, and the supplies they needed were run in to them
by the Strogonovs and the Czar. Their fortified houses on the shores of
the Arctic Ocean, or far off in Siberia, supplied shelter and protection for
any Russian peasants or frontiersmen who came into their neighborhood.
In spite of themselves they began to Russify the country around wherever
they settled.

One other important group to be added to the Cossacks and monks in
this list is the war prisoners. The Muscovites used Swedes, Poles, Germans who were prisoners of the wars of the sixteen and seventeen hundreds by putting them to work far to the east as engineers, surveyors,
and commanders of troops, even while their countries were still fighting
Russia back in the West.

The Czars also used prisoners of state for colonization, whatever the
reason for their being prisoners might be. The development of mines, of
timber cutting, of road building, were always to a considerable degree
tasks assigned the convicts. The same pattern holds true today.

The English-Dutch Opening of the Doors

As far as we can tell, it was the English who opened a gateway and
detonated Russian expansion. Certainly there were other factors which
accounted for the expansion of Russia, one of them being the relative

weakness of the Asiatic political and military powers north of the steppe belt. But what really started them off in the mid 1550's was that they began at that time, and continued thereafter, to obtain superior equipment, especially superior fighting equipment, from the English. It was not purely coincidental that the development came as it did.

Like the Dutch, the English were late in staking claims to routes from the Atlantic Ocean to the great trading centers of India and Cathay, or China. The Portuguese had what was known as the "south-east route" around the Cape of Good Hope, not only in law as against other Europeans, but also in knowledge of the route. They also held the calling stations for revictualing ships, putting the ill ashore, and the like.

The Spanish, too, had routes leading toward Asia; one was across Mexico and the other was around South America through the Straits of Magellan, if anyone dared to use it. All through the last half of the fifteen hundreds and into the early part of the sixteen hundreds the English and Dutch experimented with different projects for getting out of the Atlantic, either northeastward or northwestward, around the north of Asia or around the north of North America. Some ventures tried both in a single trip. For example, Henry Hudson, an Englishman sailing for the Dutch, tried first to go around Asia, then bumped along the ice trying to go through the polar ice cap, and finally "discovered" the Hudson River at the end of the same trip.

The curious by-product of these attempts was that in trying to reach China they found the way to Russia. It was a trip to China that was planned and hoped for when the English gathered together some money for a company, modeled on Italian trading companies. It was put together, organized, and headed by an Italian, Sebastian Cabot, who had, however, lived most of his life in England except for a period of years when he had been chief pilot for the Spanish and had made the first important attempt to colonize Argentina. Cabot, an Italian who was working for the English, played a part in the history of both Argentina and Russia.

Cabot drew up the Articles of Incorporation for the new company, and then provided the first captains trying to sail around Asia to the north with their instructions as to how to operate and what to do. Captain Willoughby's ship was lost, but Captain Chancellor got through into the White Sea by way of the warm water route which goes around the North Cape, north of Norway. This was known as the Murmansk Route in 1942 and 1943 when we were trying to move supplies to Russia.

Along the coast of the White Sea the English were treated with great coolness by the border officials. They were given the standard Iron Curtain treatment (there is no European government quite so like the seventeenth century as the present-day Russian government). Upon arrival in Russia the English expedition was kept on the edge of things, unable to get in touch with anybody, until fast couriers had run to the Czar and gotten back. Then suddenly the red carpet was rolled out, for the Czar wanted the English visitors to come down to Moscow as guests of the state. They were to be given the very best of treatment; nothing was too good for them.

Czar Ivan was delighted to find that a ship had managed to come direct from western Europe. On another trip, like ships could be loaded with gun powder and cast guns and merchandise, at a time when he was in the middle of hostile operations against Swedes and Poles. He gave the English favored treatment in every way. They could have a house. They could have a trading center. They could bring in all the merchandise they liked, and he would charge them the very lowest prices for what they bought, while he would pay the very highest prices for what they had to sell.

Furthermore, within a short time the Czar was using Englishmen as his advance negotiators in the Caucasus and in Persia. A London merchant named Anthony Jenkinson headed explorations down the Volga which flew the English flag along with the Russian. It is interesting to note that the region from which Stalin came, Georgia, had its very first contact with Russia through this English agent who negotiated with the Prince of Georgia over a treaty with the Muscovites. When the English reached Persia, hoping to open an English trade via Russia, they were opposed by the Venetians. These people had been in Persia for hundreds of years and were anxious to choke off any attempt to route trade through the Caspian, up the Volga, through the White Sea, and around to London. Except for this resistance of the Venetians in 1558 and 1559, the English exploration was a success.

In a short while the English came to be rivaled in the White Sea trade by the Dutch. For a while the Russians had been happy to have only the English; then they wished to have dealings with the Dutch also. So the Dutch and English both explored the cold oceans, trying to butt their way through the ice floes around Northern Asia or over the Pole. This went on through the late fifteen hundreds until about 1610.

On Western Europeans' maps many of the seas and islands in that part of the world today bear Dutch names. The Hudson expedition just mentioned was not unique but was one of many. The Dutch in passing went into Spitzbergen, where coal mines have been developed in modern times as well as Russian bases between Norway and Iceland. In Spitzbergen, in the sixteen hundreds, there was a tremendously rich fur trade, and an important seal and whaling industry.

Russia's Explosive Expansion over the Tundra-Taiga Lands

England's opening of the route gave Russia a tremendous market for furs, which stimulated the Cossacks on the frontier and the Strogonovs with their capital and managerial talent to push as fast as possible to the eastward and northward. Each year they took up new sections for the fur trade, exactly as the French and English fur traders, and then the Americans, pushed farther and farther to the west in North America. With the great market for furs the possibility was opened to buy fine textiles, metal goods, and other things from western Europe.

The agencies they used were the Czar's favored fur companies which provided capital and business direction. The fur companies in turn operated through subsidiaries as well as directly. They had colonization subsidiaries, and great tracts of land were opened with immense sums spent in putting in improvements such as forts, roadways, salt manufactories, and the like. There was a vigorous development of settlement planned and encouraged by the favored companies, above all by the Strogonovs.

Company (or family) merchants developed subsidiary operations by individuals or small groups of moderately well-to-do traders, who were given financing and put in charge of individual operations. Some of these went out personally to trade with the natives.

Cossacks did most of the actual pioneering, partly as employees, partly as soldiers under command. There were usually convict soldiers who had been shipped out to the frontier, given especially tough duties, and who could earn their way home in fifteen years or so by operating out there as the Czar's troops. In addition to these soldiers there were free-lance operators, mostly runaways. The Cossack habit was strong, and there was always a supply of runaways who did not dare go back, or who just liked the kind of life, free from tax collectors and other obnoxious officials found at home. In addition to these were the monasteries already mentioned, many of which had been independently founded, but most of which were colonizing enterprises on the part of older monasteries. Some of these developed around holy men as in the medieval pattern—a venerated hermit around whom disciples clustered, after which came formal establishment of the community.

The people who were already there as the Muscovites pushed eastward also conditioned the movement. Basically the different tribes were not very different from Russians, although they varied linguistically and culturally. However, it was easy for the Russian frontiersmen, barring the monks, to intermingle with the natives. A good part of this was friendly, somewhat like the intermingling which was normal on the American frontier. There were native wars, but they were not really serious, and there was little intentional extermination or removal of the natives.

These were thinly settled peoples, and about all that was necessary for a man to become a recognized Russian was that he should be baptized as a Russian Orthodox Church member. The assimilation of most of these peoples was relatively rapid through direct contact and imitation and intermarriage, and, thus, the breeding out of the local people. In the cultural sense these people turned into Russians, and came themselves to be considered Russian frontiersmen. The Russian front wave was always of mixed bloods; the one which moved into Alaska was a further cross of Asiatic-Russians with Aleuts.

The route followed east was through the forest belt. The general operation may be viewed as a wedge-shaped push forward, like the point of a great plow. The point was always farthest east, at about the middle of the line of the great north-south rivers. Along that middle line frontiersmen would be going over the portages into the next great river system, while behind them others would be going down the rivers across the tundra to the Arctic on the north, and up the rivers towards the mountains to the south, widening the belt of Muscovite control. The leaders at the point would go into a new river basin before the last two river basins they had crossed had been well explored.

It was a route of rivers and short portages of only a few miles (or a few dozen miles at most) between river systems. It was only necessary to build a few score miles of track, rather than roads, to join Moscow and the Pacific Ocean; all the rest of the way was by river.

In some ways these routes could be used even better in winter than in summer, for in winter they could run fast horse or reindeer-sleigh expeditions on the frozen rivers and across the frozen snow-covered portages. No travel at all was possible in the season of the spring breakup or of the fall close-in, partly because they could not use the rivers either for walking or boating, and also because the portages were hopelessly mucked up. In summer and winter the great routes were excellent, if rugged.

The first of the pushes past the Ural Mountain region was associated with the name of an outlaw Cossack who was trying to work off the death penalty by worthy deeds; according to Russian legend (which is a little history and a lot of legend) his name was Yermak the Cossack. He was the Daniel Boone, the great frontiersman, of Russian school-boy story. In 1581–1584 Yermak crossed into the little Mongol-Tartar khanate of Sivir, and with a few hundred Cossacks waged a victorious campaign on the Khan, commander of a few hundred soldiers whatever his claims. Facing west the Russian cannon were outdated; facing east they fired on the Mongol bowmen, formidable in the twelve hundreds, but no longer so. Yermak himself soon died violently; there are different versions of just how, in legends.

Yermak worked for the Strogonovs. After 1586 the Strogonovs had a fluctuating position and power, but soon established themselves. The Muscovites with the Czar's backing began to push through the Obi River basin. As they went, they bought all the furs they could get, encouraging natives to bring them in, as the Hudson's Bay factors and American fur traders did with the Indians in North America.

They had pushed through the Obi River valley by about the time Plymouth Colony was being established. Almost exactly at the time of Plymouth Colony, in 1618, they began moving beyond the Obi and on into the Yenissei Valley. The Muscovites were moving on beyond again by about 1620 to 1622. A single expedition could go a couple of hundred miles in a few weeks, mostly by boat. By 1630 they had explored their routes to the Far East, to the edge of the Sea of Okhotsk northward of Japan. Within somewhat less than fifty years they had gone all the way from the Czar's homeland across Asia, far faster than Western colonists went across North America. But they did not face any north-south mountain chains such as there are on this continent, and they had a river system which practically constituted a boulevard for those men who knew so well how to use it.

But the plow point continued to move. It moved into Kamchatka (the great peninsula which comes down from high in the north) and on into the Kurile Islands in the course of the late sixteen and earliest seventeen hundreds. Then it moved into the Aleutian Island chain, where Russians began to rival the Dutch and English who were already trading and raiding for sea otter and seal, especially to supply Chinese markets. The Russians arrived there in the 1730's. They had moved down the coast to Russian River (to the north of San Francisco) by eighteen hundred and just after. Their technique was good; they just kept on moving farther and farther, doing what had been done by their predecessors for a hundred and fifty or two hundred years.

Behind them there had to be consolidation work, for the frontier point could not function in thin air. Behind it were the conquered and tributary and absorbed natives who served as a basis for establishing a consolidated population. A great many of the Siberian peoples actually are not yet really fused with the Russians. But many of them soon were, and those who hold out down to the present day are not numerous or dangerous to the Russians.

In order to establish centers for their frontier activities the Russians, as they had in earlier centuries, built *gorods* like the stockaded forts built in this country by the advancing English and American pioneers. The engineers for these were often German, Scotch, or Swedish. These palisaded block houses served as storage spaces for supplies and above all for munitions; they served as refuges in case wars with the natives broke out; they also served as trading posts, and Greek trading managers were stationed in them. These Greeks did most of the business work in the Russian forts where they were in charge of trading with the natives, of keeping the books, and of making up and sending back shipments.

In addition there were, around the bigger forts and in places where the population had been established long enough, colonies of peasants who had been brought in. These people supplied more and more of the food needed locally, producing grain foods, bacon, ham, wood products, and even rough cloth. Some of them were volunteers, some were discharged soldiers who had taken up with local wives and settled down, but above all they were peasants who had been sent out, willingly or otherwise, to provide this kind of population around the forts. Many of them were convicts who were free to move about but had been told they could not come back to Russia.

The Siberian convict systems under the Czars were almost always rather open-gate affairs. To many a man sent to Siberia it was rather like being forced to move to frontier Idaho from New York. He might not want to go; he would not enjoy it when he got there; but nobody looked after him much. Nearly everyone who was sent to Siberia and wanted to return home did so. Some of them did it repeatedly. The Czarist government was very inefficient about escapes from Siberia; once the trans-Siberian railroad was built it was even possible to take a train back. Until 1917 revolutionists did this repeatedly.

The expansion of the Russian empire has to have a sort of second chapter. Beginning in the mid-eighteen hundreds and steadily until now, the Russians have been engaged in still another great forward movement. Using railroads and breech-loader rifles, machine guns and telecommunications, they were finally strong enough in the period of our Civil War and after to conquer the Mohammedan steppe and oasis states south of Siberia, and to move also on the Chinese empire. A good third of the Russian empire is a very new thing, newer than the British and French occupation of most parts of their now relinquished great empires. It was an ultramodern colonial expansion. Vladivostock was established when Lincoln was president on land seized from the Manchu-Chinese by imperialist aggression shortly before.

CHAPTER III

The
Empire of Portugal

THE Muscovites went by river boat or walked into their new salt water. In the history of European expansion the big story for empire. On the other side of Europe it was needful to sail over the fifteen hundreds was written by the Iberians under two different crowns, those of Spain and Portugal.

The leader was Portugal. In one sense, this kingdom started its expansion in the eleven hundreds and did not stop until it was played out in the sixteen hundreds. Starting from a little county along the northwestern coast of Spain, the Portuguese carved out their home kingdom southward by war and colonization. Only a short time after fourteen hundred, the Portuguese had made Portugal as we see it today on the map. Across the straits was Morocco, and out in the ocean there were islands which they had begun to hear about.

The Atlantic Islands and the African Coast

These Portuguese who had been pushing down along the west side of the peninsula had certain assets and certain patterns of approach to problems which were to be very useful to them when they started colonizing.

For one thing, the coastal peoples along the Iberian peninsula were (and are) magnificent sailors. They loved the salt sea, and were fearless and very skillful at handling their boats. The men of the coast, whether Spanish or Portuguese, were just as thoroughly able men of the sea as any Dutch or English or Norwegians. (A very large part of the salt-water fishing fleet of the United States of America is manned from the captains down to cabin boys by transplanted Portuguese.) By the thirteen hundreds their ships took them far out to sea after whale and tuna and sardines.

On these expeditions they began, apparently informally, to run across islands; the Canaries and Azores seem to have been noticed and touched on by both Portuguese and Spanish sailors before official expeditions were organized to go to them and take them in a king's name. In the history of exploration it has frequently happened that the leader of a royal expedition has hired as his guide a man who could neither read nor write but who had been there before and could show the royal expedition where to go to make discoveries.

Portugal also had merchants skilled in trade with England and the Low Countries and with Italy and the Mediterranean lands. These merchants were Portuguese and also Genoese, Florentines, and others who became absorbed into the Portuguese population. Many Genoese merchants moved to Seville and Cadiz in Spain, to Lisbon and Oporto and elsewhere in Portugal, and became natives. The hereditary grand admirals of Portugal were Genoese merchant nobles. Trade on a large scale was well understood by the Portuguese and they were ambitious to expand theirs.

Then came Prince Henry "the Navigator." That title is a modern invention; he was called Prince Henry in his lifetime—or Dom Enrique. He was an able and far-sighted man, ambitious to continue Portugal's push southward, which had just come to the end of the peninsula. He took part in a Portuguese attempt, which was not fruitful, to continue expanding by crossing over into Morocco.

So he began to organize exploration and development, and to gather a brain trust; and he started what would be known today as intelligence work. The best Jewish astronomers and map makers joined his little group. Mathematicians worked on tables for the calculation of latitude, and on devices for the calculation of longitude. He drew together and collated reports on the directions of tides and winds, the movements of fishes and birds, trying to find out what was beyond the horizons. He hired good ship builders and able captains, and gave them prizes for doing daring deeds and also for inventing new and better sailing gadgets. He went magnificently into debt, but when he died in 1460 the Portuguese were well on their way down to the Equator along the Atlantic coast of Africa. They had just learned how to pay their way in exploration by bringing slaves back for sugar plantations. They were fighting the Spanish for colonization rights in the Canaries, and they were on their way to colonization of the other Atlantic islands, the Azores,

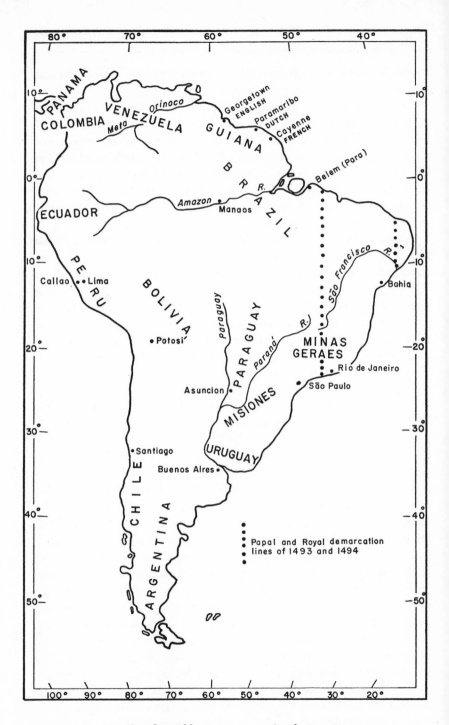

Brazil and neighboring areas in South America

Madeira, and the Cape Verde. Thanks to his leadership, the Portuguese were started toward Japan, the Spice Isles, and the upper Amazon River.

The Portuguese went south to the tip of Africa and back north into the Indian Ocean on its east side in the great expedition which took place in 1497–1498 headed by Vasco da Gama. When they set out, the Portuguese knew they were going to meet Arabs on the far side of Africa. For years they had been sending scholarly or merchant spies by the old routes into the Near East to learn all they could about the Indian Ocean and the Arabic world there. Every Portuguese ship intending to go into the Indian Ocean had carried Arabic interpreters aboard.

When da Gama reached the Indian Ocean, he kidnaped an Arab pilot and put him up at the helm. The pilot taught him how to handle the monsoon wind which made it possible to go on a straight run from the African coast to the southwest side of India.

Between 1497, when they entered the Indian Ocean for the first time, and about 1540 (that is, less than fifty years) the Portuguese had gone all the way to Japan, were trading with India and China, and had control of the exports of the Spice Isles.

Appropriation of the Arab-Malay Trading Empire

Notice was taken earlier of the Arab-Malay-Mohammedan string of trading sultanates around the Indian Ocean. Though the region they controlled was vast, from the coast of Madagascar around to Borneo and the Philippines, there was a relatively small number of Arab-Malays and of local natives who had intermarried with them and become Mohammedans. They were unorganized and their vessels and ordnance were obsolete.

The Portuguese blanketed these people with their own astonishingly small forces, which consisted of only a few thousand soldiers and sailors at any one time. But with good ships, very good command, and almost desperate bravery, the Portuguese soon dominated the Arab sultanates. They let most of them live on, as they let the Malay sultanates and Raja-ates farther east in the Spice Isles survive. They merely made the rajahs and sultans tributary, having them pay if possible in gold and spices. They actually took only about a dozen spots, where they developed their own advanced naval bases.

One was on the coast of Africa in the channel between Africa and Madagascar, Mozambique. It is still Portuguese, with a large area of subjugated land around it. Toward Abyssinia they established another,

Malinda, which they do not have any more. Across on the Indian coast they tried one or two other places first, and ended up by establishing a strong base at Goa, which is still Portuguese. They took control of the straits now called the Straits of Singapore just after fifteen hundred. Their port was at Malacca and the straits were called the Malacca Straits for a long time until the English rechristened them. (Singapore port is an English creation, raised up out of the swamps in the past seventy-five to one hundred years.) Another of their bases which is still Portuguese is Macao, situated practically across the river from Hongkong. And they still hold one part of the Spice Isles, Timor.

It is estimated that Portuguese enterprises took tremendous losses. On single ships as many as 60 and 70 percent of the men who sailed from Lisbon were no longer alive at the end of twelve months. But despite the losses, which possibly totaled about a million men during the course of the fifteen hundreds, some Portuguese became terrifically rich. The king did, for he was the chief shareholder in the big exploiting corporations. Many grandees became very wealthy, and so did some lesser persons. But by and large the country was drained not only of men but also of treasure and energy. Business tended to languish at home. Manufacture especially was neglected, and the Dutch soon began to supply the Portuguese with the things which they had made at home before— articles of clothing, household goods, and so on—while the Portuguese sold pepper and such Eastern products to the world.

In the fifteen hundreds the Portuguese supported active and influential overseas religious enterprises. At no time was the government indifferent to religion: it was quite the other way around. That became especially true after the Protestant Reformation began to draw large parts of Europe away from the Roman Catholic Church. In the 1540's the Jesuit Order began its great career, and Portuguese were active in the Order from the very beginning. The Portuguese government became very friendly to the Jesuits and gave them facilities, money, and backing for a mission enterprise to India, China, and Japan. The greatest of the Jesuit missionaries, St. Francis Xavier, worked out his career in those countries and is buried in Goa.

Under the Portuguese wing a complete Roman Catholic church organization was set up with its headquarters where they still are today, in the chief Portuguese city, Goa, on the western shores of India. A great deal of the Portuguese business profits went into the support of mission work.

Portuguese emigrants were few but there did grow up a population of Portuguese mixed-breeds and converts in India and Ceylon, Africa, China, and the Spice Isles. Those are still there, forming a population which is European in orientation and religion, although in physical appearance most individuals are like the people in whichever place they may be.

Under Dutch attack and to a small degree under English and Danish attack, the Portuguese empire lost its strength rather fast in the early sixteen hundreds. Yet that empire was never snatched from Portugal by Dutch or English annexation.

Just as the Portuguese had established control of ports and harbors all around the Indian Ocean and the Spice Isles without physically removing Arabs and Malays, so the Dutch also moved in. The Dutch established bases in the neighborhood of Portuguese holdings and drew all the business away for themselves; the Portuguese were left holding their original harbors, but little else as far as business went.

Not much later, around 1660, the English took the Portuguese under their wing diplomatically in European wars. Since 1660 Portugal's overseas empire has also been protected by the English. In return the Portuguese have supported the British state in all its wars and against all comers in Europe. This was the reason why the Americans, through Britain, were able to have use of the Azores' flying bases, which are part of Portugal, in the last war against Germany. It was the continuation of an arrangement the Portuguese and British had made almost three hundred years earlier, and which still operates.

But the Portuguese empire in effect was lost to the Dutch, for the Dutch took away the connections and trading arrangements the Portuguese had had with rajahs and sultans, usurped their spice tribute, distributing trade, and carrying trade.

Brazil

Despite the fading of the Eastern empire, which they had prized highly, the Portuguese were left with a great and important lodgment on the Western Hemisphere's shores, which they rather treated with indifference as long as they had their strong position in the East. At the time of the great voyages of Columbus and Vasco da Gama, Pope Alexander the Sixth drew a line of demarcation across the globe, giving the Portuguese the East and the Spanish the West. That demarcation line was supposed to give the Western Hemisphere to Spain, but it was so drawn as to give the little tip of South America, where it reaches nearest to Africa, to Portugal. That little tip was Brazil.

Actually the set of the winds in the Atlantic Ocean is such that Brazil is half way from Lisbon to the Cape of Good Hope for sailing ships trying to make that trip. For the first long leg of the voyage the northeast trade winds were used, the ships going down with those winds; then they continued their long run with the southeast trades coming in on the left on a long port tack. This brought them to the tip of Brazil, at which point they could pick up fresh water and vegetables. From Brazil they could go east across the Atlantic and straight around the Cape of Good Hope with prevailing westerlies pushing them. Brazil became a spot of real importance to the Portuguese on the way to the Spice Isles; but it did not at first attract very many colonists.

Especially after they lost the Indies, the Portuguese began to appreciate Brazil. In the fifteen hundreds they had set up some large sugar plantations worked by Negro slave labor along the coasts north of modern Rio de Janeiro toward the Amazon River, but otherwise the Portuguese had not done much colonizing. Then, in the sixteen hundreds, they began to move into Brazil, mostly by private migration rather than by government enterprise. They came especially from the Azores and the Madeiras and the other Atlantic islands which had become Portuguese nearly a hundred and fifty years earlier, rather than from the mainland mother country itself.

In the drier and cooler plateaus back from the coast the population became predominantly one of mixed interbred Portuguese, Indians, and Negroes, Portuguese in language and Roman Catholic in faith. These people operated small private agricultural enterprises, and engaged in stock raising, mining, and prospecting. They were a very rough element, in which there were few multimillionaires, and very few shop keepers or important merchants.

This Brazilian stock began to think of its own country as Brazil, not Portugal or the islands. It became especially proud of itself when, by its own resources, men, and enterprise, it beat off Dutch and French colonists in the 1640's and 1650's. The mother country had been helpless to prevent quite a chain of Dutch and French colonies from being established along the coasts. There are still traces of Dutch cities, such as Belem, on the north coast of Brazil.

By the eighteen hundreds Brazilians came to regard Portugal as a liability rather than an asset. At the present time the mother country has a population perhaps a tenth that of Brazil's, and the center of gravity in the Lusitanian world is in Brazil.

Brazil is not one uniform country. It has a great many quite distinct and different regions. We are familiar with the differences between the Florida Everglades country and, say, the Great Basin country of Utah, or between Southern California and Maine. In Brazil there are differences just as deep and wide between different sections.

There was a plantation section with its slaves, until the freeing of them; after which there was much the same pattern of life as holds in the old cotton and rice country of South Carolina.

A good deal of the land consisted of thinly inhabited tropical rain forest.

Then there were very important regions, especially toward the more temperate south, where grass country was perfect for cattle raising, or rich in gold and diamonds.

In that part of Brazil a breed of frontier toughs took form in the sixteen hundreds which was to play somewhat the same role in the expansion of Brazil as that played by the mountain men in American history. Coming from the southern capital of São Paulo, the Paulistas, as they were called (or *bandeiristas*), became the terror of the Indians and of the Spanish colonists all across the center of South America.

The Paulistas were frontier wanderers who lived largely by slave raiding, prospecting, and mining. It was through them that Brazilian claims inland to the Andes Mountains were created. They harassed the country, very cruelly in many places, planting the Brazilian flag as they went. They were an especial bane of the Jesuits, who were forming the extraordinary missions of Paraguay in the early sixteen hundreds. It was in fighting off the Paulistas that the Paraguayans developed their nationalism and patriotism, under the direction of Jesuit military men.

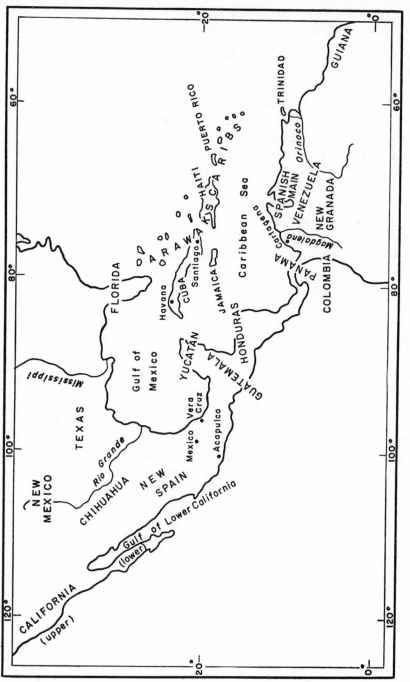

Spanish Caribbean

CHAPTER IV

Spain's Empire

THE Caribbean islands on which Columbus first touched were very quickly cleared of the native Indians by the Spaniards. The Caribs, rough cannibals on the little islands, were mostly left alone. But the soft Arawaks on the larger islands were wiped out rather like weeds off a patch of ground.

The Arawaks gone, the Spaniards were in a position to exploit the island mines; but the mines were not worth exploiting. They were in a position to develop agriculture; but that was not so promising as adventure in Mexico or Peru. Still, before the year 1520 the Spaniards began building plantations and bringing in Negro slaves to work them.

But during the years from 1520 to 1535 a large proportion of the Spaniards left Cuba, Jamaica, Haiti, and Puerto Rico, heading for new adventures in Mexico and South America. They had emptied the Indians out of the main islands and then in a curious way they themselves simply evacuated the island interiors.

In the back country which had been vacated there was good ranch and grazing country. In this back country runaways, outlaws, and sailors and soldiers who had deserted began to live in increasing numbers, raising (or, rather, hunting) wild cattle. The first colonists had brought Iberian cattle and those had gone wild. The outlaws and bush people, living in the interior and away from government, began building stockades for the trapping of the cattle and frames for the drying of wild cow meat, called *buccan,* and the men in the back country came to be known as *buccaneers.* They began to sell their dried meat to the settlers inside the big forts, such as Havana or Santiago de Cuba.

They also sold the dried meat and supplied water and vegetables to English, Dutch, Danish, Norwegians, French, and other interlopers who came by, poaching on the Spanish forbidden areas. Such traders were bootlegging European goods to the Caribbean shores in the face of Spanish prohibition, and bootlegging Spanish silver and gold back out. Many of these, the French and English especially, but also some Dutch and others, came ashore to live with the buccaneers, while many of the buccaneers took to sea in the ships which were going by.

From this the word buccaneer began to take on a new meaning, that of a special type of pirate whose home operations were around Jamaica, but who might show up in the Indian Ocean, or off the west coasts of Mexico. The buccaneers came from their own special heartland in Cuba, Haiti, Santo Domingo, Puerto Rico, and some of the small islands.

In the early sixteen hundreds the buccaneers dominated the back country of the main Spanish islands, and became a terror of the coasts. At the same time they were frequenting the north shores of South America, known as the "Spanish Main." There they operated both as traders and pirates. In the 1640's, partly influenced by wars going on back home in Europe, the buccaneers began to pull apart into quarreling subunits. The Dutch and English ceased coöperating and became enemies, and the Dutch, English, and French formed up into three separate groups. The English buccaneers seized Jamaica, and their leading captain, Henry Morgan, made peace with the English government, got himself knighted, and became the lieutenant governor. With Jamaica in English hands, backed by Cromwell who sent troops out to hold the island, other English buccaneers took over holdings on the shores of South America and established claim to English Guiana. The Dutch secured some islands, such as Curaçao, and Dutch Guiana. The Dano-Norwegians took the Virgin Islands. The English, Dutch, and French had begun to establish their own Caribbean colonies.

The Spanish held on to only the main fortified cities and clusters of nearby Spanish-style villages. They had little control save inside Havana, Santiago, and a few other big towns, and on the mainland in Cartagena down in the Colombia area. Even loyal Spaniards were nearly self-governing if they lived away from the forts. The big ranchers or *hacienderos* were fairly independent of any kind of government.

A general picture of Spanish society in those big forts was that at the top were two or three families of courtier nobles from Spain to whom the government of the fort had been granted for exploitation for a period of a few years. For the most part these men had bought their jobs, cared nothing for the local country, and looked down on everybody.

Next in rank in the neighborhood were wealthy local ranch operators,

Spanish in culture, normally Spanish in ancestry, but given to old-fashioned dress and speech. These people were not fashionable, and they too looked down on everybody else and were at odds with those who had come out from Madrid to rule.

Inside the town was a class of lesser Spanish officials and local resident businessmen, Spanish notaries, doctors, and lawyers attached to the government or the army, army officers who were captains and majors, and businessmen who were wholesalers in the trade with Spain. There would be a few hundred of these in a town like Havana, with their wives and children.

Outside and inside the city, as the lowest Spanish class, were laborers and skilled craftsmen who did most of the supervising as foremen and bosses in work, or who kept little shops, or made things for the local market. Many were partly native in ancestry.

Finally, at the very bottom were the slaves, who were above all African Negroes since the Indians had proved to make poor ones. Importation of African Negro slaves was very rapid, and they were used most of all for the heaviest and hardest work in the tropical areas. The wild Carib Indians could hardly be counted as members of that world at all, on either the islands or the mainland. They were not part of the society; they maintained their own languages and ways, in the face of everybody, for centuries.

Economies and Societies in Spanish Possessions

On the mainland of New Spain, in Mexico and in Central America down almost to the Isthmus of Panama, the social pattern, after the Aztecs had been overthrown between 1520 to 1525, was very much the same. While much of it was the same as that described above, it also was not so very different in rural areas from the Mexican Indian pattern which had been there before the Spanish came. The Aztec ruling element, the priests and commanders of the warriors, was finished off by the Spaniards, after which the villagers went on much as they had before. They were more or less in the position of villagers in Spain, except that they were more heavily burdened. A main change from their former life was that they were baptized and were no longer required to give their sons and daughters for religious sacrifices; but their taxes, rent, and interest payment went to their landlords.

On the other hand, really important changes in daily living stemmed from the introduction of European domesticated animals and the economic and social patterns connected with their raising and utilization. This was to be true of all areas in Spanish-Portuguese America where burro, horse, cow, and sheep could flourish.

In the homeland, Spaniards had long before, on similar soils with similar climates, developed the right animals and herding skills which could fit many parts of the lands they conquered.

Indians proved to be apt at horsemanship and at the herding of long-horn cows and Spanish sheep. While the village peasant Indian continued to raise corn and beans and to move about on foot even when transporting articles of every sort, other peasants were developed by their masters into ranch hands (*vaqueros*). Meat in the diet, new sorts of skills, and wool for clothing came to dominate. The transportation of officials and the well-to-do, of heavy merchandise, and of soldiers and their supplies came to be effected by horse, burro, and mule. Need for vast acreages to support each herd of animals in an arid climate imposed the ranch system, and the need to protect men and animals from beasts and wild Indians led to a general carrying of weapons and the appearance of a frontier cattle-horse population of fighters.

Mining on a large scale, using European rather than Indian techniques, developed after rich strikes were made, in the generations following the conquest. Companies to exploit them were modeled upon contemporary European patterns and supervision was in the hands of imported professionals, many of them central Europeans.

In some decades the output was tremendous. The silver shipped to Europe (and some to China) was by far the largest item in the foreign commerce, and almost alone supported the imports of articles of European manufacture. Its effects on the general European economy, especially the price levels, and on both theory and practice of governmental economic policies are matters taken up elsewhere.

In Mexico and in other areas where great mines were opened, the impact upon local societies and economies is hard to judge. Much of the mining was done in remote districts, far from centers of population, difficult of access over bad routes made more dangerous by raids of wild Indians and bandits. Food, water in some cases, and all the labor had to be transported in at great cost; defenses were always a problem. So the returns had to be very high to give profits above the very high costs.

The rather free flow of silver kept prices high for all items outside those the villagers could produce for themselves in small plots. Little of the silver ever came into their own hands; it circulated around and above them.

Humane laws protected men from slavery, save for the few Negroes.

Yet there were other laws, known in Europe, too, which placed debtors in an almost hopeless position. The economy created debtors very liberally, and debt-subordination held a considerable part of the poorest population (prohibited from running away from creditors) fixed to their localities and the creditors who dominated those localities. This was an effect accentuated by the demands for labor in the mines.

The home government was eternally pressed by the need for precious metal to support its global naval and military projects. High on the list of costs was maintenance of the very system of safe bases such as Cartagena and Havana, and the convoy-fleets needed to move precious metals to Spain and supplies and soldiers back. The royal share in newly mined silver (and gold) and the general income to the home country dependent upon silver imports bent the government to support the interests of mining operators.

The latter, pressed to recruit and then maintain their labor force, were enabled to impose a labor tax upon villages which were far from the mining areas. Few conscripts went to the hard life of the mining towns of their own choice, and fewer still went willingly into the man-killing work in the tunnels or the disease-ridden processing works. All of this went on inside a society which suffered some widespread epidemics possibly as general in their morbidity as the Black Death had been in Europe, or at least as several visitations of the Plague were in Europe itself in the seventeenth century. Imposition of forced labor service in mining did little to make the lot of villagers in the colonial world a happy one, even though it did not directly involve a large percentage of the population.

There was one appendage curiously hung onto New Spain by the Spanish home government. This was the Philippines. Because the Spanish were not supposed to sail around the Cape of Good Hope, which was a Portuguese monopoly, and did not like to sail around Cape Horn or through the Straits of Magellan, a very dangerous slow route for sailing ships, they were able to reach the Philippines chiefly by way of Mexico.

So Mexico was ruled by a viceroy from Spain, and under him was a lieutenant who in turn held authority in Manila. That lieutenant in Manila had a bodyguard of Mexican Indians who never left the Philippines; they became the ancestors of a fair part of the present day Philippine constabulary, which is Philippinized but has this Mexican Indian ancestry.

The Spanish in Manila had contact with Europe once a year when a big ship came across the Pacific from Mexico, bringing European goods and new government officials. Once a year they sent back returning government officials, letters, Chinese china which they bought in Canton, spices and other products. These products were taken in the ship to Acapulco.

It is a remarkable fact that Mexico had a large and important "colony" long before any other state in the Western Hemisphere. Traditionally, historically, and organizationally the Philippines were more a colony of Spanish Mexico than of Spain itself. As mentioned earlier, the missionaries succeeded in converting and baptizing a good part of the native population in the Philippines, turning most of them into a European-oriented Roman Catholic population during the sixteen hundreds. Spanish became a second language among Catholic Filipinos.

In the Andean highlands the Spanish established themselves much as they did in New Spain. Where the Indians were docile, and disciplined by their own civilizations and masters, the Spanish had very little trouble. The Inca local chieftain was replaced by a Spaniard who was sometimes a Spanish-Inca landlord. This situation was common enough all through Bolivia, Ecuador, and Peru. For the ordinary Indian the wrench was not very great, although the religious overturn which followed on Spanish conquest and the European and African diseases which swept those colonies combined to make the Indians miserable.

The Andean highlands were isolated, and Spaniards who went there had a long trip when they wanted to return to Madrid—from the highlands down through the coastal deserts to some port such as that of Callao, then by ship up to Panama, then across its very dangerous yellow-fever belt; from there they had to run the gauntlet of the buccaneers or privateers to reach Havana and get on one of the ships of the big fleets going back to Spain. The trip took a year or more, each way. As a result, in Bolivia and Peru there was a tendency for the Spanish settlers and upper mixed bloods to run themselves pretty much as they pleased, with little respect for the Spanish viceroy. Over the hills from him many landlords as little potentates did much as they pleased.

A few brave Spaniards went through by raft and boat from Peru to the mouth of the Amazon. Mostly, however, the Spanish stayed away from the tropical jungle. They left it as Indian country, and had little effect upon the people there.

South in the Andean highlands was the area of Chile. Chile had to be reached by boat, or else by crossing from Peru one of the worst small deserts of the world. People sailing to Chile found themselves landing on a beach with steep mountains just behind. The best country was on the other side of the range—much the same situation as that along the coast of Oregon and Washington in North America, where the rich valleys lie behind the Cascade Mountains. The first pioneers found the Indian country to the east was a lovely temperate land.

They brought in cattle and lived through the sixteen, seventeen, and most of the eighteen hundreds with rather little contact with Spain. A Castilian population grew up, speaking a very marked dialect which was distinct from all others of colonial Spain.

Southern Chileans kept crossing the mountain ranges, penetrating farther and farther inland until they emerged on the plains of southern Argentina. There their frontiersmen built up a wild East like the wild West in Texas to the west of the Pecos River a hundred years ago. There was no law east of the Andes except that which the *gauchos* themselves respected. These men simply stayed there, maintaining hardly any contact at all with home. Even the Spanish government lost nearly all control over them from the time they established themselves in the sixteen hundreds.

Another eastern enterprise was most remarkable in its own right, the Paraguayan "Reductions" the Jesuits built up on the upper waters of the Plata River system.

Several other important missionaries in the New World had suggested setting up a system of Indian reservations, and some had been worked out in Central America by the great apostle to the Indians, Las Casas. He was one of the really great figures in the history of the Western Hemisphere. Las Casas, however, did not have enough influence, and although he lived to be about ninety years old, he still did not live long enough to cure Spanish colonists of their urge to force Indians to labor without pay.

A little after his time, southeast of Bolivia the Jesuits came to work among a remarkable tribe of South American Indians. These Indians were numerous, self-respecting, and very sturdy both physically and mentally, the Guaraní. They are still an important part of the population of the Western Hemisphere.

The Guaraní took to Catholic teaching in friendly fashion and became baptized Catholics, ruled by a handful of Jesuits who had been drawn from all corners of Catholic Europe, Germans, French, Dutch, Spanish, and Italians. Only a few score handled the whole area. The Guaraní were given a good education in European crafts and agriculture. Oranges and cattle were introduced, many useful crops were brought in, and the Guaraní became what we would call in California Mission Indians. However, this was not a small mission; it was a group of missions, covering a wide area of modern Paraguay and parts of modern Brazil and Argentina.

The Guaraní were brave. From Brazil the Paulistas began to harry the Guaraní settlements during the sixteen hundreds; they were anxious to capture these natives, who made excellent slaves, being well trained and able to speak at least some Spanish. But the Guaraní fought back.

Many a Jesuit, although a learned and devout priest, had been a professional soldier in his younger days. The first of all Jesuits, Ignatius Loyola, had been a Spanish professional soldier before he became a Jesuit. Many of the fathers had only to tuck up their skirts to become again the first-rate officers they had been when younger. When the Guaraní were threatened, the Jesuits proceeded to establish a tiny frontier army. They set up blacksmith shops to make guns and powder-making establishments. They drilled the Guaraní to be privates, corporals, and sergeants, and, themselves acting as officers, beat off the Paulistas. They turned the Paraguayans into a race which calculates that one Paraguayan is worth any number of Argentines or Bolivians or Brazilians in warfare. They are somewhat mistaken in this, but they have since actually fought the Brazilians and the Argentines and the Uruguayans simultaneously. They have fought themselves pretty nearly to extermination twice in modern history. The Jesuit colony in Paraguay was a curious and model state which was never really ruled from Spain. Like the east of Chile, it was so far away that orders hardly came through.

However, in the late seventeen hundreds the Jesuits were put out of business in Catholic Europe by the pope and the Catholic kings. At about the time of the American Revolution the Spanish government took over the Jesuit colony in Paraguay for the first time. Until then it had been a special preserve little touched by other governments.

The Competition of Northwestern Europeans

Although there had been exploratory work and some colonization by the French, Dutch, and English in the fifteen hundreds, it was primarily in the sixteen hundreds that those nations began to make rapid progress in annexing lands and building up their merchant fleets. That was due in part to the lessening of Iberian strength, after the wrecking of the great Spanish Armada in 1589–1590.

It was also partly due to the rapid development of industry and shipping by the Dutch and English, who then reached the point where they could challenge the Spaniards. In addition the weakness created in the Iberian world when Spain annexed Portugal in 1580 was a factor.

On the face of it, it would seem that annexation should have strengthened both Spain and Portugal; but when Philip II annexed Portugal he actually turned the Portuguese into bitter enemies of the central Madrid government. From then until 1640 the Portuguese did not like their government by a Spanish king of alien interests. Through this combination of the two countries the Portuguese Empire was laid open to attack by Spain's enemies, who had through this unwanted union also become Portugal's enemies. The Portuguese had no quarrel with the Dutch and did not want to fight them; but they had no choice, for they belonged with Spain, both in their home country and overseas.

At this time the English and Dutch began to break up the Portuguese control of the East, fighting Spain by dismembering the Portuguese empire in the process. Poor Portugal wanted to be an innocent bystander in the wars between Spain and the English and Dutch, but instead found herself catching the heaviest blows of the latter during the early sixteen hundreds.

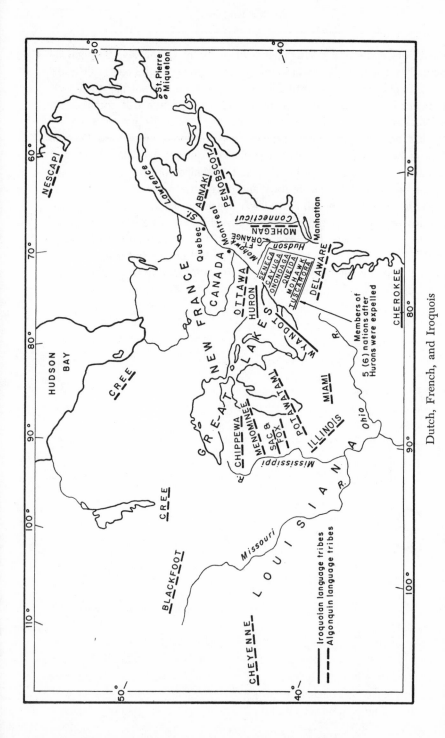

Dutch, French, and Iroquois

CHAPTER V

The Dutch

B EGINNING about 1600, a number of competitors took over leadership in the establishing of empires over tropical and semi-tropical natives, and in establishing colonies of Europeans themselves in the temperate areas which fell to their control. Leaders in this extension of western European enterprise were to be the Dutch, French, and English.

The newcomers in practically no way actually displaced the Iberian empires which they came to rival. By the end of the whole period into which we are now moving, the empires of Spain and Portugal, insofar as they were territorial holdings and governmental jurisdictions, remained intact. In fact, the empire of Spain was to remain practically as it had been created in the first few decades of the sixteenth century until after the time of Napoleon and that of Thomas Jefferson. At the same time the Portuguese Empire continued to be a series of trading posts or factories each surrounded by a modest amount of subject country along the coasts of Africa, Asia, and the Spice Isles, together with Brazil. The Dutch, French, and English made only modest efforts to annex such holdings.

A glance at a map of the world as it stood even as late as the beginning of World War II would show the tremendous territorial empires of the French, English, Dutch, Russians, Spanish, and Portuguese. However, those great empires which showed on the maps until recently, and which are still, in many areas, to be found today, were not, except in broad outline, the empires created by the empire builders of the fifteen and sixteen hundreds.

For example, students of the British colonial empire point out that because of the American Revolution by the colonies on the North American coast, much of the first British Empire as earliest established disappeared. They point out that during the course of the Napoleonic wars and the early eighteen hundreds, a second empire was brought into existence, which in turn was rather largely cast adrift; Australia, New Zealand, Canada, and other Commonwealths rose to independent status, before World War I; and further that a third British Empire, holding large parts of Africa and the Eastern world, came into existence mostly after the time of the American Civil War.

The French empire, which has stood so large on the maps in the course of the late eighteen and through the nineteen hundreds so far, was a creation of the middle eighteen hundreds and even of the nineteen hundreds, rather than the creation of the great enterprisers of whom we shall be talking.

The empire of the Dutch, which down to 1945 and 1946 was so large to the southeast of Asia, was, in the form in which it stood on the maps before World War II, a creation of the late eighteen and early nineteen hundreds.

We have already noted that in the last century the Muscovites first extended their rule over the richest lands in Moslem Asia, an area which now stands alone in the mid-nineteen hundreds, as the last of the empires established over Moslem peoples in the preceding four generations.

In great measure even the Portuguese Empire, with square surveyed boundaries in Africa such as are still seen on maps, was a creation of the eighteen and early nineteen hundreds, largely arranged by diplomats seated around European conference tables.

What we are considering, namely, the earlier empires of the Portuguese, Dutch, English, Spanish, and French, evolved either into independent branches of the European world such as, for example, Argentina, Brazil, Mexico, the United States, Canada, Australia, and New Zealand, or became the little nuclei out of which the empires of the eighteen hundreds were created.

Trade and Finance: Spice Isles, Japan, South America

The Dutch were the first of the northwest Europeans to make significant advances in the field of overseas enterprise and colonization, and partly, too, they were much the most important of the northwest Europeans until the middle and even the later sixteen hundreds. Already before 1590 there was a notable development of Dutch industry and processing at home, and of Dutch fishing operations in the North Sea. Manufacturing gave the Dutch something to trade with other peoples. The North Sea herring fisheries gave wealth, shipping, and training to seamen. Although they had to make do with a small country, and a lot of that marsh or under tide water, the Dutch nevertheless became the workmen of most of northern

Europe, getting a hold on manufacture which was unbreakable for much of the early sixteen hundreds and which is still important today.

It can be recalled here that Dutch manufactures were indispensable even to their enemies—Spain and Portugal—right through the period which we are now considering. Furthermore, in the late fifteen and through the sixteen hundreds the Dutch developed the carrying trade that has been mentioned before, moving goods all over the world for other people.

Last of all, the Dutch became extremely good fighting men on the sea. Their navy became an instrument for building an empire. Dutch privateers and plain pirates were likewise formidable to the shipping of enemies.

The Dutch were never numerous nor possessors of rich basic resources, although with man's skill they built up very rich little garden and pasture plots at home by ditching, diking, and fertilizing. They made themselves the builders and operators of ships for all northern Europe, and even for the old shipping cities of Venice and Genoa. They almost became the ship builders and operators for the globe in the course of the middle sixteen hundreds. They even carried goods from one Spanish colony to another, although it was bootleg work, and even bootleg work for the national enemy. They worked themselves into a position where their financing was indispensable, even to powerful kings making war in Europe.

Without Dutch financing, armies could not be paid, nor goods gotten together to service the troops. Dutch banking offices began to be the centers for all Europe. Down to the time of the American Revolution it was at Amsterdam that loans were floated. The American revolutionaries themselves used Dutch resources in fighting George III. The Dutch are still today a great power in the banking world.

The Dutch also did a certain amount of true colonizing. In this they had native Dutchmen to serve as colonists, but they also had available material in Protestant refugees who fled to the Netherlands from Germany and from what is now Belgium, where religious wars were a difficulty.

The Dutch built their "empire" upon a survey of the world by explorers and merchants that was about as complete as any could be. In the middle and late fifteen hundreds, before they began to operate on their own account, Dutchmen served in the Portuguese navy and as merchants in the Portuguese mercantile world. When the Dutch began to fight the Portuguese, they broke into the empire almost, one might say, from the inside. They explored the routes around Norway, and rivaled the English in opening up Russia. They explored and named the Cape Horn route to the south of South America.

The Dutch kept the trade with Japan open through the sixteen, seventeen, and early eighteen hundreds, after the Christian missions there were destroyed in the early sixteen hundreds. They maintained European contact with the Japanese and vice versa. It was through them that Japanese noblemen began to learn how far behind they were falling in the eighteen hundreds. This prepared them for the visit from Perry, and convinced them that they had to be able to make guns and ships such as those of the Americans and Dutch.

For some generations the copper exports of Japan were of world-wide economic importance. This was one of the first instances of the entry of a useful metal from an area overseas into the global market the Europeans were building. This instance also serves to illustrate the growth of interregional competition in these matters; Japanese copper mining hurt the fading production of central Europe for a while, and in turn was hurt by the rise of Swedish production.

For a little while the Dutch also did outright colonization in Brazil, until the Lusitanian Brazilians threw them out, as we have seen. There was other colonization initiated by Dutch buccaneers in Guiana and on Curaçao, which is the little island off the coast of Venezuela where today alcoholic beverages and oil are refined.

Above all, they colonized the valley of Henry Hudson's river, discovered by that Englishman when he was sailing as a Dutch employee. Finally, a little group of them settled around the tip of South Africa among the aboriginal Bushmen and Hottentots, providing the nucleus for the later Dutch Boer (farmer) population of what is today the Cape Colony.

The Hudson-Mohawk Region and the Iroquois

At the present moment we are most interested in the colony that the Dutch established in the Hudson River Valley. Curiously to us, who think of New York as so important, they first made more of Albany, or of Fort Orange, far up the river near the junction with the Mohawk River, than they did of the lower river and its island of Manhattan. For one thing, they could sail the ships of those days up to Fort Orange, and for another, it was from that point that trade routes into the interior, already developed by the Indians, were directed.

All through the westward-running trough, now known as the Mohawk Valley, lived the Iroquois tribes. The Five Nations of the Iroquois, or the Six Nations after the Tuscarora later came up from Carolina to join them, were different from the Algonquins all around them. On the whole they were hostile to the Algonquins, north, south, and west. The Dutch brought guns, iron knives, hatchets, blankets, firewater and other trade goods to the Iroquois, who in return brought their furs to the Dutch at Albany. When the Dutch came, the Iroquois had been neither more numerous nor pugnacious than the other Indians. But with Dutch backing they began to build an empire of a sort which extended all the way to Wisconsin in the course of the sixteen hundreds.

They either massacred all the Indians they could reach or forced them to trade through them with the Dutch, to the profit of the Iroquois. This "empire" of the Iroquois was to be first under the protection of the Dutch, then of the English until the Revolutionary War.

The Dutch had some idea, in their Hudson River colony, of bringing over peasants and craftsmen. In fact, they brought over a few to Manhattan Island, where they fenced them in from the Indians to the north with a wooden palisade where Wall Street now stands. Then they also founded proprietary colonies, deeding tremendous "feudal" fiefs along the Hudson Valley to rich Dutch *patroons* who could bring peasants over and develop manorial estates. Some of the patroons were successful in developing manorial setups which lasted until the eighteen-thirties, long after the American Revolution. The "manors" were late-type administrative units; there was no introduction of the original manorial cultivation system, which the Dutch had forgotten centuries before. It was the ferment of the age of Andrew Jackson which finally broke them up. Some of the patroons not only got rich, but stayed rich and are rich today. Some of them were themselves originally displaced persons, Protestants from the Belgian (Catholic) southern Netherlands driven north.

South Africa and Southeast Asia

Until quite late in the history of Dutch colonization, the lodgment which began to develop at Table Bay, near the tip of South Africa, was a poor relation. In fact, as late as the time of the American Revolution, it consisted of only a few thousand families, clustered rather near the port or spread thinly on great grazing ranches in the up-country behind. A considerable part of the population was what is called in that country "colored." "Colored" persons are not half-breed Dutch and Negro, but half-breed Dutch and Hottentot, or Dutch and Bushman and Hottentot.

The Bantu Negroes now numerically dominant in South Africa were nearly as late in reaching that country by land as the Dutch who came by boat from Europe. The original inhabitants, Bushmen and Hottentots, are not Negroes. These were subject to the pressure of the invading "Kaffir"

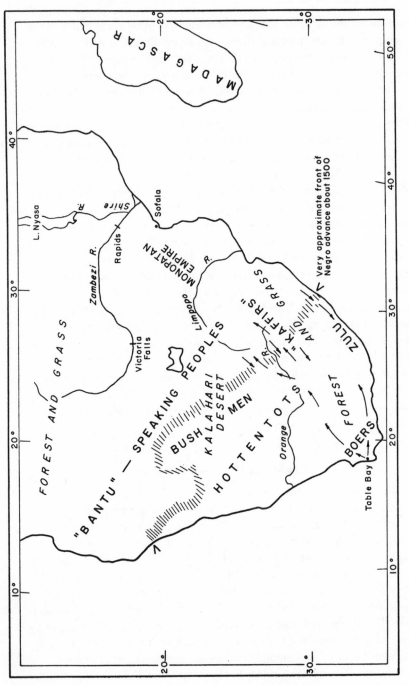

Boer South Africa

Negroes from the north and northeast during exactly the same time that the Dutch began their expansion from the south and southwest. The clash which has later developed in South Africa has been between two invaders, not between an invading nation and an aboriginal native people. The first peoples have been caught between.

The Dutch in South Africa had little to do with either the home government or with one another in the course of the first century of their settlements. They supplied foodstuffs and other goods to passing ships; they took in a few colonists with each generation, notably an infusion of French Huguenots in the course of the seventeen hundreds. They maintained themselves practically independent of all governments in the back country away from the port. The English did not take that part of the world under their control until, when at war with the Dutch who at home had fallen under Napoleon, they took the territory into custody, or at least took the port which is now Capetown.

In southeast Asia, the Dutch made some important establishments in the course of the early sixteen hundreds. In one place they outright took over control from the Portuguese. This was on the coasts of the large island of Ceylon. The Portuguese missionaries had made Catholic converts, and these Portuguese, although hated by a great part of the native population, had maintained themselves in charge of commerce with the outside world for about a hundred years. The Dutch took over, and while they did little outright colonizing, they did so establish the Roman-Dutch law as to make it to this day the basic law of the population of Ceylon. They were themselves to be pushed out of Ceylon at the same time that they lost their holding in South Africa to the British. Both Portuguese and Dutch left descendants of mixed blood, important in the local society and economy, as businessmen, clerks, and professional men.

Out in the islands where the spices were found the Dutch left the native rajahs and sultans, and the native tribes of all the different sorts who inhabit modern Indonesia, pretty much alone just so long as they did not fight the Dutch and did pay some tribute and, above all, directed their trade to Dutch merchants. The one establishment of any importance, which they called Batavia and which has now been renamed Djakarta by the Indonesian government, was founded at about the same time as they founded New York, or Nieuw Amsterdam, in the Western world, in the same way and for the same purpose.

Formosa, always interesting to merchants because it produced camphor, was long known to Chinese and Arabs, but was inhabited by tribes much like the head-hunting natives of nearby northern Luzon in the Philippines.

For a while the Dutch were lodged at a few points on the coast, supersed-
ing the few Portuguese who had come as traders in the early fifteen hundreds. Then a Chinese pirate expelled the Dutch and began the slow evolution of the island toward Chinification. The Dutch were not deeply
interested.

English Rivalry

Dutch activity in Europe and globally was not so much eliminated as surpassed by the English. The Dutch remained, through the rest of the
seventeen and the eighteen hundreds, a very important people in all
matters connected with trade, banking, manufacture, and shipping. The
Dutch, however, were not able to defeat the English navies and armies
which attacked them in the middle and later sixteen hundreds. Oliver
Cromwell fought great wars with the Dutch, and the wars continued
under the restored dynasty of the Stuarts until rather late in the sixteen
hundreds when, by dynastic chance, both states came under the rule of
one married couple, William and Mary of English history. At that point
the Dutch continued to suffer substantial losses in men and wealth because costly wars with French Louis XIV were, in considerable part, borne
as burdens by the Dutch, although by this time they were in alliance with
the English in their enterprises.

During the course of the sixteen hundreds, whether as enemies, before
William and Mary, or as friends, the English continued to take away the
leadership which the Dutch had earlier had. The latter lost colonies to
the English; one of the most notable transfers was the island of Manhattan, together with the other Dutch settlements in the neighborhood,
in the sixteen-sixties. The English attacked there when technically the
two countries were at peace and the Dutch in the colony were forced
more or less willingly to bow to English leadership. The Dutch government was unable to recover the lost lands. From that point on the Dutch
in the Nieuw Amsterdam colony had been transformed into "English
colonists."

On the whole the Dutch did not conduct very important transplantations of Europeans proper to any overseas settlements. The small establishments mentioned, in the Hudson river region and on the tip of South
Africa, both of them in temperate areas, were about the only enduring
colonies in the true sense that the Dutch ever did establish.

Generally speaking, in their tropical colonies the Dutch, like the Portuguese, filled a few small port towns with merchants, seamen, and ad-

ministrators and with an employee population of half-breeds. Native nobles and practically unchanged villagers or tribal peoples in the hinterland were not governed. The very thinness of Dutch occupation in the first place is one reason why, where they have since been eliminated, they have left relatively minor traces of their occupation.

CHAPTER VI

The French
—and the Africans

I N THE course of the later Middle Ages the French nation had built
itself into Europe's most powerful single political entity. However, it
was not quite the unified state that the kingdom of the English was,
or that most modern states are.

The king of France shared his power with a great many extremely rich
and powerful noblemen more or less closely related to him, and with
various institutions such as the Estates or Assemblies of southern France
or of northern France. He also shared his authority in part with those of
his own officials who had made their positions hereditary and who, controlling the law courts, were able on occasion to thwart his will or even
defy it outright.

In the middle of the fifteen hundreds, when the Spanish and Portuguese
were most active in colonial expansion, France was wracked by serious
civil wars. Partly these were wars of Calvinist-Protestant Frenchmen,
called Huguenots, against the more numerous Roman Catholics; partly
they were wars of great noblemen who wished to keep the monarchy from
direct control over them and their estates; partly, also, it was a war
between various branches of the French royal family itself. In any case,
civil wars greatly cut down French activity overseas until late in the
fifteen hundreds.

However, that did not mean that no Frenchmen sailed the seas, or
that no Frenchmen took part in preliminary exploring and settling activity. French merchants were trading even inside areas which the Portuguese and Spanish had reserved for themselves throughout the course
of the late fourteen and early fifteen hundreds. In the sixteen hundreds

French buccaneers in the Caribbean came to play an active part, along with the Dutch and Englishmen.

Finally, only a little after Columbus had discovered the New World, French fishermen began to have a share in the great cod fisheries on the Newfoundland Banks, and in that area established some shore posts; French fisheries are still to be found on the islands of Miquelon and St. Pierre near the mouth of the St. Lawrence River estuary. At all times they had some contact in that region with natives on the mainland.

After about 1596 the French civil wars were over. Then three strong governments in succession managed French affairs until 1715. These were the governments of Henry IV, Louis XIII, and Louis XIV. Under these kings served a succession of efficient, hard-working prime ministers, the most famous of them all being the Cardinal Richelieu who served under Louis XIII. The over-all result was that for over a hundred years France had a powerful monarchical government which was strongly motivated with the desire to be the leading state in western Europe in every way. This meant, of course, that most of French resources and energy went into wars in Europe itself.

There was, however, through many of the decades of that period, willingness to back colonial activity with a great deal of money and with diplomatic and military might. In this period the French became the great patrons of the Roman Catholic missionary order of the Jesuits.

These were especially active in North America, in Southeast Asia, and in China, but they were also active elsewhere. French penetration of Indo-China and Southeast Asia began. From the French Jesuits came a view of China such as Europe had never before had. Gifted Jesuit scholars and missionaries at the courts of the Manchu emperors made surveys of China's geology, geography, language, and literature. Their writings are the basis, to this day, of the study of China and Chinese literature for Westerners. But obviously they did not convert the Chinese.

However, the Jesuits were only a part of the French enterprise which Louis XIV especially backed with his money, his men, and his direction. Before him, Richelieu and others had pushed development of French claims in Madagascar and India, and, through explorers, had even established relations with Ethiopia and parts of Central Africa. Above all, efforts were made by France in this period to develop north of what is today the United States the great colony of New France, and its twin in what is now the Middle West and beyond to the Rocky Mountains, Louisiana with its base at New Orleans.

Government and Companies of New France

From the French posts at the mouth of the St. Lawrence—today the cities of Quebec and Montreal—and from the mouth of the Mississippi at New Orleans, the French began a great penetrating movement of the North American continent which, in territory surveyed, moved as fast as did the Russian movement across Asia. In the course of just one generation Marquette, Joliet, and scores of others opened up the whole of the central country, and pushed trading connections far up the Missouri River.

However, French missionaries in this New World and French governmental officials and traders who did a good deal of this sort of work were few in numbers and, on the whole, were never able to build the empire they were creating upon a numerous settlement of transplanted Frenchmen.

There were transplantations. Around New Orleans a modest colony of immigrant Frenchmen did take hold. The enterprise in the St. Lawrence Valley was much more extensive, though ultimately insufficient. In that region the general procedure was very much like the one followed by the Dutch in the upper Hudson River: seigneuries, fashioned upon the administrative rent-collecting estates then known in northern France, were established along the river front, and the seigneurs in turn were required to bring over colonists whom they found chiefly in the French areas of Normandy and Brittany along the English Channel.

Transplanted Bréton and Norman farmers and fishermen came to be thickly settled along the river edge above and below Quebec. In that region they implanted the Roman Catholic Church of their native country, established the Church hierarchy as a branch of the French hierarchy, and set going the rural economy which was the contemporary peasant economy of the regions which they had left at home. Inside the few towns, and about the trading posts, small settlements of French provincial craftsmen came into existence.

French enterprises in what is now India were to take shape only late and even after the period which we are considering here. Just before the American Revolution there were great wars, instigated by rivalry of French and English all over the globe; they were fought on the soil of India, and there, as elsewhere, by the time of the American Revolution the English had succeeded in practically eliminating the French. At the same time they succeeded in eliminating French political control from both New France and Louisiana. In the course of Napoleon's time the

French were to make some feeble attempts to re-establish a colonial empire, but in the face of the English navy and other enemies on the continent of Europe they were quite unable to do so.

By the time of the American Revolution the area in which the French had settled in North America contained a population of only a few thousand transplanted Frenchmen. There were seigneurs and peasants along the St. Lawrence of whom we spoke. Then, scattered far in the interior, there were trading posts in which the population, although French-speaking and partly French in blood, was very near to the Indians in habits and in ancestry.

Inside the towns of Quebec, Montreal, and New Orleans there was a resident population which included a few well-to-do personages with warehouses and business connections with the mother country. There were, however, few opportunities for these men to operate large enterprises on their own. The control of governmental companies, and the control of the government itself, held them down quite rigidly in the scale and nature of their operations. There were also monks and priests connected with the services of the church and with the very active missionary enterprises.

A few score officers, soldiers and government officials, nearly all from France, managed most of the colonies' activities. These served for terms of years, and in most cases expected to and did return to the mother country. The local population was not able of its own to provide much opposition to English control, once that control became established about 1763 over the French colonies in the temperate parts of North America.

African Migration and the Sugar Colonies

In the sixteen hundreds, when the buccaneers were at the height of their activities in the Caribbean, Frenchmen played roles similar in all ways to those of Dutchmen and Englishmen. When the Dutch began to separate from the others, centering upon Dutch Guiana and Curaçao, the Dano-Norwegians to center on the Virgin Islands, and the English on Jamaica, Trinidad, the Bahamas, and the other "British West Indies," the French came to center on the western end of Haiti, on Guadeloupe, Martinique, French Guiana, and other spots. The home governments ultimately rather adopted colonies and claims first thus established extra-legally.

In all such colonies the settlements of Europeans were on a small scale. Transient seafarers, garrison troops in modest numbers, a few dozen

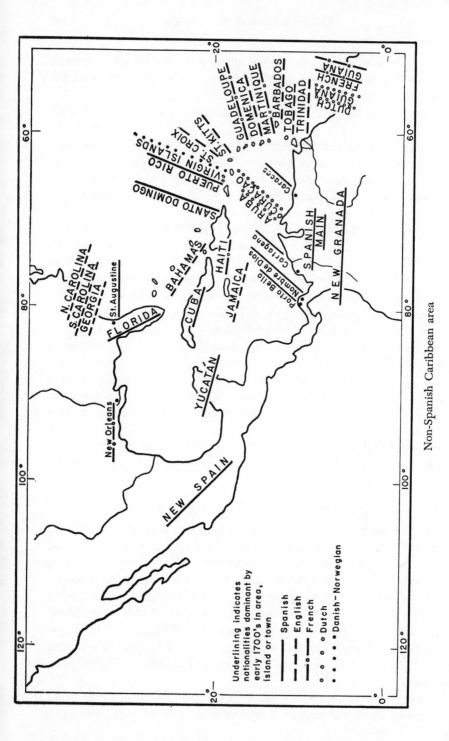

Non-Spanish Caribbean area

gentlemen, churchmen, and government officials ordered out from home for the most part represented the dominant element. Most were resident only temporarily, or hoped to be. Even planters, which was what the gentlemen mostly were, resided by preference in Europe, running their estates through managers and overseers, with a minimum of European craftsmen and clerks. The percentage of European women was always very low.

The native Indians had mostly been liquidated by massacre, starvation, disease, enslavement, or forced emigration. Some of the labor, especially at first, was supplied by enslaved Europeans, convicts, or freemen "indentured" for terms of years. Then work came to be done by slaves who were, above all, imported from the western coasts of Africa, though some other sorts of Africans and some Asians were also brought in. Nearly everywhere, by the early seventeen hundreds, the overwhelming mass of the population in the English, Danish, Dutch, and French island colonies represented migration from Africa, rather than from Europe.

All of the colonies were devoted to the production of cane sugar and its by-products, molasses and rum. In all of them the hard labor was performed by slaves, working in gangs of men and women. Sugar plantations were large, and the requirements for strong backs were unremitting. It was not a sort of production process which demanded a high proportion of skilled or literate employees.

The slave quarters were settlements of uprooted forest-village Africans. But in the first stages of enslavement, individuals from many different linguistic and cultural groups had been mixed helter-skelter. They were also broken in spirit or soon came to be. They could not transplant intact their speeches, customs, art, religions, or social patterns. Only a few shreds of such things could go on into the cultural make-up of their great-grandchildren.

Instead, they everywhere took over use of the language of a colony's masters, Dutch, English, French, Dano-Norwegian (or Spanish or Portuguese). They also were baptized into whatever European church their masters favored. Government as it touched them was the will of the overseer; they had no share in it, nor any chance to receive training in its operations. A few would receive training in simpler European crafts and in the art of domestic service, but otherwise they had no economic functions save to work, eat, sleep, and reproduce their kind.

From the earliest times on there were individuals of part-European blood in the slave population; slave women bore slave children whatever the status of the father. The mixed bloods were mingled as a matter of course with the other plantation hands, passing down, wider and wider but thinner and thinner, European ancestry to the rest of the slave population and thereby sending it along lines of physical differentiation from the related Africans proper. In the opposite direction, many of the mulattoes, quadroons, and so on acquired European skills by favor of masters or overseers who were related to them. Such individuals grew numerous enough, with sufficient education and skills, to form into an in-between layer in the plantation world and in the colonial port cities. Legal freedom was not too uncommon among them, and individuals could become slave owners and even estate proprietors themselves. For the most part they took care of craft-manufacture for local buyers, of petty trade, of coastal shipping and fishing, and served as foremen and even as overseers or small proprietors.

In all the colonies the economy was entirely integrated with the European economy. Sugar was the one crop. It was all exported to Europe, or to mainland settlements in the Western Hemisphere. In return, cheap preserved fish, textiles, grains, meats, metal goods, gold and silver for money, all wood-products, salt, and luxuries had to be brought in. European investors sent out capital and direction and took back each year as heavy profits as possible. The largest single element in the capital investment was the inventory of slaves.

The investors in Europe were mostly merchant capitalists of the port cities of the mother countries, backed by courtiers and other participants in the ventures of such merchants. In France, capitalist merchants who also owned shares in ships and who carried on general wholesale businesses within and without the homeland were the leading figures in the developing of sugar plantations, carrying on the African trade, the creation and operation of sugar producing estates, the supplying of necessities to the colonies, of shipping, and of the selling of the sugar in Europe. In the ports of the colonies, the resident managers of their mercantile and producing businesses were a local upper class, but below the churchmen and army and civil officials. They were recruited from business communities at home; they were younger brothers, or trusted employees, or junior partners, or all of these at once, of the great investors, but they were not nobles. Rouen, Nantes, and other provincial trading towns in France were most important; Liverpool furnished like personages in Jamaica, and Amsterdam did the same for Dutch colonies.

CHAPTER VII

The English

SINCE the English were to have, in the long run, such tremendous success in colonial enterprises in the temperate region of the world, it is rather necessary to emphasize that, in the first period of English overseas activity, trade was the principle objective of nearly everyone concerned. Hopes for a profitable trade or mines of either gold or silver led the English into their first steps as overseas colonists and empire builders.

Earlier, when speaking of the great expansion of the Russians, there was need to mention the fact that in the 1550's English merchants established very lucrative and, for both countries, very important trading relations.

Those activities of the English in the direction of Russia were only part of all the activities into which Englishmen plunged during the reign of Queen Elizabeth I. The successes of the Muscovy Company stimulated the founding of similar trading companies centering on other parts of the globe. The Baltic Sea attracted both individual enterprisers and company groups. The Mediterranean came to be of great interest to Englishmen who sought native products such as raisins and wines, or to find there products brought through the sleazy Portuguese network of controls to the old medieval trading centers of Alexandria, Aleppo, Smyrna, and Constantinople from the Spice Isles and China. The Mediterranean was a most important field for English activity beginning in the early sixteen hundreds, and from then until the present day.

Almost at once, as the Dutch began their own penetration of the Spice Isles, the English tried to rival the Dutch there. For a while the English and Dutch along the coasts of India, in the Malay Straits, and in the Spice Islands, were in the curious position of being at war with one another, while at home in Europe their countries were not only friends but even near-allies. In that far-off colonial world the Dutch, at that time, were definitely the top dogs. After about 1630 they drove the English out of the Spice Isles, cut off most English attempts to reach China and Japan, and confined the English in general to the area west of the Bay of Bengal.

India

Their fortunate combination with the Portuguese in the course of the middle sixteen hundreds opened to the English the opportunity to work out from Bombay into the lands of the Mogul Empire, chiefly as traders permitted by the masterful Moguls to travel and to trade. The English were to establish, from Bombay, in the course chiefly of the later seventeen hundreds, the great empire of John Company, as the English East Indies Company was known in those parts.

This was a curious subsidiary to the English government as well as being a great trading, profit-making organization in its own right. Penetration of India was never an activity of the government of the home country itself; it was never supported by a large migration to India of Englishmen or even other Europeans; instead, it was an enterprise managed entirely for profit or to protect profits by a group of directors in the business center of the City of London, and handled on the ground itself by a few hundred Company employees and army officers in the service of the Company. Trade rather than settlement was at all times the major interest and activity of the English in India. It was never a colony.

Hudson Bay, the Caribbean

Much the same thing was true of English activity, which blossomed after 1660 in the wide northern tundra and forest regions of what is today Canada. A relative of the king, Prince Rupert, who had served very valiantly in the royal cause in the English Revolution, was made head of a company of courtiers, squires, and merchant capitalists chartered to exploit a monopoly of the trade in the Hudson Bay area.

The Hudson's Bay Company, as it has commonly been known, was to establish from that time on a series of trading posts along the coasts of the great bay itself, and in the rivers away from salt water, where a profitable trade in furs could be carried on. Again, the English, under that company, did very little outright colonizing. As a matter of fact, they did none whatsoever except to establish a few Scotch traders in the posts to which the Indians and half-breeds brought furs from the deep interior. Few of those traders established in the posts showed any curiosity about the country behind. The posts had been in active operation for about a century before very much came to be known at first hand by Europeans at the posts about the lands to the south and west toward what is now the American border and the Rocky Mountains.

Although the English did not penetrate the country, their activities there tremendously modified the native economies. The Indians went over very largely to the service of the Hudson's Bay Company as its fur catchers. They came to rely on the company for their own desperately needed supplies of guns and powder, of traps and blankets, iron tools and weapons, and their luxuries such as spirits and tobacco.

The English penetrated still another area, as buccaneers this time, and with great success. Here there were no companies chartered and managed at home, but rather there were outlaws and plain pirates who established themselves together with Dutch and French on the Bahama Islands, Santo Domingo, on the coast of what is now British Guiana, and elsewhere in the neighborhood, and above all, after the 1660's, in the island of Jamaica. Those who got into the Caribbean islands, once they had firmly established their colonies, developed Negro slave sugar-producing enterprises on a grand scale. As in the French and other sugar islands, the white population was at all times a modest part of the total, although mulattoes and other mixed elements came to be a considerable fraction of the whole.

English trade with the North American continent rested in the first place on the contacts of English fishermen, who were often part-time traders and who came along the coasts between Newfoundland and the Carolinas in the middle and late fifteen hundreds. To a remarkable degree these persons showed little curiosity about the natives with whom they traded.

North American Colonies, and Ireland

Colonizing for the English proper, that is, colonizing of land by Englishmen, began in Ireland rather than on the North American continent or elsewhere. In the middle 1500's under Queen Mary (and her husband, King Philip, who was Philip II of Spain and lord of the Spanish colonies), two colonies had been established for Englishmen in the heart of eastern Ireland. The natives there were driven off, and English colonies established which were, in many ways, to be the prototypes of English colonies in Virginia or Massachusetts.

Still further colonizing activity in Ireland on a grand scale took place shortly after 1600, when a large part of northern Ireland was cleared of its natives, and great numbers of Englishmen and of Lowland Scotch were brought over, given large proprietary interests or small yeomen farms, and settled down as a kind of everlasting garrison to hold the whole island in obedience to the English Crown. Many of those who promoted the Irish colonizing were to take an active part in promoting like enterprises for settlements in Virginia and New England in the same period or immediately following. Much the same money, and the same organizing talent and personnel, went into them as into the promotion of the North American enterprises.

The development of active colonial enterprise by the English is associated with the activities of late Elizabethan and early Stuart courtiers and businessmen. English colonizing activity was always done in a kind of partnership between courtiers, such as Sir Walter Raleigh or some of the greatest English peers, London businessmen, many of whose incomes came from fabulously successful investments in the East Indies Company, and seamen and ship owners of places like Bristol, Plymouth, and London itself. However, although all of these persons were interested in quick profits, and above all in the profits which might come from gold and silver mines and the fur trade, there was, to a degree not known in other countries, a feeling that, along with the traders and miners, there should be a population of resident yeomen and craftsmen in any colony where such persons could survive.

The colonists who took hold along the coasts of North America after 1607 and after 1620 were drawn in considerable measure from the craftsmen class and from the lower levels of the rural population (often enough rural craftsmen themselves trained in cottage industry), but at all times there were enough of the upper-class gentlemen, businessmen and officials to take care of the transfer into the new colonies of English institutions— law, church, and so on.

However, the word "church" as used just now is not quite the right term for what was transferred in the religious sphere. In England various dissenting groups, some of them nearly reconciled with the Church of England, some of them bitterly opposed to it, including the Roman Catholics, provided colonists who went to various of the temperate colonies of their own volition, or at least with a willingness to go to escape persecution in the mother country.

Institutionally, just as they had done in Ireland, the English established a number of large lordships in the Western Hemisphere. They erected

great proprietary feudal holdings such as those of the Calverts in Mary-
land, of Lord Penn's family in Pennsylvania, and of an association of
aristocrats in the Carolinas. In this they followed Dutch and French, and
of course even earlier Spanish, Portuguese, Venetian, and Genoese models.

They also made extensive use of the chartered company, on the model
of the Muscovy, Levant, and East India Companies, and in general like
those of the French and Dutch. Trade, mining, and fishing were major
objectives; colonial settlement was calculated to serve such ends. The
colonists could supply the garrisons and naval bases, and in their towns
could gather and rough-process furs, metals, timber, and other products,
and distribute the mother country's manufactures to local traders. We
have noticed that the Muscovites settled peasants in Siberia for the same
reasons.

However, the peculiar development in the New England region of a
trading and colonizing and governing company as a locally managed affair
gave a curious twist to the history of Massachusetts Bay, and provided
a government which had surprisingly little to do with the mother country
through a considerable part of the seventeenth century. It might be
added that the Massachusetts Bay and other colonies did not follow the
government at home by retaining the Church of England as the Established Church, but had instead their own established, dissenting churches.
(In the one colony of Rhode Island the "establishment" was general
dissent!)

The English populations in the New World showed an ability to forage
for themselves which was quite equal to that of the French, Portuguese,
or Spanish populations in the parts of the world where they established
themselves. From the beginning there were English traders deep in the
back country, there were English cattlemen far behind the settlements,
and there were also outlaws and renegades who preferred the Indian mode
of life to that of a proper European. However, to a degree not found in
the case of any other colonizing Empire, the English colonies filled with
yeomen and other citizens or subjects from different classes in the mother
country. The cities, which began to be fairly well populated all the way
from Boston to Charleston, resembled English county towns of about the
same time and the same size. Around them there were solidly filled-in
settlements of English yeomen farmers, even in most of the Southern
colonies where the slave plantation economy was to take hold rather later.

After 1763 the French were eliminated from the political scene in North
America. While the English were given superior rights as against other
Europeans north of Florida and westward to the Mississippi, and then

northward through the lands dominated by the Hudson's Bay Company, the Spanish fell heirs to the lands west of the Mississippi, extending over the Great Plains toward the Rockies. By and large the whole of the world of the Indians north of Florida and the Gulf of Mexico was under the influence of Europeans, English or Spanish, as the case might be, but direct government extended only where the settlements were thick enough for administrators and garrisons to be maintained.

The Great Plains Indians had never thickly settled in the vast area which they controlled; they dwelt mostly along the water courses and lived on small game and by patch agriculture. But long before the Europeans in any effectual way penetrated the Plains, they had obtained horses and begun to devote their attention primarily to hunting buffalo and other game in the open grasslands. The richness of the returns from this new mode of life attracted Indians from farther east (and also from the plateaus to the west) to move toward the Plains. To a degree, in the seventeen and eighteen hundreds, this was to provide an escape for the Indians nearer the Atlantic who were under pressure from the French and English settlements.

The Indians of the woodlands had been under the control and trading influence of the French, especially of the French in the St. Lawrence region. When the English government took over the French hegemony in those parts after 1763, the desire of the Indians to maintain a hunting, trapping mode of life in dependence upon the European economy was supported by the desires of the established trading interests of the French-Canadian area to maintain the same situation. The English government, pressed by its own traders, and desiring to reconcile both the Indians and French in the new provinces, attempted to protect the Indians against further pressure from the Atlantic seaboard's English-speaking colonists. This was to be one of the bones of contention between the rebelling colonists and the home government in London at the time of the American Revolution.

The tensions, which began to play a prominent part in the relations between the English mother government and the European settlements in the eastern part of what is now the United States, were in part economic and social. The mother country existed institutionally, governmentally, and linguistically. But a fairly considerable part of the population in the colonies consisted of Germans, Scotchmen, Irishmen, and even of Englishmen whose antagonism to the English Church had been a factor in their decisions to leave the home country. Nor was the mother country particularly loved by those who were the grandsons of her own paupers and bond servants sent involuntarily overseas.

The mother country followed, of course, the mercantilistic policies which had been worked out especially since about 1650, designed to promote the welfare of the "prince"—of the mother country and of the Empire as a whole, conceived from the point of view of policy-makers in Westminster and the City of London. Heavy debts had to be paid to take care of the long wars for the establishment of English control in both India and the Western Hemisphere.

Money was a problem, not only money to make the government go and to supply the navies and diplomats, but money as a medium of exchange and standard of value. The colonists hoped the policies of the mother country would in various ways promote colonial interests primarily. The mother country was oftener interested in policies which would promote the welfare of those in England who had great amounts of colonial indebtedness on their books and wished to collect, in effect, one hundred cents on the dollar.

Of course English shipping and taxation programs were designed to bring a maximum return to the mother country on her ships. The shipping organization of the world which the Dutch had built up was being in measure taken over by the English at just this time, and the shipping of colonial enterprisers was already competing in that activity. Rivalry between the English and the New English became acute in some respects in these two fields.

Manufacture of iron goods and textiles, and a great list of other goods, had been established in the colonies. There were colonials who knew how to produce many of these articles; still others with the necessary skills could easily be imported from the mother country or the Continent. Nevertheless, to a degree the new manufactures in the colonies were discouraged by various fiscal and licensing regulations so that the colonists would remain dependent for such goods upon the mother country.

The resident upper class among the colonists felt, as was true of their counterparts in Spanish, Portuguese, French, and Dutch colonies, that they should have a larger share in the local government. It was not at all difficult for a colonial who had achieved high station in his home society, and considerable wealth, to go to England and cut a wide swathe in English artistic, literary, political, or court circles. In this way he would be doing what a well-to-do gentleman or man of talent from Yorkshire or Devon might do. And, as far as the home government could see, this would and should be quite enough for him. Men and families did do this.

However, many of the leading citizens in the colonies felt that in their own communities they should have the sort of power and position which men of the first rank had in the mother country, rather than having to go to England to enjoy lives based upon such activities.

Government in the colonies was itself to a degree in the hands of such persons, but all the key positions—and most of what we should call the patronage—lay in the hands of officers sent out from the mother country to make their way for a few years at most in the colonies before returning to play the roles their birth and fortunes entitled them to at home.

The leadership for a rebellion against the mother country when it came was provided by these discontented colonial "aristocrats," by the well-to-do merchants and would-be manufacturers in the colonial towns, as well as by the frontiersmen who felt the mother country was pampering and coddling the native Indian population instead of looking after the best interests of the frontiersmen—the best interests of the frontiersmen being interpreted by themselves as the right to dispossess and dislocate the Indians as they moved their own squatting settlements ever farther to the westward through the gaps in the Allegheny and Appalachian highlands.

The very first of all of Europe's overseas colonies to indulge in governmental and military revolt against its metropolis was the English settlement which extended from Maine to Georgia. In this region a New Europe, a New England, had come into being. This was no revolt of subjugated natives against European invaders; the natives were powerless and not of much importance until one got considerably west of the mountains; in fact, the native Indians favored the English government by and large. It was, instead, a revolt of the New Europe against the Old Europe, in the matter of government and in all matters touching the economy and social position of the colonists.

INDEX

INDEX

Italic numbers indicate reference to maps.